THE MEDIEVAL CITY

Titles in the Series
Greenwood Guides to Historic Events of the Medieval World

The Black Death

The Crusades

Eleanor of Aquitaine, Courtly Love, and the Troubadours

Joan of Arc and the Hundred Years War

Genghis Khan and Mongol Rule

Magna Carta

Medieval Castles

Medieval Cathedrals

The Medieval City

Medieval Science and Technology

The Rise of Islam

The Puebloan Society of Chaco Canyon

THE MEDIEVAL CITY

Norman Pounds

Greenwood Guides to Historic Events of the Medieval World
Jane Chance, Series Editor

GREENWOOD PRESS
Westport, Connecticut • London

Library of Congress Cataloging-in-Publication Data

Pounds, Norman John Greville.
  The medieval city / Norman Pounds.
      p. cm.—(Greenwood guides to historic events of the medieval world)
    Includes bibliographical references and index.
    ISBN 0–313–32498–0 (alk. paper)
    1. Cities and towns, Medieval—Europe. I. Title. II. Series.
  HT115.P68   2005
  307.76'094'0902—dc22   2004028021

British Library Cataloguing in Publication Data is available.

Library of Congress Catalog Card Number: 2004028021
ISBN: 0–313–32498–0

First published in 2005

Greenwood Press, 88 Post Road West, Westport, CT 06881
An imprint of Greenwood Publishing Group, Inc.
www.greenwood.com

Printed in the United States of America

The paper used in this book complies with the
Permanent Paper Standard issued by the National
Information Standards Organization (Z39.48–1984).

10 9 8 7 6 5 4 3 2 1

CONTENTS

ILLUSTRATIONS

SERIES FOREWORD

The Middle Ages are no longer considered the "Dark Ages" (as Petrarch termed them), sandwiched between the two enlightened periods of classical antiquity and the Renaissance. Often defined as a historical period lasting, roughly, from 500 to 1500 c.e., the Middle Ages span an enormous amount of time (if we consider the way other time periods have been constructed by historians) as well as an astonishing range of countries and regions very different from one another. That is, we call the "Middle" Ages the period beginning with the fall of the Roman Empire as a result of raids by northern European tribes of "barbarians" in the late antiquity of the fifth and sixth centuries and continuing until the advent of the so-called Italian and English renaissances, or rebirths of classical learning, in the fifteenth and sixteenth centuries. How this age could be termed either "Middle" or "Dark" is a mystery to those who study it. Certainly it is no longer understood as embracing merely the classical inheritance in the west or excluding eastern Europe, the Middle East, Asia, or even, as I would argue, North and Central America.

Whatever the arbitrary, archaic, and hegemonic limitations of these temporal parameters—the old-fashioned approach to them was that they were mainly not classical antiquity, and therefore not important—the Middle Ages represent a time when certain events occurred that have continued to affect modern cultures and that also, inevitably, catalyzed other medieval events. Among other important events, the Middle Ages saw the birth of Muhammad (c. 570–632) and his foundation of Islam in the seventh century as a rejection of Christianity which led to the imperial conflict between East and West in the eleventh and twelfth centuries. In western Europe in the Middle Ages the foundations for modern nationalism and modern law were laid and the concept of romantic love arose in the Middle Ages, this latter event partly one of the indirect consequences of the Crusades. With the shaping of national identity came the need to defend boundaries against invasion; so the castle emerged as a military outpost—whether in northern Africa, during the Crusades, or in Wales, in the eleventh century, to defend William of Normandy's newly acquired provinces—to satisfy that need. From Asia the invasions of Genghis Khan changed the literal and cultural shape of eastern and southern Europe.

In addition to triggering the development of the concept of chivalry and the knight, the Crusades influenced the European concepts of the lyric, music, and musical instruments; introduced to Europe an appetite for spices like cinnamon, coriander, and saffron and for dried fruits like prunes and figs as well as a desire for fabrics such as silk; and brought Aristotle to the European university through Arabic and then Latin translations. As a result of study of the "new" Aristotle, science and philosophy dramatically changed direction—and their emphasis on this material world helped to undermine the power of the Catholic Church as a monolithic institution in the thirteenth century.

By the twelfth century, with the centralization of the one (Catholic) Church, came a new architecture for the cathedral—the Gothic—to replace the older Romanesque architecture and thereby to manifest the Church's role in the community in a material way as well as in spiritual and political ways. Also from the cathedral as an institution and its need to dramatize the symbolic events of the liturgy came medieval drama—the mystery and the morality play, from which modern drama derives in large part. Out of the cathedral and its schools to train new priests (formerly handled by monasteries) emerged the medieval institution of the university. Around the same time, the community known as a town rose up in eastern and western Europe as a consequence of trade and the necessity for a new economic center to accompany the development of a bourgeoisie, or middle class. Because of the town's existence, the need for an itinerant mendicancy that could preach the teachings of the Church and beg for alms in urban centers sprang up.

Elsewhere in the world, in North America the eleventh-century settlement of Chaco Canyon by the Pueblo peoples created a social model like no other, one centered on ritual and ceremony in which the "priests" were key, but one that lasted barely two hundred years before it collapsed and its central structures were abandoned.

In addition to their influence on the development of central features of modern culture, the Middle Ages have long fascinated the modern age because of parallels that exist between the two periods. In both, terrible wars devastated whole nations and peoples; in both, incurable diseases plagued cities and killed large percentages of the world's population. In both periods, dramatic social and cultural changes took place as a result of these events: marginalized and overtaxed groups in societies rebelled against imperious governments; trade and a burgeoning middle class came to the fore; outside the privacy of the family, women began to have a greater role in Western societies and their cultures.

How different cultures of that age grappled with such historical change is the subject of the Greenwood Guides to Historic Events of the Medieval World. This series features individual volumes that illuminate key events in medieval world history. In some cases, an "event" occurred during a relatively limited time period. The troubadour lyric as a phenomenon, for example, flowered and died in the courts of Aquitaine in the twelfth century, as did the courtly romance in northern Europe a few decades later. The Hundred Years War between France and England generally took place during a precise time period, from the fourteenth to mid-fifteenth centuries.

In other cases, the event may have lasted for centuries before it played itself out: the medieval Gothic cathedral, for example, may have been first built in the twelfth century at Saint-Denis in Paris (c. 1140), but cathedrals, often of a slightly different style of Gothic architecture, were still being built in the fifteenth century all over Europe and, again, as the symbolic representation of a bishop's seat, or chair, are still being built today. And the medieval city, whatever its incarnation in the early Middle Ages, basically blossomed between the eleventh and thirteenth centuries as a result of social, economic, and cultural changes. Events—beyond a single dramatic historically limited happening—took longer to affect societies in the Middle Ages because of the lack of political and social centralization, the primarily agricultural and rural nature of most countries, difficulties in communication, and the distances between important cultural centers.

Each volume includes necessary tools for understanding such key events in the Middle Ages. Because of the postmodern critique of authority that modern societies underwent at the end of the twentieth century, students and scholars as well as general readers have come to mistrust the commentary and expertise of any one individual scholar or commentator and to identify the text as an arbiter of "history." For this reason, each book in the series can be described as a "library in a book." The intent of the series is to provide a quick, in-depth examination and current perspectives on the event to stimulate critical thinking as well as ready-reference materials, including primary documents and biographies of key individuals, for additional research.

Specifically, in addition to a narrative historical overview that places the specific event within the larger context of a contemporary perspective, five to seven developmental chapters explore related focused aspects of the event. In addition, each volume begins with a brief chronology and ends with a conclusion that discusses the consequences and impact of the event. There are also brief biographies of twelve to twenty key individuals (or places or buildings, in the book on the cathedral); primary documents from the period (for example, letters, chronicles, memoirs, diaries, and other writings) that illustrate states of mind or the turn of events at the time, whether historical, literary, scientific, or philosophical; illustrations (maps, diagrams, manuscript illuminations, portraits); a glossary of terms; and an annotated bibliography of important books, articles, films, and CD-ROMs available for additional research. An index concludes each volume.

No particular theoretical approach or historical perspective characterizes the series; authors developed their topics as they chose, generally taking into account the latest thinking on any particular event. The editors selected final topics from a list provided by an advisory board of high school teachers and public and school librarians. On the basis of nominations of scholars made by distinguished writers, the series editor also tapped internationally known scholars, both those with lifelong expertise and others with fresh new perspectives on a topic, to author the twelve books in the series. Finally, the series editor selected distinguished medievalists, art historians, and archaeologists to complete an advisory board: Gwinn Vivian, retired professor of archaeology at the University of Arizona Museum; Sharon Kinoshita, associate professor of French literature, world literature, and cultural studies at the University of California–Santa Cruz; Nancy Wu, associate museum educator at the Metropolitan Museum of Art, The Cloisters, New York City; and Christo-

pher A. Snyder, chair of the Department of History and Politics at Mary-
mount University.

In addition to examining the event and its effects on the specific cultures involved through an array of documents and an overview, each volume provides a new approach to understanding these twelve events.
Treated in the series are: the Black Death; the Crusades; Eleanor of
Aquitaine, courtly love, and the troubadours; Genghis Khan and Mongol rule; Joan of Arc and the Hundred Years War; Magna Carta; the medieval castle, from the eleventh to the sixteenth centuries; the medieval
cathedral; the medieval city, especially in the thirteenth century; medieval science and technology; Muhammad and the rise of Islam; and the
Puebloan society of Chaco Canyon.

The Black Death, by Joseph Byrne, isolates the event of the epidemic
of bubonic plague in 1347–52 as having had a signal impact on medieval
Europe. It was, however, only the first of many related such episodes involving variations of pneumonic and septicemic plague that recurred over
350 years. Taking a twofold approach to the Black Death, Byrne investigates both the modern research on bubonic plague, its origins and
spread, and also medieval documentation and illustration in diaries, artistic works, and scientific and religious accounts. The demographic, economic, and political effects of the Black Death are traced in one chapter,
the social and psychological patterns of life in another, and cultural expressions in art and ritual in a third. Finally, Byrne investigates why
bubonic plague disappeared and why we continue to be fascinated by it.
Documents included provide a variety of medieval accounts—Byzantine,
Arabic, French, German, English, and Italian—several of which are
translated for the first time.

The Crusades, by Helen Nicholson, presents a balanced account of various crusades, or military campaigns, invented by Catholic or "Latin"
Christians during the Middle Ages against those they perceived as threats
to their faith. Such expeditions included the Crusades to the Holy Land
between 1095 and 1291, expeditions to the Iberian Peninsula, the "crusade" to northeastern Europe, the Albigensian Crusades and the Hussite
crusades—both against the heretics—and the crusades against the Ottoman Turks (in the Balkans). Although Muslim rulers included the concept of jihâd (a conflict fought for God against evil or his enemies) in
their wars in the early centuries of Islam, it had become less important
in the late tenth century. It was not until the middle decades of the

twelfth century that jihâd was revived in the wars with the Latin Christian Crusaders. Most of the Crusades did not result in victory for the
Latin Christians, although Nicholson concedes they slowed the advance
of Islam. After Jerusalem was destroyed in 1291, Muslim rulers did permit Christian pilgrims to travel to holy sites. In the Iberian Peninsula,
Christian rulers replaced Muslim rulers, but Muslims, Jews, and dissident
Christians were compelled to convert to Catholicism. In northeastern
Europe, the Teutonic Order's campaigns allowed German colonization
that later encouraged twentieth-century German claims to land and led
to two world wars. The Albigensian Crusade wiped out thirteenth-cen-
tury aristocratic families in southern France who held to the Cathar
heresy, but the Hussite crusades in the 1420s failed to eliminate the Hussite heresy. As a result of the wars, however, many positive changes occurred: Arab learning founded on Greek scholarship entered western
Europe through the acquisition of an extensive library in Toledo, Spain,
in 1085; works of western European literature were inspired by the holy
wars; trade was encouraged and with it the demand for certain products;
and a more favorable image of Muslim men and women was fostered by
the crusaders' contact with the Middle East. Nicholson also notes that
America may have been discovered because Christopher Columbus
avoided a route that had been closed by Muslim conquests and that the
Reformation may have been advanced because Martin Luther protested
against the crusader indulgence in his Ninety-five Theses (1517).

   Eleanor of Aquitaine, Courtly Love, and the Troubadours, by ffiona
Swabey, singles out the twelfth century as the age of the individual, in
which a queen like Eleanor of Aquitaine could influence the development of a new social and artistic culture. The wife of King Louis VII of
France and later the wife of his enemy Henry of Anjou, who became king
of England, she patronized some of the troubadours, whose vernacular
lyrics celebrated the personal expression of emotion and a passionate declaration of service to women. Love, marriage, and the pursuit of women
were also the subject of the new romance literature, which flourished in
northern Europe and was the inspiration behind concepts of courtly love.
However, as Swabey points out, historians in the past have misjudged
Eleanor, whose independent spirit fueled their misogynist attitudes. Similarly, Eleanor's divorce and subsequent stormy marriage have colored
ideas about medieval "love courts" and courtly love, interpretations of
which have now been challenged by scholars. The twelfth century is set

in context, with commentaries on feudalism, the tenets of Christianity, and the position of women, as well as summaries of the cultural and philosophical background, the cathedral schools and universities, the influence of Islam, the revival of classical learning, vernacular literature, and Gothic architecture. Swabey provides two biographical chapters on Eleanor and two on the emergence of the troubadours and the origin of courtly love through verse romances. Within this latter subject Swabey also details the story of Abelard and Heloise, the treatise of Andreas Capellanus (André the Chaplain) on courtly love, and Arthurian legend as a subject of courtly love.

Genghis Khan and Mongol Rule, by George Lane, identifies the rise to power of Genghis Khan and his unification of the Mongol tribes in the thirteenth century as a kind of globalization with political, cultural, economic, mercantile, and spiritual effects akin to those of modern globalization. Normally viewed as synonymous with barbarian destruction, the rise to power of Genghis Khan and the Mongol hordes is here understood as a more positive event that initiated two centuries of regeneration and creativity. Lane discusses the nature of the society of the Eurasian steppes in the twelfth and thirteenth centuries into which Genghis Khan was born; his success at reshaping the relationship between the northern pastoral and nomadic society with the southern urban, agriculturalist society; and his unification of all the Turco-Mongol tribes in 1206 before his move to conquer Tanquit Xixia, the Chin of northern China, and the lands of Islam. Conquered thereafter were the Caucasus, the Ukraine, the Crimea, Russia, Siberia, Central Asia, Afghanistan, Pakistan, and Kashmir. After his death his sons and grandsons continued, conquering Korea, Persia, Armenia, Mesopotamia, Azerbaijan, and eastern Europe—chiefly Kiev, Poland, Moravia, Silesia, and Hungary—until 1259, the end of the Mongol Empire as a unified whole. Mongol rule created a golden age in the succeeding split of the Empire into two, the Yuan dynasty of greater China and the Il-Khanate dynasty of greater Iran. Lane adds biographies of important political figures, famous names such as Marco Polo, and artists and scientists. Documents derive from universal histories, chronicles, local histories and travel accounts, official government documents, and poetry, in French, Armenian, Georgian, Chinese, Persian, Arabic, Chaghatai Turkish, Russian, and Latin.

Joan of Arc and the Hundred Years War, by Deborah Fraioli, presents the Hundred Years War between France and England in the fourteenth and fifteenth centuries within contexts whose importance has sometimes been blurred or ignored in past studies. An episode of apparently only moderate significance, a feudal lord's seizure of his vassal's land for harboring his mortal enemy, sparked the Hundred Years War, yet on the face of it the event should not have led inevitably to war. But the lord was the king of France and the vassal the king of England, who resented losing his claim to the French throne to his Valois cousin. The land in dispute, extending roughly from Bordeaux to the Pyrenees mountains, was crucial coastline for the economic interests of both kingdoms. The series of skirmishes, pitched battles, truces, stalemates, and diplomatic wrangling that resulted from the confiscation of English Aquitaine by the French form the narrative of this Anglo-French conflict, which was in fact not given the name Hundred Years War until the nineteenth century.

Fraioli emphasizes how dismissing women's inheritance and succession rights came at the high price of unleashing discontent in their male heirs, including Edward III, Robert of Artois, and Charles of Navarre. Fraioli also demonstrates the centrality of side issues, such as Flemish involvement in the war, the peasants' revolts that resulted from the costs of the war, and Joan of Arc's unusually clear understanding of French "sacred kingship." Among the primary sources provided are letters from key players such as Edward III, Etienne Marcel, and Joan of Arc; a supply list for towns about to be besieged; and a contemporary poem by the celebrated scholar and court poet Christine de Pizan in praise of Joan of Arc.

Magna Carta, by Katherine Drew, is a detailed study of the importance of the Magna Carta in comprehending England's legal and constitutional history. Providing a model for the rights of citizens found in the United States Declaration of Independence and Constitution's first ten amendments, the Magna Carta has had a role in the legal and parliamentary history of all modern states bearing some colonial or government connection with the British Empire. Constructed at a time when modern nations began to appear, in the early thirteenth century, the Magna Carta (signed in 1215) presented a formula for balancing the liberties of the people with the power of modern governmental institutions. This unique English document influenced the growth of a form of law (the English common law) and provided a vehicle for the evolution of representative (parliamentary) government. Drew demonstrates how the Magna Carta came to be—the roles of the Church, the English towns, barons, common law, and the parliament in its making—as well as how myths concerning its provisions were established. Also provided are biographies of Thomas Becket, Charlemagne, Frederick II, Henry II and his sons, Innocent III, and many other key figures, and primary documents—among them, the Magna Cartas of 1215 and 1225, and the Coronation Oath of Henry I.

Medieval Castles, by Marilyn Stokstad, traces the historical, political, and social function of the castle from the late eleventh century to the sixteenth by means of a typology of castles. This typology ranges from the early "motte and bailey"—military fortification, and government and economic center—to the palace as an expression of the castle owners' needs and purposes. An introduction defines the various contexts—military, political, economic, and social—in which the castle appeared in the Middle Ages. A concluding interpretive essay suggests the impact of the castle and its symbolic role as an idealized construct lasting until the modern day.

Medieval Cathedrals, by William Clark, examines one of the chief contributions of the Middle Ages, at least from an elitist perspective—that is, the religious architecture found in the cathedral ("chair" of the bishop) or great church, studied in terms of its architecture, sculpture, and stained glass. Clark begins with a brief contextual history of the concept of the bishop and his role within the church hierarchy, the growth of the church in the early Christian era and its affiliation with the bishop (deriving from that of the bishop of Rome), and the social history of cathedrals. Because of economic and political conflicts among the three authorities who held power in medieval towns—the king, the bishop, and the cathedral clergy—cathedral construction and maintenance always remained a vexed issue, even though the owners—the cathedral clergy—usually held the civic responsibility for the cathedral. In an interpretive essay, Clark then focuses on Reims Cathedral in France, because both it and the bishop's palace survive, as well as on contemporary information about surrounding buildings. Clark also supplies a historical overview on the social, political, and religious history of the cathedral in the Middle Ages: an essay on patrons, builders, and artists; aspects of cathedral construction (which was not always successful); and then a chapter on Romanesque and Gothic cathedrals and a "gazetteer" of twenty-five important examples.

The Medieval City, by Norman J. G. Pounds, documents the origin of the medieval city in the flight from the dangers or difficulties found in the country, whether economic, physically threatening, or cultural. Identifying the attraction of the city in its urbanitas, its "urbanity," or the way of living in a city, Pounds discusses first its origins in prehistoric and classical Greek urban revolutions. During the Middle Ages, the city grew primarily between the eleventh and thirteenth centuries, remaining essentially the same until the Industrial Revolution. Pounds provides chapters on the medieval city's planning, in terms of streets and structures; life in the medieval city; the roles of the Church and the city government in its operation; the development of crafts and trade in the city; and the issues of urban health, wealth, and welfare. Concluding with the role of the city in history, Pounds suggests that the value of the city depended upon its balance of social classes, its need for trade and profit to satisfy personal desires through the accumulation of wealth and its consequent economic power, its political power as a representative body within the kingdom, and its social role in the rise of literacy and education and in nationalism. Indeed, the concept of a middle class, a bourgeoisie, derives from the city—from the bourg, or "borough." According to Pounds, the rise of modern civilization would not have taken place without the growth of the city in the Middle Ages and its concomitant artistic and cultural contribution.

Medieval Science and Technology, by Elspeth Whitney, examines science and technology from the early Middle Ages to 1500 within the context of the classical learning that so influenced it. She looks at institutional history, both early and late, and what was taught in the medieval schools and, later, the universities (both of which were overseen by the Catholic Church). Her discussion of Aristotelian natural philosophy illustrates its impact on the medieval scientific worldview. She presents chapters on the exact sciences, meaning mathematics, astronomy, cosmology, astrology, statics, kinematics, dynamics, and optics; the biological and earth sciences, meaning chemistry and alchemy, medicine, zoology, botany, geology and meteorology, and geography; and technology. In an interpretive conclusion, Whitney demonstrates the impact of medieval science on the preconditions and structure that permitted the emergence of the modern world. Most especially, technology transformed an agricultural society into a more commercial and engine-driven society: waterpower and inventions like the blast furnace and horizontal loom turned iron working and cloth making into manufacturing operations. The invention of the mechanical clock helped to organize human activities through timetables rather than through experiential perception and thus facilitated the advent of modern life. Also influential in the establishment of a middle class were the inventions of the musket and pistol and the printing press. Technology, according to Whitney, helped advance the habits of mechanization and precise methodology. Her biographies introduce major medieval Latin and Arabic and classical natural philosophers and scientists. Extracts from various kinds of scientific treatises allow a window into the medieval concept of knowledge.

The Puebloan Society of Chaco Canyon, by Paul Reed, is unlike other volumes in this series, whose historic events boast a long-established historical record. Reed's study offers instead an original reconstruction of the Puebloan Indian society of Chaco, in what is now New Mexico, but originally extending into Colorado, Utah, and Arizona. He is primarily interested in its leaders, ritual and craft specialists, and commoners during the time of its chief flourishing, in the eleventh and twelfth centuries, as understood from archaeological data alone. To this new material he adds biographies of key Euro-American archaeologists and other individuals from the nineteenth and twentieth centuries who have made important discoveries about Chaco Canyon. Also provided are documents of archaeological description and narrative from early explorers' journals and archaeological reports, narratives, and monographs. In his overview chapters, Reed discusses the cultural and environmental setting of Chaco Canyon; its history (in terms of exploration and research); the Puebloan society and how it emerged chronologically; the Chaco society and how it appeared in 1100 c.e.; the "Outliers," or outlying communities of Chaco; Chaco as a ritual center of the eleventh-century Pueblo world; and, finally, what is and is not known about Chaco society. Reed concludes that ritual and ceremony played an important role in Chacoan society and that ritual specialists, or priests, conducted ceremonies, maintained ritual artifacts, and charted the ritual calendar. Its social organization matches no known social pattern or type: it was complicated, multiethnic, centered around ritual and ceremony, and without any overtly hierarchical political system. The Chacoans were ancestors to the later Pueblo people, part of a society that rose, fell, and evolved within a very short time period.

The Rise of Islam, by Matthew Gordon, introduces the early history of the Islamic world, beginning in the late sixth century with the career of the Prophet Muhammad (c. 570–c. 632) on the Arabian Peninsula. From Muhammad's birth in an environment of religious plurality—Christianity, Judaism, and Zoroastrianism, along with paganism, were joined by Islam—to the collapse of the Islamic empire in the early tenth century, Gordon traces the history of the Islamic community. The book covers topics that include the life of the Prophet and divine revelation (the Qur'an) to the formation of the Islamic state, urbanization in the Islamic Near East, and the extraordinary culture of Islamic letters and scholarship. In addition to a historical overview, Gordon examines the Caliphate and early Islamic Empire, urban society and economy, and the emergence, under the Abbasid Caliphs, of a "world religious tradition" up to the year 925 C.E.

As editor of this series I am grateful to have had the help of Benjamin Burford, an undergraduate Century Scholar at Rice University assigned to me in 2002–2004 for this project; Gina Weaver, a third-year graduate student in English; and Cynthia Duffy, a second-year graduate student in English, who assisted me in target-reading select chapters from some of these books in an attempt to define an audience. For this purpose I would also like to thank Gale Stokes, former dean of humanities at Rice University, for the 2003 summer research grant and portions of the 2003–2004 annual research grant from Rice University that served that end.

This series, in its mixture of traditional and new approaches to medieval history and cultures, will ensure opportunities for dialogue in the classroom in its offerings of twelve different "libraries in books." It should also propel discussion among graduate students and scholars by means of the gentle insistence throughout on the text as primal. Most especially, it invites response and further study. Given its mixture of East and West, North and South, the series symbolizes the necessity for global understanding, both of the Middle Ages and in the postmodern age.

Jane Chance, Series Editor
Houston, Texas
February 19, 2004

PREFACE

This book is about the city, not a specific city, nor about the city through-out the several millennia of its existence. It is about that kind of city which emerged in Europe from the ruins of the Roman Empire and was transformed out of all recognition by the coming of manufacturing industries in modern times. This was the medieval city. It possessed qualities that distinguished it from those cities that had gone before it and that were to come after it. It was distinct also from contemporary cities in other parts of the world, such as those of the Middle East and south and east Asia.

One can debate endlessly the extent of the debt—unquestionably great—the medieval city owed to the classical cities of Greece and Rome and also the extent—probably small—of borrowings from the Middle East and the rest of Asia. By and large the medieval city was *sui generis*: it belonged to a type that was peculiarly its own. It was a response to conditions—social, economic, technological—that existed at the time and were radically changed during the following centuries.

Briefly defined, a city is a nucleated settlement that must engage in manufacturing and service occupations for the simple reason that agriculture could neither support nor employ all of its population. Before the city emerged, people lived in smaller settlement units—villages, hamlets, even isolated homesteads—and had subsisted almost wholly by cultivating their surrounding soil. Why, then, did the change occur from small agricultural settlements to large communities in which craft industries, the exchange of goods, and the performance of services played an increasingly important role?

This transition was no simple process. An increase in population and the need for protection unquestionably played a part. The classical Greeks rationalized the process, claiming that, because the growth of the city improved the quality of life, this must have been why rural settlements joined together to create an urban settlement. They even created a name, *synoicism*, to define the process. But this is to confuse cause with consequence. The creation of cities was a stage in the long progress of humanity from its hunting and collecting ancestry to the present. Like most such giant steps in the ladder of human progress, however, the creation of cities owed more to accident than to premeditation.

Cities emerged in Europe, the Middle East, and south India as early as the second millennium B.C.E., if not earlier. We recognize their remains today by their defenses and the scraps of buildings that have survived all the way from the hillforts of England to the walls of Jericho and the walled towns that once graced the plains of the rivers Tigris and Euphrates. The prehistoric town merged into the classical town with important changes in plan and composition but serving the same basic functions. There was often a change from a site whose chief recommendation was that it could be defended with relative ease to one more suited to the strictly urban functions of manufacturing and trade.

In the fifth century C.E. the urban civilization of Europe—that of the Middle East and beyond was less affected—came almost to an end. It is difficult to say how many Roman cities there may have been. Their definition is obscure; small towns merged into large villages. In Roman Britain there could have been as many as fifty or sixty towns, and they were far more numerous in Italy and southern France. The boundary of Roman authority lay along the rivers Rhine and Danube, and the sophisticated Roman town was never to be found beyond that line. Even within the bounds of the empire there were very few towns in the Balkans. Perhaps as many as a thousand places within the European provinces of the empire could have claimed the title of *urbs* (city), *civitas* (tribal capital), or *oppidum* (fort).

At intervals in the biological history of life on earth there has occurred a great dying off, when most species disappeared, leaving only enough to initiate a general renewal and a fresh evolutionary process. The same has happened to the cities of the Roman Empire. Most succumbed to invasion or to the economic forces that invasion set in motion, and those that did not wholly disappear were very much depleted. The decline and "fall" of the Roman Empire consisted essentially of the decay of towns and the disappearance of their urban functions. In extreme cases the former towns ceased even to be inhabited places, and they are marked today, if marked at all, only by banks and ditches and a few scraps of masonry.

During the following centuries the urban cycle began anew. Slowly, haltingly, small rural settlements adopted craft industries and became centers of exchange in a growing pattern of trade. This renewed growth sometimes took place on sites which, until recently, the Romans had once occupied and where they had left an infrastructure in the shape of roads and bridges. Most, however, were on virgin sites more suited to their newly developing economy.

This new urban pattern began to take shape in the seventh, eighth, and ninth centuries. There were many false starts, but the process was well under way during the eleventh and twelfth centuries, and was in full flood during the thirteenth. By the fourteenth the urban pattern was complete. There was neither space nor need for more cities, and the pattern which had been established by then was to remain little changed until the eighteenth or even the nineteenth century. The Industrial Revolution, the use of mechanical power, and the creation of the factory system—only vaguely hinted at toward the end of the Middle Ages—not only transformed many of the existing cities, but also brought about the creation of a new and, as far as Europe was concerned, final wave of urbanization.

It is with this intermediate phase in urban history, from the centuries following the decline of Rome until the completion of the urban pattern by the end of the Middle Ages, that we are primarily concerned in this book. Enough remains of these cities in the physical sense to allow us to construct a fairly complete picture of what they were like. Literary sources—narrative, legal, administrative—are abundant and give insight into the ways in which people lived within them.

It is no easier to estimate the number of cities that may have existed in medieval Europe at the height of their development in the fourteenth century than it is for the classical period. Their number fluctuated, as new towns were founded to meet new demands and older towns fell out of contention as, with changing economic circumstances, there ceased to be a need for them. And again, as in classical times it is often difficult to draw a line between small towns and large villages. They merge into one another, and if we say that the distinction is a legal one, lying in the possession, or the lack, of a charter of incorporation, this is as close as we are likely to come. If we say that, during the closing centuries of the Middle Ages, there were from four to five thousand cities and towns, we should probably be not too wide of the mark. There would, furthermore, have been relatively few large cities and a very great number of small towns. There is a tendency to use the terms *city* and *town* indiscriminately. In Great Britain the difference between them is technical, even legal. In the common use of these terms, however, *city* usually denotes a large settlement and *town* a small.

Whatever their size, each city or town was unique in plan, in function, and in social structure. Yet they all had enough in common for generalization to be possible, and it is a generalized picture of the medieval urban settlement that this book seeks to portray. Each was by definition distinct and cut off from its surrounding country not only in the functions it fulfilled but also in its legal and administrative standing. This is what F. W. Maitland meant when he claimed that the definition of the town was a legal matter (see p. 99). The city or town had acquired a charter or is presumed to have done so, and this charter conferred on it certain legal and economic rights. The city or town was cut off in these respects from the surrounding countryside. It was subject to the authority of a council, usually elected, whose jurisdiction was precisely defined and was separate from and independent of the feudal jurisdiction of the several lords of the rural manors and estates that surrounded and enclosed it. But there were various levels of independence, ranging from the city-state, which was in most respects sovereign and independent, to the very restricted independence enjoyed by most small towns. The possession of a limited degree of local autonomy is only one of the defining features of the town, but it is precise. The settlement either does or does not possess a degree of autonomy that to some extent removes it from the system of landholding we know as feudalism.

The second essential feature of the city, which distinguished it from the rural settlement or village, was the possession of certain economic functions. Its population was engaged to a variable extent in nonagricultural activities, though here there is less precision. Many villages possessed craftsmen; it is all a matter of degree. No city was ever completely divorced from the land and agriculture, but, except in a very few specialized cases, its population was greater than could be profitably employed in the fields within a reasonable distance of it. If fields were very distant, travel time would have consumed too great a part of the working day for their cultivation to have been profitable. Every city had thus to import and to pay for some part of its total food consumption, and this it could do only by making and selling goods or by performing services for which it received a monetary reward. It can be argued that there were cities, among them some of the largest and most important, which solved their problem of the balance of payments by levying taxes or exacting tribute. Foremost among them was medieval Rome, where a very high level of consumption was maintained by the contributions of the faithful throughout Catholic Europe. But Rome was not altogether an exception; it can be argued that the city maintained itself by performing a spiritual service for which it was paid, somewhat generously, by the Church at large.

Every city and town had a range of activities we can define as "basic" in the sense that they provided the export commodities and earned the revenues without which the city could not continue to import foodstuffs and industrial materials and thus preserve itself. At the same time, every city had nonbasic industries and services, which the city provided for the convenience of its own citizens. The baker and the butcher thus served almost exclusively the needs of their neighbors, while the armorer or the silversmith sold most of his wares beyond the city limits.

At the opposite end of the urban spectrum were the countless small towns, few of them with more than a thousand inhabitants, which proliferated in England and throughout central Europe. Here the food deficit was supplied by the villagers of the surrounding countryside, whose carts brought produce to their weekly markets. The town reciprocated by selling them the common articles of everyday life that could not readily be produced in their native villages.

This is the urban model that this book seeks to examine and exemplify. Examples are cited of basic products and activities, since these differed from one town to another. Their production or performance, however, called for a complex infrastructure. Goods had to be transported, some of them over very great distances, by a combination of ships, wheeled vehicles, and pack animals. Warehouses were needed for their storage and cranes for loading and unloading goods onto and off of boats. There were contracts and bills of exchange to be drawn up, and notaries and scriveners to prepare them. The multiplicity of currencies and the varying rates of exchange among them raised problems and called for expert handling. The fourteenth-century Italian merchant Francisco Balducci Pegolotti compiled a handbook—the *Pratica della mercatoria*—to guide merchants and others through these intricacies. But such commercial refinements were found mainly in the larger cities, rarely occurring in the small towns, where peasants and townsfolk engaged in a noisy barter or at most passed a few coins from hand to hand. These matters are discussed more fully in the following pages.

The city or town in which these activities were carried on was compactly built and, at least in continental Europe, was contained for its own security within an enclosing wall with towers and fortified gates. The walls had the symbolic effect of cutting off the city from its encircling countryside. The walls emphasized the contrast between town and country and gave to the city an almost personal quality. The citizens saw their city as something with which they could identify; it had a personality, represented by the heraldic display which decorated its entrance and sealed the documents drawn up on its behalf. Its walls also exercised a physical constraint on its expansion. It was, of course, always possible to build a later line of walls, enclosing a greater area. This happened in several of the largest cities in Europe. Before this could happen, however, it was usual to occupy all the open spaces: the courts, gardens, and yards which lay behind the existing rows of houses. Most towns became increasingly densely built up, until the only way to accommodate an increasing population was to build upward—to add second, third, and even more stories to the existing buildings. Village houses generally had only a single story; town houses were similar at first, and when additional floors were added it was often without first strengthening the ground floor. Town houses, and especially the larger among them, were notoriously unstable. Walls were thrown out of the vertical, and floors were uneven, partly as a result of the use of unseasoned timber, partly because too great a burden had been placed on their lower members. Only when there was no more space available within the walls did its citizens begin to build suburban—"below the city"—quarters and thus to risk living unprotected outside its walls.

The hazards of urban life were greater than those in the countryside, however. The medieval town was, more often than not, congested in the extreme, so that the supply of water and the disposal of sewage became matters of the greatest importance. Most urban structures were timber-framed, and the wood, in the absence of any kind of preservative, rotted quickly, leading to the collapse of the buildings themselves. Heating and cooking were done over an open fire; thus, domestic fires were frequent, sometimes leading to widespread conflagrations. Disease also spread rapidly through the congested urban homes. Mortality was great, higher by far than that normally experienced in rural areas. One is left asking why people were so ready to desert the country for the town. The answer must lie in the greater rewards the latter had to offer. There was wealth to be had from trade. Not all who migrated to a town made a fortune or even a modest living, but there was always the chance of doing so, and most people are by nature gamblers.

The city was a continent-wide institution, and this book seeks to give some attention to most parts of Europe. The writer claims some firsthand knowledge of most of the significant towns in almost every country and has explored their streets and alleys, their public and private buildings during well over half a century. But his deepest familiarity is with the cities and towns of England. The documentary sources he has used over this long period have been English. This is reflected in the choice of illustrative examples and documentary sources. If it is complained that there is no mention of medieval towns in Slovakia or Norway or Portugal, it can only be replied that the towns found in those parts generally conformed with the model presented in the preceding text and that lack of space prevents any particular examination of them.

These paragraphs have sketched a model of the medieval city, one to which all in a greater or lesser degree conformed. The following eight chapters explore this model and conclude with a discussion of the place of the medieval city in the history of western culture and its contribution to the society of the present.

This book has been written between bouts of illness, and the writer is deeply grateful to Professor Jane Chance, editor of this series, for her kindness and forbearance. He is also indebted to Liz Wetton who has read much of it with the hawk-like eye of an experienced editor and has corrected many blemishes in style and judgment. He is also grateful to Cambridge University Library, not only for the use over a long lifetime of its superb collections, but also for making copies of the engravings by Schedel and Braun and Hogenberg, copies of which it holds. All artwork has been prepared by the author.

CHAPTER 1

ORIGINS

When several villages are united in a single complete community,
large enough to nearly or quite self-sufficing, the [city-]state comes
into existence, originating in the bare needs of life, and continuing
in existence for the sake of a good life.

—Aristotle[1]

The town or city—the words are almost synonymous[2]—is a human settlement, larger than a village and not primarily dependent on agriculture
for the employment and support of its inhabitants. Indeed, the multiplicity of its functions—manufacturing, commerce, services, even agriculture itself—is one of its distinguishing features. Another feature of the
town, at least of the medieval town, is that its fields, cultivated by its
own citizens, could not possibly have produced enough food for their subsistence. It always had to import foodstuffs from areas beyond its direct
control. And, because these had to be requited or paid for, the citizens
necessarily had to produce goods or perform services for outsiders. Every
successful town established over the course of time a complex of relationships not only with its surrounding areas, but also with distant places
which in turn supplied it with both food and the materials needed for its
crafts. This was its hinterland.

All towns before modern times were to some extent engaged in agriculture, but a strict limit was set to the extent of this agriculture's development. Each morning citizen-farmers would lead their wagons and
carry their tools to the surrounding fields, returning each evening to the
security of their urban homes. But how far would they be prepared to

travel? The answer must be no greater distance than they could travel in an hour or little more; the farthest cultivated field could be no more than what a citizen could walk in an hour or so, whether the town covered only a few acres and had less than a thousand inhabitants or was by medieval standards a giant city of 50,000. Renaissance engravings of towns show them surrounded by the cultivated fields of their citizens.

In the course of European history, there have been four periods or phases when the foundation and development of towns was a major preoccupation of European peoples. The first was during the prehistoric period, from the Bronze Age to the Iron, when the so-called hillforts were constructed. These were large areas, enclosed by bank, ditch, and palisade. For the inhabitants of nearby farms and hamlets, the hillforts were places of refuge to which they could retreat in time of war. They served also for the storage of food and the practice of simple craft industries, which may have included tanning, weaving, and metalworking.

Such a hillfort was Danebury, lying amid the rolling hills of southern England. It is a rounded site with multiple banks and ditches and a highly sophisticated entrance that an attacker would have found very difficult to penetrate (Figure 1).

The enclosed area was about twelve acres, closely similar to that of many medieval towns. The dating of Danebury fort is difficult. The carbon-14 method was used with fragments of wood found in the foundations of huts within the banked perimeter. This showed that the site was occupied, perhaps not continuously, from the seventh century B.C.E. until the period of the Roman invasion in 43 C.E. Excavation revealed huts in which stores of food might have been kept and people might have lived during an emergency. There was also evidence for crafting within the enclosure, especially potting, weaving, the manufacture of wooden articles such as plows and even wheeled vehicles, and the fabrication of tools and weapons of iron. Most of the raw materials used came from the local agricultural activities, but iron ore was not among the local resources. It was probably obtained by the Danebury people from as far away as the Weald of Kent—some forty miles—in southeastern England, a region important for its ironworking from prehistoric times until the eighteenth century. In this and in other ways, Danebury had become a center of long-distance trade. We know from the finds retrieved in the course of excavation that a variety of goods was imported by the Danebury people.

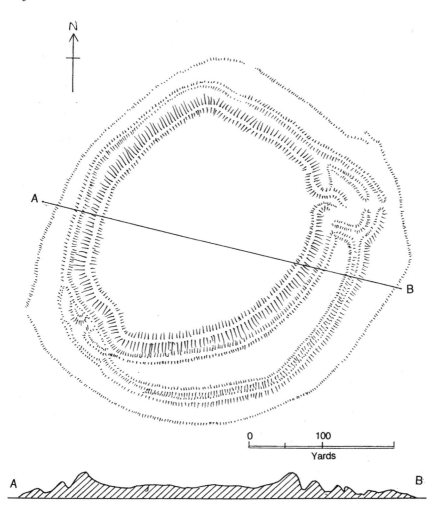

Figure 1. Danebury, an Iron Age (c. 800 to 400 B.C.E.) hillfort in southern England. It can be seen as a proto-urban town, serving as a place of safety for the inhabitants of the surrounding area. Based on Barry H. Cunliffe, *Danebury: Anatomy of an Iron Age Hillfort*, London: Batsford, 1983.

Hillforts like Danebury were proto-urban towns, and they continued to be used in many parts of northern and central Europe until, in both form and function, they were superseded by the classical city of the Greeks and Romans. In Gaul (France), Julius Caesar was obliged to overcome the resistance of the hillforts of Alesia, Bibracte, and Gergovia, which he succeeded in capturing only after prolonged sieges. The Romans replaced them with towns of classical type on nearby but less defensible sites. In England the stupendous Iron Age fort Maiden Castle was replaced, though without a siege, by the low-lying city of Durnovaria, the modern Dorchester in the county of Dorset.

The second phase in the history of European urbanization began in classical Greece, though it owed much to earlier developments in the Middle East, and was continued in Roman Italy, Spain, Gaul, and even Britain. In the view of Aristotle the city or *polis* was created when those who inhabited the villages within a small, discrete area agreed to pool their resources and come together to form an urban community. This process they called *synoecism*. In reality, however, it was probably less simple than Aristotle's model suggests. The need for protection played an important part, as it was also to do in most subsequent urban developments. The configuration of Greece, with its many small coastal plains, each of them suited for a city-state, also contributed to the growth of towns. There were hundreds of *poleis* in the Greek world, reaching from the western Mediterranean to Anatolia and Cyprus. Some, like Athens and Corinth in Greece and Syracuse in Sicily, grew to be too large to be supported by their own small territories and developed overseas trade to supply their populations, but hundreds remained, even during the period of high Greek civilization, small and self-sufficient. Most fell under the control of the Athenian or Delian League after the Persian wars of the early fifth century B.C.E. They paid tribute to the league for their common defense against the Persians. These payments were recorded on marble tablets set up in the *agora* or central square of Athens and show both how numerous these cities were and how small. It was, however, characteristic of all of them that citizens took an immense pride in their respective cities and adorned them with temples, theaters, and public places. Aristotle claimed that urban living was the natural way of life for civilized human beings, a view of the city reaffirmed many times from that age to this.

Urbanization spread from Greece to Sicily and from Sicily up the Italian peninsula to Rome and beyond. The Roman legions carried the idea of the city to most of western Europe until Roman civilization had become as much a matter of living in and beautifying the city as Greek civilization had been. The Roman city was generally larger than the Greek city. The Romans saw the city as an instrument of civilization, as a means of taming the wild barbarians whom they had incorporated into their empire. The city replaced the hillfort. It was, as a general rule, carefully planned with straight streets intersecting at right-angles. Generous space was allowed for temples and basilicas or large halls, which served as public meeting places, for the *forum*, or central square, around which these buildings were grouped, and for the theater, where dramatic shows were performed, and the amphitheater or arena, where more brutal games were staged.

The peace, which the might of Rome had ensured, made it unnecessary at first to build defensive walls around cities. But late in the third century this began to change. Groups of barbarians broke across the Roman frontier along the rivers Rhine and Danube and threatened cities in the west and south of Europe. Walls were hastily built. Archaeology has shown how temples and similar buildings were raided for stone, so urgent was the need for protection. All towns of any importance came to be walled; nevertheless, most continued for a century and more to be centers of social and economic activity. Few were actually deserted, if only because their walls, towers, and fortified gates offered some protection against invaders. But their days were numbered. Their wealth, which had allowed and encouraged the construction of their monumental structures, was dependent on the peaceful exchange of goods and services between town and country, province and province. This interchange was the first victim of insecurity and war, and the decline of the Roman Empire was marked by the contraction, even the abandonment, of cities.

The North African Moors, a Berber people under Arab leadership, perpetuated urban life in those parts of Spain they invaded and settled. The Moors also preserved elements of Greek and Roman civilization and maintained and even enlarged some of the cities the Romans had established, such as Cordoba and Seville. This was not the norm, however; other invaders were Germans from central Europe, Vikings and Varangians from northern Europe, Slavs from eastern Europe, and Turkic peoples from Asia. Most of these invading peoples had been accustomed to living in small village communities and to packing up their possessions at intervals and moving to new sites, where they cultivated virgin land for a period before moving on again. They showed little inclination to settle in towns which the Romans had built, and, if they did not destroy them, they at least allowed them to fall to ruin. Crafts, which had been prosperous in an urban environment, decayed after their urban settings had fallen to ruin. Some former Roman towns disappeared, and in others the high quality of workmanship which had once prevailed was sadly diminished.

It is doubtful whether any towns in Roman Britain, with the exception of Londinium (London) and perhaps Eboracum (York), survived as functioning urban settlements. An Anglo-Saxon poem, probably written about the eighth century, described the crumbling remains of a once prosperous Roman city—probably Aquae Sulis, or Bath (see Document 1, "The Ruin"). The invaders could only marvel at the civilization of Rome and the structures it had created. It was beyond their capacity to copy them, even to keep them in good order. The decay and sometimes the disappearance of cities was a dominant feature of the decline and fall of the Roman Empire in the West.[3]

Yet this decay was not uniform over the whole territory of the Roman Empire. A few cities in both the East and the West survived and redeveloped into thriving centers of manufacturing and trade. This was most marked around the shores of the Mediterranean Sea. The Belgian historian Henri Pirenne once argued that sea-borne trade in the Mediterranean basin survived when overland trade had declined or disappeared, because in the nature of things the ship was safe from the depredations of land-based invaders. Both Rome and Byzantium survived and even prospered during the "dark" ages that followed the end of the western Roman Empire. Venice was founded by refugees from the destruction of the Roman city Aquileia by the invading Huns. Indeed, most cities that were to dominate Italy during the late Middle Ages had survived in some diminished form from the Roman period. In France also most of the provincial capitals of Roman Gaul, though pillaged by the invaders and ruinous, nevertheless survived as inhabited places. Only in Britain and in parts of Spain were Roman cities in large measure abandoned. In the Balkan peninsula most cities—there were in fact very few—were neglected, though their ruined sites may have continued to provide some degree of protection for small agricultural communities. In the midst of modern Sofia in Bulgaria lie the scanty remains of Serdica, the Roman capital of the province Thrace. The citizens of Salona in Croatia fled to the Adriatic coast on the appearance of invaders, and there they established a more secure settlement within the walls of the huge palace the Emperor Diocletian had built for himself at Split. But most of the small towns of the Balkans merely fell to ruin and disappeared. Stobi in Macedonia is today known only through excavations carried out in modern times.[4]

A few towns of the Graeco-Roman world continued to perform some attenuated urban functions. They had been during the later years of the empire the seats of authority, and as such had an appeal to the Germanic invaders who established their petty kings within their ruined walls. When Augustine brought Christianity to England in the year 597 C.E. he made his way to Canterbury, where the remains of the Roman town Durovernum had become the seat of Ethelberht, king of the minor Saxon tribe the Cantii.

Christianity became an accepted faith within the Roman Empire about 313 and was recognized as the only religion several decades later. Wherever Christianity had been accepted, its local representative, the bishop, established himself in one of the more important towns, and his diocese conformed more or less with the service area of the preceding Roman city. Where towns lay close together, as they did in southern Italy, bishops became numerous and their dioceses extremely small. The bishop's cathedral replaced the temple or basilica, and the activities of the church attracted a small population of traders and craftsmen. When the economic depression of the early Middle Ages began to lift in the ninth or tenth century, this urban nucleus became once again a populous and many-sided settlement.

Foremost among the cities that began to grow again and to flourish in this way were Rome and Byzantium. Rome had been the chief seat of the Caesars and continues still today to be adorned with their monumental architecture. The Bishop of Rome established a preeminence among other bishops just as the emperors had themselves ruled over the provinces of the empire. The Pope as Bishop of Rome was seen in some sense to be the heir to the Caesars. In the seventeenth century, Thomas Hobbes said that one "will easily perceive, that the Papacy, is no other than the *ghost* of the deceased *Roman Empire*, sitting crowned upon the grave thereof."[5] The empire of Rome was divided by Diocletian about 285 C.E. into an eastern and a western part. The western part was overrun by Germanic invaders, and ultimately succumbed in 476, leaving the Pope or Bishop of Rome as symbol of what unity there was in the Christian West. The eastern empire continued for another thousand years; its capital city, Byzantium, was perched above the cliffs bordering the

Bosporus, the waterway linking the Black Sea with the Mediterranean and separating Europe from Asia, and was impregnable to invaders whether by land or by sea. Byzantium continued to be the seat of authority within the eastern empire, providing a home for both secular and spiritual leaders. But in most of the eastern empire in Europe, urbanism declined or even disappeared. Only in its Asiatic provinces, in Syria and Egypt, Galatia and Cappadocia, did urbanism retain some vitality. And much of the small volume of trade that continued to circulate in the Mediterranean Sea and western Europe emanated from these regions.

The third urban revolution occupied much of the Middle Ages and is the primary subject of this book. Urbanism had not wholly disappeared during the centuries following the decline of the empire in the West. Some cities survived as human settlements, and a few became the tribal seats of government for the invading peoples. But their commercial and industrial life had been drained, and they had to be rebuilt slowly. By the end of the Middle Ages a vast number of cities and towns had emerged, varying greatly in size, in mode of origin, and degree of specialization. Counting them is an impossible task because the boundary between town and village was often vague and uncertain. In central Europe alone their number must have run into the thousands.

This was an age when society was organized feudally. Land was held by territorial lords in return for service—in government or in war—to their king. Under them were subtenants who held smaller units of land again in return for service to their masters. There may have been more separate, social layers before the servile underclass, which lived by actually cultivating the soil, was reached. The social structure was in reality very much more complex than this short definition suggests. There were classes that were neither wholly slave nor wholly free. Beside those who were *adscripti glebae*—"bound to the soil"—were others who were free in respect of all except their masters. There were what have been called "degrees of unfreedom." But the general social trend was upward; more and more of the underclass became free. By the end of the Middle Ages there were, in effect, no more unfree peasants in the land of England, but they survived in central Europe; in Romania and Russia there remained serfs until the 1860s. It was from these peoples that, in one way or another, the earliest medieval towns were populated. Once the bonds of serfdom were relaxed the peasant might move to the city hoping to become lost in its anonymity. There was a saying that *Stadt Luft macht frei*—"the air of the town makes you free." It was also said that an unfree peasant who had escaped and lived in a town for a year and a day could not be dragged back again to semi-slavery on the land. In one way or another, legally or illegally, country folk made their way to the towns, established their right to live there, and became the citizen body.

The town was a paradoxical institution. It was an exception to the feudal order of things. Its citizens were free. They could not be hauled before the court of a feudal lord. They had law courts of their own, which could hear cases that arose between them. When a lord granted a char-ter to a body of townspeople, he gave away his right of jurisdiction over them or at least the greater part of it. Henceforward they lay outside the sphere of feudal law and custom. Feudal custom barely recognized the town, and yet feudal lords saw profit in promoting new towns. It is prob-ably true to say that more than half the towns of late medieval Europe had been established by feudal lords and that the feudal lords engaged in this process because they gained financially from it. The feudal lords thus connived in the creation of institutions that lay outside the feudal order and in the rise of a bourgeois class, which was destined finally to over-throw them.

Yet there is no simple explanation for the origin and development of towns and cities. The following pages represent an attempt to classify the ways in which the institution took root and flourished. We have in the first place those cities which had survived as inhabited places, with some semblance of urban functions, from the Roman period. They were not numerous, but they included some—Rome, London, Paris, Cologne—which later grew to be among the largest in late medieval Europe. To these must be added those that emerged during the centuries immedi-ately following the end of the western empire in response to the slowly developing trade of both western and northern Europe. They included places in Scandinavia where the Vikings exchanged the loot, which they had acquired in their raids, for the more refined products of the eastern empire and the Middle East. Such were Birka, Jumne, and Haithabu, all lying around the shores of the Baltic Sea, and Ipswich and Norwich ("wich" in Anglo-Saxon denoted a trading place) in England. Not all survived, because they were dependent upon a particular pattern of trade that might not long endure. Those established in Scandinavia have long since disappeared, and even their sites are in some instances uncertain. Other towns arose at this time in response to the needs of defense. Such were the "burghs" founded in England by the Anglo-Saxon kings of the ninth and tenth centuries. These were built for defense against the invading Scandinavian peoples. Some completely disappeared after their usefulness had ended, but others succeeded in attracting craftsmen and traders by the protection they could offer and in consequence grew to be important towns. In central Europe the eastward spread of German settlement was accompanied by the foundation of urban settlements that combined commercial and defensive functions. The foundation of monasteries, most of them of the Benedictine Order, also provided nuclei around which traders and craftsmen settled. The monasteries themselves, together with those who visited them as pilgrims, created a demand for goods and services that were provided by small urban communities.

These towns—Roman survivals, trading and monastic communities, and defensive settlements—all had this in common. They were prefeudal in the sense that they had their origins before the feudal occupation of the land and at a time when there was, in effect, some freedom of movement and the social restrictions of the feudal system had not yet been imposed. They did not need authorization from secular or ecclesiastical authority in order to establish a town, though this may later have been requested and was granted in their retrospective charters. Such towns are here defined as "prescriptive," meaning that their authority derived from long-standing usage. In few instances can one say when these towns began, and when they first appear in the records, they were usually already well established. As feudalism developed from the tenth century onward, these towns were seen as anomalies, as institutions that lay outside the feudal concept of society, almost as a threat to its well-being. How then to reconcile the prescriptive city with the feudal view of society?

This quandary was resolved in two contrasting ways, both admirably demonstrated in England. In the first, feudal authority might impose a castle on the urban foundation, as if to keep the radical urban population under control. In England and France almost every significant city that had survived from the Roman and Anglo-Saxon periods had a castle, built usually in a corner of its walled perimeter. London may be the best example, with the Tower of London within its southeastern angle and bordering the river Thames, but the list would also include Canterbury, Exeter, York, Chester, Winchester, and Norwich as well as numerous cities throughout France and Italy. The Domesday Book of 1086 records how many houses were destroyed in order to make way for these castles. Furthermore, the king, as a general rule, retained these castles in his own hands. They became the seat of his chief local official—the sheriff, or "shire-reeve." The urban castle remained until late in the Middle Ages a bastion of both feudal and royal power against the radical population of the towns.[6]

The second method was to absorb the town into the feudal order: to restrict its powers and to make it a source of profit. This was achieved by the grant of a charter of liberties. This was not, in these instances, a foundation charter, since the town already had been in existence, perhaps for centuries. The charter of liberties was an attempt to define and also to limit the rights and privileges of the town and to prescribe its mode of government. The charter usually provided for the election of a mayor or chief executive together with a body of councilors; it defined its commercial rights, authorizing them to have, in addition to shops, a weekly market and an annual fair. It defined the legal standing of the town, which ceased in large measure to be amenable to the civil and criminal jurisdiction of the surrounding region. The charter was a kind of contract between the feudal order and the new mercantile order, the bourgeoisie, which was eventually to replace it.

In some parts of Europe, however, the assimilation of the preexisting city to the system of feudal law and custom that prevailed was generally never fully accomplished. The city retained its earlier practice of self-regulation. It remained politically and juridically cut off from the feudalized countryside, and its citizens sometimes referred to it as a "commune." This raised problems of food supply, access to water, and means of transportation. These problems could be solved in part by the extension of urban control and the jurisdiction of urban courts for a mile or two into the surrounding countryside. Thus was formed the medieval "city-state." In some respects it replicated the *polis* of the ancient Greeks. It usually recognized the shadowy authority of a distant emperor or king, but for all practical purposes it was self-regulating and self-governing. There were numerous rebellions, especially in Italy, as citizens tried, often unsuccessfully, to establish themselves as a commune. Even London attempted—and failed—to do just this.

Italy, a land in which centralized political authority had dissolved in the years following the collapse of the western empire, was characterized for much of the Middle Ages by its city-states. The same tended to happen in Germany, where urban independence, in the absence of a strong central authority, came to be emphasized at the expense of feudal control. There was a tendency, especially in Italy, for the city's control of its immediate hinterland to be extended until the city-state had become a far more extensive territorial state. In this way the duchies of Florence, Ferrara, Mantua, and others were formed, as well as the urban republics of Genoa and Venice, which both displayed a ravenous appetite for neighboring territory.

PLANTED TOWNS

The great majority of medieval towns originated in none of these ways. They were the conscious and deliberate creations of territorial lords, always for their own profit. The lords might fear the pretensions of an urban population, but they nonetheless envied the towns' wealth and were eager to acquire the goods they traded or produced. How then to create a town and to harness its productive capacity for their own profit? The answer was to create a new wave of urban foundations as territorial lords strove to profit from urban institutions and from the urban way of life. Their method was to grant a charter, to proclaim that future citizens were wanted, and to declare that the conditions under which they would live would be generous and their privileges extensive. Sufficient land would be set aside for a town, and in some instances streets were even planned and "burgage" or building plots delimited for the anticipated settlers. There were always footloose people. Many had made good their escape from manorial villages, and others had never known the constraints of the manorial economy. Such were attracted by the prospect of urban living and the relative freedom this offered. And so plots were taken up and an urban community gradually took shape. No incipient town could have prospered without a market, to which peasants of the neighborhood could bring their surplus products for sale and where they might obtain the few goods ranging from salt to cooking pots which they could not make themselves. A fair might also be allowed, held less frequently than the market but attracting traders from very much farther afield and dealing in more unusual goods. These towns are sometimes termed *planted* towns to distinguish them from the *organic* towns, which had grown up spontaneously.

But what if settlers did not come and the market and fair generated little business? The town was then still-born, its charter a hollow pretense and quickly forgotten, and as an inhabited place the would-be town reverted to a small agricultural settlement. There were many such *villes manquees*, or "failed towns," throughout western and central Europe. What the territorial lords, who had hoped to earn a revenue from burgage rents and market tolls, had failed to realize was that the number of urban settlers, the demand for urban products, and the volume of urban trade were all strictly limited. If chartered towns increased in number, then the volume of trade that could be carried on in each inevitably grew smaller. There were many ways to cut the cake, but its size nevertheless remained the same.

In the thirteenth century, Totnes was a prosperous town on the west bank of the river Dart in the English county of Devon (see Figure 2). It had been founded about 1100 by Judhael of Totnes, lord of the castle whose ruins still dominate the town. Across the river the land belonged

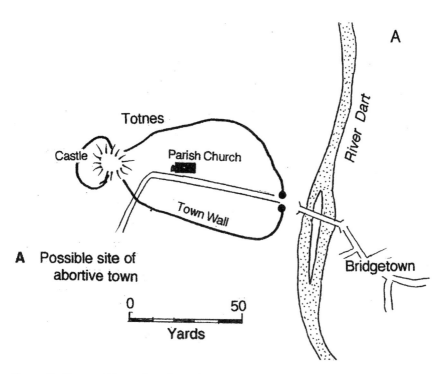

Figure 2. Totnes (Devon) and its abortive or unsuccessful satellites.

to other lords who supposed that if they also granted charters and laid out the streets of a new town they too would reap a steady income just as the lord of Totnes was doing. First came the borough of Bridgetown, at the distant end of the bridge across the river Dart. It achieved a very modest success at first, but then decayed and is today represented only by a small cluster of houses. Another attempt at town foundation was located a mile or so to the north. It was entirely unsuccessful, and no town ever materialized. The amount of business available in this part of Devon was not adequate for two incorporated boroughs, let alone for three.

In England, where government was more centralized and more effective than in almost any other part of Europe, it became the practice for the king to authorize the establishment of a town or market and fair. Before he did so, however, the king usually instituted an inquiry known as *ad quod damnum*. It asked the simple question: what harm might the proposed market do to the trade and profitability of markets already in existence? Only if there would be none was the proposed market, in theory at least, allowed to proceed. In continental Europe the same practice broadly prevailed. Market and fairs were established and given protection by territorial lords who profited from their activities. It became the general rule that no town could be founded closer to another existing town than a day's market journey (see p. 71).

Those who granted charters of foundation to medieval towns can have had little knowledge of the theoretical basis of their distribution. Only by a prolonged process of trial and error did they learn that some towns would fail if they were too closely spaced or if located in unproductive areas incapable of generating any significant trade. Yet hope springs eternal, and the tally of unsuccessful and failed towns runs to hundreds. Nor did they understand the institutions and infrastructure that made for a successful town. In this they looked to those that had—fortuitously perhaps—achieved a measure of success and imitated their practices or "laws." Many towns in England adopted the "Laws" of Breteuil, a small town in upper Normandy, which seemed to the Norman invaders of England to have achieved a certain degree of success. (See "Biographies and Places," pp. 174–75.)

The biggest wave of town foundations during the Middle Ages was in central and eastern Europe. Here it was part of the eastward progression of German-speaking peoples from the Elbe Valley to that of the Oder, and from the Oder to the Vistula, beyond which it petered out in the forests and steppe of eastern Poland and Russia. Certain well-established and successful towns in Germany served as models. Towns close to the Baltic coast derived their laws from those of the port city off Lubeck. Farther inland, Magdeburg was the most popular prototype, while others followed the customs of Nuremberg, Vienna, or Goslar. The practices followed in the Bohemian mining town of Jihlava (Ger. Iglau) were copied in the mining centers of upper Hungary and Transylvania.

There was a distinct periodization in the creation of medieval towns. Most organic towns had their origin during the early Middle Ages. One can rarely point to a date when they had their beginnings, but most were in existence by the year 1100. Far more is known of the origins of planted towns because they had their beginnings in a charter that bore a date. This is as true of southern France, Germany, and Poland as it is of England.

In England the first clear evidence for planted towns occurs in the Domesday Book itself (1086 c.e.). At Tutbury in Staffordshire, a borough had grown up *circa castellum*, "around the castle," and, since the castle had been a Norman innovation, the borough itself must have been at that time only a few years old. At several places along the Welsh border small boroughs were springing up close to the castles of the Norman invaders who almost certainly had founded them. Planted towns were least numerous, though far from unknown, in areas where there were already a number of older, organic towns as was the case in France and Italy.

Town foundation continued in England through the twelfth century and then peaked during the years 1190–1230. By this time, it might be said a sufficient network of towns had already been established to satisfy the needs of manufacturing and commerce. Few towns were founded between 1250 and the end of the century, by which time a number of those that had already been founded failed to survive. By 1300 the movement had for practical purposes run its course.[7]

Other areas where planted towns were especially numerous were southwestern France and Germany. In southwestern France, some ninety small, walled towns were founded in the period 1270–1350. They owed their origin chiefly to the English king Edward I (1272–1307) and his immediate successors in their roles as dukes of Aquitaine or rulers of southwestern France. Their motives were at least as political as they were economic, and the security of the English-held territory against other feudal lords was probably foremost in their minds. These towns, or "bastides," as they were called, resembled the Anglo-Saxon "burhs" of the ninth and tenth centuries in that their purpose was largely defensive and that some never succeeded in developing a significant commercial role and so reverted to fortified villages.

The most significant area of town foundation was central and eastern Europe north of the river Danube. Here there had never been any Roman towns to focus later urban growth, and few settlements had emerged in response to the needs of defense and commerce. The region was thinly peopled, and its development awaited settlers. These came from the tenth century onward in the form of immigrants mainly from the German lands between the rivers Rhine and Elbe. German lords from the west had conquered the land, but land without people was valueless. The lords therefore conducted a campaign to recruit settlers. It was like the populating of the American West during the middle years of the nineteenth century. According to Helmold, a twelfth-century chronicler, Adolf, count of Schauenburg, had acquired wide lands in what is today the north German province of Mecklenburg, and "[a]s the land was without inhabitants, he sent messengers into all parts, namely, to Flanders and Holland, to Utrecht, Westphalia, and Frisia, proclaiming that whosoever were in straits for lack of fields should come with their families, and receive a very good land,—a spacious land, rich in crops. . . . An innumerable multitude of different peoples rose up at this call and they came with their families and their goods into the land of Wagria [Holstein and Mecklenburg]."[8]

The newcomers laid out fields and planted towns which focused the business of their respective districts. The dates of rural settlement may be obscure, but the towns can be securely dated from their foundation charters. We can thus trace this wave of urban settlement as it spread from western Germany, where towns first appeared, to the basin of the Vistula, and from the Vistula into the wastes of Lithuania, Belorus, and Ukraine. Most of these towns were small and served only to exchange the products of urban crafts for the surplus grain and animals of the countryside. A few stood out as the centers of a long-distance trade, visited by merchants from much of Europe. They handled the animals driven westward from the steppe and gathered the grain that the merchants of the Hanse (see pp. 171–74) shipped to the large consuming centers of central and western Europe. This trade was for climatic reasons seasonal, and much of it was carried on by means of fairs that were held for only short periods at the appropriate times of the year.

This eastward movement for which the Germans use the overly dramatic name of *Drang nach Osten*—"the Drive to the East"—began during the eleventh century, if not before. By 1300 it was spreading across Poland, Bohemia, and Moravia, and by 1400 it had reached east Prussia and the Vistula. The following century took it to the borders of Lithuania. But its force was still not spent until in early modern times it reached Ukraine. Those who had been attracted mainly by mineral wealth penetrated the mountains of Slovakia and Transylvania and founded a number of towns that prospered with the mining boom of the Renaissance. This spread of urbanization, however, had little effect on the Hungarian Plain and almost none in the Balkans. Its failure here is explained by the incessant warfare that characterized the region, particularly after the coming of the Ottoman Turks in the fourteenth century. It was not that the Balkans lacked agricultural and mineral resources, but that these resources were being developed by local peoples and were handled by traders based on the coasts of the Adriatic and Black seas, where Venice, Zadar, Dubrovnik, and Varna grew rich on their profits.

Such was the progress of this, the third urban revolution in Europe. The fourth and last, which occupied much of the eighteenth and nineteenth centuries, was characterized not so much by the foundation of new towns, though these were in fact numerous, as, under the influence of the Industrial Revolution, by the selective growth of towns that had originated in the Roman or medieval periods. This was the origin of the industrial cities that reached their fullest development in the late nineteenth century, but that subject is beyond the scope of this book.

The medieval town assumed many forms and served a variety of functions, and its contribution to the development of western civilization is incalculable. At the same time the medieval town created problems that in many cases it proved unable to solve. The size of towns sometimes outgrew their ability to organize adequate supplies of water, food, and fuel. Large numbers of people living in close contact with one another contributed to the spread of epidemic disease. The disposal of sewage was managed only by sending it downriver to the next town. Congestion led to the building of multistoried houses of wood that were both highly unstable and very flammable (see pp. 39–40). Towns, last, never solved the problems of street crime and maintaining adequate policing. All these matters are examined in greater detail in later chapters of this book.

How many cities and towns were there in the continent of Europe when, about 1500, the Middle Ages drew to a close? It will be argued in Chapter 3 that they must have numbered two to three thousand or more. Each was unique, differing from all the others in its physical qualities, economic development, and institutions of government. All the larger cities have been the subjects of major books, and a history could be written for each of them. A short book about the medieval city can look only at those features that were common to most if not all of them. It is impossible in so short a space to delve into their peculiarities and idiosyncrasies. It is not possible even to mention by name all those of greater size and importance. What follows is necessarily a model showing what it was like to live and do business in a medieval city.

NOTES

1. Aristotle, *The Politics*, ed. Stephen Everson, Cambridge Texts in the History of Political Thought (Cambridge, UK, and New York: Cambridge University Press, 1988), p. 3.

2. In England the term *city* originally denoted a town that was also the seat of a bishop, that is, a "cathedral town." It is now an honorific title conferred by the government. A common convention is to reserve the term *city* for the largest and most important settlements.

3. The dividing line between the empire in the West and that in the East ran from the river Danube upstream from Beograd southward through Bosnia to the Adriatic Sea. The Eastern or Byzantine Empire claimed authority over all lands lying to the east of this line.

4. Ernst Kitzinger, "A Survey of the Early Christian Town of Stobi," *Dumbarton Oaks Papers*, no. 3 (1946): 81–162.

5. Thomas Hobbes, *Leviathan*, ed. J.C.A. Gaskin (Oxford and New York: Oxford University Press, 1998), p. 463.

6. Norman John Greville Pounds, *The Medieval Castle in England and Wales: A Social and Political History* (Cambridge, UK, and New York: Cambridge University Press, 1990), pp. 207–15.

7. Maurice Warwick Beresford, *New Towns of the Middle Ages: Town Plantation in England, Wales, and Gascony* (New York: Praeger, 1967).

8. Helmold, *The Chronicle of the Slavs*, ed. and trans. Francis Joseph Tschan, Records of Civilizations, Sources and Studies, no. 21 (New York: Columbia University Press, 1935), p. 168.

CHAPTER 2

The Urban Plan:
Streets and Structures

[T]he most excellent proporcion therof: being devyded
in to xxxix quarters the most part square, with streats
very large and broad, all strayght as the same wear
layd with a line.

Report to the privy council on New Winchelsea[1]

It was claimed in the last chapter that medieval towns each conformed
to one of two distinct plans, which in turn derived from the ways in
which the towns themselves had originated. One was the planned town,
the other the unplanned. This is, of course, a gross simplification of a
very complex reality. The best planned town became in the course of
time distorted in the absence of any effective regulatory authority. Con-
trariwise, there was more design in the unplanned town than is sometimes recognized. Nevertheless, this distinction has value and forms the
basis of this chapter.

THE PLANNED TOWN

The earliest human settlements were unplanned in the sense that the
layout of streets, houses, and public buildings was not controlled by a
local authority in accordance with an overall plan. Urban settlements
had grown by slow, unordered accretions from villages just as the latter
had grown from hamlets. But change was on its way. According to Aristotle (384–322 b.c.e.), Hippodamus of Miletus introduced "the art of
planning cities" and applied it to the construction of Piraeus, the port

city that served Athens.² This is usually taken to mean that Hippodamus laid out straight streets, intersecting at right angles, and thus enclosing rectangular blocks. This is, indeed, the street plan demonstrated in Piraeus even today. Such a planned town implies the existence not only of an overall authority, but also the need to create a relatively large center of population. In 443 B.C.E. the Athenians founded the city of Thourioi in southern Italy, divided by four streets lengthways and by three street crossways, as well as other cities similarly planned in Italy and Asia Minor. In fact the Hellenistic period of the fourth and third centuries B.C.E. was characterized by an active program of founding cities—all of them, so it appears, characterized by their planned layout.

The Greeks had not, in all probability, invented the regularly planned city. It had appeared much earlier in the cities of the Middle East, in the Tigris and Euphrates valleys. Nor did it end with the Greeks. The tradition was continued by the Etruscans in central and northern Italy. Indeed, the Etruscans may have discovered the planned city before the Greeks did. Rome itself was created by the *synoecism* or "coming together" of the villages that had previously crowned the seven hills, the *Septimontium*, of ancient Rome, but the towns the Romans established throughout their empire for the primary purpose of bringing civilization to their subject peoples were mostly built according to a regular plan of streets intersecting to enclose rectangular blocks. The best preserved of these cities—and by far the most familiar—are Pompeii (It. Pompei) and Herculaneum (It. Ercolano), preserved only because they were buried beneath the mud and ash spewed out by Vesuvius in 79 C.E. Throughout the empire, from the Rhineland to North Africa, there were planned towns. Many, perhaps the majority, fell to ruin and either were abandoned or survived only as villages after the collapse of the empire itself. In Italy, however, a large number continued as functioning towns. But even where they had been largely abandoned as inhabited places, their street plan survived in some form and imposed itself on the settlements that grew again on their sites during the Middle Ages.

In every such town, the plan became distorted. Buildings intruded into the streets, forcing the streets to make small detours. Whole blocks were cleared and became markets or were occupied by ecclesiastical foundations. Nevertheless, the ghostly plan of a Roman city shows through even today in the street plan of a Winchester, Trier, or Modena.

The planned European city was not restricted to those that derived from the Greeks or the Romans. Similar conditions during the Middle Ages contributed to similar developments. The medieval king or baron might found a city on an empty tract of land. It might be nothing more than an open-ended street, its houses aligned along each side with their "burgage" plots reaching back behind them. It might consist of streets intersecting at right angles. The one pattern would be straggling, the other compact. It might be that agriculture was more important in the one than in the other, or, more likely, that the need for security in a hostile environment dictated a more compact plan around which a wall could be built. Such towns could be found in all parts of medieval Europe.

THE UNPLANNED TOWN

No town was ever wholly unplanned in the sense of being a randomly distributed assemblage of houses and public buildings. Every town once had a nucleus that defined its purpose. This might have been a natural feature such as a river crossing or a physical obstacle that necessitated a break of bulk, the transfer of goods from one mode of transportation to another—from ship to land, from animal transportation to a wheeled cart. The nucleus might also have been a castle or natural place of security or defense, a church or an object of pilgrimage. The streets would probably have originated in the paths by which people approached this nuclear feature and would have formed a radiating pattern, interlinked by cross streets and passageways. Some roads would have derived from the ways by which people walked or drove their animals to the surrounding fields.

Such was the Athens of the *Pseudo-Dichaearchus*, clustered at the foot of the defensive hill we know today as the Acropolis. So also were countless towns in western and central Europe that grew up in response to the needs of travelers and traders or to the need for security in an uncertain age. In a few instances the origins of these towns are enshrined in legend, as is the case in the beginnings of Rome. One cannot point to any particular creative act. Unknown people at a time that can only be guessed came together and formed a settlement. They built in whatever way best suited their needs. If shipping and maritime trade were of primary interest, then their properties would in all likelihood be close to the water's edge. If security was foremost in their minds, then a naturally defensible site would be chosen. If they saw profit in serving the needs of a religious foundation such as a monastery and the pilgrims and others who would be likely to visit it, then they would settle and build as close as possible to its main entrance.

Soon after the Battle of Hastings in 1066, the new king of England, William the Conqueror, founded a monastery on the site of the battle. A small town took shape around it. A charter was granted and a market established. Today there is a large, triangular open space, dominated by the large and impressive gateway that leads to the former monastic precinct. This was the town's marketplace, though today no market is held there and the business that was once transacted has been transferred to the shops, which line the streets radiating from it. The town of Battle was an unplanned growth. It responded to the needs of the monks and of the traders who did business there. It is unique in that the pattern of its streets and buildings is not precisely replicated elsewhere. The unplanned town usually has an individuality that is the source of its interest and charm.

Superimposed on the pattern of streets, whatever their origin, were institutions of another kind: public buildings, both secular and religious, and open spaces needed for economic or ceremonial purposes. In the case of planned towns these needs had usually been anticipated when the towns were founded. A block may have been left clear to serve as a marketplace or for the construction of a town- or gild-hall. Local pride required that it should be centrally placed, ornate, and conspicuous. It was the focus of local authority, the seat of local government, and the expression of the independence guaranteed when the town was granted its charter.

Nearby, and also occupying at least the larger part of a block, was the central church. In a planned town the church is likely to have been established at the time of the foundation of the town itself. In an unplanned or organic town the church may have been even older, part of the nucleus around which the town itself gradually took shape. In a large town other churches—parochial, monastic, mendicant (that is, belonging to the orders of friars), together with the private chapels of the elite members of the community—intruded among the houses and shops wherever there was the need for them and wealth with which to build them. One must never underestimate the importance of the church in the urban landscape of the Middle Ages. For this reason a whole chapter is given in this book to the subject of the urban church.

THE WALLED TOWN

Security was a major factor in the creation and growth of most towns. The Middle Ages were a lawless time, and most citizens had much to lose not only from the activities of the common thief, but also from the depredations of ill-disciplined armies who made it a practice to live off the country. There was, therefore, some safety in numbers, and, added to this, the medieval town usually took steps to defend itself against these evils.

This necessity was not new. Classical Athens had protected itself against its enemies and had built the "Long Walls," a sort of fortified corridor linking it with its port, Piraeus. Throughout the Hellenistic world, towns were walled, towers were built, and their gateways—always the weakest point in their perimeter—were fortified. The art of fortification spread to the Greeks of southern Italy, the Etruscans, and the Romans themselves. Not all towns established within the jurisdiction of Rome were protected by walls, however. The empire was, for much of its history, relatively peaceful. But from late in the third century conditions deteriorated, and there is good evidence in the reuse of masonry, torn from temples and public buildings, that walls were hastily built in anticipation of invasion. During the closing years of the western empire, towns were in economic decline but were at the same time becoming increasingly strongly fortified.

During the "dark" centuries that followed, urban housing and public buildings decayed, but walls survived, though doubtless increasingly ruinous. When urban life began to revive, their walls were still there, an object lesson in fortification and urban security. In town after town in western Europe the walls that had given their citizens protection under the empire were patched and repaired and, here and there extended to take in a newly developed suburb, again made to serve. Take London, for example. Short segments of London's medieval walls still survive, but if their foundations are examined carefully today they are found to be of Roman workmanship.[3] The walls of imperial Rome, built under the Emperor Aurelian (215–275 C.E.), remained in use through the Middle Ages, and fragments of them are still to be seen today.

Most towns that had survived from the late Roman period retained not only their walls but also some semblance of their former street pattern. When urban life revived, only a part of the former Roman enclosure was occupied by houses and other buildings. There were open spaces between the new town and the old walls. Gradually the settled area expanded to fill out the area of the Roman town. Take, for example, the city of Winchester, the Venta Belgarum of the Romans. It had for practical purposes been abandoned when the Roman legions left Britain in 410 C.E. It became an inhabited place again a century or two later. But throughout the intervening years it had retained an aura of authority. It became the capital, if such a term can be used at so early a date, of an Anglo-Saxon kingdom. The Roman walls were again made to serve; their gates and protective towers served as fixed points on which the newly developing street pattern converged. It is not surprising, then, that the medieval streets (and also their present-day successors) replicated with only minor distortions the regular plan the Roman surveyors had laid out. Throughout western and also much of southern Europe, towns of Roman origin continue today to show a regular pattern of rectangular or subrectangular blocks, little disturbed by the passage of time and the operations of unregulated builders (Figure 3).

The population of some towns increased greatly during the Middle Ages, filling out the space within their walls and even spreading beyond

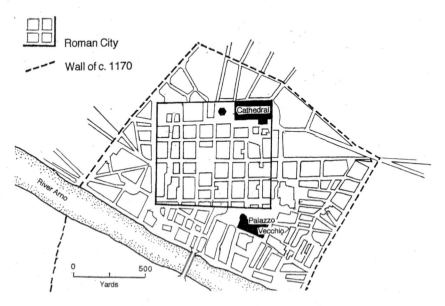

Figure 3. The expansion of Florence, showing extensions beyond the Roman walls.

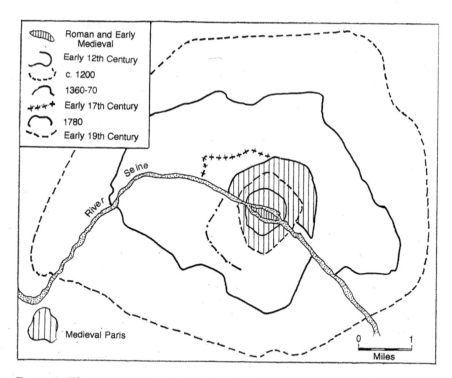

Roman and Early Medieval	
Early 12th Century	
c. 1200	
1360-70	
Early 17th Century	
1780	
Early 19th Century	

Seine

River

Medieval Paris

0   1
Miles

Figure 4. The expansion of Paris, showing the successive lines of the city walls.

them to form suburbs. In these cases it became necessary to build a fresh line of walls enclosing or partially enclosing that which had been inherited from the Romans. We thus have three kinds of walled towns. The first consisted of those in which the growth of population had necessitated the extension and rebuilding, wholly or in part, of their original line of protective walls. Among them were Paris, the largest city in western Europe (Figure 4), and Cologne (Köln) (Figure 5). In each of them, successive lines of walls embraced an ever-expanding area.

Second, there are those towns in which the extension of urban space was overgenerous. Their walls enclosed a greater area than could be populated, and the towns did not grow as had been anticipated. Such was Winchelsea, near the coast of southern England. The town and port of Old Winchelsea had been overwhelmed by the sea and destroyed during a storm in 1297. It was replanned on higher ground and on too lavish a scale, and here we can see today the vacant or only partially occupied blocks that resulted from the failure of reality to match the hopes and

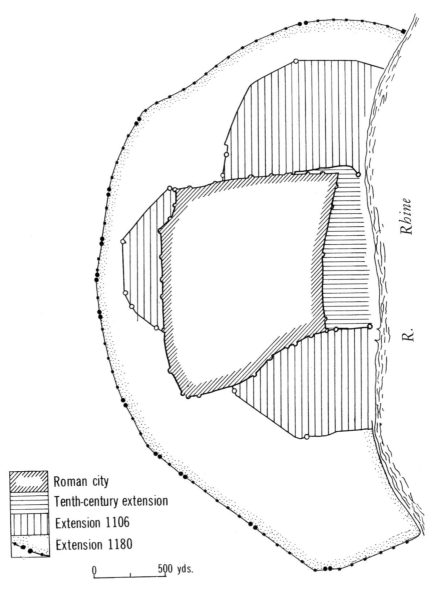

Figure 5. Cologne (Köln), showing successive extensions of the enclosed area beyond the subrectangular Roman room.

expectations of the city founders. Last, we have the great majority of Roman towns whose fortunes revived until their buildings, streets, and markets just about filled out the space that the Romans had occupied. Here the Roman walls, or what was left of them, continued to do service throughout the Middle Ages.

The effect of a wall was to set a limit—temporary in some cases—to urban expansion. If there was any threat to urban security, and there was throughout most of continental Europe, few citizens would venture to live outside the line of the town's protective walls if they could avoid it. Even the smallest of towns had walls, and there was an assumption that if a place was not surrounded by a ring of masonry, it could not then be considered a town. During the sixteenth century it became a common practice for engravers and mapmakers to produce panoramic views of cities. Most were drawn with great care and attention to detail. The biggest market for such drawings, it is said, was among the artillery masters who might be called upon to besiege the towns thus pictured and who required to know how the walls were arranged and the locations of important buildings. A series of these engravings was produced in the fifteenth century by Hartmann Schedel as illustrations to a history of the known world.[4] Another and very much more accurate series was produced in the sixteenth century by Georg Braun and Franz Hogenberg.[5] Others came from the Dutch cartographers Hondius, Ortelius, and Mercator. During the following century the brothers Merian did the same for even very small towns in central Europe. These collections, totaling hundreds of engravings, have two things in common: first, they all show in great detail the encircling walls with their towers and well-defended gatehouses, and second, they all show a broad, open space in front of the walls. This gave a clear field of fire to the defenders without at the same time offering any protection to the attackers.

Walls were functional. People were prepared to live in the utmost congestion within the walls rather than face the dangers of life in the open country beyond them. When unprotected suburbs began to take shape outside the walls, we may be sure that the need for protection had ceased to be uppermost in the minds of their citizens. And yet, even though siege craft was a well-developed branch of the art of war, there is little evidence that most walled towns were ever subjected to attack. It was the castle, the fortified home of an individual, that was most likely to be besieged. The siege of a town might be prolonged, difficult, and costly, and in feudal warfare, which was almost by definition carried on by the barons and their retainers, the castle was more important than the town, whose citizens did not readily involve themselves in feudal disputes. Furthermore, to lay siege to a town with perhaps as much as a mile of defended walls called for very large forces, which few medieval kings or barons could command. An urban siege was likely to be a long, drawn-out affair, and feudal armies were, by the conventions of the age, in the field for only a short period in each year. This is illustrated by one of the very few well-documented urban sieges of medieval Europe: that of Byzantium by the Ottoman Turks. The Turks had occupied the hinterland of Byzantium (Istanbul) for almost a century before they dared to make a direct assault on the city, and even then the siege lasted for many months.

If urban sieges were so few, why then did the towns' citizens go to the immense cost and inconvenience of constructing walls? The answer must be in order to provide effective defenses against their potential attackers. Walls were a very significant form of insurance. They served another purpose also—giving protection from lesser evils, from the small bands that occasionally terrorized the countryside. Then, too, there was the small matter of local pride. The town walls were pictured in a town's heraldry, and were replicated each time the town seal was used to authenticate a document. Last, walls were a matter of convenience. They set a limit to urban sprawl, and the walkway behind the ramparts served as a means of getting across the town without having to negotiate its busy streets. The citizens of Coventry once complained that the wall-walk was so decayed that people were obliged to resort to the unpaved streets deep in mud.

THE MULTI-FOCAL TOWN

According to legend, which may not have been so very far from the truth, the city of Rome grew from the merger of a small number of villages that had previously crowned its hills. The space between them was gradually drained, the *Cloaca Maxima* (the Great Drain) taking the water that lay on the lower ground, where the Forum was later to be established, down to the river Tiber. An enclosing wall, the Servian Wall of some six miles, then converted the seven hills into a single city. The Aurelian Wall, constructed under the empire, was, at over ten miles, even longer. This pattern was to be replicated in many other European towns. Most often their constituent quarters or wards derived from differing institutional nuclei—a castle, cathedral, monastery, or market—which in time came to complement one another. At Hildesheim in northwest Germany, one can detect no less than four independent quarters, each having had a distinctive origin, plan, and function. First came a cathedral settlement, the *Domburg*, followed half a mile away by the monastic settlement of St. Michael's. Then came an unplanned medieval settlement, the Altstadt, or "Old Town," and finally the planned Neustadt, or "New Town." Each was distinct in plan and function, but all came to be enclosed by a single perimeter wall, until they all disappeared with the destruction of Hildesheim during the Second World War.

In many of the larger cities of continental Europe a "new" town was established alongside the "old," which had had its origin under very different social and economic conditions. Krakow, in Poland, illustrates this sequence to perfection (Figure 6). Its nucleus was the Slav fortress, or *grod*, known as the Wawel. It crowns a bluff above the river Vistula (Wisla) and was eminently defensible. Below it to the north there developed an unplanned urban settlement, characterized today by its narrow, twisting streets. Then, even farther to the north, the planned town according to German "law" was laid out, consisting of regular blocks, four of them omitted in order to give space for one of the most spectacular marketplaces in all of central Europe.

Similar double towns are to be found in France. Here the Roman city had been the focus of local government; here also, after Christianity had become the recognized religion in the fourth century, the head of the local church, the bishop, also established his seat. His cathedral faced across the central square to another basilica in which secular affairs were carried on. Then came the earliest monastic orders. They rarely established themselves inside the crowded city; there may not have been room for them, and in any case they may have wanted some degree of privacy. Instead, they established their church and community just outside the town walls, and there they surrounded themselves with walls of their own. In the course of time their monastery attracted a body of merchants and craftsmen, which in some instances came to exceed that of the original city in size and importance.

Arras, in northern France, typifies this double development (Figure 7).

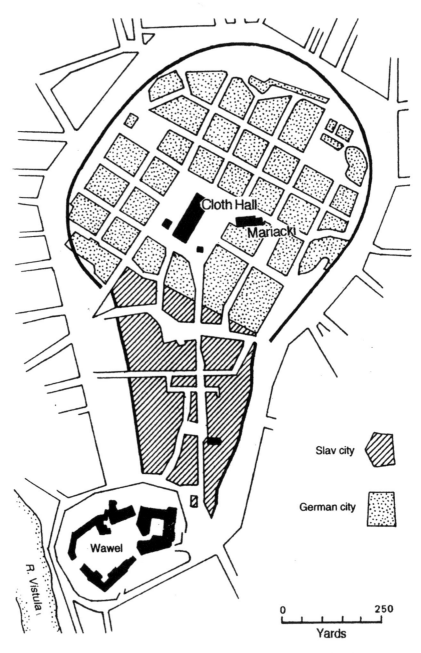

Figure 6. Krakow in the late Middle Ages. The plan shows the three stages in the development of the city beside its castle nucleus, the Wawel: the unplanned Slav town, the planned town according to German "law," and modern suburban development.

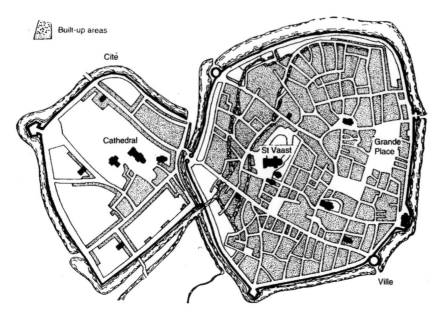

Figure 7. Arras, a binary town. The Cité derived from the Roman civitas and came to include the cathedral. The medieval town to the east of it grew up around the monastery of Saint-Vaast and became the commercial quarter. Based on a plan of c. 1435 in J. Lestocquoy, *Les Dynasties bourgeoises d'Arras*, Mem. Comm. Dept.-pas-de-Calais.

The more westerly Cité derives from the Roman *civitas*, and has retained something of the quiet contemplative atmosphere of the cathedral city.[6] The monastic town, known as *la ville*, grew faster and became a large and thriving commercial and industrial town, clustered around the former monastery of Saint-Vaast.

A similar pattern of development can be traced in other French cities, such as Reims and Troyes, in each of which a commercial town, sometimes with a monastic nucleus, grew up beside the earlier administrative and episcopal city. In England there was a similar situation at Canterbury, where the Cathedral of Christ Church was established by St. Augustine within the former Roman city of Durovernum, while a monastic suburb to the east housed St. Augustine's Abbey, one of the most important monastic foundations in England. There was, however, an important difference. In the continental examples already mentioned, the monastic suburb became the commercial hub; in Canterbury it was the former Roman *civitas capital* that became the commercial hub.

Two more prominent examples of multifocal development are London and St. Albans. London emerged from the Londinium of the Romans. It had probably never been completely abandoned, and when Augustine came on his Christianizing mission in 597, he had been instructed by Pope Gregory I to establish bishoprics in other towns that had once been Roman cities. Augustine stopped off, however, at Canterbury, and only many years later was a cathedral established in London. London grew, but still within the line of its former Roman walls, to become the capital of England and then of Great Britain. When a Benedictine monastery was established in the early eleventh century, it was not in the close proximity of the city, but two miles away to the west, at Westminster; it was the "western" minster. The same distant suburb also became the chief palace of the English kings, the "Palace of Westminster," which as their primary residence eventually replaced the cramped and uncomfortable Tower of London. The kings have left, and the site has been since the Middle Ages the place where the English (later British) Parliament has met because it was originally summoned there to confer with the king. In this case it would be many centuries before the open country with its fields and meadows, which separated the city with its cathedral (St. Paul's) from the monastic and governmental center at Westminster, became filled with palaces, domestic houses, and shops.

The second example, St. Albans, is 20 miles northwest of London. Here the city of Verulamium, one of the largest in Roman Britain, spread over the valley floor of the small river Ver. The city had decayed during the late Roman period and had been abandoned. Today only its scanty ruins survive. Then in the eighth century a monastery was founded on the hilltop to the north, where allegedly St. Alban had been martyred in the third century C.E. In this instance, the Roman city vanished as a human settlement, while the monastic suburb, helped by the miracle-working relics of its saint, grew to become a commercial town of some importance.

RIVER AND BRIDGE TOWNS

Most towns in western and central Europe grew up on the banks of a river. In southern Europe, towns were more likely to have been located on a hilltop, or at least on higher ground. This may have been because of the need for a naturally defensible site, but just as likely it was to escape the malaria-carrying mosquito, which bred in the lakes and marshes of the valley floor.

A riverside location offered great advantages. The river itself served both as a source of water and as a sewer. River navigation was in much of Europe the cheapest, the easiest, and the safest form of transportation, and, furthermore, simply being on the banks of a river gave the town some protection on at least one side. There were even towns that had their origin on an island encircled and protected by the branches of a river. Paris, which developed first on the Ile de la Cite, may be the best known, but there are others, such as Amsterdam in the Netherlands and Wroclaw (Breslau) in Poland.

Few towns that had grown up on one bank of a river failed to spread to the opposite bank. A bridge became a necessity, and the land on the far side of the river quickly became part of the urban hinterland or service area of the town. Indeed, there are instances where the bridge itself was the focal point around which the town grew. Many a town today displays this fact in its name: Bridgetown, Newbridge, Bridgend, the many place-names in France incorporating the element *pont*, and those in Germany incorporating *bruch*, both terms meaning "bridge." Always, however, there was a social and sometimes also an economic difference between the two or more parts of a city that was divided by a river. Sometimes the difference extended also to city government. London, for example, inherited the site, the walls, and in part the street-pattern of Roman Londinium. It lay at a crossing point of the river Thames. Julius Caesar's legions had forded the river at this point. A dangerous ford was soon replaced by a bridge, and there has been a London Bridge for much of the time from that day to this. At the south end of the bridge there grew up the "southern ward" or Southwark. The river is wide, and until modern times there has been only a single bridge. This contributed to a large social distance between the city on the northern bank and its suburb across the river. London Bridge was the only crossing of the river before the nineteenth century. Southwark thus distanced itself from London, and was for many centuries quite distinct for administrative purposes.

A comparable divided city is Budapest in Hungary. Buda grew up on a hill west of the river Danube and became the seat of the Hungarian kings. The steep topography of the site hindered the development of markets and the infrastructure of a commercial town. These grew up on the east bank of the river, where the level plain of the Alfold stretched away to the horizon. This was the town of Pest, differing in form, function, and every other respect from the aristocratic Buda. The Danube's fierce current held the two cities apart. They became one, it was said, only in the depth of winter, when the river was frozen and people could walk—or skate—from one bank to the other. Attempts to build a bridge across the Danube had been defeated by the engineering difficulties until the 1860s, when success was achieved and the first bridge was opened. Intercourse between the two towns at once became more intense, so that in 1872 they merged, together with their names, to give us Budapest.

The history of Prague (Praha) is, superficially regarded, not very different from that of Budapest (Figure 8). West of the river Vltava the land rises steeply to a plateau on the edge of which the kings of Bohemia had built their castle and palace, the Hradčany, which embraced also the cathedral of Prague. The town, the Mala Strona, straggled down the hill to the river, but the commercial center of Prague was established on the bank of the river opposite, where the land is relatively flat. Here was the Staré Město or "Old Town," enclosed by its walls. The river Vltava never presented a serious obstacle, and a bridge, the Kaluv Most or "Charles Bridge," was built in the fourteenth century. The Old Town was subsequently enlarged by the addition of the Nové Město or "New Town," with its formidable walls and gates that still survive in part. Unlike Budapest, the four units that comprised the city of Prague were always treated as a single administrative unit.

There was scarcely a limit to the patterns of relationship that might develop between double towns such as those that have been discussed. Each represents a permutation on a common theme—how to bring together diverse human settlements and to weld them into a single, functional unit. In most instances subtle differences in atmosphere today still distinguish the former quarters of these cities. They differed not only in their street plans but also in their styles of architecture, in the quality of housing and shops and commercial outlets, and in the ways in which their inhabitants see themselves and are perceived by outsiders.

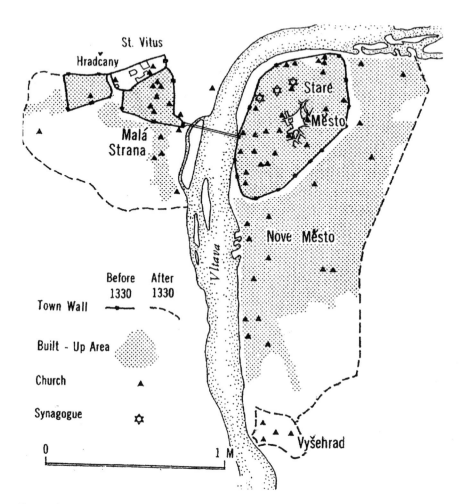

Figure 8. Prague in the late Middle Ages. Its nucleus had been the hilltop castle of the Hradčany. This attracted the small walled settlement to its south, followed in turn by the Staré Město (Old Town) farther to the south and by the Staré Město across the river Vltava and, toward the end of the Middle Ages, by the Malá Strana (Small Side) and the Nové Město (New Town). Vyšehrad, at the southern edge of the New Town, was a defended prehistoric site, which had preceded the Hradčany.

STRUCTURES OF THE MEDIEVAL TOWN

As the medieval town grew in population and assumed ever more diversified functions, so it became more congested. The area confined within its walls was limited; it came to be fully built-up with housing and other structures, but not until the danger of war and siege had diminished did most of its citizens venture to live in the open country beyond its walls.

Immigrants from the countryside who peopled the earliest European towns brought with them rural styles of building and continued to use the materials to which they had become accustomed and to handle them in traditional ways. Well might the town have looked like the village writ large. In the course of time, however, urban building began to grow apart from what was normal in the countryside. The town imposed its own constraints, the most important of which was space, or the lack of it. Urban population and urban housing became ever more dense. More houses were crowded onto each acre of urban land. Spaces between houses were gradually filled up, and the yards behind them were built over until there ceased to be space for more construction. People then began to build upward. An extra floor was added to the single-story house and then a second and a third and even more. In many an urban house the lower stages were not strong enough to bear the added weight that was imposed on them. The result was the collapse of the whole building with the consequent loss of life and property.

BUILDING MATERIALS

The growing congestion of the city necessitated a change in the materials used. The Roman cities in most parts of the empire had used a combination of stone, brick, and timber, but stone and brick were always the preferred materials. Such urban buildings that have survived from the Roman period are of stone. The towns of Pompeii, Herculaneum, and Ostia in Italy and the ruins that remain today of the Roman Forum or that crown the Palatine hill are all of masonry. Provincial towns also showed masonry construction not only in their public buildings but also in townhouses and urban villas. Stone may often have been supplemented with brick, whose use was in large measure a function of local geology, since it had to be molded from clay.

The impression derived from Roman remains may be deceptive, because only stone and brick could have survived for close to two thousand years. Timber was unquestionably used, not only to support the roofs of buildings of all kinds, but also for walls. Fragments of woodwork may have survived in the drier conditions of southern Italy and of North Africa, but timber has rotted and disappeared from northern and western Europe. Clay tiles of varied shapes and sizes were used for roofing, or, in their absence, wooden shingles and even thatch. The medieval town, following the example of the village, made the greatest use of wood, usually, but by no means always, on stone foundations. The timber was all too often green and became distorted, leading to the twisted walls and floors, which are so conspicuous a feature of surviving timber-framed buildings. The town houses of the Middle Ages were frequently rebuilt, following their collapse, their destruction by fire, or the simple desire of their occupants for a more ambitious home. Only in a few instances— Scandinavian settlements around the Baltic Sea, for example, and in the lowest strata excavated in surviving towns—can one find post-holes and traces of the decayed timber of the homes of their earliest inhabitants.

Timber construction was quick, easy, and convenient, and, in terms of cost, relatively cheap. But it had its inherent disadvantages: it had to be protected from the damp soil; it rotted quickly in the absence of any preservative—and there were no preservatives before modern times—and, above all, it burned. The most important enemy of the town was not the hostile army or the robber band; it was fire. There can be scarcely a town in northern, wood-using Europe that does not remember a devastating fire. Medieval people took it for granted that their town might some day be consumed in this way. Arson was rarely, if ever, suspected. Fires usually arose from accident:

> And we've all seen sometime through some brewer
> Many tenements burnt down with bodies inside,
> And how a candle guttered in an evil place
> Falls down and totally torches a block.[7]

Little could be done to insure against fire, except to keep a few buckets on hand filled with water and, of course, to build in materials that would not easily burn. Ordinance after ordinance in town after town prescribed the thickness of party walls and the use of stone and tile and forbade the butting of one structure against a preexisting building. As early as the twelfth century, London enacted the law that buildings should be of masonry. All of this was to little avail, however. Medieval cities—and not only London—legislated wisely, but failed completely to institute any mechanism of inspection and control. Only when one citizen brought suit against another did the courts take cognizance of a breach of the town's ordinances. Even the Great Fire of 1666, which destroyed the greater part of the city of London and demonstrated how its building ordinances had been violated, failed to bring home to everyone the need for the most elementary precautions against fire and the collapse of buildings.

Medieval growth in urban population brought about not only an increasing density of housing but also a need to build higher. Floor was added to floor, the upper floors being superimposed on the lower, which had never been intended to support their weight. Medieval builders pressed the strength of materials and structures to their limit. They lacked the mathematical skills to calculate the stresses generated. Sometimes they overcompensated, as in the three-foot party walls, which were at one time required in London; more often they failed to allow for the weakness of some of their materials, with the result that floors collapsed. Timber-framed buildings—and most urban housing was of wood on masonry foundations—crumpled as their timbers decayed, and those which had been built of masonry disintegrated from the weakness of the mortar used to bond the stonework. Nevertheless, structures grew ever taller as their builders tried to combine under one roof both shop and warehouse as well as family home. Cellars under a house, combined with four or even five stories aboveground, were in many instances a prescription for disaster.

During the late Middle Ages, building stone must have been one of the most abundant commodities in long-distance transportation. In parts of Europe, however, building stone was almost totally lacking and could be obtained for building only if a relatively cheap means of transportation, as by river barge, was available. Fortunately most areas that lacked stone possessed clay in abundance. Brick and tile thus replaced stone and slate. In the cities of northern Europe, especially those of the Hanseatic League, the raw material of brick was present in abundance in the boulder clay, which covered much of the region. In consequence many towns such as Amsterdam, Lubeck, and Gdansk (Danzig) became cities of red brick and have remained so until the present. Even the churches were of brick, with molded bricks used to give the illusion of Gothic tracery.

THE CITIZEN'S HOME

In the medieval town, streets generally came before housing, and the first houses were aligned along them. They were like those of the village, single-storied and consisting of two basic elements: the living space and the sleeping space. Chaucer knew this well. Of his poor widow's "narwe cotage" he could write:

> Ful sooty was hire bour and eek [also] hir halle,
> In which she eet ful many a sklendre meel.[8]

Whatever may have been added during the Middle Ages and after, these two elements remained the dominant features of the home. The hall was where its inhabitants lived and cooked; the bower was where they slept. This remained true of every social class.

Urban society was structured with a wide gulf between rich and poor, but their respective homes each embraced these two elements, however large they may have become and however fanciful their decoration. In the course of time the house became more complex, but it did not abandon its basic units of hall and chamber. Broadly speaking, these units assumed one of two forms according to their relationship to the street. In their earliest form the two elements lay end to end and parallel with the street. This was often wasteful of space, though, and, except in the upper-class houses, was abandoned in favor of a house plan at right-angles to the street. The house then had a narrow frontage, but extended a variable but considerable distance toward the rear. This was to become the typical town house plan in most of the larger and more congested cities, but the earlier plan survived in the smaller towns in which there was less pressure on space and was retained as upper-class housing even in the larger.

In the "parallel" house plan, the great hall, open to the roof and with tall windows along each side, stood parallel with the street (Figure 9). At one end was the kitchen; at the other, the solar, parlor, or chamber. Wings might protrude from the ends to serve as additional bedroom accommodation, as stables, or, in the case of a merchant, as storage space.

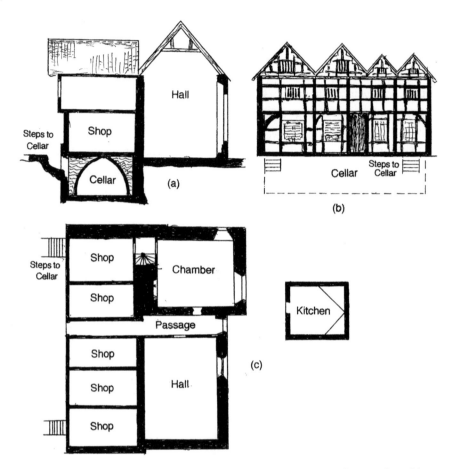

Figure 9. A row of townhouses, based on the surviving evidence of Tackley's Inn, Oxford. Primary Documents, p. 199, is a contract for building such a structure. Windows and roofs are entirely presumptive.

These might partially enclose a courtyard or even a garden. Much depended on the width of the plot. Whatever its size, every attempt was made to make the house as similar as possible to the aristocratic manor house of the countryside.

Houses of this type may have been most common in northern Europe, but they were once to be found over much of the continent. The plan was also used for gild halls and town halls in which the councils of gild and town met and held their deliberations regarding urban and gild affairs, but it was always associated with the prosperous local elite of merchants and businessmen. They were not averse to using part of their ample space as a warehouse for the goods in which they traded or to building a row of shops, cutting off their courtyard from the street, as, indeed, had happened at Norwich.

At the uppermost level of these parallel houses, and only in the larger and more important cities, stood the urban palaces of the aristocracy and ruling classes. They differed from the parallel houses chiefly in their greater size, their higher level of refinement, and their provision for large numbers of retainers. They were in particular a feature of capital cities, especially of Paris and London, of Rome and Florence and, at a much later date, of Warsaw and Prague, where they became the town houses of the landed aristocracy and the princes of the Church.

The alternative house plan to evolve during the Middle Ages was the so-called right-angled type. It was adapted to the narrow urban lot or burgage plot, and became by far the most common urban house plan. It owed nothing to any rural progenitor, deriving wholly from urban crowding and congestion. The lords who controlled or influenced urban development divided up their territory into elongated plots, which were leased to the citizens at an accepted rental. There was competition for as broad a frontage on the street as was practicable, since this was where the shop or business quarters were established. A wide frontage cost more and was taxed more heavily than a narrow one, but in very few instances was the frontage of a burgage plot wide enough to build a parallel house. Each house butted against its neighbor on each side and extended back as far as was practicable. It was, indeed, the predecessor of the rows of conjoined houses of the nineteenth and twentieth centuries. There might be generous window space fronting on the street, but little light penetrated beyond the front room, and there could be no windows in the thick party walls, which formed the sides of the house. If more space was needed—and it usually was—the house could be extended room behind room, into the space or yard behind the house. But this only intensified the darkness of the interior. The only alternative, if more floor space was needed, was to pile floor upon floor, until houses of four, five, or even more stories had been built, very often on foundations designed for only two or three.

Such houses raised serious structural problems. Party walls were usually of masonry, as was necessary to provide a rigid framework and to reduce the risk of fire spreading uncontrollably. But all internal fittings—including stairs, floor-joists, and floors—were mainly, if not wholly, of

Figure 10. Arnhem, a late medieval walled town, relatively lightly built up within its walled perimeter. Note the single line of walling facing the river Rhine which gave some protection, but the double line, together with water defenses on the landward side.

wood. The construction of the roof always taxed the skills of the builder. Since the house was long and narrow, a ridge roof running its entire length and terminating at each extremity in a triangular gable was the easiest and cheapest to construct. In consequence, drawings of medieval towns display a mass of pointed gables like a forest of conifers (Figure 10). During a storm, water accumulated in the gully between each pair of ridge roofs. It overflowed at the ends onto the heads of people in the street below. Water spouts were sometimes fitted to project the water farther into the street below, but the discharge of water was nevertheless a nuisance and was prominent among the complaints addressed to the city courts.[9] The gully between adjoining ridges was also a serious weakness. Water seeped through the gully into the rooms below, and in winter it gathered as snow, which was very difficult to remove.

The merchant was often compelled to adopt the narrow, right-angled house for lack of anything better and was obliged to cope with the problem of finding sufficient storage space for his wares. It thus became a common practice to add a cellar or basement beneath the house, sometimes even digging the basement *after* the house had been built. The cellar or basement necessarily had to be of masonry. It was sometimes reached by a small stairway located in the sidewalk or road in front of the house. It clearly presented a hazard to the unobservant pedestrian, as the *Coroners' Rolls* testify. Where it survives today, it still constitutes a minor hazard against which its owner has to protect the public with some form of railings.[10]

The practice developed, probably by the thirteenth century, of allowing the upper stories to overhang those below or, in the jargon of vernacular architecture, to "jetty." Why? This practice made extravagant use of timber and shut out the light from lower windows, but it added to total floor space and, as contemporary building contracts demonstrate, was a mark of good building practice and an object of personal pride. There can be no doubt that a timber-framed, jettied house is considered today, and probably always has been, a thing of great beauty.

Arrangements within the narrow, right-angled house varied with economic needs and personal preference. The space on the ground floor adjacent to the street was commonly a shop, which, according to the type of goods handled, might have served also as a workshop. Alternatively, a workshop may have been placed behind the shop, though the lack of natural lighting often made this undesirable. Instead, there might have been a "hall," where the family lived. The need for business premises may, on the other hand, have forced the family to make their living quarters above the shop. A third and even more floors would have given ample space for chambers in which the family, not to mention journeymen and apprentices, were accustomed to sleep. The uses to which the rooms of a medieval house were put must have varied greatly, and doubtless changed with personal preferences and needs.

A high proportion of urban houses must have embraced shops, since buying and selling were the dominant functions of every town. It is clear that the medieval shop was not a space that the customer could enter and look around in order to appraise the goods on display. There was probably little range of choice within any particular type of goods. The shop was rather an arched opening, closed by a wooden shutter, which was hinged at either the top or the bottom so that it could be lowered to serve as a display area or raised to give some protection from the weather. At night it would have been closed and bolted into place, while the owner slept above in relative security. If more space was needed a wooden stall was added, protruding into the street and further obstructing the passage of people and vehicles. The records of the London *Assize of Nuisance* are filled with complaints of such intrusions onto the public space of the street. Some streets were permanently narrowed by the unauthorized extension of shops in this age of poorly regulated private activity.

Every house in the medieval town required two particular offices: a kitchen, or at least a place in which to cook, and a toilet. In a rural home, food would have been prepared over a fire placed either in the middle of the floor of the hall or in a niche in a side wall. In some parts of Europe it was the practice to build a dome-shaped oven of stone, brick, and clay, which had to be preheated. In other words, wood was burned within it and then, when the oven was hot, the ashes would have been scraped out and the food, principally bread, inserted. In the case of the central hearth the smoke was allowed to circulate and escape through a lantern in the roof or through the manifold cracks and crannies of the structure. The fireplace built against a side wall required a chimney for the evacuation of smoke. This was so in the right-angled town house, which clearly demanded a fireplace against a side wall with a chimney running the height of the building. A development that first became apparent in the twelfth century was to build a separate kitchen projecting from the back of the house or even freestanding in the yard behind. The latter plan was always favored because it reduced the ever-present danger of fire, but it was a luxury for which there was frequently too little space.

The other necessity was what a Renaissance writer termed a "house of convenience."[11] The public toilet, discharging into a large cesspit or even built out over a river, was far from unknown in the medieval town. There are references to their maintenance in the urban documentation. Heavy reliance on a public or communal toilet seems not to have been a feature of the industrial housing until the eighteenth and nineteenth centuries, however. Thus, reliance was placed mainly on the private, domestic toilet, and every home had to have its own facility. A contract for constructing such a convenience in London in 1405 required that the latrine pit be dug before the building of the house had begun. It was to be sixteen feet by ten feet. It was in fact a cesspit. Holes would have been left for fluids to drain into the soil, and periodically its wooden cover would have been lifted and the contents shoveled into a cart that would have conveyed them to the cultivated land around the city or to the nearby river. Here it would have been sent downstream to the next settlement, which probably used the river as its source of water. There was no attempt before modern times to construct a masonry sewer for the discharge of human waste. Occasionally a toilet was constructed as a protrusion from the wall of a house or other building, so that the excrement merely accumulated on the ground below. Not all houses were able to accommodate a masonry-built cesspit. Many used only a basket-like container, woven of withies, which permitted its contents to drain into the ground. Figure 11 was drawn from a photograph of such a woven cesspit, which was preserved by the damp soil and revealed when the house site was excavated.

Not every craftsman was able to pursue his craft within the narrow confines of his home. Some crafts required a quite extensive space. The potter's kiln and the metalworker's furnace and forge could not possibly be confined within a burgage plot, even if it was not prohibited by the fire hazard they posed. Others, such as the craft of the tanner, were antisocial, and yet others, like milling and fulling, had to be practiced close to the flowing water that supplied their power. These were all squeezed toward the periphery of the settled area of the town, where space was likely to be both cheaper and more abundant. But most handicrafts called for little space. They could be pursued in the front room or in the yard of the traditional house. The butcher and baker, the cordwainer or fine leatherworker, the weaver, the dyer, and even the more esoteric craftsmen such as the furrier and the goldsmith pursued their respective crafts under the public eye and interrupted their work to chat to a passer-by. The butcher often slaughtered his beasts in the street in front of his shop and under the scrutiny of his customers. In all these instances the shop was also the workshop.

Such was the crowded, congested town in which most of the manufactured goods were made and almost all of them were sold. It was into

Figure 11. A domestic cesspit, excavated within a house in Basing Lane in the City of London. It was built of rough stones, without mortar, so that fluids might drain into the soil.

this confusion of living, working, and storage space that the patrician class intruded. How the patrician acquired his land we do not know— probably by purchase. He often succeeded in putting together space enough to build the kind of home that matched his station in life. Such a house, developed from one of humble beginnings, was the Strangers' Hall in Norwich, mentioned earlier (see p. 43). It was the late medieval rural manor house translated, very little altered, to the urban setting. An- other such a house is the Old Hall in the midst of the town of Gains- borough, Lincolnshire, now a splendid survival, encroached upon on all sides by modern, squalid, urban, and industrial buildings. All large cities once had such houses, most of them timber framed on masonry founda- tions, with elaborate facilities for every aspect of medieval life. The kitchen at Gainsborough Hall must be one of the largest and finest of its kind surviving today. The practice of building luxurious town houses con- tinued through the following centuries, though their styles changed from

Gothic to Classical and their material from a timber studding or frame-work infilled with lath and plaster, to stone and brick. Warsaw and Prague, Paris and London, Florence and Venice still contain relics of this medieval past. Not until the late eighteenth and early nineteenth centuries did the aristocracy begin to abandon the city and return to their homes in the countryside where their roots had been.

PUBLIC STRUCTURES

In addition to the domestic and commercial structures, there were two other categories of building in the late medieval town: the ecclesiastical, and the secular and administrative. Domestic architecture has already been discussed (see pp. 41–49). Chapter 4 will be given over to the ecclesiastical, and it remains here to discuss the miscellaneous secular buildings that punctuated the medieval skyline. Most conspicuous were the walls, gates, and mural towers, built as much to impress the visitor from other parts as to protect the citizenry and to give it a sense of security. As has already been seen, town walls in western and southern Europe derived in many instances from the example of the Romans. In central and eastern Europe they were the creation of medieval people, and here they had a serious military intent. Sieges were a feature of most wars from the early Middle Ages to the Thirty Years' War of the seventeenth century. In England, though not necessarily in the rest of the British Isles, town walls were built for show rather than for any serious military purpose. One cannot point to an important urban siege later than the twelfth century, and there is little evidence for one before that date. Urban sieges were more numerous in continental Europe, but even here there were very few. Walls were allowed to fall to ruin long before the end of the Middle Ages, and in most instances modern urban growth has obliterated all trace of them. In town after town, however, the line of the vanished walls can be traced because a road had once run inside but very close to them. Similarly, as suburbs grew up outside the walls, another space was left. These spaces, both within and immediately outside the line of the walls, have often survived as boulevards, with trees growing where once there had been massive walls. Outside the line of the vanished walls, where there was less pressure on space, streets are commonly found to be wider and development more spacious than within, where there often survives a kind of medieval congestion. Nevertheless, the walls survive, almost complete, at

Chester and York, and, in more fragmentary fashion, at Norwich, Exeter, London, Winchester, Chichester, and elsewhere. In continental Europe there are many examples of a more or less complete circuit of walls: in France at Aigues Mortes and Avignon, in Spain at Avila, and in Germany at Nuremberg and many small towns in Swabia. Fortified gates have survived more frequently, perhaps because they could offer some kind of accommodation and serve also for the control of admission to the town and the collection of market tolls. Many of the smaller towns of continental Europe still retain traces of their walls, and they survive almost intact in some of the hill-towns of Italy.

Streets may not have been structures, but they were an essential feature of the urban scene. Streets of former Roman towns had once been paved with stone sets, slabs, and cobbles, and, where they have in recent times been excavated, they are often seen to have been worn into grooves by the wheels of carts and wagons. The streets of medieval towns sadly fell far short of the standards set by the Romans. They were not always paved, though occasionally one finds in medieval records a note of the payment for some kind of stone surface. Most of them, however, were at best given an occasional dressing of sand or ash. They were usually made to slope, not, as is the practice today, toward a gutter on each side, but toward the middle. Water was thus kept away from the buildings which lined the streets on each side. In this way, after heavy rain a street might be turned into a miniature watercourse. Nor was there any sidewalk; pedestrians could only keep as far as possible from the middle of the road, but were always liable to be splashed by the passage of animals and vehicles. Conditions were made worse by the widespread practice of disposing of household waste by throwing it into the street, where it was collected at irregular intervals by so-called rakers and disposed of in that receptacle for all waste materials—the river.

Except in southern Europe and the Mediterranean region, most towns had been built on the banks of a river. Whether the towns had originated at crossing points, where merchants and travelers gathered, or whether the crossing was established for the convenience of the town may remain uncertain. In any case, few towns did not possess a river bridge, which was usually built and maintained by the city authorities. Some river crossings had earned an almost legendary fame, as, for instance, London Bridge, now dismembered and re-erected across a dry river-bed in Arizona, and that built across the Tiber during the early days of Rome. A few bridges were fortified and made to serve as part of the town's defenses. The Pont Valentre at Cahors in southwestern France is a particularly impressive example of a fortified bridge, with three massive towers barring its narrow road.

Other secular buildings within a town were largely concerned with its trade and other economic activities. The gilds, whose role will be discussed in Chapter 5, possessed in many cases a building that served as a kind of clubhouse, where members met to conduct the business of their gild and, on a less formal basis, to celebrate their feasts and to initiate new members. Gild halls usually took the form of large town houses, with hall and kitchen and a number of smaller rooms. London, for example, still has several, which continue to serve their traditional purposes, though the gilds that use them are no longer associations of craftsmen and have become honorific societies of well-heeled London businesspeople.

More directly linked with the economic activities of the gilds were the warehouses in which merchants stored the raw materials and finished articles in which they traded. Even today small hoisting devices are seen to protrude from the gables of the tall brick-built houses lining the canals of Amsterdam. In many other cities one can discover the warehouses of medieval merchants, now converted to other uses.

Since most towns lay on the banks of a river, which provided the easiest and cheapest mode of transport, they are likely to have had a quay, revetted or covered with stone, at which river boats could tie up and load or unload their cargoes. Many would have been equipped with a crane, a curious contraption of wood, its windlass operated by a "man-engine," for lifting the heavier items. Such a primitive crane survives in some of the small towns along the Rhine.

Another mechanical device that formed part of every medieval town was the mill. Every grain, whether wheat, barley, or rye, had to be milled before it could be baked into bread. In the countryside this had once been done by means of a quern or large stone mortar, which called for no power beyond that of the baker's strong right arm. This was gradually displaced by the water- and windmill. Milled flour was difficult both to transport and to store, and it became necessary for townsfolk to mill their grain shortly before baking it into bread, which was the most common item in their diet. Windmills were sometimes mounted on the town walls, where the breeze blew more strongly, but more often the town relied upon a water-mill, either built on the bank of the river or mounted on a boat moored in midstream, where the speed of the current turned its massive wheel.

The only other secular structures likely to stand out amid the huddle of roofs and gables filling the late medieval town were those associated with the market. The market, as has been seen, was an open space, sometimes rectangular, more often irregular in shape, where stalls for the display of goods were erected on market day. Above them there often stood a market cross, a monument with religious connotations, which, as it were, extended its benediction to the activities carried on around it. There might also have been a market hall, where market officials met and where tolls were collected and debts settled. It might also have given shelter to at least some of those who did business in its shadow. Many towns had been authorized to hold an annual fair, when stalls and benches would have been set up in the streets and surrounding fields. Few fairs continued to be held in the late Middle Ages. They had been associated with the itinerant merchant, but he was now doing his business more and more from his urban counting house rather than by traveling the roads and facing the tumult of the fair. Specialist fairs did continue to serve special interests, as, indeed, they continue to do today, but everywhere they were becoming more convivial than commercial, more fun-fairs than centers of continent-wide trade. Where they continued to be held, they filled the urban streets for a short period in each year with their stalls and their merchandise and their turmoil.

NOTES

1. Qtd. in Maurice Warwick Beresford, *New Towns of the Middle Ages: Town Plantation in England, Wales, and Gascony* (New York: Praeger, 1967), p. 16.

2. Aristotle, *The Politics*, ed. Stephen Everson, Cambridge Texts in the History of Political Thought (Cambridge, UK, and New York: Cambridge University Press, 1988), p. 36.

3. On English walled towns see: Hilary L. Turner, *Town Defences in England and Wales: An Architectural and Documentary Study, AD 900–1500* (Hamden, CT: Archon Books, 1971); Alfred Harvey, *The Castles and Walled Towns of England* (London: Methuen and Company, 1911).

4. Hartmann Schedel, *Liber Chronicarum* (Nuremberg, 1493).

5. Georg Braun and Franz Hogenberg, *Civitates Orbis Terrarum*, 6 vols., 1572–1618. Twenty-four illustrations were republished as *Old European Cities: Thirty-two Sixteenth-Century City Maps and Texts from the "Civitates Orbis Terrarum" of Georg Braun and Franz Hogenberg*, ed. Ruthardt Oehme (London: Thames and Hudson, 1965), and there is a modern facsimile edition of the whole work, published as *Civitates Orbis Terrarum: "The Towns of the World,"* *1572–1618*, ed. R. A. Skelton (Cleveland, OH: World Pub. Co., 1966).

6. Jean Lestocquoy, *Études d'Histoire Urbaine: Villes et Abbayes, Arras au Moyen Âge*, Mémoires de la Commission Départementale des Monuments Historiques du Pas-de-Calais (Arras: Impr. Centrale de l'Artois, 1966).

7. William Langland, *William Langland's "Piers Plowman": The C Version: A Verse Tranlsation*, ed. George Economou, Middle Ages Series (Philadelphia: University of Pennsylvania Press, 1996), p. 25, lines 104–7.

8. Geoffrey Chaucer, "The Nun's Priest's Tale," in *"The Cantebury Tales" Complete*, ed. Larry D. Benson (Boston and New York: Houghton Mifflin Company, 2000), p. 235, lines 2, 12–13.

9. Robert Ricart, *The Maire of Bristowe Is Kalendar*, ed. Lucy Toulmin Smith. Camden Society Publications, n.s., vol. 5 (Westminster: Camden Society, 1872), p. 43.

10. *London Assize of Nuisance, 1301–1431: A Calendar*, ed. Helena M. Chew and William Kellaway, London Record Society Publications, vol. 10 (Leicester: London Record Society, 1973), pp. xxi–xxx.

11. Such openings, each with a few steps leading down into the basement, are still to be seen (and fallen into by the unwary) in the small coastal town of Winchelsea in Sussex, England.

CHAPTER 3

THE URBAN WAY OF LIFE

Towns came late in the long span of human history. They were imposed on a landscape of small settlements, from which they drew their earliest inhabitants. The town has been throughout its history a pole of attraction to the rural population. It was their "promised land," tempting the country dweller with its range of employment and experience, far beyond anything that the countryside could offer. But the attraction of the town was deceptive. Beneath its glossy facade lay crowding, disease, high mortality, and a shorter lifespan. All too often the peasant who had migrated to the town came to look back ruefully to the rural bliss which he had left. This was as true of Aristophanes' Attic peasant as of Wladislaw Reymont's nineteenth-century Polish peasants in his aptly named *The Promised Land.*[1] In modern demographic terminology, its net reproduction rate—the average number of female children born to each woman—was less than unity. This means that women each had on average less than a single female child. In other words the population was not fully reproducing itself. The reasons for this—both social and environmental—are complex. Among the former, in all probability, was the greater age at which people married in the town than in the countryside. The nature of urban employment and the restrictive influence of the gilds led to the postponement of marriage—at least for young men. Then, too, it may have been difficult for the journeyman who had just completed his apprenticeship to establish himself in society and to accumulate enough resources to acquire a home. Environmental factors were probably more important than social, but also more difficult to evaluate. The town was densely settled; people lived closely packed in their crowded quarters. In contrast with the rural environment, any infectious disease that might take hold would be likely to spread quickly with disastrous consequences. Of no medical catastrophe was this more true than of the Great Plague, the Black Death of 1348–1350. Once it had taken root in a congested town, it spread rapidly, giving rise to a disastrous mortality.

The Black Death, otherwise known as the Great or Bubonic Plague, deserves more than a cursory mention. It was spread by the symbiotic re-lationships between the black rat, the flea, and their human victim. It has been argued—implausibly, it appears—that the great plague of Athens late in the fifth century B.C.E. was the bubonic plague. It is far more likely that the disease that decimated Byzantium under the Em-peror Justinian (527–565) was the bubonic plague. It raged in the city, but seems not to have spread into its Balkan hinterland. There may have been other occurrences before 1348, but they were contained, not by the science of medicine, which was at this time almost nonexistent, but by the vast, unpopulated distances that its vectors, the rat and the flea, were unable to traverse.

We have fairly reliable statistics relating to mortality in a few cities, especially those in Italy and southern France (Figures 12 and 13), and they demonstrate without question how great was the urban death toll. It is sometimes said that a third or half the population perished. This is no exaggeration for the cities, but such figures must not be extrapolated for the countryside. Here the Plague's spread depended on the movement of people from town to village and from village to village, and such move-ments were severely reduced as the rumor of plague spread. In conse-quence, some villages and regions were scarcely touched by the disease.

The Plague was brought to Europe in the trading ships of the Genoese, who did business with the caravan traders from Asia in Caffa and other ports of the Black Sea. They brought their goods to Italy, dropping them off at ports all the way from Sicily to Genoa itself. Infected rats and fleas harbored in the clothing of sailors also went ashore with them, and so the Plague spread up through the Italian peninsula to France and was then borne overland by traders to the Rhineland, central Europe, and the British Isles. At last this wave of infection died away in Scandinavia and the Baltic region where the population was so sparse that the Plague could spread no more.[2] But the disease was only dormant. It reasserted itself at intervals throughout the late Middle Ages and early modern times in bouts of frenetic activity, mostly in the larger cities. Each re-

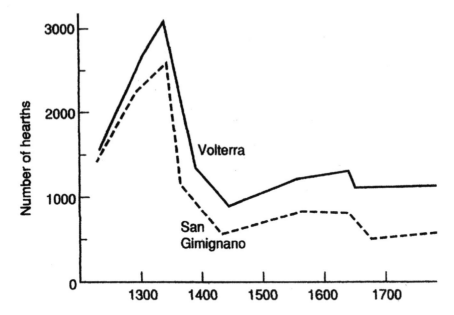

Figure 12. At both Volterra and San Gimignano in central Italy the number of hearths (or households) increased until c. 1340. The Plague then cut their number to a third or even less.

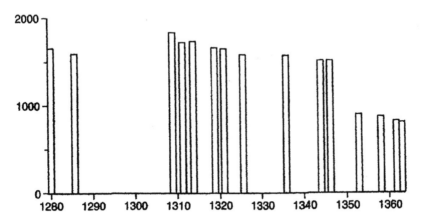

Figure 13. The number of hearths in the town of Millau in southern France at various dates. Note that their number was very nearly halved between 1326 and 1353—the period of the Black Death. Based on a table in Philippe Wolff, "Trois etudes de demographie medievale en France meridionale," in *Studi in Onore di Amando Sapori*, Milan, 1947, v. 1, 493–503.

currence decimated the urban population afresh and offered renewed opportunities in the shape of empty homes and opportunities for employment for more immigrants from the countryside. The last major outbreak in England, in 1665, was largely—though not completely—confined to the city of London, and the last outbreak in France was at Marseilles in 1720. Thereafter, the Plague disappeared from western Europe but remained endemic in the Balkans into the nineteenth century. The urban population recovered after each outbreak—in part through the birth of larger families, in part by increased immigration from the countryside.

Other urban diseases derived from congestion and the lack of cleanliness. Foremost among them were typhus and tuberculosis, the former transmitted from person to person by the microscopic body louse, the latter endemic in dark, damp, and crowded tenements. In addition there were diseases transmitted by the polluted water supply that was normal in most towns and especially in the larger and more crowded ones. Cholera, which was to become the most dangerous of all water-borne diseases, had not yet reached Europe in the Middle Ages, but it was endemic in the far East, waiting only for a fast boat from China in order for it to reach the West. Gastric and pulmonary diseases were also rife and without doubt caused a high mortality among all age groups. Not until the eighteenth century did the scientific and environmental revolution begin to bring these demographic catastrophes to an end.

There were many other infectious diseases in medieval Europe, but their relationship with the environment was not recognized before modern times and no refuge from them was found. Typhus was spread among unwashed humanity, especially during the winter months when people were crowded more closely together for warmth. There were diseases of the bronchial and digestive tracts that became more virulent during the hot, polluted summer months, when pathogens multiplied in cesspits and stagnant water and when food deteriorated quickly. Tuberculosis was rampant in damp houses with rotting timbers, and smallpox was spread "on the breath" when people were crowded together for warmth or shelter. We know now how these diseases were communicated and the defenses that can be erected against them. But to medieval people they were the inevitable lot of sinful humanity; at the most they were seen as discharges from the planets. It never occurred to anyone that their own physical environment was to blame or that they were themselves capable of preventing or curing many of them. These revelations remained unknown until Louis Pasteur and the discovery of pathogens late in the nineteenth century.

THE SOURCES OF URBAN POPULATION

In the face of this variable but generally high mortality, the towns had always to recruit population from their surrounding countryside. How extensive, one may ask, was the sphere from which the town drew its immigrants? The only certain measure is the possession of a locative personal name. Town dwellers before the twelfth or thirteenth century had no last or surname. They were known by some physical trait or, more often, by the craft they practiced: William the Short, John the Smith, Peter the Porter, and Thomas the Tailor. Alternatively they might be known by the name of the village or even of the country from which they came: William from Wickham or Ralph from Repton. In the course of time the preposition was omitted, and their names became William Wickham and Ralph Repton. There is at least a high probability that such individuals (or their ancestors) had come from the village whose name they bore. There are, however, pitfalls in this line of argument. The person named, or his or her forebears, may have migrated more than once, and women, who participated in this movement no less than men, lost their locative names on marriage. This method may be rough, but it nevertheless defines an area from which a significant part of the urban population is likely to have come. The names of townspeople can be found in tax records, in the proceedings of borough courts, and, at least for the late Middle Ages, in wills, contracts, and churchwardens' accounts. It was from such sources that the raw material of Figures 14 and 15 was obtained. These maps show the places from which locative family names had been derived for Toulouse in southern France and for Beauvais, which was not far from Paris. The maps show how far these families or their forebears had traveled in order to reach their respective "promised lands."

These maps suggest that most immigrants to the growing towns came relatively short distances and that the farther one went from the city, the fewer were the place-names commemorated in the names of migrants. The pattern of movement, in other words, conforms to the so-called gravity model, which suggests that larger cities have greater attraction as do closer ones. This, however, leaves unanswered questions: who were the people who first made the journey to the site of the future town, why did

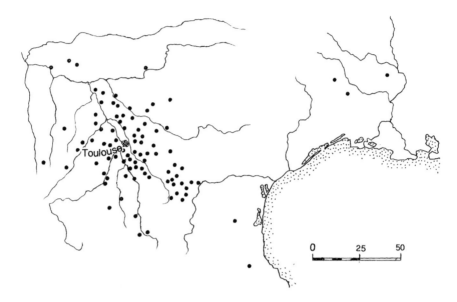

Figure 14. The source of the population of Toulouse, France, based on locative personal names.

they gather there, and what fraction of the immigrant population continued to bear the name of their ancestral village? There are no satisfactory answers. There was no one to leave a record of events and to ask why they had left the relative security of their rural homes for the uncertainties of urban life. We do, however, know very roughly what happened in the planted towns. We have seen how some of the planted towns were populated. Their lords advertised for settlers, just as the early railroads did in the settlement of the American West. But what of the countless towns that emerged during the early Middle Ages, some of them among the largest in Europe today? We must see their origins in the gatherings—which were perhaps only irregular—of merchants who had come together to buy and sell their wares. Gradually the temporary and periodic became the permanent and regular, and a merchants' settlement was born. Many of the port towns around the North Sea and the Baltic Sea almost certainly originated in this way. Many of them still bear in their names the place-name element "wich," meaning a trading place. Norwich, Ipswich, and Woolwich are today large and populous places, but their origins lay in small clusters of houses where merchants agreed to meet at intervals and do business. Not all the "wiches" prospered. Ford-

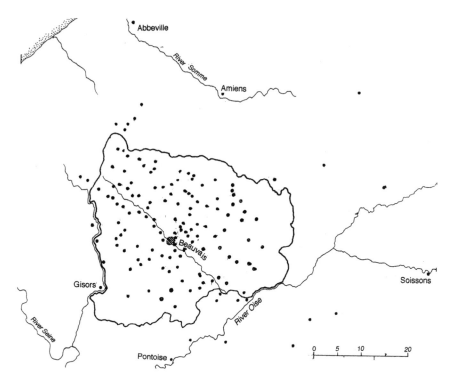

Figure 15. The known sources of migrants to Beauvais, France, based on locative personal names. The heavy line indicates the boundary of Dépt. Oise, which in turn repeat those of medieval feudal units.

wich was once the port serving the city of Canterbury but has since declined to a very small village, and ships no longer sail up its silting creek and tie up at its long-abandoned quays.

Some towns were once villages where a small population tilled the soil and benefited from some local advantage, such as a river crossing or a local resource, which could be exploited. Whatever may have been the spark igniting the growth of a town, merchants were there almost from the start, and the market became the focus of urban activities. There developed a demand for labor, both male and female, in building homes, transporting merchandise, preparing food, and practicing craft industries. And so medieval towns began their unchronicled growth—some to reach populations numbered in their tens of thousands, others to reach barely a few hundred. Each town is unique, the product of local opportunities and the initiative some possessed to exploit them.

THE SUPPLY AND PREPARATION OF FOOD

The medieval village community derived most of its food from its surrounding fields. It was a farinaceous diet, rich in bread-grains and low in protein. The chief grains were wheat, barley, and rye, varying in their relative importance with the soil and climate. Corn did not make its appearance in Europe before the sixteenth century. Animals were the chief—indeed the only—source of protein, though it must be remembered that cattle were bred not for meat, but primarily to pull the plough or the wagon, and the chief role of sheep was to provide wool. Only the pig was reared exclusively for the food it could supply, and then it was raised chiefly in northern Europe. The horse, the donkey, and the mule were not, under normal conditions, seen as sources of food. They were draft animals, and the horse—most aristocratic of animals—served, first and foremost, to carry its master into battle. Honey was the only source of sweetening, and spices, rarely seen in the rural community but imported and sold by the urban merchant, were used to give some piquancy to the otherwise bland diet. Under normal conditions of weather the village community was able to satisfy its needs and still have a small surplus, which it passed into the local market where it was sold to help feed the urban population. The town had no such advantage. If even a small town were called upon to feed itself, its cultivated lands, meadow, pasture, and woodland would have stretched so far beyond its walls that its farming population could not have made the daily journey to its most distant fields. It was of necessity a food importer.

The mechanism of food supply grew in complexity with the increasing size of the town, until in the largest the problem of feeding its people was one of the most difficult facing its authorities. Small towns could usually draw on the food-producing capacity of its surrounding villages. That was the purpose of the weekly market. Peasants brought what foodstuffs they could spare from their total production and sold them directly to the urban consumer. Where it became necessary to obtain supplies from a greater distance, the middleman had to intervene, buying in the villages, transporting supplies to the town, holding them in store for a while, and eventually selling them to the consumer. In an extreme case the merchants of the German Hanse transported Baltic rye for sale in the clothing towns of Flanders, and Italian merchants brought spices from the Middle East for sale throughout the West.

Bread-grains had a long shelf-life; it would have been very unfortunate if this were not the case, for there would have been no store of food during the months before harvest. As it was, the grains—wheat, barley, and rye—were running low when spring came, and so the joys of spring were always tempered by some degree of belt-tightening. Once baked into bread or boiled in a rather thin gruel or soup, which was a basic item of diet, the food grains could be stored for only a short time. In the village, if not also in the town, bread was commonly baked in the home, usually in a dome-shaped, preheated oven, often constructed out of doors. In the town, however, this was a dangerous process owing to the ever-present risk of fire. And so the task of baking was transferred to the professional baker. The size of the bakers' gild in all except the smallest towns suggests that baking was carried on by a professional class and that bread was sold in public from shops or market stalls. The problem facing the butcher was less tractable. Meat did not keep for more than a few days. Animals had to be kept alive and fed until they were slaughtered, butchered, and sold, and then their meat had to be cooked and eaten within a relatively short period. Both the rural and the urban domestic kitchens were adjusted to the roasting of meat and the boiling of a kind of stew made from grain, vegetables, and a little meat or animal fat, together with whatever "companage"—the term used for anything added, such as onions, to give flavor to what was, in fact, a very bland diet—might be available and seasoned with salt and whatever spices and herbs could be obtained. "Wel loved he garleek, oynons, and eek lekes,"[3] wrote Chaucer of his Summoner, and the old man's daughter in the "Clerk's Tale,"

> And whan she homward cam, she wolde brynge
> Wortes [roots] or othere herbes tymes ofte,
> The whiche she shredde and seeth [boiled] for hir lyvynge.[4]

The diet of the upper classes differed from that of the masses only in having a greater quantity of meat together with more exotic spices. The Grocers' Gild of London had in its heraldry nine cloves, one of the spices favored by the well-to-do and imported by its members. The diet of the town dweller was broadly similar to that of the rural peasant, but may have contained more exotic foods such as spices, while the country dweller had a more ready access, whether legally or by poaching, to a supply of edible wildlife, such as the rabbit.

Most foodstuffs were seasonal. The basic food grains were always abundant in the late summer and fall. They had then to be stored in granaries and protected from the depredations of rats, mice, and other vermin until the next harvest. Late spring and early summer were always a period of increasing scarcity and rising prices, when there was not always enough food, at least for the poor. Even the supply of meat was seasonal, conditioned by the supply of fodder, of which hay was the most conspicuous part. There was a gigantic slaughter of animals at the beginning of winter, as the peasant calculated how many beasts he could keep alive until the grass again began to grow in early spring.

It was, as a general rule, unsafe to drink water; thus, the process of fermentation not only rendered a drink more palatable, but also a great deal safer. The alcoholic drinks favored over most of Europe were wine and beer (or ale). The grape-vine had a restricted range, dictated by soil and climate, but within its range it was almost an urban crop. Engravings of towns of the Renaissance period often show vineyards close to the town walls. Brewing was more widespread because it could use whatever grain was available. During times of scarcity there was a competition for the grain crop between the baker and the brewer. Both brewing and wine-making could be carried on domestically, but the equipment needed—vats and a good water supply—tended to limit urban brewing to the professional brewer. Many of the larger towns had a brewers' gild.

The food supply of both village and town was always at the mercy of two factors over which the consumer had no control. In the first place, marauding armies—of which there were many in continental Europe—were accustomed to living off the land and to destroying whatever they could not themselves consume. The urban censuses, taken so frequently in many Italian cities, did not arise from any curiosity regarding the size of the population, but from the harsh necessity that each person represented a "mouth" to be fed. They did not enumerate people but *bocca*—"mouths." The urban granaries had to be well stocked if the city was to be sure of surviving periods of warfare and even the occasional siege.

The second cause for concern lay in the uncertainty of the harvest. There were bad years as well as good; years when the crop was diminished by drought, washed out by floods, or blighted by insect pest or plant disease. Against these visitations of nature there could be no protection other than a well-stocked granary. This was made all the more difficult by the irregularity and the uncertainty of the weather. Medieval people fully recognized this, as Piers the Plowman noted:

> And before a few years finish famine shall arise,
> . . . .
> Through floods and foul weather fruits shall fail;
> Pride and pestilence shall take out many people.[5]

Prices would rise; those who had money would purchase foodstuffs, usually grain, and store it, thus driving prices yet higher. It was for good reason that engrossing—the hoarding of more foodstuffs than was necessary—was accounted one of the deadly sins. The countryman rarely suffered from extreme privation, because there was always some food to be obtained from the land, but the townsman knew what it was to face starvation. The descriptions of feasts, whether given by gild members or by merchant families, betoken not a superfluity of food, but its scarcity and the desire to enjoy it to the full whenever it was available. The spring or Eastertide feasts and foods were the last occasion to enjoy them to the full before the next harvest replenished granaries and larders, and early summer was a time of increasing scarcity.

WATER AND SANITATION

A supply of water was an absolute necessity in every town. Many crafts—tanning, dyeing, brewing—required an abundant supply of water, and food could not be prepared without it. The Romans had developed hydraulic engineering into a science. Even in the small towns of provincial Britain, a supply of water was brought by a combination of pipe and aqueduct from whatever distant source there may have been. When the Roman Empire in the West collapsed, its elaborate systems of water supply were abandoned. The works that supplied the city of Rome aroused the excited admiration of medieval visitors who nevertheless proved to be incapable of emulating them back in their own homes. The new masters of Europe lacked either the skills to maintain them or the vision to realize how important they were. Medieval people relied overwhelmingly on natural springs, artificial wells, and whatever streams and rivers lay within reach. The water carrier was part of the urban scene, and leather water bottles sometimes formed the charge in a medieval coat-of-arms.

Springs and wells were rarely adequate to supply the needs even of a small town. In the fourteenth century the inhabitants of the very small English town of Penrith, in Cumberland, complained that they had "no water save a little rivulet," in which the tanners were accustomed to soak their hides.[6] Such instances could be multiplied endlessly from medieval sources. Andrew Boorde, an English writer of the early sixteenth century, advised his readers not to drink water at all. "Ale," he wrote, "for an En-glysshe man is a naturall drynke." And if water must be drunk, Boorde explained that "[t]he best . . . is rayne-water, so be it that it be clene and purely taken."[7] But capturing the rainwater from the roofs of town houses and conducting it to a cistern was not easy and seems rarely to have been attempted except in Mediterranean regions. Furthermore, water from the roofs was no less polluted than that from other sources. And so towns struggled on from one crisis to the next, from one epidemic to another until in the mid-nineteenth century the sources of infections were tracked down to a polluted water supply. The classic case was the identification of the source of the cholera epidemic of mid-nineteenth-century London. It was a street pump in the populous district of Soho, which had become contaminated. A similar outbreak at the very end of the nineteenth cen-tury in the German city of Hamburg ended in exactly the same way.

The urban water supply was always of doubtful quality but was made incomparably worse by medieval methods of sanitation and waste dis-posal. This has been a perennial human problem, of small consequence in a rural environment but desperately important in the town. The big-ger the town, the more important it became. In a congested urban envi-ronment, it was not unusual to dig a domestic cesspit and to cover it with wooden boards through which a small hole had been pierced. Such de-vices were endlessly described in the *Assize of Nuisances* of the City of London.[8] Such contrivances gave rise to countless problems, many of them described in graphic and horrifying detail, as far as London was con-cerned, in the records of the Coroners' Courts and the *Assize of Nui-sances*. The London coroner, for example, heard the case of a man who had fallen through the boards covering his cesspit, which had rotted with the damp, and was drowned in the cess beneath. Such stories appealed to the crude medieval sense of humor, and a similar incident occurs in one of Boccaccio's stories in the *Decameron*.

There was abundant space in the countryside for the digging of cesspits, but within the walls of a town building, plots were becoming ever smaller as the density of housing increased. Unless they were periodically cleared, cesspits quickly filled up and had to be replaced. Soon there was room for no more, and, as the records of the City of London show, they were even dug beneath the floors of houses and were reached by a small hole in the floor. It is difficult for us to conceive of the inconvenience—quite apart from the smell—such facilities created.

The cesspit, little more than three or four feet deep, was often lined with wickerwork like a basket and sometimes with masonry. Many such pits have been excavated and their contents analyzed by today's archaeologists. Even after five or six centuries their contents have much to tell us about the diet of medieval people, as well as yielding domestic articles such as cutlery and broken pottery which had been thrown into them. Where there was no regular refuse collection, there was every temptation to toss unwanted articles into the cesspit, which lay so conveniently beneath the kitchen floor. In a well-managed town the cesspits were regularly cleared and their contents carted away—sometimes to be dumped into the nearest river, sometimes to be spread over the suburban fields which yielded produce for the urban market. In Paris and London this traffic in "cess" was well organized to the great benefit of the gardens and of horticulture outside the cities, as well as to that of the health of the town.

In matters of water supply, sanitation, and hygiene the Church, especially the monasteries, provided an object lesson few seemed able to follow. It is possible that churchmen had been able to profit from the example of classical Rome, which some of them must have seen in the course of their visits to the Holy City. Where possible, a piped water supply was established, a siphon being used to circumvent such obstacles as a river. In Cambridge, England, the Franciscan friars drew their water supply from a spring well outside the city limits, taking it across the river Cam by means of a siphon. Unfortunately, the friars found that it was all too easy for others to tap into their supply, and not all of it ever reached their friary house.

Personal hygiene was not rated highly. Water was scarce, and the coarse soap, made by boiling wood ash with animal fat, had an unpleasant smell and was little used. There was, at least among the upper classes, a perfunctory washing of hands before a meal, and in monasteries there was usually a *lavatorium*, or wash-place, located close to the refectory, thus demonstrating the association of cleanliness with food. Here the monks at most dipped their hands into a shallow stream of water in a perfunctory fashion. Thomas Coryat, a Europe-wide traveler of the sixteenth century, urged diners not to touch the dish in which their food was served because he said that all men's fingers were not clean.[9] As cutlery came to be more widely used during the Renaissance there ceased to be any need to touch either the dish or the food.

It was customary to dispose of domestic waste merely by throwing it into the street, from which it was recovered by "rakers" who usually disposed of it in the nearest river. Even the expression "Gardez l'eau" (beware of the water), usually contracted to "loo," relates to the practice of disposing of liquid from an upper room by emptying it onto the passersby in the street below. The casual attitude of medieval people to matters of cleanliness and sanitation can be excused by their ignorance of the nature of infection and the reality of pathogens. Yet their failure to associate morbidity with filth is indeed surprising. They were quick to associate "bad air"—malaria—with the exhalations from swamps and marshes, but failed to recognize in the stench of cesspits the source of something a great deal worse. The worst of water-borne infections—cholera—was endemic in Asia, and probably had been for very many centuries, but its pathogens were unable to survive the long voyage to Europe before the early years of the nineteenth century, when the speed of ocean transport became fast enough for the pathogens to survive the journey.

ACCIDENT AND MISFORTUNE

Not only were morbidity and mortality more severe in the town than in the countryside, the ordinary hazards of life were greater. In England any unexpected death had to be examined by the coroner—the Keeper of the Pleas of the Crown (Corona) in order to ensure that the king received whatever dues and compensation might be due to him.[10] The resulting records show how precarious life was in the Middle Ages. Scores of building workers fell from their flimsy scaffolding, brewers were drowned in their own vats, and countless people, both young and old, lost their lives in the frequent fires which arose from carelessness in the kitchen or the forge and spread with the greatest rapidity from house to house. There were doctors, physicians, bone-setters, and pharmacists, whose activities, in the absence of precise diagnoses, were at best neutral and at worst lethal.

Many towns had rudimentary building regulations governing the thickness of walls and the distance by which upper floors might be allowed to "jetty" over the lower. But enforcement was never easy. Frequently we find that walls, built of unbaked clay, could not support the structures imposed upon them or were undermined and weakened by the effluent of nearby cesspits. The gables that frequently fronted onto the streets were frequently found to be crumbling and about to collapse. Streets were narrowed by the unauthorized extension of existing buildings and obstructed by accumulations of wood and of other materials. There was never any sidewalk, but the surface of the street sloped downward toward the middle, where refuse was allowed to accumulate until at irregular intervals it was swept up by the rakers.

Any serious illness was likely to be fatal. Wills, the preparation of which became common in the late Middle Ages, were rarely made until the individual in question felt himself or herself to be close to death. There was a superstition against making a last will and testament while in good health. The writer once examined a large bundle of early wills, comparing the dates when they were drawn up, signed, and witnessed with the dates when they were presented to the Church court to be "proved" (i.e., "approved"). The interval was sometimes as little as four weeks, and the average was only seven. One can only conclude that there were few illnesses from which one could recover and that most were fatal.

The disposal of the dead presented little problem in the countryside. Each parish had its cemetery, usually surrounding the parish church, where every parishioner in good standing with the Church had a legal right to be buried without charge beyond that of digging a hole and filling it in afterward. In towns, burial was more difficult. The pressure on space meant that cemeteries were small, that burials were superimposed one above another, and that the digging of one grave was likely to disturb the long-deceased occupant of another. How well we recognize this in the graveyard scene in Shakespeare's *Hamlet*. Urban cemeteries thus became intensely crowded, raising the ground level to a considerable height above that of the church floor or even of the surrounding streets. In many a medieval church one has now to step down into it from the level of the churchyard. Shallow and superimposed burials meant that dogs could scrape away the soil to reach the bones buried beneath. Even

more disastrous were the activities of the pigs that roamed the streets of
at least the smaller towns and invaded the cemeteries. All too often a
cemetery was strewn with the bones of the anonymous dead. For this reason it became the practice to build a "charnel house" in which the bones
of the ancestors of the community could be more reverently deposited.
It is impossible to quantify the dangers to health that arose from the ways
in which cemeteries were managed, but in all probability they were significant.

Most towns, including also many of the smallest, possessed "hospitals."
Some were of great size, like that at Beaune and Tonnere in Burgundy,
France. Hospitals were not, as their name suggests, places where the sick
were sent in order to recover under the solicitous care of devoted "sisters." The sick rarely recovered. Hospitals were, rather, places where the
aged could spend their last days in relative peace and comfort. The typical hospital resembled a church. In the body of the building the "sick"
lay on their beds, while at the east end a priest said mass day after day,
not for their recovery, but for the salvation of their souls after death. Such
hospitals had usually been founded and endowed by the wealthy and well
disposed, but were quite inadequate for the needs even of a small town.
How then were those too old or too disabled to work, or even to tend to
their own bodily needs, supported in a medieval society? Some were cared
for by members of their own families. It was expected that most would
have children who could perform this service, but not all were so fortunate. Not infrequently a son accepted a contractual obligation to share
a house with an elderly parent, allowing the latter the privacy of a room
and the produce of a small tract of garden. Others lived by begging and
the charity of others; the Church continually enjoined on the faithful
the duty of charitable giving. They quickly became part of that dark underworld that was present in every town. But their problem was short-
lived. They quickly succumbed to starvation and disease.

ECONOMIC RELATIONS

The area controlled by a city and thus subject to its laws and liable to
its taxation varied greatly. Nuremberg probably spanned an area of more
than 400 square miles, while Augsburg, scarcely less important as a commercial city, embraced only a small area of meadow and gardens outside
the line of its walls. In France and in England it mattered little how ex-

tensive the area under the control of any one town was. The central governments were relatively strong and were able to ensure that the market area of each was as extensive as was necessary to maintain a regular supply of foodstuffs and other commodities. Their "city limits" were effectively of little or no importance. In central Europe, where, in the absence of a strong central authority, there could have been a deep hostility between a town and its surrounding territories, the possession of a large contado was highly desirable. Augsburg, for example, had to maintain good relations with the lords of surrounding lands. It might otherwise have quite literally been starved into surrender.

Every town was the focal point of a region, as it had been since urban history began. The extent of this region was a function of the city's size and the range of its economic activities. It would also have been influenced by the terrain, by transportation facilities, and by obstacles to movement such as mountains and rivers. It would also have been affected by political considerations: relations with surrounding territories and treaty privileges and obligations. But let us assume that the area in question was homogeneous, that the quality of the land and ease of movement over it did not vary in any direction. No area on this earth could have satisfied these conditions. Perhaps the nearest approach would have been the plains of eastern England and of northern France. In these areas every small town, which, by definition, was unable to supply its own needs in foodstuffs and at the same time required a market for its own products, was surrounded by its market region. The extent of this market region would have been determined primarily by the distance peasant farmers were prepared to travel to their nearest urban market. The medieval English jurist, Bracton (d. 1268), enunciated a simple rule. A man could walk twenty miles in a day (at least, he was able to do so then). He would be required to spend at least a third of a day at the market, thus leaving him with two-thirds of the day for his outward and homeward journeys. During this period he could cover at most two-thirds of the twenty miles that made up the hypothetical day's journey. He would thus have to live not more than six and two-thirds miles from a market. Our hypothetical, homogenous land would thus be divided up into market areas, all of them of the same size and within each of which the peasant was guaranteed access to a market within the limits just described. Since, however, the land surface cannot be divided into circular areas without their overlapping, it is assumed that they must be hexagonal, as in Figure 16.

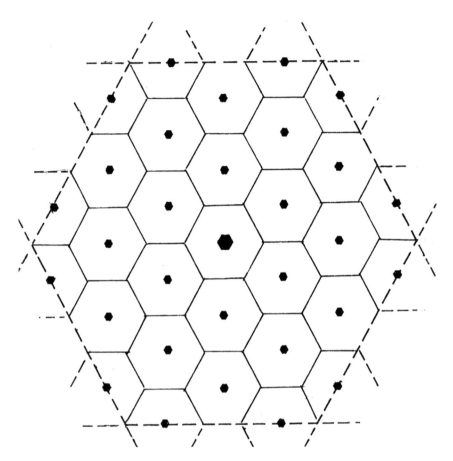

Figure 16. Theory: The theoretical distribution of market centers in a homogeneous landscape.

An examination of the urban pattern in any moderately uniform region is likely to show a scatter of market towns not inconsistent with this theory, whether we base it on contemporary evidence or on that of the Middle Ages (Figure 17).

Many urban functions, however, were not required in every small town. There might be so little demand for a goldsmith or a silversmith, for a dealer in expensive fabrics or imported spices, that none had established themselves. It might have been sufficient if only one town in a dozen or twenty possessed these crafts. The same would have been true of merchants who engaged in long-distance trade or of service occupations, such as those of the scrivener who inscribed deeds and inedited ac-

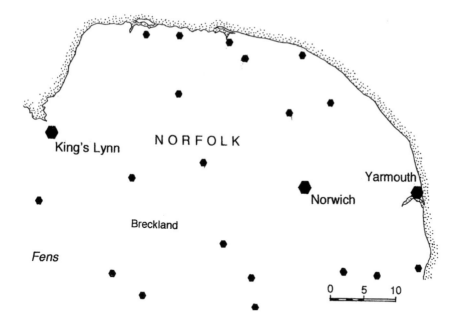

Figure 17. Reality: The actual distribution in the English county of Norfolk.

counts and letters for a predominantly illiterate populace. And so we find
a higher order of towns, each with a larger service area and a greater
range of functions, occupations, and professions than simple market
towns. One can go further and postulate an even higher order. These
might include the seats of government, the major ports, and the centers
of highly specialized manufactures. The higher the order of a town the
greater the range of its activities, the larger its population, and the wider
its effective region.

This is theory—commonly called central place theory—and theory is
distorted, first and foremost, by physical circumstances and, second, by
political considerations. But when allowance is made for these factors it
is surprising how close reality comes to what can theoretically be expected. Let us consider two towns at opposite extremes of this urban hierarchy.

Rheinfelden was, during the late Middle Ages, a small walled town
lying on the river Rhine some ten miles upstream, that is, to the east of
the Swiss city of Basel. Rheinfelden had belonged to the Dukes of Zähringen,
to whom it owed its charter. Its walls, built during the thirteenth cen-

tury, enclosed an area of about twenty-five acres, and its population could not have been much more than 220 households or a thousand people. The crafts were well represented and probably supported almost two-thirds of the families. There were weavers, tanners, leather- and metalworkers, and a number of carpenters and builders. There was, of course, a market that was frequented by peasants from the surrounding countryside. Fortunately, a list has survived of the places from which the peasants traveled each week to the Rheinfelden market.[11] Its market region appears as a rounded area extending almost ten miles from the town into the Jura Mountains to the south, but a shorter distance northward into the Black Forest (Figure 18). The town lay on the south bank of the

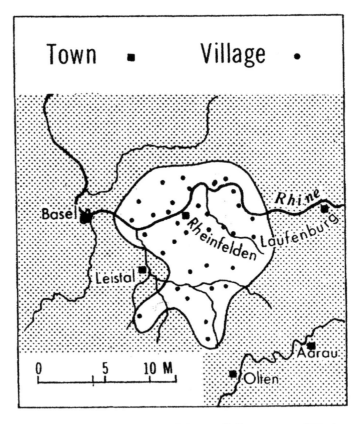

Figure 18. The service area of the small Swiss town of Rhein-felden.

river Rhine. There was a bridge at this point, but the perceived obstacle the river presented, together with the fact that a toll had to be paid to cross it, restricted the service area of the town on the northern side of the river.

At the opposite end of the hierarchy of cities lay Nuremberg.[12] It was an imperial city, subject only to the emperor, whose remote and ineffective authority the city's fathers could afford to ignore. Nuremberg had succeeded in extending its authority over a far greater area than was necessary to satisfy its needs. The Reichswald, which lay close to the city, supplied timber for its domestic building, and no less than thirty quarries contributed masonry for the ambitious building projects that included several miles of city wall with a large number of towers and gates. Bricks and tiles were made from a clay that occurred to the north at the foot of the Swabian Jura. Wine was brought from farther afield along the several rivers that joined the Pegnitz. Supplementary supplies of grain, made necessary by the city's population, which grew to some 40,000–50,000 at the end of the Middle Ages, came from Bohemia and Saxony, and meat came from animals reared on the plains of Poland and Hungary.

By the late Middle Ages Nuremberg had far outgrown its local supplies of food, large as these were, and had come to depend on merchants who bought in distant markets and transported their goods by whatever means were available to the markets of the city. Similarly the crafts located in Nuremberg satisfied not only the local demand for manufactured goods, but also a market, which was as large as southern Germany, with the more esoteric products of its craftsmen. Nuremberg was one of the highest orders of cities in Europe, embracing as it did not only the functions of the lower- and middle-order towns, but also those of the highest. We do not, unfortunately, have a list of the gilds or of the crafts practiced in the city, but there could have been no commodities that were unavailable in its shops and few merchants in the whole of Europe who did not do business with those of Nuremberg.

Between Rheinfelden and Nuremberg lay hundreds, even thousands, of towns organized in the map illustrated in Figure 19. It is easy in theory to allocate particular towns to their appropriate level in this hierarchy, but reality is more complex. There was an urban spectrum ranging without clear demarcation lines from the largest and most varied down to the smallest and most narrowly based.

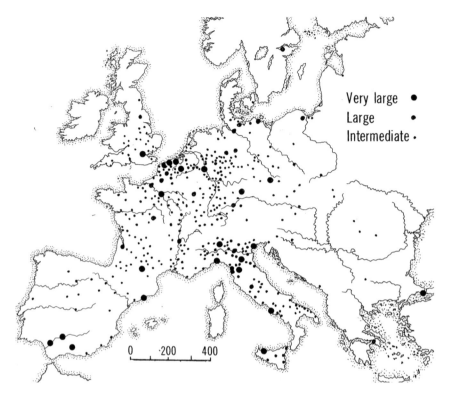

Figure 19. The distribution of large and intermediate cities in late medieval Europe. Note their concentration in the Low Countries and in northern and central Italy.

HOW BIG AND HOW MANY

In this section we address three important questions: how many towns there were in medieval Europe, how large they were, and what fraction of Europe's population lived in cities and towns and what was its social structure. On the question of size we are very ill-informed. No country instituted a true census before the eighteenth century, with one important exception. Many Italian cities depended heavily on imported grain and were frequently at war with one another. Attempts to count the population were therefore made in order to determine how many "mouths" there were to feed and how large a store of bread-grains should be kept to feed them.[13] Indeed, the word *bocca* came to be used for "people." For the rest of Europe, however, we are dependent for estimating population on a surrogate, most often the number of taxpayers, sometimes of communicants or of men of military age. Each such person must be regarded as the head of a household and supposed to have had a family. What we need to know in order to obtain a rough estimate of the size of the population is thus the average size of the household or family, and this is very difficult to determine. Tax rolls often listed the "hearths," which must be assumed to have been the groups of people living in a single home. This may have been more than a single family, especially in the crowded conditions of the larger cities. What we have in such cases is not a household or family, but what has been called a "houseful," a kind of tenement for which the average population cannot possibly be determined. The results are highly unreliable, and, as in all medieval statistics, we must allow for a wide margin of error.

The population of medieval towns was in a constant state of flux, increasing with immigration from the countryside in times of uncertainty, depleted by disease in times of major epidemics. If it is difficult to generalize regarding rural population, it is almost impossible for urban. But it can be said with some certainty that urban population increased overall until about 1300. Its growth then flattened off and may even have begun to decline before it was in 1348 hit by the Great Plague. The extent of losses from this cause is uncertain, but was far greater in most towns than in the countryside. Italian evidence suggests that some towns may have lost up to a half of their population. In eastern and northern Europe, however, where towns were more widely spaced and their conditions less congested, the ravages of the Plague were less severe, and there were large areas where it does not appear to have been experienced at all.

There were few very large cities in medieval Europe, perhaps no more than a dozen or fifteen, each with populations of more than 50,000, and some of these may have fallen below this level in times of plague. The reasons are clear. It was difficult to feed cities of great size, and the craft industries were not able to employ so great an urban population. Byzantium was a probable exception. Byzantium could be provisioned by ship from the wheat-growing lands around the Black Sea; similarly, the cities of Flanders relied on grain brought from the region of the Baltic Sea. The Italian cities had greater difficulty, as is apparent from their frequent head counts. Much of their grain supply came from the plains along Italy's east coast and from Sicily.

An intermediate category of towns had, let us say, from 5,000 to 25,000 inhabitants before the time of the Black Death. Thereafter, if we may judge from the few well-documented examples, the population fluctuated greatly, as did the number of cities and towns which fell into this inter-mediate group.

Last, there were towns of less than 5,000. Some were prosperous and important; a few narrowly failed to qualify as cities of intermediate size. Others, with less than a thousand inhabitants, were barely distinguish-able from large villages in either function or social structure. Some even failed completely to maintain their urban status. The writer well re-members stumbling quite by accident on the minute German town of Mainbernheim in the province of Bavaria. Mainbernheim lay within a ring of high walls with tall, slender towers spaced at intervals and a sin-gle defended entrance. Within, there seemed to be nothing more than a very few farmhouses with their barns and animal shelters. This had once been a town. There was room for a resident population of considerably less than a hundred, and the "town" had probably never held more. One is left wondering how so small a community was able to build fortifica-tions of such magnitude. South and central Germany and also Switzer-land were notable for their number of "dwarf" towns or Zwergstadte, all of which had elaborately constructed walls and towers.

Putting this information together allows us to compile a rough table that answers two of the questions which were posed earlier, how many and how large. But this must be seen for the greater part as nothing bet-ter than an intelligent guess. It relates to the years before the Great Plague. Totals would have been very much lower during the years fol-lowing 1350, though some towns might have regained their earlier size before the end of the century.

On this precarious basis the following table (Table 1) has been com-piled and the map (Figure 19) drawn. Cities and towns are for conven-ience grouped into five categories. In reality they form a continuum reaching from the largest with a population of over 50,000 to the small-est with less than a thousand. Byzantium, before its siege by the Turks in 1453, may once have been the largest city in Europe, with perhaps close to 100,000 inhabitants, but this population was greatly diminished, first after it was besieged and looted by the Crusaders in 1204 and then after its conquest by the Ottoman Turks in 1453.

Table 1
The Size of Towns in Northern Europe

Town Size	Number	Total Population
Giant (over 50,000)		
Very Large (25–50,000)	15	400,000
Large (10–25,000)	45	570,000
Intermediate (2–10,000)	350	1,100,000
Small (under 2,000)	3–4,000	2,250,000

For two countries—England and Italy—we have sources of unequaled importance. The Domesday Book of 1086 and the Poll-Tax of 1381 both covered most of England. Neither is a census in the strict sense; both were compiled primarily for taxation purposes and give the numbers of either adult males or of households. Nevertheless, it is possible to multiply the figures given by the estimated size of an average family in order to obtain a total population. Domesday Book is far from consistent in its terminology. In some towns it enumerated *mansurae*, or houses; in others, *burgenses*, or citizens. In most of the towns for which these data are given there were different categories of townspeople. The smallest town was credited with only seven burgenses—perhaps about 30 inhabitants; the largest—Norwich—with 665 burgenses and 480 *bordarii pauperes* (meaning perhaps "poor husbandmen"), thus suggesting a total population of between 5,000 and 6,000. The two most important cities in twelfth-century England—London and Winchester—were, for reasons which we do not know, omitted from the Domesday survey.

Another important source is a tax roll of 1334. This gives not the size, but the aggregate wealth of communities. Furthermore, boroughs were taxed at a different rate from rural settlements, and their definition is very arbitrary. The resulting list of towns is useful for purposes of comparison, but tells us nothing about their size.

Poll taxes were levied in 1377, 1379, and 1381. Of these the records for 1377 are the most complete and are used here. Even so, there are many omissions, and many small towns were accounted only as parts of the parishes in which they lay. The tax was payable only by adults—those over 14—and only by laymen. Clerics and the very poor were exempt,

Table 2
Urban Population of England as Percentage of Total

Year	National Total	Urban Total	Percentage Urban
1086	1–1.5 million	66–82,000	5.5–6.5
1377	1.2–2 million	c. 90,000	8.5–10

and no one can say what proportion of the total population these com-prised. After the Great Plague, it appears that the population of those towns, which had survived the three centuries since the compilation of Domesday Book, had increased by from 2 to 3 percent, a very slow rate of growth.

The last question—what proportion of the total population lived in towns—is almost impossible to answer, except for a few, small, well-documented areas. The answer calls for a reliable estimate of the popu-lation both of every country and of the towns within each of them. The English sources discussed earlier allow acceptable estimates to be made for that country, but for other countries we have no certain knowledge. Table 2 lists the estimated urban population in England in the years 1086 and 1377 as a percentage of the total population.

These figures, based on Domesday Book and the Poll Tax returns of 1377, are estimates only, and may contain a wide margin of error. Apart from the uncertainties of the records, it is impossible to arrive at an agreed figure for the average size of the household. The 1377 figures are, of course, post-Plague. The extent of the losses in 1348–1350 and of the recovery by 1377 are equally indeterminate. It seems evident that the urban population increased considerably more rapidly than the rural dur-ing the period 1086–1377.

Despite the evident shortcomings in the sources, the medievalist J. K. Russell has made a brave attempt to estimate the population of Europe as a whole.[14] Table 3 lists the total European population during the Mid-dle Ages according to Russell's estimate and the estimated urban per-centage of that total. The proportion would have varied greatly over the continent and would without question have been largest in Flanders and Italy.

The map (Figure 19) shows all towns that have been placed in the in-

Table 3
European Urban Population

Year	Total Population	Urban Percentage
1000	52,200,000	1–3%
1340 (pre-Plague)	85,900,000	5–10%
1400	52,000,000	5–8%
1500	70,000,000	9–12%

termediate and higher categories. It shows a kind of urban axis reaching from London to Naples and passing through Flanders, the Rhineland, and northern and central Italy. It also shows lesser branches that extended respectively down the Rhone valley to the Mediterranean coast and eastward across central Germany to Magdeburg and Prague. By contrast, central France (basically the Auvergne) and much of Spain except the extreme south, which was then ruled by the Moors, and eastern Europe from the Baltic Sea to Greece were almost devoid of towns. Urban growth was inhibited in central Spain by the wars between the Christian states of the north and the Moors, and did not revive until after the expulsion of the Moors from Spain in 1492. The data for the three large, Moorish towns in southern Spain (Cordova, Seville, and Granada) are very uncertain.

This distribution of large towns was closely related to that of the chief manufacturing industries. The most highly urbanized parts of Europe, Flanders, and northern and central Italy, were outstanding for their cloth manufacture. Cities and towns were numerous, and some were very large. Urban population formed overall only a small proportion of the total population, however. Precise estimates of the actual figures are impossible; the population of both town and country was liable to very considerable fluctuations. Urban population constituted the highest proportion in the manufacturing regions of Flanders and Italy. Here it may have approached a quarter of the total. In France, England, and central Europe it would have been a great deal less, perhaps 10 to 15 percent at most, while over the vast extent of northern and eastern Europe it was probably less than 5 percent.

NOTES

1. Wladyslaw Reymont, *The Promised Land* (*Ziemia obiecana*), trans. M. H. Dziewicki (New York: A. A. Knopf, 1927).

2. There is a very large literature on the subject of the Black Death and of plague in general. Particularly important are John Findlay Drew Shrewsbury, *A History of the Bubonic Plague in the British Isles* (London: Cambridge University Press, 1971) and Philip Ziegler, *The Black Death* (New York: John Day Company, 1969).

3. Geoffrey Chaucer, "Prologue," in *"The Canterbury Tales" Complete*, ed. Larry D. Benson (Boston and New York: Houghton Mifflin Company, 2000), p. 15, line 634.

4. Chaucer, "Clerk's Tale," in *"The Canterbury Tales" Complete*, ed. Larry D. Benson (Boston and New York: Houghton Mifflin Company, 2000), p. 122, lines 225–27.

5. William Langland, *William Langland's "Piers Plowman": The C Version: A Verse Translation*, ed. George Economou, Middle Age Series (Philadelphia: University of Pennsylvania Press, 1996), p. 79, lines 346–49.

6. "Northern Petitions Illustrative of Life in Berwick, Cumbria, and Durham in the Fourteenth Century," ed. Constance Marie Fraser, *Publications of the Surtees Society*, vol. 194 (Gateshead: Surtees Society, 1981), p. 107.

7. Andrew Boorde, *The Fyrst Boke of the Introduction of Knowledge Made by Andrew Borde, of Physycke Doctor. A Compendyous Regyment; or, A Dyetary of Helth Made in Mountpyllier, Compyled by Andrewe Boorde, of Physycke Doctour. Barnes in the Defence of the Berde: A Treatyse Made, Answerynge the Treatyse of Doctor Borde upon Berdes*, ed. F. J. Furnivall (London: N. T. Trubner & Company, 1907), pp. 253, 256.

8. *London Assize of Nuisance, 1301–1431: A Calendar*, ed. Helena M. Chew and William Kellaway, London Record Society Publications, vol. 10 (Leicester: London Record Society, 1973), pp. 5, 38.

9. Thomas Coryat, *Coryat's Crudities*, ed. William M. Schutte (London: Scolar Press, 1978).

10. The coroner was an officer of the crown (corona) charged with the task of seeing that, on the unexplained death of any of his subjects, the king received all that was due to him. In the case of an accident the instrument of death was due to the king.

11. Hektor Ammann, *Wirtschaft und Lebensraum der Mittelalterlichen Kleinstadt: I. Rheinfelden* (Frick: A. Fricker, 1948).

12. Based mainly on Fritz Schnelbogl, "Die wirtschaftliche Bedeutung ihre Landesgebiet fur die Reichstadt Nurnberg," *Beiträge zur Wirtschaftsgeschichte Nürnbergs*, 2 vols. (Nürnberg: Stradtrat, 1967), 1:261–31.

13. On the population of the Italian cities see Julius Beloch, *Bevölkerungsg-eschichte Italiens*, 2 vols. (Berlin: De Gruyter, 1965).

14. Josiah Cox Russell, *Late Ancient and Medieval Population*, Transactions of the American Philosophical Society, n.s., vol. 48, pt. 3 (Philadelphia: American Philosophical Society, 1958).

CHAPTER 4

THE CHURCH IN THE CITY

And I'll have your church roofed and build you a cloister,
Have your walls washed and your windows glazed
And pay those that paint and make pictures for you
So that all men will say I'm one of your order.

—Piers Plowman[1]

Some towns grew up around a church; others had churches thrust upon them. Whatever the relationship between them, the Church has played a very important role, both physical and cultural, in the development of urban life. In its origin Christianity was an urban faith. It was borne by its earliest missionaries from city to city. The epistles of St. Paul were addressed to townsfolk, and the first Christian cells were in the greater cities of the Roman Empire. Only slowly did the faith penetrate the countryside, which long remained the sphere of the *pagani*, countryfolk or "pagans," and it came even later to mountainous and thinly peopled regions. These remained dark corners of the land until late in the Middle Ages. And yet Christianity always had a certain affinity with wastelands and solitary places. The wilderness was where Christians went for contemplation and spiritual refreshment. It was the resort of the "desert fathers" and the first home of certain religious orders. There were thus two strands in the evolution of the Christian Church: that which attracted people to the company of others and carried on its activities in crowded cities and, by contrast, that which sought the solitary life—monastic in the strict meaning of that term. The latter is not important in the present context except insofar as here and there it contributed to the settlement and development of such wasteland areas and thus stimulated urban growth. Places of pilgrimage became the nuclei of some towns, and remote monasteries sometimes became centers of commercial, even of industrial, activity. One thinks of Santiago, the reputed burial place of St. James of Compostela in northwestern Spain; of Bobbio in the Italian Apennines; of Sankt Gallen, which even became the capital of a Swiss canton; of Maria Lach in the German Eifel, and, in Great Britain, of Ely on its island amid the Cambridgeshire Fenland and of Glastonbury similarly placed in the Somerset marshes.

But such instances were few. Far more important in the development of the Church were the regional capitals, the *civitates*, of the Roman Empire. These became the administrative centers of the Church, just as they had been of Roman governors. In them bishops established their sees, or seats. Here they built their cathedrals and, at a later date, their palaces. Foremost among such cathedral cities was Rome itself, ruled after the departure of the emperors by the bishop of Rome, the Pope. Few Roman imperial *civitates* did not become episcopal dioceses, and, during the centuries of invasion and turmoil following the eclipse of the Roman Empire in the West, it was the bishops who provided some kind of institutional continuity and preserved much of what was left of Roman culture.

The cathedral, as became a great public building, was centrally placed. It was, like the Roman basilicas and temples that preceded it, open to the public and graced with whatever art and decoration were available. In that part of Europe that became subject to the Catholic Church— which eventually was all of Europe with the exception only of Russia and the Balkans—cathedrals were of two kinds: secular and monastic. The former were staffed by secular priests who lived in the world and rubbed shoulders with ordinary people; the latter were houses of monks who led cloistered lives of prayer and study despite their location in the heart of crowded cities. By their very nature monastic cathedrals were in large part cut off from whatever settlements lay around them. The focus of their lives was the cloister. Secular cathedrals, on the other hand, may have had cloisters, but life was focused more on the people outside their walls. In fact, monastic cathedrals became significant only in Sicily (Palermo and Cefalu) and curiously in England, where about half the medieval cathedrals were monastic. It is difficult not to attribute this fact to the influence of the Norman conquerors who in the eleventh century overran both areas.

A cathedral city was dominated physically by its cathedral, as, indeed, many of them remain today. Its towers and spires dignified its skyline as much as the tall buildings do in any modern city, and the cathedral now attracts tourists as it once drew pilgrims to its shrine and sacred relics. It is impossible to exaggerate the economic importance of the medieval pilgrims. They brought their contributions to the building of the church just as their presence filled the inns and hostelries. Chaucer's jovial band, which gathered at the Sign of the Tabard in London's southbank suburb of Southwark and wound its loquacious, story-telling way to Canterbury,

> The hooly blisful martir[2] for to seeke,
> That hem hath holpen whan that they were seeke[3]

brought profit to the city. The distance from Southwark to Canterbury is only some sixty miles; they must have traveled very slowly indeed to have been able to spin so many lengthy tales. Canterbury, like Santiago, Reims, St. Albans, and Rome itself, did very well from this medieval form of the tourist business. Canterbury was the foremost English center of pilgrimage, but there were many others scattered throughout Catholic Europe. They passed in and out of fashion, and their importance tended overall to decline toward the end of the Middle Ages. Nevertheless, their importance in urban development cannot be overestimated.

THE URBAN PARISH

The cathedral stood at the peak of an ecclesiastical hierarchy. At its base was the parish, the smallest territorial unit in the administrative system of the medieval church. Every parish, whether rural or urban, had a church that served the spiritual needs of its parishioners.[4] Parishes varied greatly in area, but there was a certain consistency in the size of their populations. They had to be large enough to support a priest and maintain a church, but at the same time small enough for the priest to attend to the parishioners' spiritual needs and for the parishioners to go to their parish church on those occasions the Church had ordained. The parish had its origin in the establishment of a church. In rural areas the founder was likely to have been a local lord who built a church, probably at first only a wooden structure, and endowed it with a tract of land, which, for the foreseeable future, would yield an income to support the priest and maintain the church. In very few instances do we know the name of the founder, but in the town of Cambridge, England, a church was built by three named persons who, around 1140, obtained a tract of land from the Abbot of Ramsey Abbey.[5] The founders probably saw the church as a family possession in which they would worship during their lives and where masses could be said for the repose of their souls after death. The church they built still stands, despite thoughtless restoration. It is round in plan, unlike the pattern of most other city churches, and may have been modeled on the supposed plan of the Holy Sepulchre in Jerusalem. This was the time of the Second Crusade, which aimed to rescue the Holy Places from the Turks, and this event would have been present in the minds of at least the better educated citizens. During the early centuries of Christianity, dozens of churches must have been founded in this way. Most were small. Some churches succumbed, their minuscule congregations unable to bear the cost of maintaining them. Other churches, especially those in the more prosperous quarters of a town, were rebuilt and extended until in scale and elaboration they even rivaled the cathedrals themselves. In any medieval city the scale of its church building is a rough measure of its wealth and prosperity. Medieval churches, with their tall windows, towers, and spires, gave a city a distinctive skyline. Panoramic drawings and engravings, which began to multiply toward the end of the Middle Ages and during the Renaissance, depicted the churches prominently, even exaggerating their scale and allowing them to dominate the urban landscape.

These remarks regarding the proliferation of parochial or communal churches relate only to what we have termed organic towns, those towns that either redeveloped from the ruins of Roman towns or grew up in response to local needs and opportunities during the following centuries. Their population consisted mainly of freemen who could come and go as they wished, and if they desired and could afford the spiritual luxury of a church on the street corner, they were able, like the three burgesses of Cambridge, to have one. These early towns were dotted with churches. It is easy to say that their number greatly outnumbered the needs of the population. London, which at this time could not have had more than 50,000 inhabitants, had acquired about 120 churches, most of which perished in the Great Fire of 1666.[6] Only a fraction of them were rebuilt. Winchester, with at one time some seventy churches, was even more richly endowed in relation to its population, which could never have been more than 5,000, and Huntingdon, which throughout the Middle Ages consisted of little more than one long, twisting street, had at least four. Those who founded churches in the medieval city did not, like those who organized church developments in the nineteenth century, think in terms of the future growth of population and the amount of church seating that would be needed. The possession of a church was a mark of status. The group of families that collectively owned a church and occasionally visited and used it could hold their heads high within the local community. But many of these urban churches had only a short life. The families that had supported them might die out, or the descendants of the founding families might be unable or unwilling to make the financial sacrifice necessary to continue to support them, or, in an extreme case, the church might no longer be necessary owing to a decline in the local population. The city of Winchester had, by the end of the Middle Ages, thus lost almost half of its original churches.

In most of the large cities, which had boasted many parishes with their individual churches, ecclesiastical functions eventually came to be concentrated in a small number of large and pretentious churches. It is not always easy to determine how many smaller churches were lost in this way. In Winchester, as we have seen, about half had disappeared by the end of the Middle Ages. Cambridge lost only two out of its original fourteen, but York, for instance, lost many more.

In the nonorganic or planted towns, of which there were a far greater number, the way parishes and churches came to be founded was quite different. These lay in the open countryside, which had been Christianized and in which a loose network of rural parishes had already been established. The whole countryside had perhaps previously been divided very roughly into parishes, even if their boundaries had not yet been precisely determined. The newly founded town necessarily lay within a parish, where there was already a parish church. The church might have been incorporated into the town, or the town might have been laid out in its close proximity. There was thus no need to make provision for a new church exclusively for the new town; to have done so would have been to detract from the revenue by way of tithe and glebe (its landed endowment) of the original church. The new town would necessarily have

been within a parish and might even have been shared between two
neighboring parishes, but its church did not necessarily lie within the
town. The church may have been situated on land across the fields, and
its parishioners may have been faced with a long journey on Sundays and
other feast days in order to fulfill their spiritual obligations.

This situation was especially common in England, where many planted
towns owed their spiritual obligations to churches that sometimes lay at
a considerable distance across muddy fields and along ill-made roads.
Their inhabitants might appeal to their bishop for some redress. They
protested that the journey was long and dangerous; that the aged, to the
peril of their souls, sometimes failed to make the journey; and that new-
born infants taken to the church for baptism might succumb to the dangers and difficulties of the journey. Townsfolk became adept at inventing
reasons for establishing a church right in their midst whether the local
priest and his bishop approved or not. Sometimes the bishop's heart was
touched; sometimes he resisted the most powerful persuasions. The problem was financial. Parishioners contributed, or at least were presumed to
do so, a tithe (one-tenth) of their income to their parish church, whether
it be close by or distant. To create a new parish would be to diminish the
income of the rural church, and bishops were very protective of the rights
of parishes and of their parish priests. At most the bishops would allow
the town to have a chapel-of-ease, the financial burden of which would
fall upon the community that used it, while at the same time the citizens continued to pay their tithe and other spiritual obligations to their
distant parish church.

There are in England many towns, some of them large and commercially important, in which the only church was of this lowly status right
up to the reforms of the nineteenth century. Hull, the large industrial
and port town in northeastern England, was one of them. The town was
itself founded by King Edward I in 1296 to aid in the war against the
Scots. It lay on both banks of a small river, the Hull, and its original
name was Kingstown-on-Hull. But the river Hull had constituted the
boundary between the two rural parishes of Ferriby and Hessle, and the
new town of Hull lay at some distance from their respective churches.
Permission was given by the Archbishop of York, in whose diocese Hull
and the rural parishes lay, to establish a chapel-of-ease for the town on
each bank of the river. Hull was a prosperous port, and could well afford
the cost not only of supporting two churches of its own, but also of build-

ing them on such a lavish scale that they survive today and are among the largest and finest in the country.

Some planted towns had been established before the parochial system was fully established. These towns might then each have a church of its own, independent of the parishes that might be established around it. It was intended to satisfy the needs of a fairly large community and was of necessity larger than the many churches found in one of the older organic towns. The local elite invested in it, adding to its fabric and decorating it elaborately. Although examples have been taken from England, the situation regarding the urban parish church was broadly similar in continental Europe. Here, too, the older cities contain a multiplicity of churches, while those of late medieval origin have as a general rule only a single large and impressive church. As planned towns emerged along Europe's eastern frontier, the planners often left a town block free for the construction of the church, which was thus fully integrated with the rest of the town.

CHURCHES MONASTIC AND MENDICANT

The monastic movement originated very early in the Middle Ages from the desire of some—both women and men—to withdraw from society and to live a life of contemplation and prayer. Their earliest monasteries were in the desert. Although some orders, notably the Cistercian, continued this practice of withdrawing from the society of ordinary people, others, especially the Benedictine, never carried matters to this extreme. They established their houses close to inhabited places, even within or very close to populous cities. We have seen how in western Europe a cathedral might be founded within the walls of a once Roman town, followed by a monastery just outside. Very few of the larger and more important cities of western and southern Europe were without a monastic settlement, and some—London and Paris, for example—had several.

The urban monastery was, unlike most cathedrals, usually enclosed by a perimeter wall, pierced by formidable gatehouses. Within there would be the monastic church, together with its cloister, dormitory, refectory, and other ancillary buildings: chapter house, kitchen, infirmary, store house, and rooms for guests. The whole complex would have occupied a very considerable area. The "close" of Norwich cathedral-priory, for example, occupied more than eighty-five acres, about ten percent of the total area of the city.

It was, however, no easy matter to acquire a piece of real estate of this extent, and most monasteries founded in urban areas were a great deal less extensive than that of Norwich and furthermore were obliged to occupy an extramural site, just beyond the protective line of the city's walls. The example of Westminster Abbey, outside the walls of the city of London, has already been mentioned. Other instances would include the Parisian monasteries of Saint-Germain and Saint-Denis, just outside the built-up area of Paris.

Few monasteries, whether urban or rural, were founded after about 1300, except perhaps on Europe's expanding eastern frontier. Society in general had ceased to have a high regard for the totally reclusive monk, and turned to newer orders with a more developed social conscience. Among them were the friars. Their friaries may have resembled monasteries in some respects, but the friars themselves participated in urban activities. They undertook pastoral duties, and their churches were primarily for preaching to large urban congregations. They slept in dormitories, ate in refectories, and usually possessed a diminutive cloister, but much of their time was spent outdoors, in the streets and marketplaces, where they carried on their spiritual battle for the souls of men and women. The friars of the Dominican Order were noted for their campaign against heresy in the thirteenth and fourteenth centuries. Friaries were nevertheless an important element in the urban landscape. Their conventual buildings may have been relatively small and inconspicuous, but their churches were usually large, with a preaching nave capable of holding an audience of many hundreds.

Friaries were not established much before the middle of the thirteenth century and were not numerous before the fourteenth. By this time the larger cities were closely built up, and little space could be found within their walls for new religious foundations. Least of all could a mendicant order secure land near the urban center where most of the people could have been found. Its buildings usually had to be squeezed into whatever vacant space happened to be around the periphery of the town, and some were obliged even to locate outside its walls.

From their very nature the mendicant orders were attracted to the larger towns where they were likely to find an impoverished but susceptible population. The countryside, which could never have furnished large audiences for their oratory, held little attraction. Their choice of towns in which to locate thus reflected their perception of the need for their services. The French historian Jacques Le Goff has argued persuasively that the number of mendicant orders established in a town was a measure of its social and economic importance.[7] Le Goff demonstrated this from France, but it is no less applicable to England (Figure 20) and to many other parts of Europe.

There were four major mendicant orders: Dominican (founded 1220–1221), Franciscan (1209), Carmelite (c. 1254), and Augustinian (1256), together with a number of lesser orders that attracted few brothers and little money and were generally short-lived. In England the orders of friars were suppressed during the Reformation, and their buildings were sold and used for whatever purpose seemed profitable at the time. The map (Figure 21) shows the distribution of the houses of the four major mendicant orders on the eve of the Reformation. The possession of a house by each of the major orders can thus be seen as a measure of a town's importance. In England there were no less than fifteen cities with this mark of distinction. London, of course, was one, as were the archiepiscopal cities of Canterbury and York and the university towns of Oxford and Cambridge.

It is not surprising to find Lincoln, Norwich, Winchester, and the port towns of Bristol and Newcastle in the list. What may appear strange is the inclusion of Boston (Lincolnshire), King's Lynn (Norfolk), and Stamford, also in Lincolnshire, which today are all relatively small towns. During the Middle Ages, however, Boston and King's Lynn were the most important ports outside London, carrying on what was for the time a large trade with continental Europe, while Stamford was the site of one of the largest commercial fairs in northwestern Europe. This map also demonstrates the contrast between the developed east of the country and the less developed west.

There were other orders besides the monastic and the mendicant, which established themselves in medieval towns. Foremost among them were the fighting orders, the Knights of the Temple of Jerusalem, or "Templars," and that of the Hospital of St. John of Jerusalem—the Hospitallers. They had been founded during the twelfth century and were dedicated to the recovery of the Holy Places of Jerusalem, which had recently been lost to the conquering Seljuk Turks. When this was seen as a hopeless undertaking, they turned their energies against pagan and other nonconformist Europeans, especially those of eastern Europe. The Templars were sup-

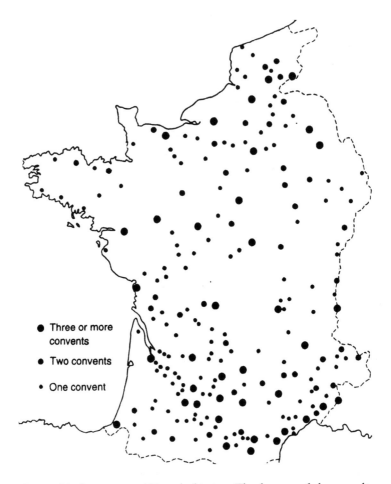

Figure 20. Locations of French friaries. The houses of the mendicant orders (friaries) were almost exclusively urban. There were four
major orders, and their representation was a measure of a town's importance. The map of French friaries has been based on Jacques Le
Goff, "Odres mendicants et urbanisation dans la France medievale,"
Annales: Economies—Societies—Civilisations, v. 25 (1970), pp. 924–46.

pressed early in the fourteenth century, and most of their assets were transferred to the Hospitallers. Other orders, such as those of Alcantara and
Calatrava, were formed in Spain for the more practical task of resisting
the North African Moors, who, since the eighth century, had overrun
much of the country. In western Europe these fighting orders established
monastic houses or "preceptories" in many of the larger towns as well as

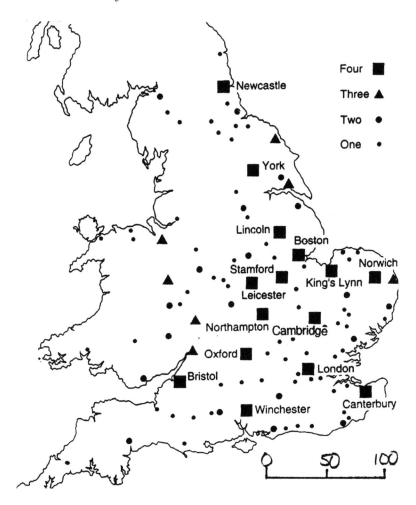

Figure 21. Locations of English friaries.

in the countryside where they had acquired land. Their purpose was to raise money and to stimulate recruitment, but they nevertheless contributed to the religious tapestry of the larger cities. Their churches were both grand and conspicuous, because many—but not all—were circular in plan in imitation of the supposed plan of the Holy Sepulchre church in Jerusalem. Such a church survives intact in the hilltop city of Laon in northern France, but perhaps most famous of all is the Temple Church in London. It was severely damaged by bombing during the Second World War but has now been restored to its former splendor.

THE ROLE OF THE CHURCH IN THE TOWN

The Church has, since the early Middle Ages, played an important role in urban history. Its institutions have always been seen as forming a kind of government parallel with the town's secular administration. The relations at a higher level between church and state have not always been cordial, but at the lower level of city and town there was little for them to disagree about. The Church authorities generally supported the secular government of the town, and in return the latter involved the Church in all its ritualized and formal occasions. These included processions through the urban streets, participation in masses within the church, and even financial assistance from the secular authorities in building or rebuilding the foremost church. There were even occasions when the secular authority was charged with nominating the priest to serve the urban church. One reads much about conflicts between the Church authorities and the urban populace. Of course, such conflicts occurred and were often very violent. As a general rule, however, they arose from the excessive zeal of the ecclesiastical—usually monastic—authorities in exacting to the full the feudal obligations that were due them. There were such disturbances in England, notably in the towns of Exeter and St. Albans where the issue was the exaction of labor dues for work on Church land.

More important in many ways were the attitudes and sympathies within a city. Communication was easier and swifter in the city than in the countryside. New ideas—social, political, and religious—could circulate more easily in the city than in the countryside, and most revolutionary movements have had their roots in urban conditions and were first spread through the urban proletariat. To what extent, we may ask in this context, was religious reform motivated by urban activities? Of course, there were explosions of rural discontent, for the condition of the peasant was in many ways worse than that of the townsfolk. Excessive rents and unreasonable demands for peasant labor were sufficient grounds for revolt, but these cannot be said to have had any intellectual basis. But intellectual grounds for revolution was abundantly supplied in the towns, where people could congregate in large numbers, and orators, whether religious or secular, could inflame the minds of crowds. It can be argued that most religious movements—reformist or heretical—had their roots in the towns. The Hussite movement among the Czechs derived from Prague, and the not dissimilar English movement, the Lollards, originated in Oxford and London. If Martin Luther had not affixed his theses to the door of the urban church of Wittenberg in Saxony, but to that of a remote country parish church, would the Reformation have taken the course it did? In Switzerland it was the urban cantons who accepted the Protestant teachings of Luther and Calvin, while the countryside remained predominantly Catholic.

Schools and the pursuit of education were features of the town rather than of the countryside. The printed book originated in the town, and almost all the early printers and publishers were to be found in the larger cities. The first "grammar schools" were urban. Their purpose was to train a class of literate people for the service of business and the state, even though the "grammar" they taught was that of the classical civilizations. Most radical movements originated in the town where there was likely to have been an underclass ready to support revolutionary change and an intellectual class capable of understanding and leading it.

NOTES

1. William Langland, *William Langland's "Piers Plowman": The C Version: A Verse Translation*, ed. George Economou, Middle Age Series (Philadelphia: University of Pennsylvania Press, 1996), p. 24, lines 64–67.

2. Thomas à Becket, Archbishop of Canterbury, murdered in his cathedral in 1170 at the behest of King Henry II.

3. Geoffrey Chaucer, "Prologue," in *"The Canterbury Tales" Complete*, ed. Larry D. Benson (Boston and New York: Houghton Mifflin Company, 2000), p. 5, lines 17–18.

4. Norman John Greville Pounds, *A History of the English Parish: The Culture of Religion from Augustine to Victoria* (Cambridge, UK, and New York: Cambridge University. Press, 2000), pp. 3–6.

5. C.N.L. Brooke, "The Churches of Medieval Cambridge," in *History, Society, and the Churches: Essays in Honour of Owen Chadwick*, ed. Derek Beales and Geoffrey Best (Cambridge, UK, and New York: Cambridge University Press, 1985), pp. 49–76.

6. Mervyn Blatch, *A Guide to London's Churches* (London: Constable and Company, 1978), p. xxii.

7. Jacques LeGoff, "Apostolat Mendicant et Fait Urbain," *Annales: Economies-Societes-Civilisations* 23 (1968): 335–52.

CHAPTER 5

CITY GOVERNMENT

What is it that makes a borough to be a borough? It is a legal problem.

— F. W. Maitland[1]

This yere the said . . . maire, bi assent of al the Counseile of Bristowe, was sende vnto the Kynges gode grace for the confirmacioun
of the fraunchises and preuilegis of the saide Towne, whiche Maire
spedde ful wele with the kynges gode grace, confermyng and rate-
fieng al the libertees of the said Towne, with newe speciall addicions
for thonour and comen wele of the same.

— Robert Ricart, c. 1462[2]

The Palazzo Pubblico in the city of Siena in central Italy was built during the thirteenth century as the seat of the city's government. During
the 1330s it was decorated with a fine series of frescoes that are among
the highest achievements of the Siena School of painting. Foremost
among them is an allegory of good and bad government, a theme common in western thought from classical times. Good government is represented by a seated figure, flanked by other figures representing the civic
virtues of Peace, Fortitude, Patience, Magnanimity, Temperance, and Justice. Elsewhere are seen the consequences of good government: citizens
going about their daily business within the city and in the fields, which
reach right up to the city walls. On the opposite side of the hall and facing the representations of orderly government is a picture of bad government. A grim, horned figure is flanked by others that reflect Tyranny,

Treachery, and Vainglory, and below them the representation of the vices: Cruelty, Treachery, Fraud, Wrath, Dissention, and War. This theme is continued in the pictorial depiction of the consequences of bad government: strife and disorder, plunder, massacre, and looting. The lesson these frescoes had for the "Nine" who formed the Council of Siena was clear enough, though it was one neither they nor the governing bodies of other Italian towns found it easy to learn.

The medieval city, as a general rule, lay outside the system of land tenure and political control we know as feudalism. It may not have been the most peaceable of institutions. It had to protect itself in a hostile world, and this all too often led to its involvement in local wars. The central Italy of the Renaissance was far from being the most peaceful of lands. In England, by contrast, the strength of the central government prevented the worst excesses of feudalism and encouraged the emergence of an intermediate order of society—the bourgeoisie. In central Europe, where royal control was least effective, cities had the greatest difficulty in protecting their independence and the welfare of their citizens, and they tended to form leagues or alliances among themselves for their mutual protection. Foremost among these city leagues was the Hanseatic, an extremely important association of trading towns around the Baltic Sea that existed to protect their trade between eastern and northwestern Europe. There were other urban leagues in Germany, which were smaller and less powerful. Most were short-lived. They formed to resist a particular foe and often broke up through their mutual jealousy and distrust. Cities were capable of pursuing a policy aimed at securing their own commercial well-being. This implied the existence of a governing body that made decisions on behalf of the urban community. Where central government was weak or almost nonexistent, as was the case in Germany, cities pursued whatever courses were thought necessary for their own protection, and this in turn necessitated a strong and purposeful urban government.

CITY AND GILD

The citizen was governed in two ways. In the first place, the citizen was a member of the urban community. He was taxed in order to maintain urban services and was subject to urban courts. In the second place, the citizen was a craftsman or tradesman and subject to the officials of a gild, which supervised his economic activities. There were, of course, many who failed to achieve gild membership, but all had the considerable obligations and doubtful privileges of membership of the urban community. These two—citizenship and gild membership—overlapped. Many of those who comprised the council, the city's governing body, were also the masters and leading members of their respective gilds. What they did as members of the city's governing body was often to the advantage of their craft or gild. Urban disorder may often have been prompted by the exploitative actions of those who controlled the gilds, but it was suppressed by the actions of the council and at the expense of the community. Never were the actions of the one wholly divorced from the interests of the other.

THE INCORPORATED TOWN

The foremost line of defense of a town against the feudal world that enveloped and threatened it was its possession of a charter. The charter had always been granted by the feudal authority that claimed some kind of jurisdiction over the region in question. It might be given to a town that in some rudimentary form already existed, or it might have been granted in anticipation of potential townsfolk coming together to establish a town. The effect of a charter was to give the town a personality, to permit it to exist as if it were an exception to the feudal system of land tenure. The primary function of a charter was to allow its citizens to have their own form of government, separate and distinct from that of the surrounding countryside. The charter separated the town from the system of legal jurisdiction prevailing in the countryside. There were also, as a general rule, certain economic—specifically commercial—concessions. But there were degrees in the separateness of the town from the country. Some towns, for example, might have only the lower forms of jurisdiction, not unlike those possessed by a manorial court, while the higher forms were reserved for the agents of the crown or for the greater territorial lords; in others the king's local representative, the sheriff, was excluded and the city even had its own sheriff. This graded system of the administration was especially important in England and, by extension, in Wales and Scotland. At the same time the town assumed some of the privileges of the territorial lord. The territorial lord possessed his heraldry, his coat of arms, made up of the emblems and symbols by which, in this illiterate age, he chose to be known. In battle they were painted on his shield. The town never had occasion to bear a shield, so they were engraved in the seal by which the town authenticated contracts and other documents. The town developed a ritual of its own, made up of processions and feasts in which its councilors participated; it had its formal occasions and its officers wore, as they continue to do today, the badges and chains of their office. In short, the town was quick to acquire a personality of its own and to attract the loyalty of its citizens.

A village community, at least in most of western and central Europe, was part of a manor, the lowest unit in the system of land tenure. Even though the village community could, in such matters as crop management, run its own affairs, it remained subject to its territorial lord in most other respects. The lord's court had jurisdiction over all the petty disputes regarding land and personal relations that were likely to arise in a peasant society. The grant of a charter severed this link. The village community became a town and was henceforward allowed to manage most, if not all, matters touching its social and economic well-being. In order to do this it was allowed to have an executive officer—a mayor, provost, or portreeve (he bore a variety of titles)—together with a council to advise and assist him. These were normally elected, but by whom and how frequently was not always specified in the charter. We cannot assume that there was a democratic form of government within the town. In almost every town the franchise was very narrow. The council, rarely consisting of more than twenty members, was elected by the local notables from among their own number, and when a vacancy occurred through death or resignation, they were filled by nominees of the remainder of the council members. They formed a self-perpetuating group, and the rest of the urban population could play little or no part in urban government except by the threat, which they always posed, of civil disturbance. In some cities, as in London, for example, the gilds played a very prominent role in government, and their respective leaders or aldermen actually comprised the city council.

And what did the lord gain in return for relinquishing his executive and judicial control over the community? The answer is money. If his community was a newly established or planted town, then the lord received a form of rent, known in England as a "burgage" rent, commonly fixed at a shilling for each building plot. In other cases, the lord received an annual payment, the so-called *firma burgi* or "farm" of the town.[3] Eventually these payments lapsed, and by the end of the Middle Ages they were rarely demanded. And then there were always tolls and taxes that arose from the economic activities of the town, payments for setting up a market stall or a levy rather like a sales tax on the business done in the market. The self-governing rights enjoyed by towns over much of Europe all derived from those that had been granted in their original charters. In many instances the charters themselves became out of date as the burgesses in one way or another widened their claims and extended their rights and privileges. The burgesses might then petition for a new charter, which would give legal definition to their more extensive claims. Many towns possess more than one charter, though there has been an unfortunate tendency to lose or to destroy the one that had been superseded and had thus become obsolete.

The town, second, was usually authorized by its charter to establish its own courts of law and to exercise a jurisdiction over certain categories of cases and offenses. These rights varied with the seriousness of the case or the nature of the offense. All petty offenses would have been justiciable in the urban courts, and in the larger and more important cities the local courts would also have heard cases of the gravest order. Little distinction was made between criminal and civil jurisdiction; the same courts handled both. A clear distinction was drawn between breaches of the civil code and the ecclesiastical or canon law, however. A range of cases that are today in most countries within the jurisdiction of the secular courts were in medieval Europe subject to the courts of the Church, and the law these courts dispensed was Church or "canon" law. These included all cases relating to matrimony and testamentary matters. The will of a deceased had to be "proved" (i.e., approved) before a Church court before it could be implemented. The Church also claimed, but generally failed, to exercise jurisdiction over matters that involved debts and contracts. It also claimed that lending money at interest was contrary to canon law and subject to the Church courts. But in this respect wily merchants generally succeeded in evading the strict interpretation of Church law, usually by arguing that there was a degree of risk in their undertakings and that they were entitled to payment to cover the possibility of loss.

The charter also commonly facilitated and provided for commercial activities. Buying and selling were the lifeblood of the medieval town, and most urban charters did what they could to protect and encourage them. The town had, of course, its craftsmen with their shops, in which they sold the products of their crafts. But these were also to be found in the largest of the unincorporated villages, and they called for no particular protection. It was the trade carried on with and between outsiders from beyond the limits of the town that created the largest profit and called for the greatest protection. This was accomplished by two different aspects of the charter. In the first the townsfolk were given permission to organize and hold a weekly market and at the same time a fair—sometimes more than one—each year. At the same time the rights of merchants from elsewhere were restricted, and the local merchants and tradesmen were protected from competition from beyond the limits of the town. No lord could grant the merchants and tradesmen privileges in lands beyond his control, but the lord was able to state in his charter that they were free to trade in all places over which he had jurisdiction. Free trade was not the objective of urban policy in medieval Europe, only freedom within a specified group, namely the citizens of the town in question.

The market was the medium through which the town carried on its business within its own local area. The market was held in almost every instance known to us once a week, the day having been prescribed by the charter or fixed by custom. In all towns there was an open space reserved for it. In planned towns it was usually a rectangular block, or even two or more blocks. In others it was of a more irregular shape, triangular or polygonal. In yet others, usually those in which the market needs had not been fully anticipated in their formative years, there may have been more than one market enclosed within their twisting streets. These were often distinguished by the names of the more important commodities handled in each, as, for example, the "Corn Market" and the "Hay Market," or by the days of the week on which they were held, like the Friday and the Saturday markets in King's Lynn in England.

Once in each week, in wintertime as well as summer, the peasant wagons would make their slow progress from village and farm to the town. They were mostly four wheeled, built according to local tradition, and hauled by oxen, which at other times were used to pull the plow. Those to be seen in the small town markets in eastern Europe and the Balkans today differ in no essential respect from what were used by the medieval peasant throughout Europe. They were lined up in the marketplace, and produce was sold directly from them or from adjacent stalls to the local populace, just as happens today from Poland to the Balkans. As a general rule a charter also authorized a fair at least once a year. This was more important than the grant of a market because it attracted merchants and traders from far and wide and handled a far greater range of commodities. The total volume of long-distance trade was inadequate to support more than a few fairs, however, and most urban fairs failed and were abandoned.

The charter sometimes granted even more favors to especially privileged cities. Its citizens might have freedom to travel and to do business without molestation or the payment of tolls in a number of other places. These places, of course, had to have been within the jurisdiction of the lord who was granting the charter. In England charters granted by the king not infrequently specified that the merchants in question had a similar freedom in all the chartered towns of his realm, a very extensive and valuable concession. The grantor in this way created a kind of free-trade area. Another privilege might be exemption from the tolls payable for navigation on a certain stretch of a river or for crossing it by bridge or ferry. The river Rhine, for example, became so encumbered with toll stations that their effect was to stifle trade. Here, however, no local lord had jurisdiction over the whole region. There was no one who could grant any exemption from the burdensome tolls, which were exacted from the countless castles built by petty lords along the banks of the river.[4] Here a lord could give the right to use only what was his own, and the lords who controlled the banks of the Rhine were a law unto themselves.

Such were normally the contents of the thousands of urban charters that were granted throughout the Middle Ages. They varied greatly in their detail, in the extent of the privileges they conferred, depending on both the status and the possessions of the lords who granted them and on the needs of the town being incorporated. Periodically they were renewed and their conditions modified in order to accommodate changed political and economic circumstances. Charters were of the greatest value during the early phases of urban growth when towns were a new and fragile institution in an unfriendly and often hostile world. The need for this kind of legal protection declined during the later Middle Ages, and in modern times charters, granted only infrequently and rarely renewed, have had little practical value. The right to trade and to do business became ever more widely extended until it became state-wide. Today political efforts are instead turned toward securing the right to trade without constraint between nations. This is nothing more than a worldwide extension of the medieval demand for the freedom to trade in neighboring towns.

A charter guaranteed the freedom of the citizens who had received it. They could travel, pursue a craft, and do business without fear of being dragged back to the village from which their ancestors had come. But a charter did not promise the citizens equality. Few societies were less egalitarian than those of a medieval city. The charter it had received was not an urban constitution. It did not prescribe in detail how each city was to be governed. No attempt was ever made to separate the roles of members of the city council from that of the judges in the city court or from the mastership of a gild, to define the ways in which they were to be elected, or to prevent conflicts of interest from tearing the citizen body apart. The practices in medieval cities in these respects was often so ambiguous and so confusing that they seemed to encourage venality and corruption.

PATRICIANS AND CITY GOVERNMENT

Charters usually required that there should be a mayor and council. The charter might specify the number of councilors, but rarely, if ever, did it define the electorate and the basis of the election process. Did the councilmen—councils were exclusively male—each represent a district, a ward, or a parish, or were they each put forward by a gild or craft, or did the council merely co-opt new members from among their friends as vacancies occurred? All these methods were to be found among medieval towns. The extent of the council's authority was never defined with precision before the nineteenth century. The extent of its authority, it might be said, was limited only by what it could get away with. In cities, such as the German Imperial Cities,[5] the extent of authority was restricted only by the feeble authority of the distant emperor, who was usually too concerned with other matters to take this responsibility seriously.

In the larger cities, their councils wielded immense power, and the leading families schemed and even fought one another to be included among their members. Urban society was dominated by the small number of elite families who rivaled one another and competed for positions in the city's governing body. Their wealth derived from trade—not, as a general rule, the petty trade of the small shopkeeper and craftsman, but that which came from large-scale dealing in wool, cloth, or spices and other commodities imported from distant or foreign lands or acquired at the great international fairs. They understood the markets. They could buy cheap and sell dear. They dominated, even controlled, those gilds that were relevant to their business, and they manipulated the rules of their gilds so that no simple gildsman could ever compete with them in their most profitable lines of business. They took great risks and inevitably they took great losses, but many also became rich and survived to establish charities for the benefit of their communities. Most cities and towns had their merchant dynasties, which for generation after generation dominated the trade, the gilds, and the councils; they also built churches, established schools, and endowed charities to perpetuate their memory and to relieve the pains of purgatory, which, no doubt, they richly deserved. Many an urban charity, hospital, or school continues to bear even today the name of the late medieval family that founded and endowed it.

One must not be too critical of the urban patriciate. They had no rules and few precedents to guide them. They may have been without scruple, but they took great risks and had no means of insuring their ventures against loss at sea or on land. Shakespeare's representation of the merchant class of Venice, constantly concerned for the security of their ventures and borrowing in order to finance their commercial activities,[6] could easily have passed for those who managed the trade of Antwerp, of Cologne, of Florence, or of London. Some made great fortunes but had no regular means of investing them except in the next venture. Sometimes they built princely homes or bought up urban real estate and assumed the grave risk that it might be consumed in the next urban fire. There was little else they could do with their money except to purchase the material things of this life and ensure their well-being in the next. The only recourse was to invest in their own future salvation by establishing chantries and endowing them with priests who would for all eternity sing masses for their souls.

As the Middle Ages drew to a close, however, other avenues of investment opened up. There were always the poor to be helped by the foundation of hospitals. There was a growing need for educated men as commerce became more sophisticated and double-entry bookkeeping was adopted. Schools were needed to train them at least in the language, Latin, in which much of the business was carried on. And so grammar schools were helped into existence. Last, there was always the land. A market in agricultural land came late in the Middle Ages. It was a mark of the decline of feudalism. The old landed families were gradually relinquishing their grip on the land as they ceased to require the service of knights and foot-soldiers which it had been the land's function to provide. The successful merchant might thus become a landholder and abandon the city and the counting house for the rural manor, which yielded perhaps a smaller income, but one which could be relied upon to continue undiminished by the risks and accidents of trade.

From the thirteenth century onward the commercial activity on which the merchants' fortunes had been based called increasingly for servants who could read and write, keep accounts, and dispatch written instructions to agents in other countries. Even the merchants themselves were becoming literate; they were developing a taste for literature, and, whether or not they understood what they were doing, they were contributing to a literary and artistic culture. Fortunately the correspondence of some urban merchants has been preserved. Particularly noteworthy are the letters sent and received by Francesco di Marco Datini, a merchant of the Tuscan town of Prato,[7] and of the Bonis brothers of Montauban in southern France.[8]

Urban culture was basically secular. Of course, the patricians built churches and funded masses for the welfare of their souls, but they also looked askance at the religious structure, as well as its endowments and activities, which were so conspicuous a part of the urban scene. In some cities, churchmen might have accounted for some 10 percent of the population, yet in a material sense they contributed very little to the urban economy. Indeed, their presence was a negative factor. They benefited from urban services, including the protection afforded by the city's walls, and yet paid few or no taxes to support them. There were towns, especially in central Europe, where this situation contributed to a degree of anticlericalism. It is indicative of this that most cities welcomed Martin Luther and accepted the Lutheran and Calvinist reformations.

The patrician class built town houses that were large, pretentious, and expensively decorated. They lived well, and desired it to be known that they were doing so. Many of their houses have survived from the fifteenth and sixteenth centuries in cities such as Goslar in central Germany, Amsterdam, and Bruges, which happily escaped the bombing and destruction of the Second World War. This social phenomenon was not new, nor did it end with the *nouveaux riches* of the late medieval city. But how did the rural nobility regard these upstart urban parvenus? It is difficult to generalize, but it would probably be true to say that they were received with a mixture of amusement and contempt. Nevertheless, many urban patricians succeeded in joining the rural aristocracy, helped by the fact that so many of the old aristocracy were killed off during the wars of the late Middle Ages. Some, like the Fuggers, merchants of Augsburg, even acquired titles of nobility. Meanwhile, many of the merchant class had adopted the outward symbols of the aristocracy. They assumed a heraldic device, which they had carved or illustrated on their domestic furnishings and fittings. They might endow a chantry in their local town church, where they would be buried while priests sang masses for the repose of their souls. If they did not rise to a marble recumbent effigy, they at least had themselves commemorated in a monumental brass (Figure 22). Here they were shown in short tunic or long gown, just as the knight had been represented in chain- or plate-mail. Their clothes and those of their wives and children were of the finest fabrics from the Fairs of Champagne or the markets of Flanders, and by the fifteenth century they were paying artists to produce overly flattering portraits of themselves. Albrecht Durer (1471–1528) painted the burghers of Nuremberg, and his portrait of Jakob Fugger, merchant of Augsburg (1459–1523), is witness to this ruthless, hard-headed merchant capitalist.

The patrician class was all the while receiving a procession of new members. Most would have come from the more illustrious gilds, for there was, at least in the larger towns, a clear division between the more elite gilds and those whose members produced the cheaper necessities of life. Contemporaries clearly distinguished between those whose members engaged in such refined crafts as silk weaving, the finishing of expensive fabrics, and gold- and silversmithing and those concerned with commodities of everyday use. The former had to be well-to-do; their capital equipment and their stock-in-trade alone represented a very large investment, and their daily business was with the patrician class and the landed gentry of the surrounding countryside. In town after town we find that such people were socially upwardly mobile, and the least that they would have expected to achieve would have been a place on the common council.

Members of the lower crafts played little part in urban government, and those who made up the ranks of journeymen and unskilled workers played none. There was often a simmering discontent among them. They paid their local taxes, but had little prospect of ever participating in local

1460. J. Browne and wife,
All Saints, Stamford, Lincs.

Figure 22. Memorials of prominent citizens: John Browne and his wife, c. 1460, at All Saints Church, Stamford, Lincolnshire (left). An anonymous notary of c. 1475, Saint Mary-Le-Tower Church, Ipswich, Suffolk (right). A pouch suspended from the notary's waist contains the writing materials that were tools of his trade.

government. Occasionally this tension broke into civil strife, sparked by the attempts of the journeymen and other workers to encroach on the business spheres of their betters or to engage in "foreign" trade, which the patricians regarded as their own preserve. City ordinances, usually inspired by the merchant class, were passed restricting the amount of goods a gild member could take out of the town or sell to a "foreign" merchant. In such disputes the merchant class almost always won. When the Middle Ages drew to a close, most of the larger cities were each firmly in the grip of a small group of merchant capitalists whose wealth was based on trade and whose power derived from their ability to bribe, coerce, or intimidate all who might stand in their way. Urban government was throughout Europe based upon a narrow oligarchy, and most attempts to overthrow it ended in disaster.

The government of the city of London from late Anglo-Saxon times until long after the Middle Ages had ended provides an insight into the factions, classes, and interests that fought for control within the city. We find at first a fluctuating group of notables—they may have constituted a gild—in charge of the city, supported, if that is an appropriate term, by a periodic folkmoot, or open-air gathering of citizens. From these notables there emerged the aldermen, who each exercised some authority in one of the wards or divisions of the city. They owned property there, and some even possessed a court and exercised a local jurisdiction, known as sac and soc.

After the Norman Conquest (1066), royal or feudal control was imposed on the city, and three castles—Bayard's, Muntfichet, and, of course, the Tower of London—were built. Of these three, only the Tower of London survives today. This control was resisted by the citizens, who succeeded in playing off the barons against the king and profiting from each in turn. In 1319 the citizens of London obtained a charter from King Edward II (1307–1327). Government of the city was to be henceforward in the hands of an elected mayor and the aldermen; the urban electorate was to consist only of the "freemen" of the city, a status which could be acquired only through membership in a gild. Doubt has been cast on the validity of this charter. Nevertheless, the gilds remained in complete control of the city government. Even today the titular lord mayor is always the alderman of one of the now honorific city gilds.

GILDS AND FRATERNITIES

Medieval life was dominated by fraternities or brotherhoods. Their purpose was both social and economic, but underlying all of their activities was the urge to protect the interests and to further the ambitions of a group of like-minded people. They admitted women as well as men, though women were never numerous among their membership and were largely absent from the craft gilds. When a gild member died, it was quite common for his widow—if he left one—to continue to manage his business, if not always to practice his craft. Gilds, however, were in general very solicitous of the welfare of their members' families and were often found to have provided for the welfare of widows and dependent children. Gilds were to be found in the countryside as well as in the towns, and most were able to combine a religious purpose along with their secular pursuits of supervising conditions of manufacture and trade. But the chief urban gilds were primarily economic. They were associations of producers. They would have claimed that their purpose was to maintain standards of craftsmanship. At the same time, they were monopolistic. They discouraged competition and unquestionably kept prices higher than they might otherwise have been. Their generally restrictive practices led to their widespread suppression in modern times.

It is impossible to separate the government of a medieval city from the organization of the gilds to which most of its patricians belonged. Mastership of an important gild and membership of the governing council were two sides of the same coin. The obvious conflict of interest was never a matter of concern to the urban governing class. They acted in different capacities, but their action in the one always had some relationship to their role in the other, and all too often one finds that the actions of the city authority were those that best served the interests of gild members.

A list of London crafts or gilds was compiled in 1422 for the convenience of one of them. It named no less than ninety-two crafts. Another list, made in 1518, gave the names of forty-seven, but made no claim to be complete.[9] Other lists exist for the larger English cities and for many in continental Europe. Some gilds were ephemeral, absorbed into the ranks of others, or even lapsing through lack of members. Furthermore, gilds differed greatly in their social and economic importance. A small group of gilds, known as the "greater misteries," contained among their membership men of very great wealth. They dominated the Common Council, and it was from their ranks that the mayor was most often chosen. They included the drapers, mercers, grocers, fishmongers, woolmongers, skinners, and goldsmiths. These were merchants rather than craftsmen, and their wealth derived in part from foreign trade. Their interests were different from those of the craftsmen, who made goods for sale through the city shops. There was always a degree of tension between the greater and the lesser misteries. In modern and not wholly inapplicable terminology, the greater misteries favored free trade, while the lesser tried to protect their members from outside competition.

A comparable division of gilds was to be found in most of the larger cities in western and southern Europe, with the politically important gilds in the hands of the merchant class. Only in the smaller towns was the wealthy patrician element small or even absent, and only there was the simple craftsman likely to have a role in the government of his town.

Urban records portray the gilds as fulfilling almost exclusively secular functions. Their purpose was the management of their respective crafts and the protection of the interests of their members. And yet most also had a religious function. Their origin lay far back in the early Middle Ages, in the associations formed by individuals for a special purpose. In some instances all the local notables formed a gild. There is evidence for such gilds even before the Norman Conquest. Cambridge, for example, had its Cnichtengild, or gild of knights, and there is some slender evidence for such gilds elsewhere. In many towns for which early evidence survives, a "Gild Merchant" united all engaged in trade or the crafts, whatever their nature. They were, to quote a modern analogy, a very primitive Chamber of Commerce. They broke up, perhaps under the weight of their own increasing membership, into the more specialized gilds that have already been mentioned. Religion pervaded all walks of life in medieval Europe, and even the secular gilds, whose primary interest was the successful prosecution of a craft or trade, had marked religious overtones. Its members often had a patron saint and attended mass in a church, which they came to regard as their own, usually on the dedicatory feast of the saint whom they had adopted.

Gilds were associations of producers. Their actions, they would have claimed, were aimed to secure the "just price" for the commodity in which they dealt and a fair reward for their members' labor. But the effect, whether or not they admitted it, was to keep prices up and to restrict competition. Their further claim that they ensured quality in the product by the proper training of apprentices and the constant regulation of their crafts may also be disputed. Their alleged failure in these respects led in the eighteenth century to their abolition in some countries and their decay in others. There is no basis for the claim sometimes made that the work of the gilds was directly continued in that of the trade union movement. But from the thirteenth to the sixteenth centuries the gilds dominated the urban scene both politically and economically. In most towns they were closely linked with urban government, and the way to political influence and power was all too often by way of the mastership of an important gild. The number and complexity of gilds depended usually on local circumstances. In the larger towns gilds tended to divide and their number to increase with the growing complexity of the technical processes involved. In small towns there were usually few gilds because there were not enough craftsmen to constitute a separate gild for every profession.

In the 1250s, one Etienne Boileau, chief magistrate of Paris, was called upon by his king, Louis IX, to compile a list of the city's gilds with a tabulation of their respective ordinances. Boileau listed well over a hundred, but unfortunately did not specify the numbers of members in each.[10] We know, however, from other sources that some were very small; that of the blasoniers, men who decorated shields with the heraldry of their owners, had later in the century only two members. Gild ordinances defined minutely the conditions under which gild members might work. Locksmiths, for example, could copy a key only if they had the lock in their own hands. Such a requirement might well have been dictated by the local authority, intent on preventing burglary. There were probably gilds that escaped Boileau's inquiries, but then Paris was the largest city in western Europe with enough craftsmen to be able to organize the most unusual of activities. There was, for example, a gild of those who made buckles for belts, but it is difficult to explain the presence of about 250 members of the goldsmiths' gild, unless we can assume that their market covered much of France.

Only in the larger cities was there a comparable proliferation of gilds. In the smaller towns the numbers participating in a particular craft were too small, and several related crafts often merged to form a single umbrella organization. Where there was a multiplicity of gilds a distinction was usually drawn between the more prestigious crafts and the more menial. Very broadly the former embraced the merchants who traded in cloth and spices and other valuable commodities. They controlled the market and made great profits, it was alleged, by exploiting the craftsmen who actually made the goods in which they traded. London, as we have seen, had its greater misteries and its lesser. Almost everywhere there was conflict between the two groups, resolved by compromise or by conflict, usually to the advantage of the merchant or patrician class. In Florence, chief center of the Italian cloth industry, there were the *popolo grasso*, the rich and well-fed merchant class, who managed the Arti Maggiori and controlled the manufacture of the superior cloths and thus the commercial destinies of the city. They were opposed by the *popolo minuto*, the "little people," who wove and finished the cloth and yet could barely afford to clothe themselves. The conflict between them came to a head in the bloody riots of the Ciompi (1378–1381), and ended with a compromise by which some of the lesser crafts gained official recognition while the rest were suppressed. But it was in the long run a victory, as it almost always was, for the merchant capitalists.

The humbler crafts—weaving, food preparation, and woodworking— were proportionately more prominent and more stable because they provided for the basic needs of the mass of the population. Even so, their number fluctuated. In Frankfurt-on-Main, a city whose population probably did not exceed ten thousand, there were fourteen gilds in 1355, increasing to twenty, and eventually to twenty-eight at the end of the Middle Ages. Liege, in Belgium, was comparable in size, and had at most thirty-two gilds, while Mulhouse, a small town in eastern France, with considerably fewer inhabitants, had only six, respectively the bakers, butchers, smiths, tailors, vine-growers, and agricultural workers. Duren, in the lower Rhineland, a town of similar size, had seven gilds, among them bakers, brewers, shoemakers (probably including tanners), smiths, weavers, and woodworkers. Such must have been the industrial organization of most of the intermediate and small towns of medieval Europe.

URBAN FINANCES

The finances of a medieval town are little understood, in part because few records appear to have been kept, in part because the task of providing services for the urban population was itself shared among several institutions. In rural parishes the Church authorities, specifically the churchwardens, handled secular as well as ecclesiastical financial affairs, and in the towns the rural practice seems to have been perpetuated. Furthermore, certain fields of activity were left to the charity of individuals and institutions. The urban authorities were very reluctant to assume any responsibility for education, public health, or the very poor.

What, then, were the financial obligations of those who managed the affairs of the city or town? Practice varied, but the answer might well have been as few as possible. The urban officials, like the parochial, usually served voluntarily, whatever may have been the benefits and perquisites they derived from their offices. The chief expenditures made

by those who governed the cities are likely to have been in wages to employees and to masons and others engaged in the building trades. Street
cleaning, for example, was an obligation that scarcely arose in a rural setting, and a payment had to be made to the "rakers" who gathered and
disposed of the urban refuse. The building of town walls was a major obligation, and we know that they were often in a bad condition owing to
the reluctance of the authorities to authorize expenditure on them.

Towns had no budget specifically for education. This, generally speaking, was left to the Church, though late in the Middle Ages endowed
schools began to be established, owing their origin to the generosity and
enterprise of individuals. Apprenticing an orphan to a craft was about as
far as most urban authorities were prepared to go. The same can be said
of welfare. There was no mechanization whereby the urban authorities
assumed any responsibility for the poor, the sick, and the destitute. Insofar as these were looked after, it was by the Church. The parochial
churchwardens and monastic and mendicant institutions gave small sums
in charity, but there was no organized provision, and the urban authorities never saw any reason to intervene. England was one of the foremost
countries to institute some form of poor relief, and here it was imposed
on town and parish by the central government late in the sixteenth century. The Elizabethan Poor Law was at the time one of the most forward-
looking institutions in Europe. It was the nineteenth century before some
parts of the continent began to follow the English example.

Over most of England, the expenses of local government were largely
covered by the parish. Churchwardens, whose primary obligation was to
look after the affairs of the Church, also assumed responsibility for maintaining roads and bridges and, though unwillingly, supporting the poor
and sick. This shows through in the accounts they kept, showing their
petty expenditures and how these were covered by the varied parochial
impositions. Indeed, the parish, an ecclesiastical institution, remained
until the nineteenth century the chief vehicle for these activities. It
would probably be true to say that during the late Middle Ages the greater
part of urban expenditure on secular matters was by the parochial authorities, and it was not until the early nineteenth century that the balance tipped the other way.

Nevertheless, all towns incurred some expenditure and required a
budget. Usually debts were incurred, and the city council then turned to

the question of how to discharge them. Money was spent on building and cleaning, on entertaining prominent visitors, and by the councilors on entertaining themselves. The whole town participated in periodic or seasonal festivities, among which Carnival was often the most prominent and the most costly. This celebration of the last day before the beginning of the Lenten fast had a very respectable antiquity. How Carnival was paid for was a matter of local custom, but it appears that some contribution toward its cost came from the city itself. There were other expenditures, some of them regular, others only occasional, dictated by local circumstances. The purchase of a store of bread-grains by Italian cities as an insurance against war has already been mentioned. There were occasions when the city council assumed responsibility for the local church that had fallen by default under their care.

There were many ways by which the city raised the small sums needed to discharge its many petty debts. The town, like the parish, sometimes possessed property, which it let at a rental. There was an income from market tolls and from the rent of stalls in the marketplace. Then, too, the administration of justice was made into a source of income for the town. Few offenses could not be redeemed by the payment of a fine. And if in a particular year obligations looked as if they would exceed income, it was always possible to levy a tax on every "head" or every home. Among the obligation of the urban community was, in England at least, a payment of taxes to the crown. A lump sum was usually imposed and was paid by the city and recouped from the community's varied tax income.

NOTES

1. Frederic William Maitland, *Domesday Book and Beyond: Three Essays in the Early History of England* (London: Collins, 1961), p. 214.

2. Robert Ricart, *The Maire of Bristowe Is Kalendar*, ed. Lucy Toulmin Smith, Camden Society Publications, n.s., vol. 5 (Westminster: Camden Society, 1872), p. 43.

3. *Firma burgi*—literally farm [rent] of the town; the sum paid by the town annually to the king.

4. On the obstacles to the navigation of the Rhine see Norman J. G. Pounds, "Patterns of Trade in the Rhineland," *Science, Medicine, and History: Es-

says on the Evolution of Scientific Thought and Medical Practice Written in Honour of Charles Singer, ed. E. Ashworth Underwood, 2 vols. (London: Oxford University Press, 1953), 2:419–34.

5. The German or Free Imperial Cities were those which owed allegiance only to the German or Holy Roman Emperor. Others were dependent in some way on a dependent lord. The former were virtually independent.

6. See especially William Shakespeare, *The Merchant of Venice*, in *The Complete Works of Shakespeare*, ed. David Bevington (New York and Reading, MA: Longman, 1997), 1.1.

7. See Iris Origo, *The Merchant of Prato, Francesco di Marco Datini, 1335–1410* (New York: Alfred A. Knopf, 1957).

8. See Edouard Forestiè, Barthélemy Bonis, and Géraud Bonis, eds., *Les Livres de Comptes des Frères Bonis, Marchands Montalbanais du XIVe siècle*, Archives Historiques de la Gascogne, 3 vols. (Paris: H. Champion, 1890), 2:xix–cxliii.

9. On the London gilds, see George Unwin, *The Gilds and Companies of London* (London: Methuen & Company, 1908), Appendix A, pp. 370–71.

10. Étienne Boileau, *Réglemens sur les Arts et Métiers de Paris, Rédigés au XIIIe siècle: et Connus sous le Nom du Livre des Métiers d' Étienne Boileau, Publiés pour la Premiè fois en Entier, d'Après les Manuscrits de la Bibliothèque de Roi et des Archives du Royaume*, ed. G.-B. Depping, Collection de Documents Inédits sur l'Histoire de France (Paris: Impr. De Crapelet, 1837).

CHAPTER 6

URBAN CRAFTS AND TRADE

Now men are drawn together upon sundry causes and occasions thereunto them moving: some by authority, some by force, some by pleasure, and some by profit that proceedeth of it.

—Giovanni Botero[1]

The town or city was one of the most complex, versatile, and many-sided of all human creations. It was a mirror to human activities, reflecting the attitudes, the wealth, and the well-being of society, and, like human society, its roles were forever changing. Those factors that had brought it into existence were not necessarily those that shaped its growth and kept it in existence. It was shaped, molded by successive generations, which in the course of time changed its landscape, transformed its functions, and gave it a personality with which its inhabitants were usually all-too-willing to identify. Just as the feudal classes chose their heraldry and displayed it on their shields and their funerary memorials, so cities and towns also adopted a coat of arms, using and adapting the same charges or motifs as the secular and religious lords had done. They displayed it over their town gates as if announcing to the visitor who they were and what their pretensions were, and they impressed it in wax whenever a document was authenticated on their behalf.

Foremost among the functions served by cities and towns were the craft industries and trade. Other functions such as defense in a hostile world, monetary and other services, the spiritual welfare of large segments of the population, and even cultivation of the surrounding fields played their roles in the life of the city, but manufacturing and trade were always present, and without them there could be no town. Of these two, trade was in most instances the older and the chief contributor to the wealth of the urban community. But trade is inseparable from the specialized crafts, if only because those who made goods, whether a loaf of bread or a piece of cloth, had to sell them in order to acquire materials of their craft and the necessities of life.

CRAFT INDUSTRIES

Most crafts have traditionally been seen as urban pursuits, but they began in the countryside and in some respects have remained rural even in modern times. Some, such as mining and the metalliferous industries, were rural from the nature of their raw materials; others, such as milling and fulling of cloth,[2] came to depend on flowing water to operate their mechanisms. Yet others, like spinning and to some extent weaving, remained rural, domestic crafts because they could be fitted into the farming calendar, which notoriously had periods when there was little to do on the land. Furthermore, these rural, domestic crafts provided work for women who were as a general rule underemployed in a rural environment. How, then, was the change made from village cottage to urban workshop?

The answer must lie in the increasing sophistication of the craft industries themselves and the growing professionalism of the craftsmen who practiced them. There was a world of difference between the coarse woolen cloth woven on a vertical loom within the darkened space of a cottage and the elite fabrics finely woven by the Florentine Arti di Calimala or the expert weavers of the Flanders cities. The emergence of a class of professional craftsmen was in turn a response to the rise of an aristocratic class able and willing to pay for quality products. Not all urban products were of the highest quality; many were intended for an expanding mass market. Nevertheless, the structure of the gilds that emerged in most European towns aimed at maintaining the highest standards and excluding poor and shoddy workmanship from the market.

A few basic industries remained rural, including the extractive industries and those heavily dependent on fuel and bulky minerals. Tanning was attracted to the countryside that was the source of both the skins and hides it used and the abundant water supply needed by its processes. Furthermore, tanning was an unsociable industry owing to the smells and pollution it caused, and citizens would not have welcomed it into their midst. Spinning never ceased to be a rural industry; there was a wider range of occupations open to women in the cities, and one rarely hears of an urban spinster. Urban crafts increased in number through the Middle Ages as formerly unified manufactures divided into distinct processes, with each process under the charge of a particular craftsman. The craft of making knives was, for example, shared among those who forged the blades, those who fitted the handles, and, last, those who made the leather sheaths in which to carry them. Clothworking involved a multitude of separate crafts according to the degree of refinement required. In addition to the spinners, there were combers, dyers, weavers, fullers, and shearers. Some of these crafts have been perpetuated in the names of the descendants of those who had practiced them. The art of fulling, or thickening the cloth so that it became in some degree felted, is commemorated in the "Fullers," "Tuckers," and "Walkers," while the "Shearers" were employed in wielding the giant shears used to obtain a smooth and even finish to the cloth. Metalworking showed a similar division of labor, ranging from the blacksmith who forged the simplest of wrought-iron wares, such as horseshoes, to the armorer who crafted a suit of armor to fit snugly on the body of his client. When the production of a single article required the services of several distinct craftsmen, it was desirable, if not essential, that they should live in close proximity to one another.

THE GILDS

Medieval crafts were, with very few exceptions, controlled by craft gilds or associations of craftsmen who pursued the same profession. One might expect to be able to trace the range and variety of the crafts pursued in any town from the number of gilds, for it is axiomatic that very few urban craftsmen escaped the obligation to become a gild member and to share in the management of their craft. But it is rarely possible to compile a list of gilds for any but the largest towns. Many crafts had so few practitioners that one cannot conceive of them as organized in any way. In such cases several closely related crafts were usually represented by a single gild. Only in this way could its members secure the advantages of collective action and participate in urban government. The urban gilds performed two very different functions: the control of productive activities and the government of the town in question. The government of the town has been discussed in the previous chapter. It is the role of gilds as associations of producers and traders that is discussed here.

The urban manufacturing unit was always small. Traditionally it consisted of the master, a journeyman, and an apprentice, obligated to work for a term of years for a minimal payment and thus to acquire a knowledge of his craft. At the end of this period of training, traditionally seven years but usually a good deal less, the apprentice produced his Meisterwerk, or masterwork, proof that he had acquired the necessary skills and could be allowed to pursue his craft on his own and without supervision. But this is only the idealized state of affairs: reality was always more complex. Some crafts—dyeing, for example—called for more labor than could be brought together under this system. More wage-earners were needed and there came to be in most towns a proletariat with no hope of ever setting up in business on their own account and of becoming gild members. They were the *popolo minuto*, among whom there was often rumbling discontent, punctuated by outbursts of violence. But, however large the employment, there was never any question of mass production or of any organization approaching the factory system of modern times. When anything resembling a "factory" did appear, there was still no mechanization of production, only a large number of traditional craftsmen gathered under one roof and subject to a certain degree of supervision and discipline.

In most instances, the craftsman did not occupy a workshop separate from the house in which he and his family lived. He worked in the full glare of the public to whom he sold his wares, interrupting his task to serve a customer and doubtless to gossip about local affairs. Few craftsmen required mechanical power of any kind. The bellows of a forge were most often worked by hand. Only the milling of grain called for a unit of power greater than the strength of a workman, and grain mills usually made use of water power, which took them beyond the limits of the town. Even so, most towns had a "town mill" down by the river and just outside the town walls.

The urban-domestic system of production lasted with no fundamental change into the eighteenth century. By that time two fundamental innovations were beginning to change both the location and the scale of manufacturing. These innovations were the adoption of larger units of production or "factories" and the introduction of steam power, and these were to dominate manufacturing from the nineteenth century onward.

The range of crafts pursued in medieval towns varied very roughly with the size of the town itself. Certain branches of production were present in every town, however small. Food was a universal need, and every town had its bakers; about one baker to every hundred or so of the town's population seems to have been roughly their density. Then there were butchers, who bought live animals from the country and, if we may trust medieval illustrations, butchered them in the street in full view of the public. Cloth- and ironworkers were always present, as were woodworkers, not only those who fashioned wooden furniture and vehicles, but also the carpenters who erected the framework of homes. As towns grew larger, their service areas became more extensive and the range of demand in their markets more varied. Clothworking was divided into its more specialized crafts, and more refined types of cloth began to be made. Towns began to have their particular specialties, distinctive in weave, texture, and color. The Bonis brothers, merchants of the town of Montauban in southern France, handled the distinctive cloths of no less than fourteen places, scattered over the whole of France from Flanders to the Pyrenees.[3] In the large towns one would find goldsmiths and silversmiths, whose clients were to be found only among the aristocracy and the wealthy patricians, and the leatherworkers, who made Cordovan[4] and other types of leather which they passed on to the makers of superior footwear, pursemakers, beltmakers, and saddlers. The range of industrial production was the surest measure of the importance of a town and of the extent of the region it served.

A common decorative motif, found in churches over much of Europe, is the so-called Christ of the Trades (Figure 23). It shows the figure of a scantily clad Christ surrounded by the tools of the craftsmen. It has sometimes been seen as a representation of Christ blessing the workers in all trades. This, however, is incorrect. It shows, in fact, Christ suffering again because people were working on the Sabbath, which they had been told to observe as a day of rest and prayer.

The medieval craftsman worked on every day of the week except Sundays and certain feast days of the Church. These feast days varied from place to place but usually did not seem to have included Christmas. In the late Middle Ages the feast of Corpus Christi, customarily held on the Thursday following Trinity Sunday and thus in the early summer, came to be observed almost everywhere. The working day was as long as conditions allowed, and that was usually from dawn to dusk. Probably few

Figure 23. A late medieval wall painting showing "Christ of the Trades." Many of the tools remain decipherable. The playing card (center-left) is almost certainly a later interpolation. Church of Saint Breage, West Cornwall.

would have wanted to work on Sundays even if the Church had permitted it, and the gilds sometimes prohibited work after dark because the ill-lighted interiors contributed to shoddy workmanship.

URBAN TRADE

The second major function of the medieval town, whatever its size, was trade, but it is impossible to separate the tradesman from the craftsman. The craft industries were mostly specialized, and those who practiced them had necessarily to sell their products in order to support themselves. Furthermore, manufacturing units were small, and every craftsman dealt directly with his public. He was himself both manufacturer and trader. Except for a few of the more refined products, the more expensive fabrics, and the oriental spices, there were no middlemen in medieval urban trade; the producer sold directly to the consumer. Only for goods from distant regions, such as Baltic grain in the cities of Flanders, did a merchant intervene.

The trades themselves can be distinguished as intra-urban and extra-urban. In the case of the former, the craftsmen sold the products of their crafts to other craftsmen and their families. Such were those craftsmen: the bakers and butchers, who produced almost exclusively for local consumption. The extra-urban craftsman also sold to his fellow citizens, but a significant part of his business was with those who came in from the countryside or from other towns to buy his wares. There had to be a balance between these two. No town could subsist on its internal production and trade. In other words, no town could be self-sufficient; it had to carry on an external trade. This extra-urban trade was carried on mainly through the medium of the local market. The butcher and the baker worked primarily to satisfy the needs of their own fellow citizens. On the other hand, few of those who bought the products of the goldsmith or the armorer were among their friends and neighbors. Their clients were scattered widely throughout the countryside and in distant towns too small to have counted a goldsmith or an armorer among their citizens. For some commodities, notably those required every day and in fairly large quantities, the market area was small. Those who produced them were present even in the smallest town, and their market area extended no farther than the nearest villages.

As towns grew and diversified their production, so they developed institutions appropriate to whatever it was that they produced and to the scale of their production. The structures of urban trade assumed three basic forms. First, there was the shop, in which the craftsman-producer met his customers face to face and haggled over prices, except insofar as these had been fixed—as was the case in some places with bread and beer[5]—by the local authority. Second, there was the market, to which people, mostly peasants from the surrounding countryside, brought the products of their own farms and gardens for sale to the citizens and in return bought such goods—mainly the products of the urban craftsmen— as they could not obtain in their native villages. The third structure in the commercial system was the fair, held less frequently and at fewer places, but attracting merchants from far greater distances, who frequently dealt partly in goods of higher value.

1. The Shop. The urban shop required no authorization. Townsfolk had carried on business with one another since towns began. There were shops in the towns of classical Greece and of the preclassical Middle East. We can still see the shops of ancient Rome, of Pompeii, and of the few towns of the Roman Empire that have miraculously survived. They were wide, arched openings, within which there might have been some display. Behind the goods exhibited for sale and clearly visible from the street was the bench, oven, or loom of the craftsman whose wares were on sale. There was no glass window to protect the display—sheet glass did not appear until late in the sixteenth century. Instead, shutters would have been closed at night to protect the shop from intruders. The craftsman, with his family and perhaps an apprentice, lived behind or above the shop. It was an arrangement that continued little changed throughout the Middle Ages and into modern times. The shops along the main street of Dubrovnik today originated in the fifteenth or sixteenth century, but they replicate those which have survived amid the ruins of Roman Ostia or around Trajan's Forum in Rome itself. The shop, as has been seen, often doubled as workshop, so that the customer could see with what care the articles offered for sale had been made.

2. The Market. Every charter that founded or incorporated a town made provision for a market, for without a market it was no town, since the town's essential function was to provide for the sale and purchase of goods. In England there was no god-given right to establish a market, as there was to open a shop. Authority—the king, duke, or territorial lord—

conferred this privilege, which was usually defined in the town's charter of foundation. The market was usually to be held weekly, and on a specified day. It should not cause any harm to markets already in existence, though there must inevitably have been some degree of competition. The ideal situation was a regular distribution of market centers, such that no place was more than a market day's journey from a place of trade, and this came by custom to be six and two-thirds miles.

Almost every town in medieval England and in much of continental Europe made provision for its market by allocating an open space for it, usually near the center of the town. In a planned town this might be one, two, or even more blocks. In towns that grew without any preordained plan, the marketplace was less regular, but it was always present. It might be as small as an acre or two, while in some important trading towns, Arras in northern France, for example, or Krakow in Poland, it was many times this size. The marketplace might contain a splendid building in which trading could be carried on and merchants might do their accounts whatever the weather might be. In Krakow, the Sukiennice—literally the "Cloth Hall"—stands in the marketplace, evidence today of the wealth and importance of its traders. A comparable "cloth hall" dominated the market of the Flanders city of Ypres. Destroyed during the First World War, it was subsequently rebuilt and stands today as a monument to the greatness of the Flanders cloth trade during the Middle Ages. Other towns had less pretentious market buildings, and in most of them, those who came to buy and sell merely set up wooden stalls on which to display their goods. The open market survives today in many European towns from Great Britain in the west to Poland and beyond in the east, creating still as colorful and as efficient a marketing system as it did during the Middle Ages. Stall-holders paid—and still pay—a charge for the privilege of doing business on market days, and during the Middle Ages a toll was levied often proportionate to the volume of goods traded. Those lords who planted a town and granted its citizens the right to have a market were likely to make a considerable profit from what was, in effect, a sales tax. Most towns, and certainly all those of great importance, gradually eliminated this imposition by emancipating themselves from feudal control.

3. The Fair. When the king granted the right to hold a weekly market, he usually coupled with it the privilege of having an annual fair. Fairs differed fundamentally from markets. They were less frequent, the range of goods handled was far greater, and they were frequented by merchants from far greater distances. A fair, furthermore, was likely to last for several days. Goods to be sold and bought came to the fair by wagon-load, together with traders in their hundreds from all parts of Europe. Some fairs developed a specialization in the commodities they handled, in cloth, for example, or in wine, or spices, or dyestuffs. There were central European fairs that dealt in animals—chiefly cattle and sheep—driven westward from the grazing lands in Hungary or Poland to be sold to traders from the large urban consuming centers in the west. The cattle droves of the late Middle Ages and early modern times must have resembled that on the Chisholm and other trails that led from the high plains to the cattle towns of Abilene and Dodge City in the United States. The origins of fairs are obscure, because most of them began as localized but irregular gatherings of merchants who left very few records of their activities. It is even claimed—very improbably—that some fairs derived from the periodic gatherings of merchants during the late Roman Empire. Certainly fairs were present in Europe soon after the period of the Barbarian invasions had come to an end. There was a cluster of fairs near Paris—the Champagne Fairs; there were fairs at the southern and northern ends of the chief routes across the Alps, and at sites all over Europe where traditional routes converged. Swiss fairs, held at Geneva, Basel, Luzern, and at the otherwise little-known town of Zurzach, handled wine, silk, and other goods brought across the mountains from Italy, to be distributed by other merchants and different modes of transport to markets and fairs throughout western and central Europe. Goods from these fairs were retailed as far away as Stourbridge Fair on the outskirts of Cambridge in distant England. Here street names perpetuate those of some of the commodities once traded at the fairs. Most famous of European fairs, however, were those of Champagne. These were located in four cities lying to the east of Paris: Troyes, Provins, Lagny, and Bar-sur-Aube.

A fair must have looked like a market on a greatly exaggerated scale. Wooden stalls were set up along the streets or in the surrounding fields, to be taken to pieces and stored when the fair had ended. Sometimes lack of space drove the fair into the open country. Stourbridge, probably the largest in England during the late Middle Ages, spread far beyond the limits of the city of Cambridge and extended over the fields along the banks of the river Cam.

The fair as an institution belonged to a certain period in the social and economic history of Europe. It was a primitive means of handling long-distance trade. The merchant still accompanied his goods from the point at which he had acquired them to that where he sold them to the next person who would pass them on to the consumer. Toward the end of the Middle Ages, goods came increasingly to be dispatched by sea or overland in the charge of a ship's master or of a carrier, while the merchant himself sat in his counting house in Florence or Venice, Genoa, or Lyons. The business of fairs had been intermittent, lasting only for the few days during which the fair was held. It then passed to the towns where it became a continuous, year-round operation. Goods were received at any time, were held for a period, and were then sold. The warehouse replaced the market stall and became typical of the large commercial towns of the late Middle Ages and Renaissance. Most of the late medieval warehouses have been swept away to make room for later buildings, but they still survive in Augsburg—the Fuggerei, at Provins in France and Amsterdam in the Netherlands and in a few other cities.

4. Service Occupations. This is an all-embracing term, used to cover the multitude of occupations that resulted in no tangible product. Service occupations enable others to pursue their manifold crafts and occupations more efficiently and in greater comfort and security. Service occupations include such professions as those of the scriveners—the professional writers who inedited letters and charters, prepared accounts, and recorded events for a society that was still basically illiterate. Then there were teachers—very few outside the monastic schools; messengers, who, in the complete absence of any kind of postal system, carried messages and bills of exchange across town and country; street sweepers who fought a generally losing battle against the filth, litter, and excreta that accumulated in the streets; the water carriers who brought polluted water from well or river to the domestic home; the carriers who transported timber and fuel; and the broad mass of people who supplied unskilled and casual labor, drifting from one humble, laborious job to another and in doing so barely keeping themselves above the starvation line.

Such people were most numerous in the larger towns: men who perhaps had deserted their rural homes for the anonymity of the city and others who had good reason to fade unnoticed into the urban background. They were always there, the "little people," the urban crowd, always ready to engage in destructive revolt and yet totally lacking in any sense of direction or purpose. They were the original proletariat. They were less numerous in the smaller towns and almost absent from the smallest, in which anonymity was impossible. But they must never be forgotten or their importance underrated. It would not be an exaggeration to say that the urban upper classes lived in constant fear of the "little people," who had it in their power to disrupt the business and destroy the material assets of their masters and betters.

One service industry has not yet been mentioned—the Church. In the minds of contemporaries, the Church may well have been the most important service industry of them all. The Church provided a service that everyone was presumed to need, and to which most gave money and resources according to their means. Its physical structures broke the urban skyline and were, in the larger towns, to be found on almost every street corner. Its influence was pervasive and inescapable. So important was the Church in the medieval city that it is the subject of a separate chapter in this book.

5. A Seat of Authority. The earliest towns almost without exception were administrative centers, however weak and undeveloped that administration may have been. Many of the hillforts discussed in Chapter 1 were the power centers of tribal chieftains. Every Greek *polis*, or city-state, had a town at its center, and when Rome began to extend its authority over southern and western Europe, it established a town as the focus of each tribal area, or *civitas*. The empire declined, but an aura of authority continued to cling to the ruins of its more important urban settlements. Tribal leaders sought them out and made them the capitals of their domains. They built primitive palaces there, and when Christianity arrived, sometime during the fourth and later centuries, its missionaries turned for recognition to the former centers of Roman power. When Augustine brought the Gospel to England in 597, he had been directed by the Pope to head toward the former Roman city of Londinium. In fact, Augustine got only as far as the city of Durovernum, or Canterbury, and found that an Anglo-Saxon tribal leader had arrived there before him. When, following his papal instructions, Augustine began to establish churches throughout England, he turned to the former Roman towns of Rochester (Durobrivae), London, and York (Eburacum). The same was happening throughout the Christian West. Only where the Romans had never conquered and settled did the Church have to look elsewhere to found bishoprics and build its cathedrals.

Secular authority, no less than ecclesiastical, sought the aura conferred by the relics of the Roman Empire. To occupy its sites was in some degree to inherit its authority. Most of the cities of regional importance under the Romans continued, sometimes after the lapse of many decades, to be centers of government. Feudalism, on the other hand, had a rural basis. At its heart was the possession of land and the source of its power was the rural castle. But, as we saw in Chapter 1, feudal society took the town under its wing and attempted—in the end unsuccessfully—to absorb it into its system. One such method was to impose a royal or feudal residence on the town, and increasingly king and baron made the town the focus of their authority. In England, rural Windsor and Clarendon[6] were balanced by urban Whitehall and the Tower of London. The same was happening in the territorial states of central and northern Europe and in France, where Paris and a small number of provincial cities grew in political importance and eventually dominated administrative affairs. The castle epitomized royal or baronial authority. Again to cite English examples: every regional capital of Roman Britain, with the exception only of the very few that had not survived the Barbarian invasions,[7] came to have a castle, and most of them remained in the possession of the king for most of the time. In fact, the urban castle became the seat of the jurisdiction of the king's local representative, the sheriff. Often the castle had been created at the expense of the town. Domesday Book, compiled twenty years after the Norman Conquest, records in city after city the destruction of domestic houses to make space for the castle.

The system of counties that was established in England and later in Wales and Scotland very roughly replicated Anglo-Saxon tribal areas, as these had succeeded the *civitas* areas of Roman Britain. Within each county, there had been a Roman town, the *civitas*, or capital, and many centuries later this capital became the site of a Norman castle and the center of the county or shire administration. Since Anglo-Saxon times, the ruler had placed an administrator—a "reeve"—in charge of each county. He became the "shire-reeve," abbreviated at an early date to "sheriff." Every county had, and still has, its sheriff. At first the seat of his authority was in the urban castle, but this has in modern times been overwhelmed and destroyed by the growth of the town, and the county administration is today usually housed in a modern office block. But in London we can still envisage in the Tower of London the means by which the royal government once held sway over the unruly population of a great city. In Paris the outbreak of the French Revolution was marked by the destruction of the royal castle, the Bastille, even though by that date this was little more than a symbolic act.

In England feudalism seldom broke down into anarchy, and the urban castle was very rarely called into service in defense of the monarch. In continental Europe things were less orderly and regular, chiefly because the power of king and emperor was much less, and that of the barons, supported by more extensive lands, was proportionately greater. It is as difficult to generalize regarding continental Europe as it is about England, but here, too, in varying degrees the city became the seat of power and the focus of the machinery of government. In some regions, where the authority of the central government had broken down, as in the Low Countries and Italy, the authority of the city came to predominate and brought large areas of the surrounding countryside under its control. Thus were formed the city-states, in each of which the urban focus had assumed great administrative powers. Ghent and Bruges in Flanders and Florence, Lucca, Siena, Ferrara, and many others in Italy all represent the governmental role the city had assumed. In each a castle was built or, at a later date, a palace, that represented the power of the city as the Doge's Palace did in Venice and the castle of the Counts of Flanders in Ghent.

The administrative role of the smaller towns was generally restricted to the towns themselves and their immediate surroundings. They had no jurisdiction very far beyond their walls or farther afield than the land their citizens cultivated. Their local government was, by and large, in the hands of unpaid, part-time amateurs.

FROM WORKSHOP TO FACTORY: THE STRUCTURE OF URBAN MANUFACTURING

Urban manufacturing activities remained into modern times predominantly small scale. In most instances the manufacturing unit embraced at most half a dozen people and in the majority of cases they were significantly smaller. Only in nonurban pursuits, such as mining, quarrying, and smelting, does one find large units of production before modern times.

Another feature of medieval craft industries was that they were never separated far from the residence of those who practiced them. The medieval craftsman lived "above the shop," and domestic and manufacturing quarters were never clearly differentiated. In most nonwestern cultures the craftsman or retailer lives in one place and carries on his business in another. In medieval Europe, these two activities were almost always combined. A result was that for craftsmen there was never a journey to work. At the same time, the manufacture of an article, with the significant exception of cloth, was not often separated from the shop where it was sold. For most commodities the workshop was both the place of work and the point of sale.

One speaks today of industrial integration, of the union in some kind of association of all units engaged in the same branch of manufacturing—horizontal integration—or of all sequential processes within a single branch of manufacturing—vertical integration. Medieval manufacturing knew of neither of these types of industrial organization, except insofar as the gild system provided for the association in common membership of those in a particular town who followed the same craft. The cloth industry provides a partial exception. The production of a fabric involved a number of sequential stages from the shearing of the sheep to the shearing and finishing of the cloth. The more refined the fabric, the greater the number of these discrete processes, most of which were carried on by separate, independent craftsmen. But very rarely does one encounter any significant degree of vertical integration between these separate branches, each of which sold its products on to the next in the manufacturing process for which they had become its own raw material.

Nor can one detect any significant change in the structure of manufacturing before the end of the Middle Ages. The only conspicuous example of the application of mechanical power to any industrial process during the whole Middle Ages was the adoption of the fulling mill in the thirteenth century, which has already been mentioned. The process consisted of beating the cloth, to which a detergent, usually fuller's earth, had been added, with large, flat beaters. This process had at first been carried on by the fullers themselves who trod the cloth in large wooden vats (hence their alternative name of "walkers"), in much the same way that their country cousins trod the grapes to make wine. The mechanization of the process consisted in using a simple waterwheel to raise and lower the "beaters." The fulling mill represented an important piece of capital equipment, not only in the timber structure itself but also in the conduits by which the flowing water was taken from a river and returned to it after its task of turning the mill wheel had been accomplished. This often called for the services of skilled surveyors and engineers.

The flour mill used basically the same type of equipment, and it too called for the diversion of a stream so that it flowed over or under the mill wheel. Both flour mills and fulling mills had necessarily to be located in the countryside, which provided the force for their wooden machinery. These industries were nevertheless carried on as family enterprises.

The factory as a large unit of production, employing a relatively large number of people, was an invention of the very end of the Middle Ages. A modern factory depends on the employment of mechanical power to operate its machines, and this had, in effect, to await the invention of the steam engine in the eighteenth century. About 1540, one William Stumpe purchased the buildings of the dissolved monastery of Malmesbury in England, and there he established the manufacture of cloth. At this time he was visited by Henry VIII's antiquary, John Leland. Leland found "every corner of the vaste houses of office that belongid to thabbay be fulle of lumbes [looms] to weve clooth yn, and this Stumpe entendith to make a stret [street] or 2. for clothier[s] in the bak vacant ground of the abbay."[8] It was, however, no factory; it used no power beyond the fingers of the weavers who sat before their looms under the watchful eyes of William Stumpe. It was a means of ensuring quality and maintaining discipline, and it lasted for only a few years. The true factory lay two centuries in the future, and it was at first a rural rather than an urban phenomenon because it was dependent on water power.

NOTES

1. Giovanni Botero, "A Treatise Concerning the Causes of the Magnificency and Greatness of Cities," in *The Reason of State*, trans. P. J. Waley, D. P. Waley, and Robert Peterson (New Haven: Yale University Press, 1956), p. 227.

2. E. M. Carus-Wilson, "An Industrial Revolution of the Thirteenth Century," *Economic History Review* 11, 1 (1941): 39–60.

3. See Edouard Forestiè, Barthélemy Bonis, and Géraud Bonis, eds., *Les Livres de Comptes des Frères Bonis, Marchands Montalbanais du XIVe siècle*, Archives Historiques de la Gascogne, 3 vols. (Paris: H. Champion, 1890), 2:xix–cxliii.

4. A very fine leather which took its name from the Moorish city of Cordoba.

5. The Assizes of Bread and Beer were courts which sat periodically in England in order to fix the price of these commodities. Some cities in Italy and elsewhere had a similar practice.

6. Clarendon was a rural palace of the English kings, located near Salisbury. It fell to ruin and only faint traces now survive.

7. Several towns in Roman Britain failed to survive the Barbarian invasions and are represented today by at most a few ruins. Well-known examples are: Silchester (Calleva Atrebatum) and Wroxeter (Uriconium). Verulamium was abandoned, but the nearby town of St. Albans took its place. In France, Glanum is now a ruin, but was succeeded by nearby St. Remy.

8. John Leland, *The Itinerary of John Leland in or about the Years 1535–1543*, ed. Lucy Toulmin Smith, 5 vols. (Carbondale: Southern Illinois University Press, 1964), 1:132.

CHAPTER 7

HEALTH, WEALTH, AND WELFARE

And before a few years finish famine shall arise,

. . . .

Through floods and foul weather fruits shall fail;
Pride and pestilence shall take out many people.

—Piers Plowman[1]

We turn at last to the social structure and well-being of the population of the medieval town. Medieval urban society was, in contrast with that of the countryside, free. "Stadt Luft macht frei" ran a very old saying. The villein who had escaped to a town and had breathed its "free air" for a year and a day became a free man or woman and could not be hauled back to his or her village of origin by any territorial lord. There is, however, little evidence that this really happened on a regular basis. There was no "underground railroad" as there was in the U.S. antebellum South. All citizens might be free, but the town was very far from egalitarian, more unequal in fact than the contemporary countryside.

Medieval society was often represented even by contemporaries as consisting of three classes. At the summit of its social structure was the noble class of lords and warriors. Besides them were the clergy whose task it was to serve God and thereby to save the souls of all others. Below them both and at the bottom of the social pyramid were the peasant class who tilled the soil, produced the crops, and thereby ensured the welfare of the other two. No place was found in this model for those who dwelt in towns and who made and sold things. These constituted a class that emerged during the early Middle Ages, the burgesses or bourgeoisie. The burgesses in turn divided into three overlapping groups, which nevertheless constituted a social pyramid. At its summit, by the late Middle Ages, were the patricians, men who had accumulated a modest fortune, usually by trade, and used their wealth to achieve status within their respective towns. It was usually this class of person who occupied the mayoralty and comprised the common council. Below them was the class of master craftsmen, men who had their own workshops, where they worked with the help of a journeyman or two and usually an apprentice. Last, there were the laborers and unskilled workers, the journeymen and the apprentices, many of whom hoped to climb the social ladder and join the class above them. In order to do this they had to be very fortunate indeed. Nevertheless, there was a sufficient social mobility to blur the lines that have here been drawn between the classes that made up urban society. The merchant class included both the "grocer" who, by definition, made bulk purchases in gross and sold them on to lesser traders, and the man who bought a pig from a peasant, butchered it, and sold it piecemeal from a stall in the open market. The smaller the town, the fewer there were of the grocers, until in the smallest towns there were only petty traders who dealt in local produce together with the urban proletariat.

Nor was the line between merchant and craftsman clear cut. Many, perhaps most, craftsmen were traders insofar as they sold the products of their own workshops to passing customers. With few exceptions their workshop was their shop. Some required little by way of tools, equipment, and capital; others had necessarily to be well capitalized in order to carry on their business. The stock in trade of the goldsmith or the silversmith was itself worth a very considerable sum. They were craftsmen, but their personal wealth must have been far greater than that of many a patrician who dealt in simple commodities such as wool or cloth.

The operating unit was small, consisting of the master craftsman and, since his skills had to be passed on to the next generation, an apprentice, bound for a notional seven years to do his master's bidding and acquire the rudiments of his craft, even if these could have been learned in a week or two. All too often the apprentice constituted a form of cheap labor. The idealized production unit was filled out with one or more journeymen—from *journee*, because paid by the day—a class, underpaid and overworked, who had learned a craft, but lacked the capital or the influence to be able to set up shop on their own account. The journeymen were always a restless class, and it was chiefly from them that the troublesome, rebellious medieval crowd was drawn. They were, along with the unskilled and footloose, the underclass. This is the social background of the stories of the apprentice who married his master's daughter, rose in the social scale, and joined the elite of the town. Few could ever have done so well for themselves, for the master in an average lifetime would have trained far more apprentices than could ever have married his daughter and inherited his shop.

The craftsman class thus graded downward into that of workers, some of them skilled, most of them not, who accepted what work they could and lived on the margin of subsistence. They, if they were fortunate, served a master but had no hope of ever becoming more than a wage earner. Otherwise, they swept the streets, cleaned the sewers, manhandled the merchandise, or stood around waiting for the next remunerative job to turn up. They were *les classes dangereuses*—"the dangerous classes"—of medieval society. They fed the criminal class, and we encounter them in urban revolts and in the proceedings of the criminal courts.

Urban society consisted, therefore, not of three neatly bounded classes, but of a continuum, which reached from the richest merchant to the poorest of the unskilled. This fragmentation of society had emerged slowly and was in a state of constant change. There was a degree of social mobility, though this is difficult to measure and, through the tales of successful apprentices, has certainly been exaggerated. There was a kind of hierarchy into which people fresh from the countryside were constantly being fed at the bottom, some making their way a short distance up the steep slope of the social pyramid, few reaching its summit. But there were those who did. The English story of Dick Wittington, the poor country boy who made his way to London accompanied by his remarkably talented cat and there rose to fame, fortune, and the lord-mayoralty of London, is firmly entrenched in popular folklore and also has a firm foundation in fact. Such cases were rare, but nevertheless sufficiently numerous to raise the hopes of a poor country lad.

The sex ratio in the medieval town is far from clear, but there would appear to have been a surplus of men, if only because men were more likely to abandon the country and make for the city. The city held less attraction for women. There were fewer occupations in which they could find employment, and within the city, if they could not find refuge in marriage, they had little hope of employment outside what came euphemistically to be called "domestic service." The unmarried woman was a "spinster," but the spinning of yarn was not a significant urban employment.

Many of the great merchant families were remarkably short-lived. Rapid rise from the bottom to the ranks of the elite and as quick a decline was often the case if it was not also the rule. From rags to riches and back again within three or four generations was often the fate of elite families. There were many reasons. The merchant's business was a precarious one. Ships were lost at sea; goods were stolen on the highways; debts could not be collected; there was a constant fear of fire and flood, and against none of these was it possible to insure. Then too the accidents of birth and death led to the extinction of many a merchant dynasty. Last, many of those who did survive the trials and tribulations of medieval life and succeeded in accumulating a modest fortune often sought safety in the ownership of land far beyond the city's walls. When all is said, real estate was the only safe and satisfactory form of investment. Merchant families retired to the countryside, bought a small estate, and joined the ranks of the gentry. Many of the European aristocracy had their origins in that urban trade which they later affected to despise.

MEDICAL CARE AND HEALTH

The medieval town offered little by way of medical care. Toward the end of the Middle Ages the well-to-do and the well-disposed often founded and endowed hospitals and schools. The larger towns were rarely without them, but the purpose of hospitals was not to heal the sick. They were places where the old and the infirm could pass their last days in relative peace and comfort. There were no institutions dedicated specifically to healing the sick because the sick were rarely healed unless nature itself healed them. The practice of medicine consisted of little more than a few traditional methods, which, if they did no harm, nevertheless had no therapeutic value. The medical knowledge that was taught in the schools of medicine derived from the classical world of Greece and Rome and in fact had made no significant advances since the time of Hippocrates and Galen. Their writings had been transmit-

ted by way of the Arabs of North Africa and had reached Europe together with all the corruptions and additions they had picked up on the
way. For most people the practice of medicine meant following a small
number of traditional practices and remedies, which had been perpetuated through the Anglo-Saxon "leechdoms."[2] Medieval people had no
concept of the nature of pathogens. They could not understand that
disease was the product of organisms that could be carried by vectors
from person to person, city to city. One might have expected that their
experience of the Great Plague and of the pragmatic value of quaran-
tine would have taught them something along these lines, but it did
not. As late as the mid-nineteenth century, the London cholera epidemic was overcome not by medical science, but by the chance association of high mortality with the vicinity of a particular source of water.
The important breakthrough had to await the period of Pasteur
(1822–1895) and the discovery of pathogens. Medieval people talked
of *malaria*—"bad air,"—the exhalations of marshland, instead of realizing that the source of many of their ills lay in the stench of the cesspit
and the foul taste of polluted food, and they even supposed, with
Chaucer, that illnesses came from the heavenly bodies. There were doctors whose fees were out of all proportion to the value of the services
they offered. In fact, any serious illness was likely to be fatal. Despite
the existence, at least during the late Middle Ages, of schools of medicine at Salerno, Montpellier, Paris, and elsewhere, medical knowledge
was compounded of superstition and folklore. Little was known of
human anatomy, and nothing of the nature of disease. The result was
a very high death rate generally, and highest in the cities. In no field
of medicine was this higher than in childbirth. For this there is no
quantitative evidence, but it is clear from documentary sources that the
death rate in childbirth was appallingly high and remained so into modern times. And in this, as in most other aspects of medicine, the rich
suffered as much as the poor.

The medieval town made as little provision for the education of its
citizens as it did for their health. Toward the end of the Middle Ages,
schools were established primarily for the teaching of "grammar," which
meant, of course, Latin grammar. Only boys received this restricted education, which they subsequently employed in the service of either the
merchant elite or the priesthood. Previously the only schools had been

attached to monasteries, where the curriculum contained little or nothing outside the liturgy of the Church. Only in the universities was the curriculum broadened to include the elements of mathematics, philosophy, and theology, and these institutions could never have trained more than a minute fraction of one percent of the population. Not even the parish priest had been educated. His virtue lay in ordination, not in education.

THE URBAN UNDERWORLD

Every town, small as well as large, has at all times faced its problems of crime, and in this the medieval town was no exception. The city was more crime-ridden than the countryside. Crime has always been more readily practiced in the crowded, anonymous city. The inhabitants of the small town may have constituted a "face-to-face" society in which everyone knew everyone else, but in towns above a certain size this aspect of life disappeared. The individual was lonely within the crowd, and the watchfulness of neighbors and the rigors of law enforcement became less effective. There was, as a statistical study of medieval court rolls has demonstrated, relatively more crime in the city than in the village, merely because detection was less easy and the criminal could more easily melt into the anonymity of the crowd. Crimes of violence were common, and criminal law was extremely ineffective; few out of many criminals came to their appointed end.

Crimes can be divided into four categories according to their severity and how they were committed. First, there was larceny, which consisted merely in taking the goods of another person. Larceny was accomplished without violence and was often a spontaneous, unpremeditated act. It related usually to goods of little importance and low value, and often went unreported. Larceny included the actions of the cutpurse, the brewer who adulterated his beer, the baker who sold short weight, and the citizen who stole a handful of grain from a market stall, all of them, as we know from medieval court records, prevalent in the medieval town whatever its size. In England a distinction was drawn between petty larceny, which involved goods worth less than a shilling, and grand larceny. Petty larceny was treated as little more than a misdemeanor and was commonly condoned by society. Barbara Hanawalt has shown how a poor woman who stole a loaf to feed her children was let off with little more

than a caution.³ Grand larceny, however, which consisted of the theft of
goods of a higher value than a shilling—about a week's wages for a common laborer—was a very different matter and was usually visited with a
far greater penalty.

Next in order of severity came burglary, the act of breaking into a
building—a house, a shop, even a church—for the purpose of stealing its
contents. Burglary was premeditated and usually involved goods of a
higher value than those taken in a case of larceny. Furthermore, burglary
often involved more than one "professional" thief. In the German poem
of Helmbrecht we find such a professional:

> Wolfsrüssel, he's a man of skill!
> Without a key he bursts at will
> The neatest-fastened iron box.
> Within one year I've seen the locks
> Of safes, at least a hundred such,
> Spring wide ajar without a touch.⁴

A professional indeed! A locked chest nevertheless provided some security. In England, parish churches were required to have such a safe place,
ostensibly for keeping documents and silver plate such as chalices, but
we know that on occasion parishioners also stored their few valuables in
the parish chest. Furthermore, the quality of medieval building construction actually encouraged burglary. Locks, usually the crude product
of the local blacksmith, presented little obstacle to a Wolfsrüssel. Doors
were easily forced and could be secured only by drawbars or wooden bars,
which, when drawn across the doorway, prevented them from opening,
and windows were protected at best by an iron grill.

Robbery, the third type of common crime, was far more serious. Robbery involved violence, even homicide, and was committed most often
in the open countryside and on the highways, and the victim was frequently a traveler or a merchant transporting his wares across country.
Robbery was visited with the severest penalties, but was not on the whole
an urban crime. The fourth category of crime was homicide itself. It
might result from disputes of a commercial or personal nature. Homicide
was as likely to be committed in the town as in the countryside, and was
most likely to arise, whether intentional or not, in the course of a burglary. Hanawalt has analyzed the recorded crimes committed during the
first half of the fourteenth century within a limited area of England:⁵

Cases	Number	Percentage
Larceny	6,243	38.7
Burglary	3,818	24.3
Robbery	1,640	10.5
Homicide	2,952	18.2
Others	1,299	8.3
	15,952	100.0

There is no reason to suppose that these statistics would have been sig-nificantly different elsewhere in Europe. A feature of medieval crime was its simplicity, almost its crudity, and in this it reflected the low level of crime detection. Little planning went into medieval crime. There was the case of the thief who stole a silver chalice from a church where it had been left unguarded and at once tried to sell it in the local market only a few yards away, where it was immediately recognized.

The incidence of crime varied. There were some times when crime was a serious social problem, and other times when there were relatively few cases. A high crime rate, it has been claimed, coincided with periods of political unrest, when the power and authority of the government may have been weakened. But Hanawalt's study of crime during the disturbed early fourteenth century does not support this contention. Open warfare, however, certainly increased the total volume of crime, since marching armies lived off the land and, the sources tell us, committed every vari-ety of crime in doing so. The fighting soldier, in fact, expected to be re-warded with loot. The armies of the Fourth Crusade, for example, were disappointed of their promised loot when the Adriatic (and Christian) port city of Zadar (It. Zara) surrendered before their final assault. It was a military convention that a city was not to be pillaged if it had surren-dered before being attacked. The Crusaders nonetheless pillaged the de-fenseless city after it had passed into their hands. The effects of war are, however, overshadowed by other factors. Larceny, especially petty larceny, was most common when the prices of basic foodstuffs were high. There was a close correlation between the level of crime and the price of grain.

Methods of law enforcement varied from country to country, city to city, but were always inefficient and never more than moderately suc-cessful. There were constables, parochial officers, untrained and unpaid, who held office for only a year. Punishments were generally harsh. If criminals were not often caught, then it seemed only reasonable to make a horrific example of those who were.

PROSTITUTION

This, the "oldest profession," was never reckoned to be a felony, even though in the eyes of the Church it was a grievous sin. When, in the late Middle Ages, records began to be kept of the visitations of bishops and archdeacons, accusations of sexual misconduct were among the most common. But in England and in much of Europe, the Church had no sanction by which it could enforce its judgments upon the lay population. Its range of punishment was limited to penance and excommunication, and these the lay person could, and often did, ignore. The Church admitted that procreation was necessary and that sex was therefore legitimate, but many churchmen demanded that it should not be pleasurable. More reasonable counsels eventually came to prevail. Given the nature of human desire, the Church admitted unwillingly that prostitution served at least to contain it and to prevent it from becoming a social evil and a threat to society. To St. Thomas Aquinas it was a necessary evil.

The evidence that we have for prostitution is almost wholly urban. Brothels, often associated with bathing establishments, had been a feature of towns under the Roman Empire. In some form they survived the Dark Ages to become authorized and profitable institutions in many towns of continental Europe. They were commonly established around the perimeter or in the suburbs of towns. In London the "stews," as they were called, lay in Southwark on the south bank of the Thames and opposite the city itself. Here they were a source of profit to the local landowners, among whom was the bishop of Winchester. The Church at large derived a considerable income from the brothels it condemned.

Some urban authorities attempted to control prostitution and even to reform prostitutes. Their motives, however, were often less the reform of morals than the suppression of the petty crime that took place around brothels and among prostitutes. In France, King Louis IX (St. Louis) tried to outlaw prostitution, but his successors more wisely and more successfully attempted only to restrict it to specific quarters of the town. The former existence of such a "red-light district" is occasionally commemorated even today in a place or street name.

Prostitution was throughout the Middle Ages an activity of poor and destitute women for whom there was no other source of income. Such women followed armies and accompanied the crusaders. But some prostitutes had been members of middle-class families that had fallen upon hard times. Prostitutes were also employed by the authorities for the pleasure of visiting dignitaries, and, in varying stages of undress, they figured in the processions and shows staged for the populace. More is known of the mistresses who were kept by kings and people of note. They were condoned by the Church and by society and were the predecessors of the courtesan of later centuries. The number of illegitimate children of the royalty and aristocracy is some measure of the practice.

URBAN CRAFTS AND THEIR LOCATION

There was a tendency in the medieval town, just as there is in the town today, for similar businesses to be sited close to one another. This was, indeed, convenient for their customers and was probably advantageous to the businesses themselves. In small towns each category of business had so few practitioners that this aggregative tendency had little opportunity to manifest itself, but in cities of intermediate and large size there was a marked tendency for similar businesses to cluster together. In London's Cheapside, it was said, there were a dozen or more goldsmiths, and in most large towns the customer was burdened by the range of choice. In some instances, crafts were forced together by their common demand for some raw material or facility. The need for water drew tanners to the banks of a river; butchers and bakers were attracted to the most densely populated areas, which provided their customers. Conversely, smiths, metalworkers, and armorers were drawn to the urban periphery where their polluting activities would cause the least inconvenience. The luxury trades clustered together, as, indeed, they continue to do, even though in terms of the materials and techniques they used they had little in common. Merchants might gather around the marketplace or near the town hall, the focus of power and authority within the town, but their warehouses lay along the waterfront where ships unloaded and loaded. As documentation—wills, contracts, conveyances—accumulates, we can begin to put together the jigsaw puzzle that is the medieval town, but always there are missing pieces, areas for which we do not know their precise significance in the

town's economy. There are towns for which we can compile a kind of social and economic geography. We can say which were the affluent areas
where the merchants and influential people lived, and we can identify
those areas where one would not have ventured alone at night, where one
would have gone to purchase quality clothing, and where good weapons
and armor were fabricated. Urban tax records give us some idea of where
the more wealthy citizens chose to live, and this was almost always close
to the city center and near the gildhall, the seat of urban authority. Figure 24 shows the distribution of wealth in the French city of Amiens.

The richer members of the urban society tended to live in the central
area and along a north-south axis. In these respects the large city of the
Middle Ages did not differ greatly from the metropolitan city of today.
A social differentiation also becomes apparent through the tax rolls. The
houses of the rich tended to cluster around the seat of local authority.
Even today the finest medieval housing can still be found around the central square, as at Brussels, Prague, and Krakow, even though the city fathers no longer live there. The foremost instance of this tendency for like
people to live close together was the formation of the Jewish Ghetto.

THE GHETTO

One often finds that in any city similar professions and businesses tend
to locate close to one another. Banks and financial institutions, high
quality shops, and consumer services tend to have their own streets or
quarters. Whether this occurred in the medieval city for the convenience
of clients or for that of shopkeepers and salesmen is not clear. What is
certain, however, is that this was never a requirement of city government;
it was never part of public policy.

In the same way ethnic segregation has taken place in many cities,
and this too is of great antiquity. In medieval Europe the people who
were thus segregated or chose to set themselves apart most conspicuously
were the Jews. Their ghetto became a feature of many towns of continental Europe.

The Jewish people had spread across much of the Roman Empire. The
edict of Caracalla (188–217 c.e.) gave them Roman citizenship, and their
distinguishing religion was free of any kind of discrimination or persecu-
tion. Christianity did not receive comparable recognition until about

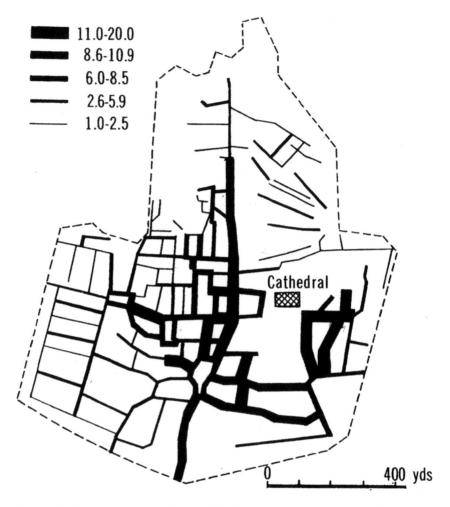

Figure 24. Amiens, northern France. The lines represent streets and their thickness indicates the tax (in *livres tournois*) paid by each house. After Pierre Deyon,
Amiens Capitale Provincale, Paris, 1967, p. 543.

313. In the Theodosian Code, issued by the Emperor Theodosius II in
439 C.E., Christianity was recognized as the religion of the empire. For
the first time the Christian hostility to the Jews and Judaism became also
the policy of the state, and so it has remained until modern times.

The Jews became almost exclusively an urban people. They could not
hold land, and thus they lived outside the feudal system. Only in the towns
could they gain some kind of acceptance, and here they came to domi-

nate certain commercial activities, including moneylending, an occupation they made their own. The Catholic Church, increasingly intolerant, encouraged their oppression and financial exploitation. The first of the many pogroms the Jews suffered occurred about 1100, when the masses, unable to participate in the First Crusade (1098–1100), turned their hatred against the Jews of the Rhineland cities. In their search for security the Jews formed ghettoes in most important European cities. The word *ghetto* derives from Venice where one of the earliest ghettoes took shape.

It is impossible to say how many Jews there may have been in medieval Europe. Many thousands lived in the cities of southern Europe, where their commercial success did nothing to endear them to their gentile neighbors. They did not reach England until after the Norman Conquest. In the twelfth century they probably numbered no more than 5,000. In 1290 they were expelled from England and from France shortly afterward. Then followed their expulsion from parts of Germany and Italy. Curiously, the ghetto in Rome survived, and the papacy showed greater tolerance than most secular states. Not until the rise of modern fascism was the Jewish population seriously threatened here.

The expulsion of the Jews from western European cities drove them eastward. They were welcomed by King Kazimierz of Poland, thus beginning the long association of the Jewish people with their "Pale" of settlement in eastern Europe. Here and in western Russia they remained until, in the nineteenth century, they began again to drift westward.

The Jews were tolerated, even encouraged, in Moorish Spain, where they did much to preserve the scientific and medical knowledge of the classical world. They drifted back into central and western Europe in modern times, but nowhere were they obliged to live segregated from Christian society until after the Reformation. There is no other case of ethnic segregation in medieval Europe; apart from the Moors in southern Spain, there were no other ethnic minorities.

NOTES

1. William Langland, *William Langland's "Piers Plowman": The C Version: A Verse Translation*, ed. George Economou, Middle Age Series (Philadelphia: University of Pennsylvania Press, 1996), p. 79, lines 346–49.

2. See *Leechdoms, Wortcunning, and Starcraft of Early England. Being a Collection of Documents, for the Most Part Never before Printed, Illustrating the History*

of Science in This Country before the Norman Conquest, ed. Thomas Oswald Cock-ayne, Rerum britannicarum medii aevi scriptores, or Chronicles and memorials of Great Britain and Ireland during the middle ages, no. 35, 3 vols. (London: Longman, Roberts, and Green, 1864–1866).

3. Barbara Hanawalt, *Crime and Conflict in English Communities, 1300–1348* (Cambridge, MA: Harvard University Press, 1979), pp. 65–101.

4. Clair Hayden Bell, ed. and trans., "Meier Helmbrecht," in *Peasant Life in Old German Epics: Meier Helmbrecht and Der Arme Heinrich*, Records of Civl-ization Sources and Studies, no. 13 (New York: Columbia University Press, 1931), p. 69, lines 1203–8.

5. Hanawalt, *Crime and Conflict*, Table 3, p. 66.

CHAPTER 8

CONCLUSION:
THE CITY IN HISTORY

The city and civilization are inseparable: with the city's rise and spread, man at last emerged from the primitive state. In turn, the city enabled him to construct an ever more complex and, we would like to believe, more satisfying way of life.

—Gideon Sjoberg[1]

In recent years the problems of the city have been the subject of count-less conferences and studies, ranging from the incidence of urban crime to the quality of urban housing. These matters, as the foregoing chapters have shown, are far from new. They troubled the medieval citizen as much as they do the modern. And yet, if we take the long view, towns owed their origin to the dangers and difficulties present in countryside rather than in the town. The classical Greeks who saw in the synoecism of sev-eral rural communities the origin of the *polis*, or city, had no doubt but that the change was for the better. The late Roman writer Isidore of Seville defined a city as a place where *vita tutior est*—"where life is safer"— but this was at a time when barbarian invasions were making life hard everywhere, and the only protection was to be found behind the line of urban walls. The Romans, furthermore, saw in the foundation of cities a means of civilizing the barbarian peoples whom they had conquered. The quality of *urbanitas*, the way of living in *urbs*—the city—was both urban and urbane, and the Romans thought it the most valuable gift they could bestow on their conquered peoples. In modern times, escape to the city from the poverty and near starvation of an overcrowded countryside was a blessed relief. The town was the "promised land," the Ziemia Obiecana of Wladyslaw Reymont's novel on this very subject, where employment could be found and food could be purchased.[2] It was where every poverty-stricken peasant hoped to go. The peasant saw the vast brick factories and the smokestacks belching their pollution over the landscape merely as symbols of that wealth, in which he hoped to share. But the peasant's views were as illusory as those of the romantics who visualized the joys of the countryside. For those near the bottom of the social ladder, both town and country were harsh, unrewarding environments in which to live, and that was where most people found themselves. For those with the means to choose between town and country, however, they each had their attractions and their advantages. For urbanites a week in the country was a welcome holiday, and for the eighteenth-century landowner a residence in London or Paris or some other city of distinction was a social necessity.

And so it was also during the Middle Ages. The city, especially a large one, was a land of opportunity, where young men could hope to make their fortunes in trade or in marriage. Few succeeded, but hope sprang eternal in their minds. The rich and highly placed built palaces, and the poor lived in squalid, rat-infested, disease-ridden tenements. The social spread in a large city was greater by far than it ever had been in the countryside. Late in the seventeenth century, the English Duke of Buckingham built for himself a grand house on the western edge of the city of London. It now serves as the town house of the English queen, who, like her predecessors, also has several rural homes. Over its facade the duke had inscribed the words *Rus in Urbe*—"a bit of the countryside in the town." He, like many others both medieval and modern, was trying to make the best of both worlds, to bridge the gap between country and town. He might claim to have succeeded, even though the vast, park-like grounds of Buckingham Palace are today enclosed within the grip of main roads and the roar of traffic is never absent.

THE MAKING OF A MIDDLE CLASS

Both rich and poor migrated to the town, the former to add to their wealth by commercial activities and financial manipulation, the latter because towns offered the prospect of a livelihood at however humble a level. They continued to come from the early, formative years of the city until, by the end of the Middle Ages, more than 10 percent of the population of western Europe were dwelling in towns, and in some well-favored areas, such as Flanders, the percentage must have risen to twenty or more. Migration from country to town intensified in modern times, and, with industrial development in the nineteenth century, more than half the population of every town in Europe soon came to be living in a town.

The urban population was drawn from every social class, but its proportion varied from one part of Europe to another. "The noblem[a]n of Italy," wrote Giovanni Botero, "divideth his expense and endeavours part in the city, part in the country, but the greater part he bestows in the city. But the Frenchman employs all that he may wholly in the country, regarding the city little or nothing at all."[3] Not entirely true, but nevertheless a perceptive observation. The town houses of the aristocracy had to be more compact in the congested Italian cities; they also had to be defensible. And so the Italians raised their slender towers a hundred feet and sometimes more above the level of the streets. In northern Europe the landed classes in general continued to live on their estates, where their fortified castles gradually gave way to the stately homes that survive today in their hundreds and are so often beyond the means of their owners to maintain. The balance of classes within the city thus varied from those in which an aristocratic class dominated, such as Florence, Siena, and Rome, to those which had drawn the bulk of their population from the overcrowded land, like Nuremberg, Cologne, and London. But whether predominantly aristocratic or plebeian or somewhere between the two, the city proved to be a social melting pot, and what came out in the end was the bourgeoisie.

Medieval social thought had conceived of society as built of three classes: the landowning, feudal, and military class, which protected the rest; the churchmen, who prayed for all; and last, the rural masses, on whose broad shoulders fell the task of supporting the other two. To these the bourgeoisie came to be added. Its very name suggests its origin in the town, "burg," or "borough." It was to become the fastest growing and the wealthiest of any division of society, and it was quick to make its influence felt at least in western and central Europe. King Edward I of England in 1295 brought the towns within the sphere of national government. Parliament, the king's legislative and advisory body, had hitherto consisted of those barons and lords who had received a "writ of summons," commanding their presence at the royal palace of Westmin-

ster or at any other place the king might designate. In that year Edward
commanded each city, together with each of the forty or more counties
that made up the land of England, to send two representatives to a parliament to be held at the palace of Westminster. This was the first English—or indeed European—parliament to be summoned, representative
if not of the whole population then at least of three of its main social
classes, the aristocratic and landowning class, the Church, and the city-
dwelling and bourgeois. Thereafter, Parliament continued in England to
be summoned at irregular intervals throughout the Middle Ages and early
modern times until, toward the end of the seventeenth century, their
meetings became more regular and their responsibilities greater. No king
could henceforward evade or avoid the obligation to consult Parliament,
since it became the law of the land that only Parliament could authorize the levying of taxation to pay for the machinery of government. Parliament divided in the course of time into two houses. One, representing
the barons and the landholding class, became the Upper House or House
of Lords, and to it were added the bishops and the abbots of at least the
more important monasteries. The other, composed of the representatives
of the towns and of the counties or shires, became the House of Commons. The latter came inevitably to be dominated by the representatives
of the towns, since they were far more numerous than the "knights of the
shires," who could never have numbered more than about eighty.

It is true that King Edward and his successors were selective in their
choice of the cities and towns which they commanded to send members
to Parliament, and that they saw in the Commons a counter to the power
and authority of the barons who made up the House of Lords. They could
never have anticipated that in time the Commons, composed mainly of
urban representatives, would dominate Parliament and in effect make law
as well as authorize taxation, but such has now been the situation for
more than many centuries. Today it is the towns, the bourgeoisie, which
effectively control the destiny of England.

The summoning of the first or "Model" Parliament was an event of
immense political importance, not only for Great Britain, but also for Europe and the rest of the world. From it derived the concept and the practice of democratic government. The earliest English parliaments were
called more to advise the king than to make law and authorize taxation,
though the latter functions crept in at an early date, because the Lords
and Commons began to impose conditions and make demands, which

the king sometimes found difficult to refuse or to resist if he was to receive the revenues he needed. Democratization was a long, slow process in which the towns, through their representatives, played a leading role. In the words of the poet Tennyson:

> Freedom slowly broadens down
> From precedent to precedent.[4]

And this we owe to the rise of the towns and the development of a bourgeois class, sufficiently wealthy and educated to play a role in government. If Westminster is the mother of parliaments throughout the world, then it was the towns that produced the personnel of the first and subsequent parliaments and gave its members the skills and the will to shape politics in the interests of the people.

The bourgeoisie, as it took shape in the cities of late medieval Europe, became a distinct class like the aristocracy, distinguished by its wealth, its occupations, and its level of education, all of which allowed it to participate in government. Its degree of freedom also set it apart from those who labored in the fields; it also separated itself from the urban underclass, which played no role in city government. To keep to the English example, the right to vote was, until the reforms of the nineteenth century, restricted to the moneyed and educated within the towns. However, the English bourgeoisie was unique in Europe, at least before modern times, in being able to send representatives to a national parliament and thus to participate in national government. The only other cities to acquire comparable privileges were those of the Swiss Confederation, in which a dozen cities each constituted a separate and largely self-governing city-state or Canton. In central Europe the Reichsstadte, or "Free Imperial Cities," also achieved virtual independence, but, though they formed leagues among themselves for their mutual protection, they never achieved a common representation in an assembly of the German Empire until modern times. There were also occasions when some French cities were consulted individually by the king of France. It must not be assumed, however, that burgesses at the time greatly relished these rights and privileges. They were costly. Members of the English Parliament were not paid for their services until the nineteenth century. They came to Westminster at their own or their city's expense, and it was to the financial advantage of the cities that parliamentary sessions should be both infrequent and short-lived. In retrospect it seems strange that medieval towns should have objected to the political process by which they achieved power and their representatives came to share in the government of their country.

Neither Edward I nor his successors ever prescribed how the urban representatives were to be chosen. We can be sure that, at least during the Middle Ages, there was nothing in the least resembling an election; there was never a group of candidates competing for the honor of representing their community. In all probability those who would represent the town at the next session of Parliament at Westminster would have been chosen by the city's council, and some would probably have made the journey to London under protest. Serving their city by attending Parliament was not at the time seen as a privilege or as an honor. Attitudes began to change, however, when members of Parliament found that through their office they could remedy grievances and influence public policy and the legislative process. Such is the nature of progress: the reinterpretation of old institutions, earlier legislation, and practices. It was like pouring the new wine of democracy into the outworn bottles of absolutism and feudalism.

Every town, as we have seen, had a controlling council, which had been prescribed in its founding charter and subsequent confirmatory deeds, but not all of them were represented in Parliament. How were parliamentary boroughs chosen? The king and his advisers invited—one might even say commanded—certain boroughs each to send two representatives to the gathering at Westminster. The king probably chose towns most likely to comply with his demands. Some were minute; a few had even ceased to have any semblance to a town. These were the so-called rotten boroughs, which, early in the nineteenth century, lost the privileged role they had acquired in the Middle Ages.

And who chose the men who were to represent the town in the Parliament at Westminster? The electors may have been the council or the leading figures in some or all of the gilds or those who managed the wards or civil divisions of the town. The system, we may be sure, was not democratic as we would understand the term today. Women could not participate in any way until the twentieth century, nor could most of the men until the nineteenth century. The importance of the medieval institution of Parliament and of the medieval practice of summoning representatives of the towns lies in the fact that the manifold systems of urban government were all capable of modification, of extension, of adjustment, so that they could slowly be made more truly democratic. The United States were far more democratic from the moment when the Constitution was ratified in 1788, but this was only because they had the British example, with all its imperfections of which the founding fathers were well aware, to guide them.

It was many centuries before the bourgeoisie had established itself in most European cities, and not until the nineteenth century did most come to be represented in some kind of national assembly. These pages have been given to the political experience of English, later of British,[5] cities and towns because it was largely through them that parliamentary representation was shown to be both effective and possible. Edward I's Parliament of 1295 was indeed the mother of parliaments.

CHARITABLE WORKS

It was characteristic of the urban middle class that it was able to accumulate capital, something which was beyond the capacity of both the rural, feudal class and the agricultural masses. To the Marxist historian this arose from the surplus value of business activities, the sum by which the value of products or of services exceeded the cost of either making or performing them. The urban merchant or craftsman always acquired, or at least hoped to acquire, a surplus value from his professional pursuits. His chief problem was what to do with it. Investment at interest, or usury, as it was called, was forbidden by canon law. Of course, the Jews could lend at interest, and Christians could on occasion make use of their services without any hurt to their souls. As for the Jews, in the eyes of the Christians, they had no souls to compromise. The middle class sometimes devised ways of evading the usury law, and in doing so were sometimes aided by the canonists themselves. Interest might be allowed, for example, if there was risk in the venture on which the money had been gambled. Shakespeare's *The Merchant of Venice* is essentially a play about the nature of usury. Metal or coins, it was said, were barren; they could not breed or increase their value: "for when did friendship take / A breed for barren metal of his friend?"[6] Such medieval concepts were, however, being abandoned when Shakespeare wrote his plays.

Nevertheless, there were no sure ways of investing capital and of obtaining a regular income from it. There was no stock exchange in which to invest, and most opportunities that did exist were accompanied by great risks. Well-to-do members of the bourgeoisie were in fact left with three courses of action during the late Middle Ages: investment in land, good living and the purchase of *objets d'art*, and investment in works of charity or religion. The land market was not at this time as fully developed as it later became, though many a merchant became a substantial landowner. To do so, however, usually meant deserting the city to live in the countryside and to join the society of the local gentry, a step not all urban patricians were prepared to take.

The gratification of personal desires assumed many forms. Clothing became more elaborate and more extravagant toward the end of the Middle Ages. To wear the latest fashion in style and material became a mark of status, a form of conspicuous consumption. So common did this practice become that some cities initiated sumptuary legislation that restricted certain articles of clothing to the patrician class. The same went for diet. The consumption of elaborate meals and exotic foods became a mark of class, and those who ate well wanted others, including their peers and those who could not afford to do so, to know how extravagantly they were indulging themselves. The twelfth-century writer Alexander Neckham urged his wealthy readers to allow the smells from their kitchens to circulate beyond their walls so that those less fortunate would know how well they were faring.

There was also an expenditure, which increased as the Middle Ages progressed, on personal memorials, mementos, art objects, and other ornaments. From the fourteenth century onward wealthy patricians had themselves commemorated in portraits. Albrecht Durer was a prominent artist in this regard, having painted the portraits of the patricians of Nuremberg as well as the portrait of Anton Fugger (see p. 109). Nowhere was the employment of artists in this way more important than in Italy, where both urban patricians and the rural aristocracy had themselves memorialized in this way. This practice ensured profitable employment for painters and sculptors and ensured a sound economic basis for the art of the Renaissance.

The expenditure on personal art and art created for the home merged with the expenditure on art created for the Church. Artists were employed to create funeral monuments and to decorate chapels and chantries erected for the celebration of masses for the souls of the deceased. One rarely if ever finds a will that does not bequeath money for some church-related activity. The doctrine of purgatory had evolved in the twelfth century, together with its corollary that its pains could be alleviated, if not wholly removed, by masses sung on behalf of the deceased. And so chapels were founded in their hundreds, each of them endowed with enough land to support a priest who would serve in it and perform the rituals.

This was, of course, an unproductive investment, since its yield was supposedly the welfare of the founder's soul. Yet very large amounts of urban capital were diverted into this spiritual activity. The second outlet for capital was socially more desirable. Public-spirited members of the bourgeoisie established hospitals and schools and left money for such charitable enterprises as apprenticing orphans to a craft and providing dowries for impoverished maidens. Few towns were without an endowed hospital. The hospital did little by way of curing the sick, but it provided a home and a very modest income for the infirm and aged, for whom society had made no other provision. Many such hospitals, each with its modest endowment in urban real estate, survive today, especially in Great Britain, and still perform the functions their founders had prescribed for them more than five centuries ago.

Of the greatest social value in the long run was the foundation of schools. In the late Middle Ages the bourgeoisie was beginning to appreciate the importance of education, not merely the liturgical education that cathedral and monastic schools provided, but more practical skills as well. Townsmen were beginning to keep accounts and to communicate their orders to merchants in distant cities and other countries; double-entry bookkeeping was developing, and there was a growing demand for literate employees. The newly founded schools taught primarily Latin, the language in which most international correspondence was carried on, but the pupils who had learned to write in Latin could readily turn their skills to English or French or whatever was the current language of business.

Investment in education most often took the form of the founding and endowment of schools for the very limited purpose of teaching Latin grammar. But the need arose for schools that specialized in other fields, notably medicine and the law. The medical traditions of the classical world had passed to the Arabs through the schools at Alexandria and other cities of the Middle East, and from here they were returned to Europe by the Arab invaders. One of the first European schools of medicine was at Salerno in southern Italy, close to areas infiltrated by Arab culture. At about the same time the study of law, both Roman and canon (the rapidly evolving law of the Church), was established in some of the cities of central and northern Italy, Bologna preeminent among them. In each case a teacher gained a reputation for his scholarship and teaching ability and soon attracted a body of students. Hostelries then appeared to accommodate the students. This development inevitably occurred in the larger and more important cities. In the course of time both students and teachers acquired some kind of organization, which in some degree was borrowed from that of the contemporary craft and professional gilds; teachers and students very broadly replicated the relations of master craftsmen and apprentices. One college at Cambridge was actually founded by a local gild and still today bears in its name the dedication of that gild. The student bodies then began to receive help from both the aristocracy and the patricians because they could in various ways assist their benefactors. Among the latter were churchmen, especially bishops and their more highly placed servants, who desired to see the number of theologians and canon lawyers increase. These institutions then began to grant degrees to those who had completed the course of studies in their schools, even though they were in origin merely licenses to teach. At this point we can think of these institutions as universities in the modern sense.

The earliest universities in Europe had emerged in Italian cities in the late twelfth and early thirteenth centuries. The idea of the university spread. It reached Paris, where a number of schools, some of them attached to Notre Dame, the cathedral of Paris, emerged. Students from Paris reached Oxford in the late twelfth century, and there established schools similar to those they had known in Paris. Oxford students migrated to Cambridge where, by the middle years of the thirteenth century, there was a similar organization.

The university came later to Spain and central Europe. In Spain it had to wait until the Moors had been driven back to the south of the country, Andalusia, where they had first settled and where their imprint has been the strongest. The first university north of the Alps was at Prague, where the Emperor Charles IV established it on the basis of less formal student gatherings. The Charles University at Prague was closely followed by those of Krakow, Vienna, Heidelberg, and Cologne. The University of Leipzig was established by the German students from the

Charles University at Prague who had left in the face of opposition from Czech students. By 1250 there were some twenty-five universities in Europe, all of them in prominent cities whose importance and prestige they increased by their presence. Many had papal authorization; all were in some way attached to the Church. A few had specialized fields of study, like medicine at Montpellier in France and canon law at Bologna, but most pursued the *Studium Generale*, or "General Studies," which, despite its name, was restricted to fields related to theology and philosophy.

URBAN PRIDE

Medieval Englishmen may not have cherished their obligation to be represented in Parliament, but they demonstrated in many ways their pride in their city. They extolled its beauty, its amenities, even the quality of the fish in its river. They praised its buildings, coupling this with remarks on the beauty of its womenfolk. Such writing became a genre in the Italian cities and was imitated in other parts of Europe. Above all they invested money in their city. In rural areas the parish church was the foremost object of pride. Parishioners, when alive, planned its expansion far beyond the needs of the community, and after death they bequeathed money to replace a window or to add a statue. So in the towns the citizens invested in town walls, towers, and gates. The town gate was that part of the town the visitor first encountered, and for that reason it was often highly decorated. Today many European cities, such as Prague, for example, still retain gate-towers, which in their size and decoration far exceed the needs of urban defense. When the king of England authorized the building of the town walls of Norwich, they were, he said, for the beautification as well as the defense of the city.[7]

THE ARCHITECTURAL HERITAGE

One of the ways this pride in the city manifested itself was in the townspeople's willingness to erect buildings and monuments for its beautification. Pausanias, who wrote a travel guide of the second century C.E., had no doubt about the nature of a city. It had to be resplendent with public buildings and facilities, serving the intellectual and leisure activities of its citizens as much as their commercial and economic needs. In this the medieval city reverted to the classical tradition of Greece and

Rome. It was on the classical model that the medieval city was built, and it became the object of a similar pride. People identified with their cities and looked upon them with a kind of reverential regard. They were prepared to expend much of their wealth on public buildings and they commissioned writings that showed them, not without a certain judicious exaggeration, to the best advantage. Such a work was the paean of praise in honor of the city of Chester (England), written by Lucian, a monk of the local Benedictine monastery.[8] Felix Fabri, a German humanist of the late fifteenth century, tells us how the rebuilding of the cathedral of Ulm, his native city in south Germany, was begun in 1377. Foundations were dug and piles driven. Then the foundation stone was laid with great ceremony, and "not by workmen, but by the august members of the [city] Council, some of them turning the great wheel,[9] others guiding the ropes, . . . and all this was done most seriously while the people prayed, the monks chanted, and the town band played. . . . And when the first stone had been laid the Lord Mayor opened his purse, took out a number of coins and adorned the hewn surface with 100 glittering gold pieces. When he had done so the other patricians stepped down, each in his turn, and covered the stone with gold and silver, and the men of the people did the same. And so, on this day, was collected a great fund for the building of the new church."[10] What is significant is not the amount of money contributed, but the fact that it was the patricians, not the Church dignitaries, who were foremost in the undertaking. In Ulm they were lavish in their support of the city's outstanding public building, but the same or similar activities were taking place in all large cities, in many of intermediate size and importance and even in some of the smallest. Ulm was not the only cathedral whose construction owed more to the lay patriciate than to the ecclesiastical hierarchy itself. The cathedrals of Cologne and Strasbourg were also built in part at least to flatter the vanity of their rich citizens. The role of the city's council, itself made up largely of the richer citizens, was dominant no less in the chief parish churches of the town. In city after city we find that the city council appointed the priest and paid for the construction of the more important parish churches, and, as if in return, used the church for its gild ceremonies and other formal occasions.

Scarcely less important in the eyes of its citizens were the town's secular buildings. Throughout Europe the management of a town's affairs was becoming more complex. There were records to be kept, taxes to be collected and accounted for, and contracts to be drawn up and enforced. These activities all demanded office space and a secretariat or chancery. There had to be a meeting place for the council. Warehouses were needed for the storage of the grain the town held for an emergency. How towns faced up to these requirements varied from one town to another, but in most there was a town hall, a *hotel de ville*, Rathaus, or Ratusz, splendidly decorated and appointed, since it was an expression of corporate civic pride. Many have survived from the late Middle Ages, among them the ornate town hall of Brussels, built during the years 1401–1456, which today still looks out over the spacious marketplace. Town halls proliferated across medieval Europe, some of them as spikingly Gothic as any medieval cathedral, as in the Ratusz of Wroclaw; others massively utilitarian, like that at Torun, built like a fortress to safeguard and protect the city's interests. The town hall represented the aspirations of the urban bourgeoisie to govern itself and to manage its own affairs. It was a challenge to the rural, feudal classes; it made a statement that the future lay with its members.

The argument of this chapter has been that the city can exist only by means of its manufacturing, commercial, and service industries; that these industries generate a surplus and that this surplus in turn both supported a leisured class and permitted those who enjoyed it to indulge their taste in art of all kinds. This included, given the prevailing spiritual inclinations of the age, church art and religious observances. It also embraced "high art," so that we must see in the urban patricians not only the source of the soaring spire of Ulm cathedral, the highest but not necessarily the most beautiful in Europe, but also the inspiration of much of the great art of the Renaissance and seventeenth century. The artistic and cultural achievement of western civilization, like its political legacy, was by and large the achievement of its cities and towns.

NOTES

1. Gideon Sjoberg, *The Preindustrial City: Past and Present* (Glencoe, IL: The Free Press, 1960), p. 1.

2. Wladyslaw Stanislaw Reymont's novel *The Promised Land* is concerned with the migration of peasants from an overcrowded land to the newly industrializing city of Lodz in Poland.

3. Giovanni Botero, "A Treatise Concerning the Causes of the Magnificency and Greatness of Cities," in *The Reason of State*, trans. P. J. Waley, D. P. Waley, and Robert Peterson (New Haven: Yale University Press, 1956), pp. 259–60.

4. Alfred, Lord Tennyson, "You ask me why, though ill at ease" (1842).

5. The terms England, Britain, Great Britain, and United Kingdom each have precise but different meanings. "England" denotes the area ruled from London during the Middle Ages; the term "Britain" is used for the whole island, including Wales and Scotland; "Great Britain" and "United Kingdom" are used for the island of Great Britain together with Northern Ireland, and "British Isles" is the inclusive term for the United Kingdom together with the Irish Republic.

6. William Shakespeare, *The Merchant of Venice*, in *The Complete Works of Shakespeare*, ed. David Bevington (New York and Reading, MA: Longman, 1997), 3.1.131–32.

7. William Hudson and John C. Tingey, eds., *The Records of the City of Norwich*, 2 vols. (Norwich: Jarrold & Sons, 1906–10), 1:xli–xlii.

8. Lucianus, *Extracts from the MS. "Liber Luciani de Laude Cestrie," Written about the Year 1195 and now in the Bodleian Library, Oxford*, ed. Margerie Venables Taylor, The Record Society for the Publication of Original Documents Relating to Lancashire and Cheshire, vol. 64 (Edinburgh and London: Record Society, 1912).

9. The great wheel must have been the medieval crane, in effect a kind of man engine in which the motive force was provided by men "walking" inside a giant wooden wheel.

10. From Felix Fabri's "Description of Swabia," qtd. in Gerald Strauss, *Sixteenth Century Germany: Its Topography and Topographers* (Madison: University of Wisconsin Press, 1959), p. 77.

Biographies and Places

Augsburg and the Fuggers

The family of Fugger typified the great trading and financial houses of late medieval Europe. It derived from a petty craftsman living at Graben, near Augsburg in south Germany. Augsburg was an imperial city, subject only to the German emperor, a fact that gave its citizens a greater freedom of action than those of lesser cities. The earliest known members of the family moved to Augsburg, only a few miles away. There they prospered and turned from the simple craft of weaving, which they had pursued in their home village, to the vastly more profitable business of trading and banking.

Jakub Fugger established the fortunes of the family in the first half of the fifteenth century. He died in 1469 and was succeeded by seven sons, most of whom entered the family business. For five generations the Fugger family dominated trade in Augsburg and much of south Germany. Then their business began to decline. The commercial revolution that resulted from the opening up of a sea route from western Europe to Asia and from the discovery of the New World greatly affected commercial firms in central Europe. Augsburg ceased to be the northern focus of a trading route that crossed the Alps from Germany to the Mediterranean Sea and the Middle East. Trade passed to the port cities of western Europe: Antwerp, Amsterdam, and London. Furthermore, the Thirty Years' War (1618–1648), which ravaged the whole of central Europe, interrupted their trade. Finally, the several lines within the vast Fugger family began one by one to die out, so that by the mid-seventeenth century the Fuggers' commercial empire had ceased to exist.

The fortunes of the Fuggers had been based first on the crafts and commerce of the Augsburg region, but in the mid-fifteenth century they began to see that profit was to be made from the mines—mostly for silver—which were beginning to open up in the Austrian province of Tyrol. This led on to the exploitation of mines, still largely under Austrian rule, in the province of Slovakia, then called upper Hungary. The Fuggers at first looked for silver, which they coined and passed into circulation. The silver from mines at Jachimov in Bohemia (now part of the Czech Republic) was minted to give coins known as Taler, from which we get the word "dollar."

From silver they turned to copper, which occurred more abundantly in the mountains of Slovakia. Copper was beginning to be used extensively in the manufacture of bronze, from which the cannon (just beginning to come into military use) were cast. The Fuggers were thus among the very first people to make money from the armaments trade. The many small towns of Slovakia, which continue today to show the attractive Renaissance architecture of the fifteenth and sixteenth centuries, are evidence of the activities of the Fuggers more than five centuries ago.

Jakub Fugger and his successors accumulated vast fortunes not only for themselves, but also for the dukes of Austria, on whose lands they were particularly active. Jakub was ennobled by the German emperor, himself an Austrian Habsburg, and became the banker or chief financial agent of the House of Habsburg. Like big corporations today, the Fuggers spread their interests into other fields. Their mining activities were extended to the mercury (cinnabar) mines of Spain. They invested their profits in land and acquired large personal estates. They also went, on behalf of the Habsburgs, into land management. This brought them into close personal contact with the German princes and gave them entrance to the aristocracy of both Austria and Germany.

Like wealthy urban merchants elsewhere in Europe, the Fuggers undertook charitable works and became patrons of art. They built the Fuggerei in Augsburg, a quarter of the city established to house large numbers of the laboring poor. Other members of the family became collectors of classical manuscripts, authors of historical treatises, and advisers and confidants of the princes of Bavaria. The churches of St. Anna and St. Ulrich in Augsburg itself became the burial places of many members of this extended family, and their family mansion, the *Fuggerhaus*, still stands within the old city, whose fortunes they had assured.

The Cinque Ports

Urban leagues were not a feature of Germany alone. There was an important association of port towns in England, the Cinque (pronounced "sink") Ports. In origin there were, as their name implies, five of them. Their purpose was not, as in the German urban leagues, the self-protection of their individual members, but rather the protection of this vulnerable coastline, which lay opposite and in places in sight of the shores of continental Europe. The defense of this stretch of coast was a major preoccupation of the English—later the British—government from at least the fifteenth century until the threatened German invasion of 1940.

This urban association began to take shape in the thirteenth century, and from its early days embraced the five small port towns of Dover, Hastings, Hythe, Romney, and Sandwich (Figure 25). To these were subsequently added, though without any change in the name of the group, the towns of Rye and Winchelsea.

These towns were not seen as bastions, protecting the coastline from invasion by enemy forces. Most had no defensive walls, though castles were built at Dover and Hastings. They were, rather, schools of seamanship and places where the broad-beamed, sail-driven, wooden ships of the time could be built, launched, and maintained. They were thus highly specialized towns. At no great distance in their hinterlands lay the forested region known as the Weald (from the German "Wald," meaning forest). We must think of the great oaks being dragged down to the coast, cut up and fabricated into "cogs," caravels, and other types of ships.

This urban association was united under the Lord Warden of the Cinque Ports. He was usually a seafaring man and was appointed by the English crown. His office still continues, but is today wholly honorific, and he resides whenever he wishes to be present amid his "ports," in Walmer Castle, a fortress built by King Henry VIII about 1540 to provide further coastal defense against the French.

Among the duties of the Lord Warden was to preside over the Court of Admiralty for the Cinque Ports. This was an important and powerful body, which coordinated the activities of the individual ports and settled the disputes that inevitably arose between them. The national obligations of the Cinque Ports declined from the seventeenth century. Shipbuilding ceased, and the protection of the realm passed to ships larger

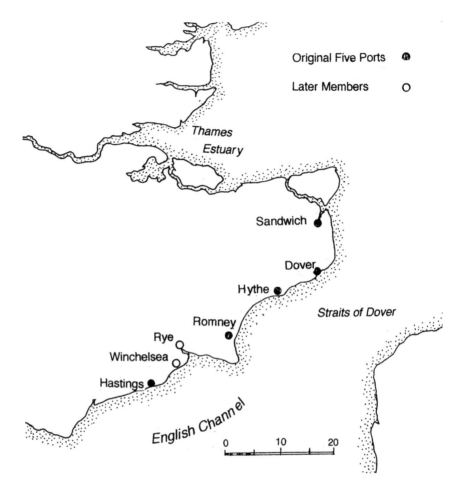

Figure 25. The Cinque Ports, which had the function of guarding the coast of southeast England. They were superseded in the fifteenth and sixteenth centuries by a series of masonry fortresses.

than those which could be accommodated within the small harbors of the ports themselves. Most of these once important port towns declined almost to insignificance. Today only Dover remains a significant port. The waterway of Romney has silted; Old Winchelsea was overwhelmed by a surge of the sea in the late thirteenth century and was rebuilt a mile or two inland. No ship could today reach the town of Tye, which nevertheless still retains its old world charm. The rest are merely coastal resorts, coming alive only during the short holiday season in summer.

The Fair Towns of Champagne

Many of the hundreds of charters granted to towns in the twelfth and thirteenth centuries conferred on them the right to hold a fair. A fair was a simple, almost primitive, means of doing business. Traders, carrying their goods by cart or pack animal, would gather at agreed places and at prearranged times and do business with one another. It was face-to-face trading. The merchants knew one another. They recognized those who were trustworthy and those who were not, and they had their own rough and ready means of settling the disputes that inevitably arose between them—the courts of "pie-powder," *pieds poudres*, or "dusty feet," whose name suggests the informality with which they were conducted.

No one knows when or exactly how that series of fairs arose that made the plains of Champagne the hub of European commerce during the thirteenth and fourteenth centuries. There had been periodic gatherings of merchants here as early as the fifth century C.E., and it appears that some of the early monasteries encouraged such meetings on the occasions of their dedicatory feasts. There was, for example, a fair at the Parisian abbey of Saint-Denis in the seventh century. It lasted no less than four weeks and attracted merchants from all parts of western Europe. Fairs were then established in the cities of Flanders and handled the cloth, which was already becoming a specialty of the region.

But no region offered greater advantages than Champagne, the extensive region lying to the east of Paris. Across it ran the most used routes between Italy and Flanders. Above all, the counts of Champagne maintained order and, in this turbulent age, gave shelter and protection to traders and travelers. There were numerous markets spread among the town of Champagne, handling the produce of their local regions. Four of them acquired a wider reputation and developed a trade with more distant parts. They were Troyes, capital of the counts of Champagne, Provins, Lagny, and Bar-sur-Aube. Each had some local advantage. Troyes itself derived from the Roman tribal capital of Augustobona and had already become the seat of a bishop. Lagny lay on the navigable river Marne and close to Paris. Both Bar and Provins had the advantage of much-used highways. The Church also contributed to the rise of the fairs by encouraging and protecting merchants, so that by the mid-twelfth century, all four fairs were in existence, and each was building a continent-wide reputation for the volume of trade conducted here.

The four towns adapted to the regular influx of traders, with carts and baggage-trains and their demands for food and accommodation. In each of them certain quarters were for a period in each year given over to their activities. Stalls were erected in the streets; warehouses were built for storage; and an infrastructure of transportation, legal, and financial services was created. At the same time the fairs generated their own underworld of thieves, prostitutes, and pimps.

The number of fairs increased and their dates became fixed and were rigidly observed. In the end a cycle of fairs evolved. There were six, more or less evenly spaced throughout the year. Two were held at Troyes and two at Provins while the lesser towns of Bar-sur-Aube and Lagny each had one. The duration of each fair was about six weeks. During the first week the merchants were gathering, setting up their stalls and getting to know others who had come. This was followed by periods devoted to specialized trades: cloth, leather goods, and so forth. The fairs ended with a period during which accounts were settled. Money did not change hands during the main part of the fair. The traders themselves had come from all parts of Europe, and they used every currency that was in general circulation. Money did not pass from one to another with every transaction. Instead, a record was kept, and a balance was struck at the end, when many transactions were found to have cancelled one another out. Little remained to be settled by the payment of coin, which was just as well because there was always a shortage of minted money.

By the end of the twelfth century, the fair towns had become adapted to the routine of short periods of intense activity, each followed by longer periods, when damage and losses were repaired, and the townsfolk prepared for the next influx of noisy, undisciplined, and grasping traders. The system reached its peak during the thirteenth century, but by 1300 its importance was beginning to decline. The volume of trade had grown to the point at which it could no longer be transported and handled at the fair towns. Varieties and qualities of woven and leather goods had become standardized, so that a merchant in distant Italy had only to order a dozen of this or of that cloth for the order to be understood and filled. It was becoming as simple as the mail-order business of today, and the necessary financial devices were developed in the shape of bills of exchange—the medieval equivalent of checks—for making payments. The face-to-face gatherings of merchants were no longer necessary, and the fairs of Champagne gradually became less important in the commerce of Europe.

The decline of the fairs was not wholly due to changes in business methods. The government of the County of Champagne, which had carefully nurtured them, passed to the French crown, which was less careful in protecting them. Civil wars deterred merchants from visiting the fairs, and in 1312 the first of the Venetian galleys conveyed merchandise between the ports of the Mediterranean and those of northwest Europe. The final blow was struck by the outbreak of the Hundred Years' War in 1337.

The Hanseatic League

Of all the associations of towns that arose during the Middle Ages, the German Hanse was by far the most important and the most successful.[1] It was, to quote its earliest title, a community of the merchants of the German empire frequenting Gotland. The term *Hanse*, which was later applied to it, was a Middle English word denoting a society or against the imperial frontier, where wide rivers and extensive marshland had given it some protection against the barbarian peoples beyond. It had been little developed under the Romans and contained few roads and no city of any great significance. It did, however, produce a certain rough cloth from the wool of the sheep which grazed the marshland, and, made up into garments, the cloth gained a certain reputation during the Dark Ages as *pallia Fresonica* (Frisian cloaks). It was on this slender basis that one of the great cloth manufacturers of the Middle Ages was built.

In the sixth century this began to change. The Germanic Franks pressed "company," and the Hanseatic League was just that: a rather informal and fluctuating group of merchants doing business in the Baltic Sea. The island of Gotland, with its chief town of Visby, was then the focus of their activities and their chief meeting place.

The merchants of Gotland, a large island in the Baltic Sea, were heirs to the Vikings who had dominated the Baltic region from before the eighth century. From Visby their commerce had extended eastward to Novgorod and thence up the Russian rivers and down the Volga to the Caspian and Black Seas. Here they encountered the merchants of the Byzantine Empire and did business in its capital city of Byzantium. These Viking traders were known as the "Rus," and it was from their settlements along the headwaters of the Volga that the first Russian state was to emerge. It was by the route they had marked out that oriental silks and spices as well as the Byzantine gold coin—the Bezant—became known in the West. At the same time loot from English monasteries passed through the emporium of Visby to Russia and the Middle East.

By the eleventh century this trade had declined, and the Vikings had ceased to threaten the coastlands of western Europe, but a small-scale commerce continued between Scandinavia and the eastern Baltic region. Its terminus was the Russian city of Novgorod where merchants established a trading base. Their penetration of the hinterland was, however, obstructed by the Prussian and Lithuanian tribes. In the twelfth century, conditions were beginning to change. German settlement was advancing slowly along the south coast of the Baltic, first to the Elbe, then the Oder, and last into the basin of the Vistula. Land was being cleared and brought under the plow. Towns were founded and commerce developed along the rivers that discharged to the Baltic Sea. In 1143 the town of Lubeck was founded and within a very short time its merchants were participating in Baltic trade alongside those of Visby.

The future was to be with the men of Lubeck and of the towns along the south Baltic coast. They had advantages which allowed them to usurp the role previously played by those of Gotland. In the first place, their hinterland was developing and becoming more populous. Its expanding agriculture generated a surplus of grain which was needed in the West, and its forests yielded timber and furs.

A further advantage arose when the Order of German Knights, having abandoned its role as protector of the Holy Places in the Middle East, looked for other peoples and realms to conquer. They were invited by a Polish prince, Conrad of Mazowsze, to turn their energies against the Prussian and Lithuanian tribes. Their success was followed by the rise of towns in the eastern and southeastern Baltic lands, and this in turn contributed to the trade of the Baltic ports.

Within the councils of the ill-organized community of Gotland merchants, the men of North Germany and of Lubeck in particular soon gained the upper hand. The earlier trade, which had been across Russia to the Middle East, diminished and eventually disappeared as the savage Tartar peoples—the Golden Horde—came to control the whole steppe region. It was replaced by the newly developing trade with Poland and the Baltic lands. The change within the Hanse, as we must begin to call this rudimentary organization, came when it was decided that disputes between member cities should be settled in Lubeck rather than

Visby and that the Hanse's chest, or treasury, should also be transferred there.

The Hanse was a loose association, never a formal league. At any given time, its membership consisted of those cities and towns that had sent representatives to its most recent assembly of *Hansatag*, which met at irregular intervals at Lubeck. The Hanse had no constitution, or regular meeting place, though this role tended to be assumed by Lubeck. Its rules were merely the decisions reached at its *Hansatage*. Yet it clearly had a policy, which its members pursued with vigor and considerable success, and that was the achievement of commercial profit. It negotiated agreements with territorial princes, and even made war on the kingdom of Denmark in protection of its right to send its ships through the Danish channels into the North Sea.

Membership fluctuated, but was generally between seventy and eighty. It included rich and powerful city-states, such as Lubeck, Rostock, and Stralsund on the Baltic and Hamburg and Cologne in the West, as well as many small towns of minimal commercial and political importance. The league also did business with towns such as London, Bruges, and Novgorod, which were outside its direct control. But it was able to negotiate treaties with the king of England, the Count of Flanders, and the prince of Moscow and was allowed to set up "counters" or *Kontor* in their respective countries. These served at the same time as domiciles for German merchants, as warehouses for their goods, and as places of business. Their *Kontor* in London was known as the *Stahlhof*, or Steelyard. There exist today in the small English town of King's Lynn considerable remains of the late medieval *Kontor* of the German Hanse.

Together with its most distant *Kontors*, the league's membership was vast at the height of its property. During the fifteenth century, the league's power and importance began to decline. Territorial states ceased to tolerate the pretensions of these autonomous cities, and in some cases the privileges of the *Kontors* were withdrawn. The Novgorod *Kontor* was closed by the Russian tsar in 1494; in London the *Kontor*'s privileges were terminated by Queen Elizabeth I (1558–1603). In Flanders, Bruges ceased to be accessible to the ships of the Hanse. Above all, the opening of sea routes to the Middle East and Asia undercut the Hansards' trade, while English and Danish merchants themselves encroached on the Baltic sphere. The wars of the seventeenth century in central and northern Europe were the final blow. A diminishing number of cities maintained the fiction of the Hanseatic League into the eighteenth century, and its last assets were liquidated early in the nineteenth.

The Laws of Breteuil

Breteuil is today a small town in upper Normandy. In the eleventh and twelfth centuries, however, Breteuil played a significant role in the urban development of northwestern Europe. About 1060, William, Duke of Normandy and the future William I of England, built a castle here to protect his dukedom from enemies to the north and placed it in the charge of his cousin, William FitzOsbern. A town then grew up in the shadow of the castle, and was in the course of time granted a charter of liberties. We do not know when this occurred, nor has a copy of the charter survived, but the liberties it granted to the men of Breteuil were to become the model for the charters that some of Duke William's followers were to grant in England, Wales, and Ireland.

The stages in this process have been reconstructed in a series of papers written by Mary Bateson more than century ago.[2] Roger, the second son of the first castellan of Breteuil, also known as Roger of Breteuil, followed Duke William to England, fought at Hastings (1066), and was rewarded by the grant of extensive lands taken from the defeated Anglo-Saxons. Among these possessions were lands along the border—the Marches—between England and Wales. It was here that Roger of Breteuil, alive to the advantages, both military and monetary, of the possession of boroughs, gave urban privileges to the settlements that had grown up beneath the castles he had founded. It is likely that the only urban privileges with which Roger was familiar were those his father had granted to his French hometown. Among the towns which thus came to be endowed with the Laws of Breteuil was Hereford, which was already the seat of an Anglo-Saxon bishop. Domesday Book, which was compiled in 1086, clearly states that Hereford enjoyed the *leges et consuetudines quae sunt . . . in bretuill* (the laws and customs which prevail in Breteuil).

At about the same time a castle was built and a town established at Rhuddlan in north Wales, but also within the Welsh Marches. Of it Domesday states that it possessed the laws and customs of "Hereford and Breteuil." More than a century later the town of Shrewsbury was stated to be governed *per legem Bretoll* (according to the law of Breteuil). The laws and customs of Breteuil were also adopted (by what agency we do

not know) in towns as far from the Welsh Marches as the English mid-
lands, the southwestern peninsula of England, and Ireland, where, a century after the Norman Conquest of England, their descendants were
striving to subdue the Irish. Altogether there were seventeen towns in
Great Britain that claimed to follow the "laws" of Breteuil, together with
eight more that may well have done so. A dozen towns in Wales derived
their "liberties" from the model FitzOsbern had brought from France.

What then were those "laws" that had proved to be so popular and
so convenient? This we do not know, since none of the confirmatory
charters have survived. Bateson, however, made a valiant effort to reconstruct them by tracing the common elements in the urban practices
of these towns during the late Middle Ages. It appears that the original
Laws of Breteuil were especially notable in one way. They were generous; they set out to attract settlers. The burgage plots were large; amerce-
ments, or fines, were low; permission was granted for citizens to take
wood from the forests belonging to the lord for building and heating their
homes.

The territorial, feudal lords were evidently competing for settlers who
would come and occupy the plots in their new towns. They were needed
not only to pay market tolls and burgage rents to their lord, but also to provision the castle and to serve its garrison, small though this may have been.
"The lord," in the words of Bateson, "offered as a bait a liberty which men
are seeking; the men who care to accept the grant, who accept it with every
security legal forms can give, will strive to defend it from all encroach-
ments."[3] From this contract, over a period of many centuries, emerged the
self-governing town of the late Middle Ages and modern times.

Ludlow, England, and Kalisz, Poland: A Contrast

Ludlow lies in the Welsh Border, that area of rare beauty, partly in
England, partly in Wales, which was fought over by the two countries for
centuries. Ludlow is therefore a defended town, founded by the Norman
conquerors in the twelfth century. Its nucleus was a castle, founded in all
probability by a local lord, William de Lacy, shortly before 1100. It
crowned a steep bluff, overlooking the river Teme and facing into Wales,
while to the east lay a flat-topped ridge over which the town itself was
to spread.[4]

The castle appears to have been built of masonry almost from the start, with a tall tower that served as a strong entrance to its inner courtyard. Work continued intermittently on the castle throughout the Middle Ages. A fine dining hall was built on the most protected side of the court, in which a circular castle chapel was built freestanding, and domestic buildings continued to be added throughout the remaining years of the Middle Ages, when Ludlow became the "capital" of the Marches or Borderland. Not until the eighteenth century did the castle cease to be inhabited.

South of the castle (Figure 26) and reaching down to the river, the small settlement of Dinham developed. It evidently prospered and was followed by the more regularly planned town that came to extend eastward over the low ridge. On the map today, Ludlow shows a regular layout, with its streets intersecting more or less at right angles. It is difficult not to see in this the work of the lord of the castle who created the street pattern, provided for a market area, and aligned the long, narrow burgage plots. On the highest ground a church was built, occupying, together with its cemetery, a whole block. Last, sometime in the thirteenth century, a wall was built to enclose the whole and to link it with the walls of the castle, together with no less than seven fortified gates.

Castle and town together occupied a strongly defensive site, though their strength was never put to the test. Wales was conquered by the English late in the thirteenth century, and Ludlow became a peaceful market town, doing business with the fertile and productive region that surrounded it.

The town must have been granted a charter, probably during the twelfth century, but it has been lost. A second charter, dated 1449, renewed the privileges the town had already received. The town was administered by a council made up of twelve alderman and twenty-five councilors, all elected by the burgesses of the town. But the town's independence was restricted. The lord of the castle continued to enjoy extensive privileges, including that of holding the chief court of justice, which provided him with a small income from fines and penalties. The lordship itself passed from one noble family to another, until it came to the Mortimers, the earls of March (i.e., the "March," or border of Wales). In 1425 it passed into the possession of Richard, Duke of York, and ultimately into that of King Edward IV.

Some 900 miles to the east and within the territory of the modern state of Poland is the town of Kalisz, about 120 miles west of Warsaw. Kalisz

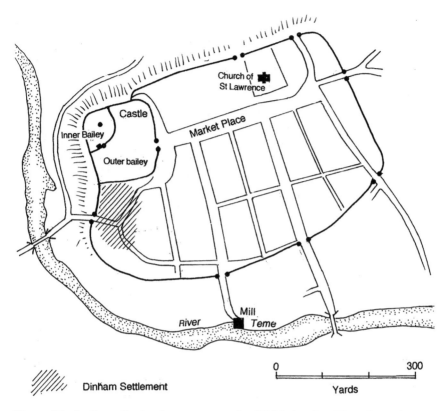

Figure 26. Ludlow, England: a town on the Welsh border. The planned town was established as an extension of the castle and of its adjoining settlement of Dinham.

was developing at the same time as Ludlow and under not dissimilar conditions. Kalisz, too, was a frontier town, founded by a local territorial lord to serve its agricultural countryside and to make profit for its master. Kalisz differed in one respect from Ludlow. It also had a castle (*grod*) as its nucleus, but this lay half a mile away along the marshy bank of the small Barcyz River. This was in all probability because there was no firm, dry site for the town above the river's level in the close proximity of the *grod*.[5]

The town of Kalisz was laid out, like Ludlow, with a network of intersecting streets (Figure 27), but their alignment has become slightly distorted. A charter was granted at some time during the twelfth century, but, as at Ludlow, the territorial lord retained a considerable degree of control, which was, however, diminished during the late Middle Ages as

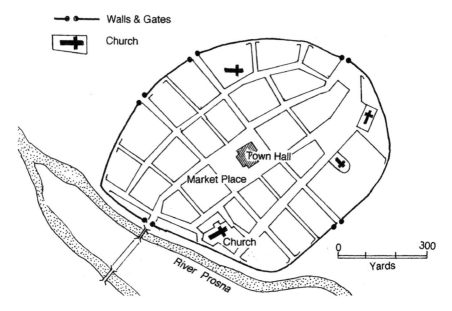

Figure 27. Kalisz, Poland: a planted, walled, and planned town.

the burgesses increasingly exercised control. Within the town, authority lay mainly in the hands of a council made up of citizens of the patrician class. These were merchants who controlled the crafts and trade of this rich region of central Poland. By the end of the thirteenth century they had organized a system of gilds. Two blocks within the town had been set aside for a market, and a town hall, or "Ratusz," was built within them. In addition to this weekly market, Kalisz also had a fair, which played an important role in the trade between the Baltic region to the north and the plains of eastern Europe and the Danube Basin.

Kalisz came to be enclosed by defensive walls, which have now entirely disappeared. There was a parish church, which at first had the whole town as its sphere of influence. But this was supplemented as the town grew during the fourteenth century, by a second parish church and by a convent of Franciscan friars.

Ludlow and Kalisz are typical of a kind of town that proliferated in most parts of Europe, except the Mediterranean region, during the Middle Ages. It was to be found from Wales to the Danube valley and from southern France to Switzerland and Germany. What these regions had in common was a feudal organization of society, which permitted a territorial lord to establish towns and set up markets wherever these might be profitable to himself. A second feature was their political insecurity. Towns were safe places, or at least safer than the open countryside, where economic activities could be pursued in relative security. Last, most of these towns showed evidence of planning, and many of them today still have their streets aligned on a regular, gridiron pattern.

The Most Highly Urbanized Region of Europe

In Flanders and neighboring parts of Brabant and Hainault, a number of towns began to emerge in the eleventh century, which were eventually to include some of the largest in Europe: Bruges and Ghent, Brussels and Antwerp, and, between them, a host of smaller towns. The only comparable region lay in northern and central Italy, where the medieval towns mostly derived from those of the late Roman Empire. The cities of Flanders and its neighboring provinces, however, owed nothing to Rome. Their roots did not lie in the distant past, but in the development of trade that took place long after Roman rule had ended. (See Figure 28.)[6]

The territory had been part of the thinly populated Roman province of Belgica, which lay across the lower courses of the Rhine and Meuse. During the fifth and sixth centuries it was invaded by the Germanic Franks, who settled over much of the region. A century or two later the Scandinavians, sailing up the great rivers, began to ravage it. The local population sought refuge in fortified enclosures, which must have resembled the burhs being built at about the same time in Anglo-Saxon England. Some may have been communal enterprises; others were the fortified homes—castles, in fact—of the local elite. Yet others were founded by the Church to protect its monastic sites. By the eleventh century, the land was dotted with strong points that attracted settlers on account of the protection they afforded. In this way, burh and castle together gave rise to a scatter of small towns, just as they were doing across the water in England. These urban settlements then developed a trade, not only locally with their respective hinterlands, but also with other parts of northwestern Europe. Markets and fairs began to emerge. They already had an important commodity in which to trade—the coarse local cloth. In the course of time, this cloth became more refined and supplied an ever-widening market. The weaving industry outgrew its local

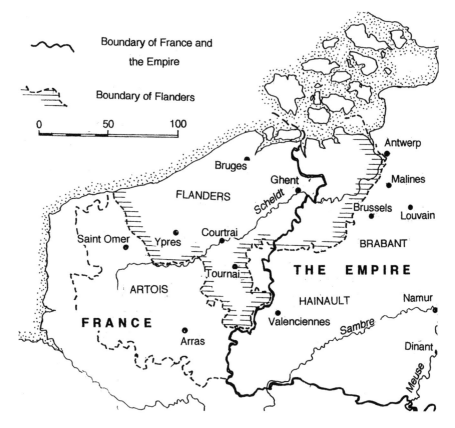

Figure 28. Flanders, the most highly urbanized and industrialized region in late medieval Europe.

supply of wool, and English and French wool began to supplement that which came from the sheep of the Flemish marshes. Related trades—especially dyeing and finishing the cloth—developed. At the same time, metalliferous mining developed in the hills to the south; a copper and brass industry appeared in the valley of the Meuse, centering in the town of Dinant, and its products also passed through the markets of the Flanders cities.

The region had, furthermore, an advantage of incalculable importance in the quality of its rulers. The Count of Flanders, who had brought much of the region under his control, recognized the value to himself of prosperous towns and developed industries. They brought profit to his lands and, through taxes and tolls, money for himself. From the mid-eleventh century, the counts pursued a policy of encouraging the growth of towns and the spread of commerce. Generous charters of liberties were granted, and the cities were allowed to develop self-governing institutions on a scale that led the eminent Belgian historian Henri Pirenne to write of the "urban democracies of the low Countries."

The liberties the count conferred upon his Flemish cities were modeled on those of Arras in northern France. The count retained ultimate control, but allowed each of the towns to be governed by a council of *echevins* (councilors), chosen from among the burgesses themselves. In the course of time the authority of the counts diminished while that of the burgesses increased. The Flemish cities did not quite become urban republics on the lines of the great cities of Italy, but there remained little external control over their activities.

The cities of Flanders carried on manufacturing industries on a quite considerable scale. They were of two kinds. First, there was the production of goods required by their own urban population and by the surrounding villages. These included the preparation of foodstuffs and articles of everyday use, and in this respect the Flemish cities differed in no way from those of the rest of Europe. Second, there were the major—the staple—industries: cloth weaving and finishing and the metal industries. These were not managed by craftsmen in small, domestic units and governed by the rules of their respective gilds. They were in the hands of merchant capitalists, men who purchased wool and metal in bulk, put it out to domestic weavers and metalworkers, and later collected the finished goods and marketed them throughout western and central Europe. Their market, by contrast with that of the craftsman, was the known world. No gild regulated their activities, and they were in a position to make vast fortunes. They were among Europe's first capitalists.

The cities in which they lived were large, their population increased by immigration from the countryside. The immigrants, mostly penniless, became the workforce of the clothing trades and were wholly dependent on the class of merchant capitalists who employed them. In all the large towns the proletarian clothworkers made up a large part of the population. The cities themselves were far larger than could have been sustained by their surrounding hinterlands and were supported by foodstuffs imported from as far away as the Baltic Sea and paid for by the export of cloth. Inevitably, strife arose between the merchant and patrician class on the one hand and the mass of the working population on the other.

City government was firmly in the hands of the patricians. Working-class discontent began to show itself from the mid-thirteenth century in outbreaks of violence, culminating in disastrous wars in the early fourteenth century. The question of the independence of the Flemish and other towns came to be wrapped up with the struggle between Flanders and France, and this was in turn a factor in the beginning of the Hundred Years' War between England and France. Flanders' dependence on English wool helped to cement the alliance between them in opposition to France.

The short-lived independence of the democratically governed cities of Flanders ended in war and confusion. This inevitably influenced the cloth industry. But there were other factors in the decline of the clothing towns at the end of the Middle Ages. The supply of English wool began to dry up with the expansion of the weaving industry in England itself, and the European market for Flemish cloth was reduced to a fraction of what it had once been. At the same time seaborne trade began to desert the Flemish towns as their rivers silted and became shallow. Commercially their heir was the great port city of Antwerp, which until late in the sixteenth century was the greatest trading center of northwestern Europe. It in turn was succeeded by Amsterdam, and in more recent years by Rotterdam.

Penryn, Cornwall, a Bishop's Town

The Cornish historian Charles Henderson described Penryn as a speculation of the bishops of Exeter. The bishops owned the surrounding land, where they possessed a manor house at which they frequently stayed during their rare forays into this remote part of their diocese. It was a bishop of Exeter, William Brewer (1223–1244), who in 1236 incorporated the small settlement that had grown up near the manor house by giving its residents a charter. This document has not survived, and the earliest record that exists today is a confirmation of it given by Bishop Walter Bronescombe some forty years later.[7]

From this record we learn that the men of Penryn held burgage plots, each of them paying the annual rent of 12 pence. In return the burgesses were to possess all liberties and free customs that they had hitherto enjoyed. The charter, unfortunately, does not tell us what these liberties were, though they had probably been specified in the earlier charter, which has been lost. They probably included the right to hold a weekly market as well as an annual fair and possibly to organize gilds for its crafts-men and merchants. The fair appears never to have been successful; there was probably insufficient long-distance trade to support it. Nor do we know what jurisdictional and administrative privileges the bishops al-lowed to their tenants; probably very few, for bishops liked to keep a tight control over the towns they founded.

The town of Penryn consisted of little more than a single street, which climbed steeply from the tidal waters of the Penryn River and then fol-lowed a ridge toward the higher ground to the northwest. Near its mid-dle, the street widened to form an open space that would have served as the market and in later centuries contained a freestanding town hall. Houses and shops would have lined the street, and behind each its bur-gage plots, long and narrow, would have reached down the slopes on each side of the ridge.

The borough lay entirely within the ecclesiastical parish of St. Glu-vias, whose church lay away on the other side of the Penryn River. It is curious that a bishop had founded his borough without any regard for the church and the parish in which it lay. The burgesses, finding the journey to their parish church longer and less convenient than they had antici-pated, obtained in 1374 permission to build a small church, known as a chapel-of-ease,* within the borough, but it appears to have been demol-ished during the Reformation, and the burgesses were left to make the journey on foot to their parish church.

The bishops took no great risk when they founded the borough of Pen-ryn. It lay on the bank of the Penryn River, which discharged into the spacious Falmouth Harbor, one of the best and most sheltered in all northwestern Europe. Its chief port had hitherto been Truro, some eight miles inland, but the port of Penryn quickly cut into the trade of Truro and enjoyed a period of prosperity until the foundation of the town of Falmouth in the early seventeenth century created a highly successful rival to Penryn. A rent roll of the bishops of Exeter of 1307–1308 showed the borough paying £7 "13 "2½ by way of rent on its burgage plots, whereas the weekly market yielded no less than £26 "7 "5 in tolls. Alto-gether it must indeed have been a profitable undertaking.

---

*A "chapel-of-ease" was a church built to relieve pressure on a parish church from overcrowding or to serve the needs of a newly developing community.

Penryn differs from those planted towns discussed earlier in that Penryn never possessed fortifications. It was sufficiently far from the coast to have had little fear of piratical raids, and warfare and civil disorder were too rare to threaten the security of the town. There were hundreds of such towns in medieval Europe, and bishops participated in their foundation as readily as other landholders. The unwalled street town was particularly common in England, though not in Wales, which never enjoyed England's level of peace and security.

Sir Richard "Dick" Whittington

It is a British custom around Christmastime to stage an entertainment known as a "pantomime." It is intended primarily for children, but is sometimes satirical and always coarsely humorous. There are a number of stock characters on whom the action depends. One of them is Dick Whittington together with his cat. In popular folklore Whittington was a poor boy from the provinces who, accompanied only by his cat, set out for London in order to make his fortune. There are many variants of the story. One has it that he took employment in the household of a London merchant by whom he was badly treated, until the cat proved its worth by exterminating a plague of mice. Another version of the Whittington saga tells us that he despaired of ever making his fortunes and had turned for home, when he heard the "Bow Bells"—the bells of the church of St. Mary le Bow (or "Beau"). They seemed to say to him: "Turn again Whittington; thrice Lord Mayor of London town." He turned, and at once his fortunes changed.

This is all popular folklore, but there was indeed a Richard Whittington. He was the younger son of a Gloucestershire squire. As he had little chance of ever inheriting his father's land, he took up the trade of mercer, or dealer in high quality textiles. This took him to London, where he married a rich heiress and quickly established himself as a member of the city's ruling elite. He continued in the cloth trade and became the chief officer of the Staple, or association of merchants dealing in England's most important or "staple" export—cloth. This led on to his election as mayor or chief executive officer of the City of London in 1398–1399. His term of office was for a year. He was re-elected for the year 1406–1407 and again for 1419–1420, but died three years later.

It was typical of such a wealthy merchant that he was called upon to lend money to both King Henry IV (1399–1413) and to his son, King Henry V (1413–1422). In the absence of any system of banking that we would recognize, kings could obtain credit only through the goodwill of their rich subjects, and Whittington was not only a financier to the king but was also well rewarded for his pains. Whittington left a vast fortune at his death for charitable purposes. He expended money for building London's Gildhall and for adding to the Grayfriars or Franciscan church. During this tenure of the office of mayor it is said that he was so disgusted by the condition of Newgate, one of the city's prisons, that he himself paid for its rebuilding. He also restored St. Bartholomew's Hospital, endowed almshouses, and established a piped water supply for at least part of the city.

How then was the memory of a good and charitable public servant transformed into the story of a poor boy who made good with the help of his cat? The latter story first appeared in a play licensed for the stage in 1605. It was frequently referred to thereafter, and even appeared in the folklore of continental European countries. The real Richard Whittington must have been a well-known and highly respected figure, a suitable person on whom to hang the story of the poor immigrant to London who had prospered and made good.

NOTES

1. Philippe Dollinger, *The German Hansa* (Stanford: Stanford University Press, 1970).

2. Mary Bateson, "The Laws of Breteuil," *English Historical Review* 15, 57 and 58 (January and April 1900): 73–78 and 302–18; "The Laws of Breteuil. Part II. The English Evidence (Continued)," *English Historical Review* 15, 59 (July 1901): 496–523; "The Laws of Breteuil (Continued)," *English Historical Review* 15, 60 (October 1901): 754–57; "The Laws of Breteuil (Continued)," *English Historical Review* 16, 61 and 62 (January and April 1901): 92–110, 332–45.

3. Mary Bateson, "The Laws of Breteuil," *English Historical Review* 16 (1901): 344.

4. Ron Shoesmith and Andy Johnson, eds., *Ludlow Castle: Its History and Buildings* (Almeley, UK: Logaston Press, 2000).

5. Pierre Francastel, ed., *Les Origines des Villes Polonaises* (Paris: Mouton & Company, 1960), pp. 179–90.

6. Henri Pirenne, *Early Democracies in the Low Countries: Urban Society and Political Conflict in the Middle Ages and the Renaissance* (New York: Harper & Row, 1963); Michael M. Postan, "The Trade of Medieval Europe: The North," *The Cambridge Economic History of Europe* vol. 2, ed. Postan and H. J. Habakkuk (Cambridge, UK: Cambridge University Press, 1952); *Ciba Review*, 2, 14 (October 1938): pp. 466–504. Issue "Cloth-Making in Flanders."

7. Roland J. Roddis, *Penryn: The History of an Ancient Cornish Borough* (Penryn: D. Bradford Barton, 1964), pp. 16–29.

Primary Documents

DOCUMENT 1
"The Ruin"

An Anglo-Saxon poem, usually known as "The Ruin," describes the condition of a former Roman city after the Anglo-Saxon invasions. The city in question has been identified from the allusions to the springs and hot baths with the city of Bath in southern England, the Roman Aquae Sulis.

Wondrously wrought and fair its wall of stone,
Shattered by Fate! The castles rend asunder,
The work of giants moldereth away,
Its roofs are breaking and falling; its towers crumble
In ruin. Plundered those walls with grated doors—
Their mortar white with frost. Its battered ramparts
Are shorn away and ruined, all undermined
By eating age. The mighty men that built it,
Departed hence, undone by death, are held
Fast in the earth's embrace. Tight is the clutch
Of the grave, while overhead for living men
A hundred generations pass away.
       Long this red wall, now mossy gray, withstood,
While kingdom followed kingdom in the land,
Unshaken 'neath the storms of heaven—yet now
Its towering gate hath fallen . . .
       Radiant the mead-halls in that city bright,
Yeah, many were its baths. High rose its wealth

Of hornèd pinnacles, while loud within
Was heard the joyous revelry of men—
Till mighty Fate came with her sudden change!
    Wide-wasting was the battle where they fell.
Plague-laden days upon the city came;
Death snatched away that might hose of men . . .
    There in the olden time full many a thane,
Shining with gold, all gloriously adorned,
Haughty in heart, rejoiced when hot with wine;
Upon him gleamed his armor, and he gazed
On gold and silver and all precious gems;
On riches and on wealth and treasured jewels,
A radiant city in a kingdom wide.
    There stood the courts of stone. Hotly within,
The stream flowed with its might surge. The wall
Surrounded all with its bright bosom; there
The baths stood, hot within its heart . . .

Source: Albert S. Cook and Chauncey B. Tinker, eds., *Select Translations from Old English Poetry* (Boston and New York: Binn and Company, 1902), pp. 56–57.

DOCUMENT 2
Anglo-Saxon Chronicle

The following extract is from the records of the foundation of fortified burhs in Anglo-Saxon England, many of which subsequently developed into chartered boroughs.

913. Here Æthelflæd built Tamworth and also Stafford stronghold. Here, around Martinmas in this year, King Edward ordered to be built the more northerly stronghold at Hertford, between the Maran and the Beane and the Lea. And then after that, the summer after, between Rogation days and midsummer, King Edward went with some of his reinforcements to Maldon in Essex, and camped there while they made and strengthened the stronghold at Witham; and a good part of the people who were earlier under the control of Danish men submitted to him. And some of his reinforcements made the stronghold at Hertford on the south side of the Lea. [from the Worcester manuscript]

914. Then in this, the next year, [was made] that [stronghold] at Eddisbury in early summer; and later in the same year, late in harvest-time, that at Warwick.

915. Then in this, the next year after mid-winter, [was built] that stronghold at Chribury, and then that at Weardbyrig; and in the same year before mid-winter that at Runcorn. [from the Abingdon manuscript]

921. Here in this year before Easter King Edward [the Elder, 899–924] ordered them to go and build the stronghold at Towcester; and then after that, at Rogationtide in the same year, he ordered them to build the stronghold at Wigingamere.

The same summer, between Lammas and midsummer, the raiding-army from Northampton and from Leicester and north of there, broke the peace and went to Towcester and fought against the stronghold all day, and thought that they would be able to break it down. However, the people who were inside there defended it until more help came to them; and then they left the stronghold and went away. . . . At the same time the raiding-army went from Huntingdon and from East Anglia and made that fortress at Tempsford, and lived in and constructed it. [from the Winchester manuscript]

Source: M. J. Swanton, trans. and ed., *The Anglo-Saxon Chronicle* (London: J. M. Dent, 1996), pp. 97, 98, 99, and 101.

DOCUMENT 3
Domesday Book

The preparation of Domesday Book was ordered by King William I of England in 1086. It was a listing of places, their feudal ownership, and their population and resources. Its purpose was fiscal; it was, in Maitland's words "a geld book, no more and no less," and the king expected to be able to use it in assessing national taxation in his newly acquired kingdom. All English towns were included, with the exception of the cities of London and Winchester, which for no known reason were not included in the completed Domesday Book. The following extract, which is typical of most English towns at this time, shows a settlement in which agriculture was probably more important than industry and crafts.

HUNTINGDON
IN THE BOROUGH OF HUNTINGDON THERE ARE 4 FERDINGS

In 2 ferdings [quarters] there were TRE [Tempore Regis Edwardi—in the time of Edward the Confessor] and are now 116 burgesses rendering all customs and the king's geld, and under them are 100 bordars who help them to pay the geld. Of these burgesses, St Benedict of Ramsey [i.e., Ramsey Abbey] had 10 with sake and soke [civil and criminal jurisdiction over them] and every custom, except that they paid geld TRE Eustace took them away by force from the abbey, and they are now, with the others, in the king's hand [i.e., possession].

Ulf Fenman had 18 burgesses; now Gilbert de Ghent has them with sake and soke, except for the king's geld.

The Abbot of Ely has 1 toft [farmstead] with sake and soke, except for the king's geld.

The Bishop of Lincoln had on the site of the castle 1 messuage [house and garden] with sake and soke, which is not there now.

Earl Siward had 1 messuage with a house, with sake and soke, quit of all custom, which the Countess Judith has now.

On the site of the castle there were 20 messuages [assessed] to all customs, rendering 16s8d a year to the king's farm, which are not there now.

In addition to these, there were and are 60 waste messuages within these ferdings, which gave and give their customs.

And in addition to these, there are 8 waste messuages which TRE were fully occupied, and gave all customs.

In the other 2 ferdings there were and are 140 burgesses, less half a house, [assessed] to all customs and the king's geld, and these had 80 closes [enclosed piece of land] for which they gave and give all customs. Of these, St Benedict of Ramsey had 22 burgesses TRE. 2 of these were quit of all customs, and 30 paid 10d each. All other customs belonged to the abbot, apart from the king's geld.

In these ferdings, Ælfric the sheriff TRE had 1 messuage, which King William afterwards granted to his wife and sons. Eustace has it now; a poor man, with his mother, claims it. In these 2 ferdings, there were and are 44 waste messuages, which gave and give their customs. And in addition to these, in these 2 ferdings Burgræd and Thorkil TRE had 1 church with 2 hides* of land and 22 burgesses with houses belonging to the same church with sake and soke, all of which Eustace has now. Therefore these men claim the king's mercy. Nevertheless these 22 burgesses give every custom to the king. Bishop Geoffrey has 1 church and 1 house of the aforesaid, which Eustace took away from St Benedict, and the same saint is still claiming them. In the borough itself, Gos and Hunæf had 16 houses TRE with sake and soke and toll and team. Countess Judith has them now.

[A passage—omitted—defines the tax obligations of the town to the king.]

1 mill renders 40s to the king, 20s to the earl. To this borough there belong 2 hides carucates and 40 acres of land 10 acres of mellow, of which they divide the rent, the king [having] 2 parts, and the earl the third [part]. The burgesses cultivate this land and lease it through the servants of the king and the earl. Within the aforesaid rent are 3 fishermen paying 3s. In this borough there were 3 moneyers paying 40s [shared] between the king and the earl, but now they are not there. TRE it rendered £30; now the same.

Source: Ann Williams and G. H. Martin, eds., *Domesday Book: A Complete Translation*, Alecto Historical Editions (London and New York: Penguin Books, 2002) p. 551.

DOCUMENT 4
Urban Charters

> Charter of King John to the Borough of Cambridge. *The charter confirms to the burgesses their right to have a gild merchant*—Gilda Mercatoria. *This was a predecessor of the more specialized craft and trading gilds, and probably embraced those citizens who were engaged in commerce or the crafts.*

John by the grace of God, King of England . . . we have granted and by this our present charter have confirmed to our burgesses of Cambridge a gild merchant, and that none of them may make a plea outside the walls of the borough . . . none of them may fight a duel and they shall plead without the walls of the borough of Cambridge concerning any plea, unless they

---

*Hide, a variable measure of land, originally a unit sufficient to support a family.

be pleas of exterior tenures, except our moneyers and servants. Moreover we have granted to them that none of them shall make [proof by] battle, and that with regard to pleas pertaining to our crown they may deraign themselves according to the ancient custom of the borough. This also we have granted to them, that all burgesses of Cambridge of the gild of merchants shall be [free] of toll and passage [road toll] and lastage [toll for attending a fair] and pontage [bridge toll] and stallage [fee for setting up a market stall], in fairs and without, and throughout the ports of the sea and beyond the sea, saving in all things the liberties of the city of London, and that none be adjudged to be in mercy as to his money except according to the ancient law of the borough. . . . And that they may justly have their lands and pledges and all debts, whosoever may owe the same. And that right shall be done to them touching their lands and tenures which are within the borough according to the custom of the borough. And of all their debts which shall have been contracted at Cambridge and of the pledges made there, pleas shall be held at Cambridge. And if any in all our land shall take toll or customs from the men of Cambridge of the gild of merchants and shall have made default in right, then the sheriff of Cambridge or the reeve of Cambridge shall take therefore a distress at Cambridge, saving in all things the liberties of the city of London. Moreover for the amendment of the borough of Cambridge we have granted to them their fair in Rogation* week with its liberties as they were accustomed to have it, and that all the burgesses of Cambridge be quit of jherescheve and of scotale** if our sheriff or any other bailiff shall make a scotale. These customs aforesaid we have granted to them and all other liberties and free customs which they had in the times of our ancestors when they best and most freely had the same. . . . And whoever shall seek the borough of Cambridge with their merchandize, whencesoever they be, whether strangers or others, they may come, stay and return in our sure peace. . . . And we forbid that any cause herein injury or loss or trouble to our burgesses aforesaid upon pain of our forfeiture of ten pounds. Wherefore we will and firmly command that the said burgesses and their heirs shall have and hold all

---

*Rogation Week, the week following Trinity Sunday, during which it was customary to bless the crops.

**Scot-ale; *scot* means "free-from." This means free of the obligation to contribute ale to the king's sheriff on certain festive occasions.

these things aforesaid in inheritance of us and our heirs well and in peaceably, freely and quietly, entirely and honorably as is written above.

Source: Frederic William Maitland and Mary Bateson, eds., *The Charters of the Borough of Cambridge* (Cambridge, UK: Cambridge University Press, 1901), pp. 5–7.

Charter of Walter Bronescombe, Bishop of Exeter to the Borough
of Penryn. *This is a confirmation of the earlier charter of Bishop William
Brewer (1223–1244), which has been lost.*

To all faithful Christians who shall hear these present letters Walter by divine mercy Bishop of Exeter, greets you.

We have examined the letters of our predecessor of pious memory, William [Brewer] . . . in these terms: To all Christian people . . . William by divine mercy . . . know ye that on behalf of ourselves and our successors I have conceded and by this charter have confirmed to the good men of our borough of Penryn and their heirs and assigns that they may hold their burgage plots freely of us and for each acre wholly and properly measured by the payment to us and to our successors of 12 pence by way of rent per year at the two terms, namely All Saints' Day [Nov. 1] and May 1st . . . for all services. We have furthermore conceded that on the surrender of a burgage or on the death of a tenant, they ought to pay a relief of 12d. for each complete acre. . . . We wish and order that the said burgesses may have all things specified, together with all liberties and free customs in perpetuity. Given at Penryn, 1236.

Source: *Exeter Episcopal Registers [Bishops Brones* combe and *Quivil]*, ed. Hingeston Randolph, vol. 2 (1889), pp. 220–21.

DOCUMENT 5
Fairs and Markets

Care was taken by the crown that no new market or fair might be established to the injury of one which already existed, as here in Essex:

In 1318 a jury at Colchester found "That the Abbess of Barking (Berkyngg) [Barking Abbey in East London] holds a market at Salcote every Monday, to the injury and hindrance of Colchester Market, by what warrant and for how long they know not.

Source: W. Gurney Benham, ed. and trans., *The Red Paper Book of Colchester* (Colchester: Essex County Standard Office, 1902), p. 45.

DOCUMENT 6
Gilds and Gild Regulations

Some gilds received charters from the patrons or territorial lords of the towns in which they had been established. Almost all devised their own rules or ordinances which governed the conduct of their members and prescribed standards of workmanship. The following extracts are from the regulations of three of the gilds of the important town of Colchester in Essex, England:

1. [T]he sise [assize]* of a Spicer is that he have no weght but thei be sised [authorized by a court] and sealed and trew beme [balance used for weighing], and that he sell by no horns [containers of indefinite size] nor ayme of hande [by the handful], nor by no nother sotilty [subtlety] to disseyve the poure commyns; and that his spice be gode and clene garbeld. and yf he do the contrary to this hys fine is at every tyme iij^s. iiij^d., and if he wil not be ware by ij warnynggs, the iij^d tyme to be juged according un to the statute.

2. The statute of a Whitetawier is that he taw no ledir [lather] but shepe ledir, gyts (goats') ledir, deris, horss, and hownde ledir, and that it be made of sufficient stuff. And if he do the contrary to this, he to be mersed [amerced or fined] according un to the forme of the statute.

3. Also the sise of a Tanner is that he tanne no shepis ledir, geyts, deris, horsh ne honnd [hound] ledir, nor he have no maner [kind of] ledyr to sell, but it be thurgh tanned. And if he do the contrary his fyn is at every tyme vjs. viij^d,** and to forfet that is forfetabull, and if he will not by . . . ware by ij warnings, the iij^d tyme to be juged according un to the form of the statute.

---

*Assize, either a law, as in the "Assize of Clarendon," or the court which administered the law.

**Values are given in pounds, shillings, and pence, shown as £, s, and d. There were twelve pence in the shilling and twenty shillings to the pound. Pence were always represented by "d," from the Latin *denarius*.

Source: W. Gurney Benham, ed. and trans., *The Red Paper Book of Colchester* (Colchester: Essex County Standard Office, 1902), pp. 19–20.

Confirmation of the Tanners' Gild at Rouen, Normandy

Henry, by the Grace of God King of England [Henry II], etc. . . . Be it known that I have granted and confirmed with this charter of mine to the tanners of Rouen that they may have their gild with all its customs, freely and quietly, fully and honorably. Furthermore, on account of the services which these tanners perform, no one may follow their craft in Rouen or its region unless they permit. Therefore I order that no one shall interfere with them or act against their craft except through me.

Source: Author's translation of *Documents Relatifs a l'Histoire de l'Industrie et du Commerce en France*, ed. M. Gustave Fagniez, 2 vols., Collection de textes pour servir à l'étude et à l'enseignement de l'histoire (Paris: Alphonse Picard et Fils, 1898), 1:89.

Cordwainers' Gild of Oxford: Charter of Henry II of the Late Twelfth Century (c. 1175)

Know ye that I have granted and confirmed to the corvesars [cordwainers] of Oxford all the liberties and customs which they had in the time of King Henry [I] my grandfather, and that they may have their gild, so that none carry on their trade in the town of Oxford, except he be of that gild.

I grant also that the cordwainers who afterwards may come into the town of Oxford shall be of the same gild. . . . For this grant and confirmation, however, the corvesars and cordwainers ought to pay me every year an ounce of gold.

Source: R. Trevor Davies, *Documents Illustrating the History of Civilization in Medieval England (1066–1500)* (London: Methuen and Company, 1926), p. 115.

> *Approval of the Regulations of the Coopers' Gild of York, 1471: The coopers were the makers of wooden barrels, in which wine and other liquids were (and are) transported and stored. The "searchers" were the officials who examined the products of gild members and judged of its quality.*

[T]he serchiours and the honest personnes of the craft of coupers . . . desired the constytucions under writen to be added to thaire saide crafte.

It is ordained . . . that no maister of the craft of coupers within the said cite shall take non alien borne oute of this royme . . . to his apprentez in the same crafte, apon payne of forfeitur of xx s.

[I]t is ordained that evere hyred man of the same craft . . . that has ben apprentez in the same craft within the said cite, shall yerely pay to the serchiours of ye same craft . . . iiij d.; and, yif he were nat apprentez within the saide cite, yerly he to paye . . . vj^d.

[I]t is enact and ordeyned that yif ony [every] maister of that craft . . . be duele warned by his serchiours . . . to com to eny place . . . touching the wele [welfare] and worshipe of ye saidez cite and craft, and therin fayles, he shall forfett . . . vj^d.

[T]hat what maister . . . is rebell and disobeysaunte unto his serchiours . . . shall forfett x s.

[T]hat . . . the serchiours [may] . . . make due serche . . . upon all maner of warke of newe wroght . . . such as is to be put to saile. [Inferior workmanship to be forfeit.]

[T]hat, yif eny straunger . . . com to this cite and will wirke in the same occupacion . . . shall aske leyfe of the serchiours . . . and than his warke to be seyn by the same serchiours yif it be warkmanly don or no; and than his hier to be extented by it for yere or be weyk, as reason and conscience will.

Source: *York Memorandum Book*, Part I, 1376–1419, Publications of the Surtees Society, vol. 120 (London: Andrew & Company, 1912), pp. 69–70.

Complaint of Poor Workmanship

The common people complain to the bailiffs of Colchester that the Tile-makers

maken her (their) tyll bi diverse fourmes, more and lesse, none of hem (them) acordaunt to nother, to gret noissaunce and harmyng of the said people, wherfore hit is ordeyned and enstablisshed bi the said Bailifs and the generall counseill that no maner Tylemaker of the said toun of Colchestr ne with inne the fraunchise of the same toun fro this tyme foorth make no maner tyll, but all of one lengthe and of one brede (breadth) . . . acordaunt to a standard abidyng in the Moothalle of the said town; upon peyne of [a fine of 20 s.] . . . half [of which is to go] to the comoun profit of the said toun, and [the other half] . . . to hym that wil compleynen [the complaint].

Source: W. Gurney Benham, ed. and trans., *The Red Paper Book of Colchester* (Colchester: Essex County Standard Office, 1902), p. 49.

DOCUMENT 7
Apprenticeship Contract

I, Peter Borre, entrust my son Stephen to you, Peter Feissac, weaver, in order to learn the craft of weaving. He is to live at your house and to work for you from the next feast of Easter for four years. I understake to see to it that my son works for you, and that he will be faithful and trustworthy in all things and will not steal from you nor run away for any reason until his apprenticeship is complete. I, Peter Borre, will recompense you for any loss or damage that might arise. . . . For his part Peter Feissac undertakes to instruct Borre's son faithfully and to provide him with food and clothing. [Dated 1248.]

Source: Louis Blancard, ed., *Documents Inédits sur le Commerce de Marseille au Moyen Age*, vol. 2 (Marseilles: Barlatier-Feissat, 1884), p. 33.

DOCUMENT 8
Urban Conditions

Information on urban housing is most readily obtained from the contracts made between householders and the builders—masons and carpenters—who had contracted to build their houses. The following extracts are from contracts published in L. F. Salzman's Building in England, *Appendix B. Most are in Latin, and have been translated or summarized by the author.*

Housing

Simon of Canterbury undertakes in the presence of the Mayor and Aldermen to build for William de Hangitone, using his own materials, "a hall and chamber together with a small chamber, and a larder between the aforesaid hall and chamber; also a solar above the chamber with a fireplace; there is to be a gallery at the upper end of the hall [*in capite aule*] and an outside staircase from the ground to the gallery, and two compartments in the cellar under the hall, and one compartment crosswise under the hall for the drain [toilet, *cloaca*] and two conduits for the said drain, and a stable of the length between the said hall and the [illegible in manuscript].

London, 1308. No. 3

Source: L. F. Salzman, *Building in England down to 1540: A Documentary History* (Oxford: Clarendon Press, 1967), pp. 417–18.

Contract to Build Four Tenements in Canterbury, 1497

This indenture between William Haute, Knt [Knight] and John Browne of Canterbury, carpenter, witnesseth that John shall build four tenements on the land of the Augustine Friars in the parish of St George, in length along the street 84 feet and 24 feet deep. There are to be 4 halls with windows on the south side, and a stair from the hall to the chamber in each house. Also four shops next the street, with 4 chambers with windows over them. Each shop is to measure 12 feet by 8½ feet. At the end of each shop there is to be a buttery,* 4 feet wide and 8½ feet long, and each buttery is to have a convenient window. There is to be a kitchen, 10 feet by 12 feet, in each tenement. The upper floors are to be jettied.

The said William is to find all timber and other materials. Payment is to be in instalments, the first being when all the premises are fully framed and ready in form to be set up. [It is clear from this that the wooden framing of the house was first laid out flat on the ground and then raised into a vertical position, a method still used in house building in the United States. It is likely that Sir William Haute was investing in urban real estate, from which he expected to obtain a regular income. It is interesting that a knight, almost by definition a rural landowner, is here engaging in urban transactions.]

Canterbury, 1497. No. 101.

Source: Salzman, *Building in England*, pp. 554–56.

---

*Place where common foodstuffs were kept.

Contract to Build the Boar Inn on the Market Place

An indenture between William Ludlowe and John Fayrebowe, carpenter of Busshopestrowe, Wiltshire witnesseth that John "will make for the said William a house within the Bore [tavern] adjoining the Market Place . . . containing in length 63 feet and within the walls 20 feet. The grounsills* are to be 15 inches wide and 10 inches thick. There are to be 14 principal posts, every post 16 feet long and 13 inches wide and 12 inches thick. Every 'somer'** to be 16 inches wide and 15 inches thick. And every joist 8 inches thick and 9 inches wide. There are to be 10 inches between every joist. Every 'byndyngbeme'*** is to be 9 inches thick and 15 inches wide, and every wallplate, 8 inches thick and 9 inches wide, and every rafter 4 inches thick at the top and 5 inches at the foot. The rafters are to be spaced at 9 inch intervals. . . .

The house is to be well and truly made of sufficient timber, clean and without sap or windshake, ready to be set up and reared by the feast of the Nativity next. The said John shall find all timber for doors and windows and studs for the walls. And William shall find all nails, wattle [withies or osiers to be daubed with clay; see Glossary], roofing and mason's work necessary, and also meat and wages for two men working with the said John for seven days at the rearing of the house, and also the meat and wages for the men carting the timber to Salisbury. William will also pay 20 li [*livres*, i.e., pounds] for building the house and finding the timber, to be paid in three installments."

Salisbury, 1444. No. 73.

Source: Salzman, *Building in England*, pp. 516–17.

---

*Timbers placed on the ground, above which the wooden framing of the house was raised.
**Bressomer, a "summer" or beam extending horizontally over a large opening, and sustaining the whole superstructure of wall.
***Cross-beam; diagonal to strengthen the wooden framework.

DOCUMENT 9
Sanitary Conditions

The London Assize of Nuisance *is a record of complaints of physical conditions within the City of London and of judicial proceedings taken to rectify them. The published record gives details of sixty-one cases heard between 1301 and 1431. The majority relate to roofing gutters which discharged storm water onto the streets below, and to objectionable cesspits within houses or close to adjacent properties.*

77. Robert le Barber complains that William le Mareschal has constructed a gutter (goterum) from which the water falls at his door (hostio), and has built a jetty (jacticium) above (ultra) his beams (trabes) opposite his door and windows (fenestrarum) which obstructs his view, and that his chimney (caminum) is too near the [plaintiff's] party-wall (parieti), causing danger of fire to his house. . . . Judgment that *within 40 days etc*. [William] remake the gutter in dispute . . . that he remove . . . the jetty . . . and that he rebuild his chimney. (March 1305)

396. The commonalty complain . . . that whereas Fisshyngwharf lane . . . used to be common to all citizens conveying their goods and merchandise . . . by horse and cart, William Trig has obstructed it with wooden stalls (trunci), wood and other things so that there is no longer access by it to the [river] Thames. . . . William comes and allows that the lane was . . . and still is . . . too narrow to be used by carts, which cannot turn in it . . . [Judgment: the jury finds for the defendant]. (February 1346)

324. William de Thorneye complains that when he hired workmen to build the cess-pit of a privy in his house . . . Andrew Aubrey and Joan his wife had the work prohibited. [They] say that the cess-pit is not built in accordance with the custom of the City, since the fence (claustura) is not 2½ ft. from their wall. . . . [T]he mayor and aldermen . . . having viewed the cess-pit, find that it is not to the nuisance of the [plaintiff], but sufficient and tolerable according to the custom of the City. (May 1333)

119. In a perambulation* made that day it was found that a stone gable (gabulam) of the house of Stephen de Abyndone . . . is ruinous, to

---

*A walk about their city to assess damage or to determine boundaries.

the danger of the neighbours and passers-by. The sheriff is ordered to warn [Stephen] to repair the wall *within 40 days etc.* (June 1307)

214. The mayor and commonalty complain . . . that whereas of old . . . a gutter (gutera) running under certain of the houses . . . so that the flow might cleanse the privy . . . Alice Wade has made a wooden pipe (pipam ligneam) connecting the seat (sedile) of the privy in her solar with the gutter, which is frequently stopped up by the filth therefrom, and the neighbours under whose houses the gutter runs are greatly inconvenienced by the stench. Judgment that she remove the pipe. (August 1314)

369. The commonalty complain . . . that [certain persons] have neglected to repair the pavement outside their tenements . . . in accordance with the City ordinance; with the result that it is broken and worn down (concavium) and crushed (quassatum) to the danger of both pedestrians and horsemen. . . . Judgment . . . that . . . each of them repair the pavement outside his own tenement. (July 1341)

394. The commonalty complains . . . that Walter de Eure has a vacant plot of land . . . which is unfenced, so that malefactors and disturbers of the king's peace and robbers lurk there by night and waylay passers-by, attacking, beating and wounding them and stealing their goods. . . . Judgment . . . that . . . he fence the plot of land. (Sept. 1345)

569. [Complaint] that Richard Bayser, [butcher], and Emma his wife have built a "skaldynghous"* in their tenement . . . in which they slaughter pigs and many other animals, and the water mixed with the blood and hair of the slaughtered animals, and with other filth from the washing (lotura) [of the carcasses], flows into the ditch or kennel in the street . . . causing a stench in many places there. [Judgment postponed.] (Feb. 1370)

617. Thomas Yonge and Alice his wife complain [that several people] built a forge (fabricam) of earth and timber, 40 ft. from the road . . . of which the chimney (tuellus) is lower by 12 ft. than it should be, and not built of plaster [mortar?] and stone as the custom of the City requires; and the blows of the sledge-hammers (grossis malleis) when the great pieces of iron called "Osmond" are being wrought into "brestplates," "quysers"** [cuirasses], "jambers" [protection for the arms] and other

---

*Scalding-house, a room in which utensils or carcasses of animals are scalded.
**Cuirass, another term for body protection; from "cuir"—leather—of which it was made.

pieces of armour, shake the stone and earthen party-walls of the [plain-tiffs'] house so that they are in danger of collapsing, and disturb the rest of the [plaintiffs] and their servants, day and night, and spoil the wine and ale in their cellar, and the stench of the smoke from the sea-coal used in the forge, penetrates their hall and chambers, so that whereas for-merly they could let the premises for 10 marks a year, they are now worth only 40s [shillings]. [The defendants] deny the [plaintiffs'] contention that chimneys ought to be built of stone and plaster, and high enough to cause no nuisance to the neighbouring tenements, and declare that good and honest men of any craft, viz. goldsmiths, smiths, pewterers, gold-beaters, grocers, pelters, marshals and armourers are at liberty to carry on their trade anywhere in the City, adapting their premises as is most con-venient for their work, and that according to ancient custom any feoffor [owner] may give . . . his property as well to craftsmen using great ham-mers as to others. [Furthermore] he has set up his anvil in what was for-merly the kitchen at a sufficient distance from the [plaintiffs'] messuage, and strengthened the chimney with mortar and clay and raised it by 6 ft. or more. (March 1378)

Source: Helena M. Chew and William Kellaway, eds., *London Assize of Nuisance, 1301–1431: A Calendar*, London Record Society Publications, vol. 10 (Leices-ter: London Record Society, 1973), pp. 16, 97, 79, 26, 45, 89, 96–97, 142, 160–61.

Construction of a Sewer in Cambridge, 1294

Thomas le Cuteler . . . of Cantebrige [Cambridge] and Margaret his wife complain of Gilbert Sys that he unfairly discharged (*levarit*) a sewer to the hurt of his [Thomas's] free tenement in Cantebridge after etc. and so unjustly, because the opening of that sewer lies bare against the walls, by reason of which the filth of that sewer causes the walls to decay so that they cannot hold them up. And also whereas Thomas and Margaret have been accustomed to let their house up to two marks a year, now no on [sic] is willing to hire it at more than one mark on account of the foul-ness of that sewer.

A sworn jury confirms that the sewage "rotted the 'grundsells' [wooden ground plate] and posts of the house, so that it will shortly fall to the ground." Gilbert is found guilt [*sic*] and Thomas and Margaret recover damages.

Source: W. M. Palmer, ed., *Cambridge Borough Documents*, vol. 1 (Cambridge, UK: Bowes and Bowes, 1931), pp. 9–10.

DOCUMENT 10
Street Life

Life on the streets of a medieval city is best seen through the records of the city's courts. It was violent; assault and murder were commonplace, and public control of urban development was at best spasmodic and ineffective. Citizens extended their properties into the street, narrowing it until traffic could no longer pass. Steps were cut in the highway to gain access to cellars and basements to the grave danger of pedestrians, and animals were slaughtered and even forges erected in the midst of the highway. Safety precautions, which would today have been normal, were ignored, and the loss of life, especially of the young, was horrendous. The following extracts from the London Eyre of 1244 throws some light on these conditions.

HOMICIDE

102. John Black "courector" was found strangled in his shop, and Thomas le Custurer who strangled him because of a wound John had dealt him, fled to the hospital of St. Thomas the Martyr across the Bridge, where he died of the wound. The value of Thomas's chattels is 12 d. [a deodand].

107. Robert of St. Osith struck Thomas de Haldham on the head with a staff, and killed him. He fled to a church [i.e., sought sanctuary] and acknowledged the deed and abjured the realm.* . . . He had chattels worth 4s.

142. Honorius le Rumunger killed Roger de Vilers with a knife, and fled to the church of St. Bartholomew, where he acknowledged the death and abjured the realm. He had no chattels and was in frankpledge in the ward of Joce fitz Peter.

---

*Left the country, swearing never to return.

Source: Helen M. Chew and Martin Weinbaum, eds., *The London Eyre of 1244*,
London Record Society Publications, vol. 6 (Leicester: London Record Society,
1970), pp. 42, 44, 46.

ACCIDENT

80. William son of Adam le Cost was crushed by a stone wall which
fell upon him, and was killed. Judgment: misadventure. No one is suspected. Value of the wall 1 mark.

81. [A] girl of two fell into a pan full of hot water and was scalded.
No one is suspected. Judgment: misadventure. Value of pan 6d.

91. [A] woman named Juliana of Camberwell fell from a solar in the
house of John de Exeport, and was crushed by the beams of the solar
which fell upon her, so that she died. No one is suspected. Judgment:
misadventure. Value of the planks 3s.

101. [A] man named William Aubyn fell into the Thames, pulled in
by a bucket which he had in his hand for drawing water, and was drowned.
No one is suspected. Judgment: misadventure. Value of the bucket 4d.

126. A boy was found crushed to death by a block of wood. No one
is suspected. Judgment: misadventure. Value of the block of wood 8d.

Source: Chew and Weinbaum, *The London Eyre*, pp. 33, 34, 38, 43, 51.

STREET OBSTRUCTIONS

350. A forge stands in the middle of the king's highway [in Farring-
ton Ward] opposite the New Temple and renders yearly to the king 12d.

351. Another forge stands in the king's highway opposite Shoe Lane
which renders to the king yearly 6d. by the hands of the same brethren.

364. Stephen of Bocking has a cellar and a pentice* above the steps
of his cellar to the nuisance [of the public]. Let it be demolished.

445. Andrew the Draper has a cellar the steps of which stand 3 ft. in
the king's highway. The same Andrew has a porch which is to the nuisance [of the public]. Let them be amended.

Source: Chew and Weinbaum, *The London Eyre*, pp. 137, 140, 148.

---

*Pentice, a lean-to shelter.

LONDON BRIDGE

344. The justices ask by what warrant the citizens of the London built upon London Bridge. The City answered that for the most part the fabric of the bridge was maintained by the alms of the citizens of London, and the wardens and brethren of the bridge built mostly from those alms upon the same bridge shops for the maintenance and improvement of the fabric; this did not however cause the deterioration of the street which is sufficiently wide everywhere and those crossing by the bridge do so the more securely and boldly for the buildings built thereon.

Source: Chew and Weinbaum, *The London Eyre*, p. 134.

DOCUMENT 11
Urban Finances

> *Most larger towns had an official in charge of its finances. He rendered an account to the city council every year, but the amount of money that he handled was usually very small. There was as a general rule no urban taxation, though there might have been a levy to cover an exceptional expenditure such as the building of the town walls. Maintenance of the streets was the obligation of those who lived along them. Many of the duties which were later to be discharged by the municipal authorities were performed by the parishes of which the city was made up. The chief source of municipal income was the property which it owned and from which it received a rent. Also important were the tolls received for the use of the market and the fines imposed for breaches of urban "laws."*
>
> *Below is the earliest treasurer's account for the borough of Cambridge for the year 1347. It shows how petty were the sources of income and how trifling the matters on which it was spent.*

RECEIPTS

20s. 9d. received of the old treasurers . . . [i.e., carried over from the previous year]

71s. received of the shops near the wall of the Augustine friars

20s. received of the new shops opposite the Gildhall

£5. 16. [*sic*] received of divers [various] men purchasing their freedom . . .

66s. 8d. received for divers fines in the Court

£15. 7s. 2d. received of the collectors of the hird penny for the armed men

72s. 11d. received for the tallage made for the archers

PAYMENTS

To the sheriff, for the new gift to him that he would not take victuals, £3; to
   the undersheriff, half mark*

To Sir Richard de Kelleshall for the new gift to him, 20s.; to his clerk, half
   mark; to his esquire, 2s.

To Sir William de Tjorp, justice, 40s.; to his clerk, 2s.

To Master John de Thoresby, for his fee, 20s.; in other expenses, 20s.; to the
   keepers of the horses of the Lord the King, half mark; in wine for the same,
   3½ d.; to John Tayllefor, messenger of the Lord the King, 2s.

To the messenger of the Lord the King, coming for the armed men, 40d.

To a page carrying the writ for the said armed men**

To a messenger carrying the writ for a ship, 2s. [meaning not clear]

Paid the mayor and the bailiffs for their fee, 30s.

To William de Horwood, clerk, for his fee, half mark

To the same William for a tallage tenth, half mark; to the same William from
   the tallage of wool, half mark

Paid William de Lolleworth and Thomas de Cottenham going to London for
   the Parliament, 20s.

In one cup sent to Matthew Hardy, 54s.

To John de Steping for three gaol deliveries, 18d.***

Paid John de Hilton for the write for the archers, 1 mark

In expenses of Thomas Wyth and William de Horwoode to Ely with the commission for having a ship, 2s. 2d.

In ale for the archers, 6d.

In clay bought for the Great Bridge, 2s.

In wine for the King's ministers, 8d.

In timber for the pillory,**** and divers expenses for the same, 12s. 9d.

---

*A mark was 6s. 8d., or two-thirds of a pound. It was a unit of value very com-
monly used.

**A legal writ authorizing the conscription of soldiers.

***A gaol delivery; the king's judges toured the royal prisons and heard the cases
against all the prisoners being held there, thus "delivering" or emptying the
gaols. Hanging was almost the only penalty inflicted on the guilty.

****Pillory, a wooden structure in which the guilty were fastened by the neck
and hands to a wooden cross and held up to the ridicule of the crowd.

To Johnde Hilton going to the admiral, 1 mark; in expenses of the same then and one horse for his esquire, 3s. 7d.; in expenses of the said John returning from the admiral, 14d.; paid the same John for his labor, 2 marks; to his esquire, 40d.

DOCUMENT 12
Citizenship

62. Be it known . . . that no one may be in the City as a citizen, and stay there and enjoy the law of the City for more than three nights, unless he finds two pledges [guarantors of his good behavior] and thus is in frankpledge; and if he stays one night longer in the City . . . and commits a felony or does anything in breach of the king's peace, and does not stand his trial, the alderman in whose ward he was, ought to be in mercy for harbouring him . . . when he was not in frankpledge.

209. The mayor and sheriffs are ordered to take into the king's hand all the houses and buildings which belonged to Bernard de Salette in the City of London, because he was a stranger [alien?] and not in lot and scot, and did not belong to the liberty of the City; and they are to enquire concerning the chattels which the said Bernard had and to answer for them.

Source: Chew and Weinbaum, *The London Eyre*, pp. 25, 86.

DOCUMENT 13
Urban Description and Illustration

While there is no lack of documentary sources for the conditions of life in the medieval city and also a small but growing body of archaeological evidence, we know little about how these cities looked. Little attempt was made to draw or paint them, and literary descriptions are few and not particularly informative. Yet there were illustrations and descriptions of a kind. Their weakness was that they were generalized. A city was not seen as a place with its own particular characteristics, its own personality. A description or illustration of one town could be reused with little change for another. Not until the early sixteenth century was any attempt made to portray the city as it actually was, distinct and different from every other.

DOCUMENT 14
The Visual Arts

*Little attempt was made before the fifteenth century to represent cities
visually. They appear in the paintings of the Italian Renaissance but are
usually so generalized that one cannot ascribe them to any particular
place.*

In 1493 Hartmann Schedel published his Liber Chronicarum, *a history
of the known world, profusely illustrated with woodcuts, among which is a
very large number of urban views.[1] The context assigns names to each of
them, but most are so alike that they must be dismissed as largely figments
of the engraver's imagination. Only a small number, including Nuremberg,
which was Schedel's birthplace, bear any relationship to reality.*

*In the second half of the sixteenth century this began to change. Just
as cartography, in the hands of the Dutch, became a precise science, so
panoramic views of cities acquired a greater precision and accuracy. For
this, it has been suggested, there was a good practical reason. Artillery
was beginning to play an increasingly important role in warfare, especially
in the sieges of cities, and it became important for artillery masters to have
some idea of the location of important buildings within any city that was
under siege. There was thus a ready market for panoramic urban views
with some pretension to accuracy.*

*Be that as it may, urban views without any accompanying text became
more numerous and increasingly accurate. They reached their highest
point in the vast, three-volume urban atlas, compiled in the late sixteenth
century by Braun and Hogenberg.[2] The Middle Ages had already ended,
but their record is the best representation of how European cities must
have looked soon after the Middle Ages had drawn to a close.*

DOCUMENT 15
Literary Descriptions

*Literary, in particular poetic, descriptions of cities became a literary genre
in classical times. Ausonius used it in his* Ordo Nobilium Urbium, *and
his example was followed, albeit unconsciously, by a few writers during the
Middle Ages. Most often the writer used it to praise the splendor and nobility of his native town. Such accounts were rarely accurate. In this age of
faith, their authors tended to stress the saints with whom their cities had been
associated and emphasized their relics and associated churches and miracles.*

This tradition, sometimes in verse, sometimes in prose, continued through the Middle Ages. It was peculiarly Italian, as if emphasizing its classical origins, and very few examples derive from north of the Alps. They were too greatly concerned with religious life and miraculous happenings and symbolism to dwell on topographical aspects of the city. A list of such writings was published by J. K. Hyde,[3] whose critical evaluation of them is of the highest value.

Among the exceptions to this generalization is William FitzStephen's description of London. It was written about 1200, and is known to us as a preface to his Life of Thomas à Becket (1118–1170), who was born in London. This account contains far more topographical material than is usual. Extracts from FitzStephen's record follow.

Lucian's Chester. The earliest urban description to be written in Great Britain is probably that in which the monk Lucian described the town of Chester.[4] It shares the characteristics of many of the Italian writings of this period. It is rhetorical, wordy, and moralizing. It opens with a religious exhortation, and continues with a discussion of the origin of the name "Chester." Lucian mentions that the city has walls and four gates, and that it stands above a beautiful river which has abundant fish and also permits ships from Aquitaine, Spain, Ireland, and Germany to unload their cargoes at the city.

The city has two straight streets, intersecting at its center, so that in plan it symbolizes the Cross. A market at the center represents the birth of Christ, the "Eternal Flood" (ad exemplum panis eterni de celo venientis). The churches of St. John the Baptist, St. Peter, St. Werburgh, and St. Michael lie respectively on the eastern, western, northern, and southern streets. Throughout the symbolism of these locations is emphasized.

This is followed by a sermon which calls upon the four dedicatory saints to protect the city and by a brief account of the other churches of Chester. Then comes a passage in praise of the abbey of St. Werburgh (now Chester Cathedral), before the author returns to the subject of the city's gates and the symbolism of the churches which lie near them. This eulogy concludes with a long discourse on the roles of priest and monk and lavishes praise on those to be met with in Chester.

DOCUMENT 16
FitzStephen's Description of London

Among the noble and celebrated cities of the world [is] that of London, the capital of the kingdom of the English. . . . Higher than all the rest does it lift its head. It is happy in the healthiness of its air; in its observance of

Christian practice; in the strength of its fortifications; in its natural situa-tion; in the honour of its citizens; and in the modesty of its matrons.

In the church of St. Paul there is the episcopal seat. . . . As regards the practice of Christian worship, there are in London and its suburbs thir-teen greater conventual churches and, besides these, one hundred and twenty-six lesser parish churches.[5]

It has on the east the Palatine castle, very great and strong: the keep and walls rise from very deep foundations and are fixed with a mortar tempered by the blood of animals. On the west there are two castles [i.e., Baynard's and Muntifichet, both now entirely lost] very strongly fortified, and from these there runs a high and massive wall with seven double gates and with towers along the north at regular intervals. London was once also walled and turreted on the south, but the mighty Thames, so full of fish, has with the sea's ebb and flow washed against, loosened, and thrown down those walls in the course of time. Upstream to the west there is the royal palace [i.e., Whitehall] which is conspicuous above the river, a building incomparable in its ramparts and bulwarks. It is about two miles from the city and joined thereto by a populous suburb.

Everywhere outside the houses of those living in the suburbs, and ad-jacent to them, are the spacious and beautiful gardens of the citizens, and these are planted with trees. Also there are on the north side pastures and pleasant meadow lands through which flow streams wherein the turn-ing of mill-wheels makes a cheerful sounds [sic]. Very near lies a great for-est [probably Epping Forest is meant] with woodland pastures in which there are the lairs of wild animals: stags, fallow deer, wild boars and bulls. The tilled lands of the city are not of barren gravel, but fat Asian plains that yield luxuriant crops and fill the tillers' barns with the sheaves of Ceres [the goddess of the harvest, hence "cereal"].

There are also outside London on the north side excellent suburban wells with sweet, wholesome and clear water that flows rippling over the bright stones. Among these are Holywell, Clerkenwell and St. Clement's Well, which are all famous. These are frequented by great numbers and much visited by the students from the schools and by the young men of the city, when they go out for fresh air on summer evenings.

The city is honoured by her men, glorious in its arms, and so populous that during the terrible wars of King Stephen's reign [1135–52] the men going forth from it to battle were reckoned as twenty thousand armed horsemen and sixty thousand foot-soldiers, all equipped for war.[6] The citizens of London are regarded as conspicuous above all others for their polished manners, for their dress and for the good tables which they keep.

[There follows an account of the schools in London.]

Immediately outside one of the gates there is a field which is smooth both in fact and in name. On every sixth day of the week, unless it be a major feast-day, there takes place there a famous exhibition of fine horses for sale. Earls, barons and knights, who are in the town, and many citizens come out to see or to buy. It is pleasant to see the high-stepping palfreys with their gleaming coats, as they go through their paces, putting down their feet alternately on one side together. Next, one can see the horses suitable for esquires, . . . [and then] there are the sumpter-horses, powerful and spirited; and after them there are the war-horses.

By themselves in another part of the field stand the goods of the countryfolk: implements of husbandry, swine with long flanks, cows with full udders, oxen of immense size, and woolly sheep. There also stand the mares fit for plough, some big with foal, and others with brisk young colts closely following them. [There follows an account of the Smithfield horse fair.]

To this city from every nation under heaven merchants delight to bring their trade by sea. The Arabian sends gold; the Sabaean spice and incense. The Scythian brings arms, and from the rich, fat lands of Babylon comes oil of palms. The Nile sends precious stones; the men of Norway and Russia, furs and sables; nor is China absent with purple silk. The Gauls come with their wines. [This fabrication appears to have derived from a classical source; it is grossly exaggerated.]

To this it may be added that almost all the bishops, abbots and magnates of England are in a sense citizens and freemen of London, having their own splendid town-houses. In them they live, and spend largely, when they are summoned to great councils by the king or by their metropolitan, or drawn thither by their private affairs.

Source: See William FitzStephen, "Description of the City of London," in *English Historical Documents 1042–1089*, 13 vols., ed. D. C. Douglas and George W. Greenaway (London: Eyre & Spottiswoode, 1953), 2:956–60.

DOCUMENT 17
Two English Towns: Lincoln and Nottingham

In 1533 John Leland, librarian to King Henry VIII, was commissioned by his master to tour England and Wales, visiting religious houses and reporting on their manuscripts and other treasures. In the course of his travels he gathered notes which were to become the basis of The Itinerary of John Leland. *This work presents a picture of England and of much of Wales as they were early in the sixteenth century. His accounts of two English cities are given here: Lincoln and Nottingham. They show us what these cities were like at the end of the Middle Ages. These extracts show how practical were the urban descriptions of Leland, and how free they were from the religiosity of Lucian and of the Italian topographers. There were very few towns which he did not visit and describe, and his work is a mine of topographical information. There are several editions of Leland's work, but the most accessible is* The Itinerary of John Leland *as edited by Lucy Toulmin Smith.*

Lincoln

He first describes very briefly the city's gates and encircling walls. The original city lay on the summit of a hill, which drops steeply to the river Witham. It was founded by the Romans as Lindum, and there are some architectural remains from this period, including the north gate, or Newport Arch.

It is very likely that in old tyme the toppe of the hille only was waullid and inhabitid.

The ryver of Lincoln breking into 2. armes [branches] a very litle above the toun passith thoroug the lower part of Lincoln toune yn 2. severalle partes of the south ende of the toune very commodiusly, and over eche of them is an archid bridge of stone to passe thoroug the principal streate.

The lesser arme lyith more southly, and the bridg over it is of one arche. The bigger armes *fert cymbas piscatorias*. Gote bride [bridge] to passe over the lesser arme. Highe bridge to passe over the great arme.

A very goodly house longging to Sutton is hard on the north syde of S. Annes chirch yarde.

A litle above Gote bridge, on the este side of the high streat, is a fair guild haul, longging to S. Annes chirch e reigione, of the fundation of Bitlyndon and Sutton, marchants.

I hard say that the lower parte of Lincoln town was al marisch [marshy], and won be policy, and inhabitid for the commodite of the water.

This part of the toune is caullid Wikerford [Wigford]: and yn it be a 11. paroche chirches, one there I saw in clene ruine, [be]side the other xi.

The White Freres [i.e., Carmelites] were on the west side of the high streat [in] Wikerf[ord].

There be in the residew of the toun, as in the north parte apon the hille, xiij. paroche chirchis yet usid. I saw a rolle wherin I countid that ther were xxxviij. paroche chirchis yn Lincoln.

There goith a commune fame [report] that there were ons 52. paroche chirchis yn Lincoln cite, and the suburbes of it.

[He then describes the suburbs of the city.]

It is easy to be perceivid that the toune of Lincoln hath be notably buildid at 3. tymes [i.e., three separate building periods]. The first building was yn the very toppe of the hille, the oldest part wherof inhabited in the Britans tyme, was the northethest part of the hille, directly withoute Newport gate, the diches wherof yet remayne and great tokens of the old towne waulles buildid with stone taken oute of [the] diche by it: for al the top of Lincoln Hille is quarre ground. This is now a suburbe to Newporte gate: in the which is now no notable thing but the ruines of the house of the Augustine Freres on the south side, and a paroch chirch of the est side: and not far from the chyrch garth apperith a great ruine of a toure [tower] in the olde towne waulle. . . . Much Romaine mony is found yn the northe [fieldes] beyond this old Lincoln. After the destruction of this old Lincoln men began to fortifie the souther parte of the hille, new diching, waulling and gating it, and so was new Lincoldn made out of a pece of old Lincoln by the Saxons.

Source: See John Leland, *The Itinerary of John Leland*, ed. L. Toulmin Smith, 5 vols. (Carbondale: Southern Illinois University Press, 1964), 1:29–31.

Nottingham

Nottingham is booth a large toun and welle buildid for tymber and plaster, and standith stately on a clyminge [i.e., steep] hille.

The market place and streate both for the building on the side of it, for the very great widenes of the streat, and the clene paving of it, is the most fairest withowt exception of al Inglande.

Ther be 3 paroches chirches; but the chirch of S. Mary is excellent. . . . Southeward as to the water side be great clifes and rokkes of stones, that be large and very good to build with, and many houses sette on the toppes of them: and at the botom of them be great caves wher many stones hath bene diggid out for buildinge yn the toune, and these caves be partly usid for dwellynge howses, and partly for cerllars and store houses.

Ther hath beene 3. houses of freres, as I remembre, whereof 2. stoode toward the west of the towne and not far from the castelle.

The towne hath be meately welle wallid with stone, and hath had dyvers gates; much of the waul is now down, and the gates saving 2. or 3.

There is no suburbe over the stone bridge . . . on the south side of the toune.

The castelle of Notingham stondith on a rocky hille as on the newest side of the towne; and Line ri[ver] goith by the rootes of it.

There is [a great] likelihood that the castelle was buildid of stones taken owt of the rokke and the great diches of it. [There follows a very detailed description of Nottingham Castle.]

Source: See Leland, *The Itinerary of John Leland*, 1:94–96.

NOTES

1. Hartmann Schedel, *Liber Chronicarum* (Nuremberg, 1493).

2. Georg Braun and Franz Hogenberg, *Civitates Orbis Terrarum*, 6 vols., 1572–1618. Twenty-four illustrations were republished as *Old European Cities: Thirty-two Sixteenth-Century City Maps and Texts from the "Civitates Orbis Terrarum" of Georg Braun and Franz Hogenberg*, ed. Ruthardt Oehme (London: Thames and Hudson, 1965), and there is a modern facsimile edition of the whole work, published as *Civitates Orbis Terrarum: "The Towns of the World,"* *1572–1618*, ed. R. A. Skelton (Cleveland, OH: World Pub. Co., 1966).

3. J. K. Hyde, "Medieval Descriptions of Cities," *Bulletin of the John Rylands Library, Manchester*, vol. 48 (1965–1966): 308–40.

4. *Liber Luciani de Laude Cestrie* [Lucian's Book in Praise of Chester], ed. M. V. Taylor, *The Record Society of Lancashire and Cheshire*, vol. 64 (1912).

5. This total for the number of parishes is approximately correct, but includes some which lay outside the line of the Roman/medieval walls.

6. This estimate of the number of armed men which London could put into the field is grossly exaggerated, and is a good example of the unreliability of medieval figures. The total population of the city could not about 1200 have exceeded 10,000.

GLOSSARY

Ale: An alcoholic drink prepared by fermenting vegetable grains, usually malted barley; differs from beer in not having been flavored with hops.

Bastide: Small, fortified town, built in southern and southwestern France by the kings of both France and Great Britain; the latter was duke of Aquitaine and thus held this part of France.

Beer: An alcoholic drink prepared by fermenting vegetable grains, usually malted barley; differs from ale in having been flavored with hops.

Bourgeoisie: The body of the inhabitants of a "bourg" or borough; usually restricted to its middle class of traders and craftsmen.

Bread-grains: The cereal grains usually used in making bread because they contain gluten, which allows the bread to rise; preeminently wheat, but also barley, rye, and on rare occasions, oats.

Burg, Burh: A town, usually referring to a town of early date, for example, Anglo-Saxon.

Burgage plot: Small, clearly defined unit of urban land, suitable for building a single house and/or shop.

Capital: The central place of a civitas.

Central-place theory: The theory that there is an even scatter of "central places" (villages or towns) over any relatively homogeneous surface of the land; that smaller or "lower order" central places are denser on the ground than larger, and that the range of urban functions is related to the size of these units.

Cesspit: Pit or hole in the ground dug to receive the effluent from a toilet, usually domestic.

Charter: A document, usually of parchment, in which its author grants prescribed lands, rights, or privileges, typically those of urban self-government.

City-state: Small, sovereign territory, focused in a single dominant city; a term used chiefly for those of classical antiquity.

Civitas: A tribal territory of the period of the Roman Empire; many survived as a Roman administrative unit and in many instances as the territory subject to a medieval bishop.

Contado: Italian for "county"; a restricted area subject administratively to a count; Fr. Comte.

Deodand: Literally "given to God." This was the value of any inanimate object through which someone had lost his or her life, for example, a broken ladder. It was assessed by the coroner at the judicial inquest, and was payable by its owner to the king, who was presumed to give it to some charitable purpose.

Domesday Book: A record ordered by King William I in 1086 for as much of England as then lay under his control, of the ownership of land and the possession of resources.

Eyre: Judicial circuit, as in "Justices in Eyre"; hence the court that made a progress through the country.

Fair: A gathering of traders, usually lasting several days and rarely held more than twice a year; from the eleventh to the fourteenth centuries, the chief medium in the long-distance trade of Europe.

Frankpledge: Every person in medieval England was presumed to belong to a Frankpledge, which was jointly responsible for the good behavior of each member. Periodically checks were made on membership; this was the "View of Frankpledge."

Geld: Literally, money; hence, tax.

Ghetto: A name deriving from a quarter in medieval Venice in which most of the city's Jews lived; by extension, any part of a town in which a particular ethnic minority settled.

Gild, Guild: An association of people for an economic, social, or religious purpose, or for some combination of these ends.

Gild Merchant: The association of traders in any one town, which generally preceded the formation of individual gilds.

Hanse: An association of people for a particular purpose; specifically the association of North German merchants trading in the Baltic Sea: the German Hanse.

Hearth: A household, or the group of people living together in a single home. It was used as a unit for determining taxation.

Hinterland: Literally the "land behind"; hence the territory served by a particular town or port.

Hospital: During the Middle Ages an endowed institution that cared for the aged and impotent, and not necessarily the sick.

Hospitallers: A knightly order of the Hospital of St. John of Jerusalem whose task it was to protect and safeguard pilgrims to the holy sites.

Jetty: The projection of an upper floor of a house over a lower; possible only in timber frame construction.

Just price: The theory that the price of a commodity should reflect the labor of producing it, and that no attempt should be made to profit from scarcity or need; the opposite to market price.

Lammas: August 1st, seen as the end of harvest, when the open fields were made available for the communal grazing of the animals of the community.

Lavatorium: The place in a monastery (usually in the cloister and close to the refectory), where hands were washed before meals; by extension, a toilet.

Market: A gathering, usually on a preordained day of the week, of peasants and townsfolk for the purpose of exchanging urban and rural products.

Osemond, Osmund: A high quality iron or wrought iron, chiefly made in Scandinavia from iron ores that were relatively free of harmful impurities; imported by some western European countries and used for making steel.

Parish: The smallest unit of ecclesiastical jurisdiction and subject to a single priest; of variable extent. The urban parish might cover only a few acres; the rural, several square miles.

Pathogen: The disease-bearing microorganism that is passed from one patient to another by means of a vector or carrier, the flea in the case of the Plague.

Pentice: A projecting or overhanging roof, sometimes extending over the street from a house in order to give shelter to a shop or basement stairway.

Plague: Strictly *pestis pestiferous*, which is spread by the symbiotic relationship of flea and rat; correctly used for the "Black Death" of 1348–1350, but also for several later outbreaks in Europe. Also used, incorrectly, for other severe epidemic diseases.

Planted town: A town resulting from the deliberate act of foundation by a territorial lord; usually, but not always, planned on a gridiron pattern.

Porticullis: An iron grill set vertically in a defensive gatehouse; can be lifted to allow passage; frequently found in urban gates.

Primate city: The theory that in any extensive area there is always one urban center that is very much larger than all others, and that there is a mathematical relationship that approximately defines this relationship.

Relief: Feudal payment for land or other concession.

Sea coal: The name used to distinguish mineral coal from "*char* coal." So named because it was imported into London by sea from the coastal coalfields of Northumberland and Durham.

Sheriff: From the Middle English "shire-reeve," meaning the king's chief representative and administrative officer in each county. The office survives, but his duties are now mainly honorific.

Studs: The wooden framework of a "half-timbered" house or other building. The intervening spaces would have been filled in with either wattle-and-daub (the pliable branches of the willow tree, woven together and daubed with clay) or brick.

Synoecism: The coming together of the inhabitants of the villages in a relatively small area to form a single city or *polis*.

Tallage: A tax or levy imposed by feudal authority; the implication is usually that it is arbitrary and unauthorized.

Tan, Taw: The process by which skins are converted into leather by soaking them in a bath of tannin, a complex chemical of vegetable origin. Oak bark was commonly used.

Templars: The Order of the Knights of the Temple; founded during the twelfth century for the purpose of protecting the Temple of

Jerusalem and the other holy places and the pilgrims frequenting them.

Tower house: Fortified house built within a city for the protection of the family which inhabited it; chiefly in Italy, where the tower houses were built to very great heights, but also to be found widely in cities and also the countryside of western Europe.

Tuberculosis: Disease of the lungs, brought on mainly by living in a damp and dirt-ridden environment, such as that found in many medieval towns.

Typhus: A disease commonly met with in damp and dirty living conditions and resulting in a high mortality; its vector was the body louse; also known as "trench" fever and "gaol" fever.

ANNOTATED BIBLIOGRAPHY

General Works and Bibliographies

Clark, Peter, and D. M. Palliser, eds. *The Cambridge Urban History of Britain. Vol. 1, 600–1540.* Cambridge, UK, and New York: Cambridge University Press, 2000. An up-to-date, multiauthor work, of the highest value.

Graves, Edgar B., ed. *A Bibliography of English History to 1485: Based on "The Sources and Literature of English History from the Earliest Times to about 1485" by Charles Gross.* Oxford and New York: Oxford University Press, 1975. Chapter 20, pp. 700–750, deals with the English city.

Lobel, Mary D. *The British Atlas of Historic Towns.* 2 vols. New York: Oxford University Press, 1969–1979.

Martin, G. H., and Sylvia McIntyre, eds. *A Bibliography of British and Irish Municipal History.* Vol. 1. Leicester, UK: Leicester University Press, 1972. A critical bibliography, of the highest value.

Singer, Charles Joseph, ed. *A History of Technology.* Vol. 2. Oxford: Clarendon Press, 1956. Old, but still of great value on medieval technology and urban material culture.

Relevant Periodicals

Annales: Economies—Societes—Civilisations (Paris)

Kwartalnik Histroii Kultury Materialnej (Warsaw)

Vierteljahrschrift fur ekonomische und kulturische Geschichte (city of publication unknown)

Origins of Urbanism

Ammann, Hektor. *Wirtschaft und Lebensraum der mittelalterlichen Kleinstadt: I. Rheinfelden.* Frick: A. Fricker, 1948.

Aston, Michael, and James Bond. *The Landscape of Towns.* London: Dent, 1976.

Ballard, Adolphus. *British Borough Charters, 1042–1216.* Cambridge, UK: Cambridge University Press, 1913.

———. "The Law of Breteuil." *English Historical Review* 30, 120 (October 1915): 646–58.

Ballard, Adolphus, and James Tait. *British Borough Charters, 1216–1307.* Cambridge, UK: Cambridge University Press, 1923.

Beresford, Maurice Warwick. *New Towns of the Middle Ages: Town Plantation in England, Wales, and Gascony.* New York: Praeger, 1967.

Collis, John. *Oppida: Earliest Towns North of the Alps.* Sheffield, UK: Department of Prehistory and Archaeology, University of Sheffield, 1984.

Cunliffe, Barry. "The Origins of Urbanization in Britain." In *Oppida, the Beginnings of Urbanisation in Barbarian Europe: Papers Presented to a Conference at Oxford, October 1975.* Edited by Barry W. Cunliffe and Trevor Rowley. Supplementary Series vol. 11. Oxford: British Archaeological Reports, 1976, pp. 135–61.

Dobson, R. B. "Urban Decline in Late Medieval England." In *Transactions of the Royal Historical Society.* London: The Royal Historical Society, 1977, pp. 1–22.

Ennen, Edith. *Frühgeschichte der Europäischen Stadt.* Bonn: L. Rörscheid, 1953.

Maitland, F. W. *Township and Borough: With an Appendix of Notes Relating to the History of Cambridge.* Cambridge, UK: Cambridge University Press, 1964. A classic study by the greatest of all legal historians.

Meyer, Erwin T. "Boroughs." In *The English Government at Work, 1327–1336.* Edited by James F. Willard and William Alfred Morris. Cambridge, MA: Mediaeval Academy of America, 1950, pp. 105–41.

Miller, Edward, and John Hatcher. *Medieval England: Towns, Commerce, and Crafts, 1086–1348.* London and New York: Longman, 1995. An excellent summary with a good bibliography.

Postan, M. M., and H. J. Habakkuk, eds. "Trade and Industry of the Middle Ages." In *The Cambridge Economic History of Europe.* Vol. 2. Cambridge, UK: Cambridge University Press, 1952.

Rorig, Fritz. *The Medieval Town.* Berkeley: University of California Press, 1967. A translation of a German classic.

Russell, Josiah C. "Late Ancient and Medieval Population." *Transactions of the American Philosophical Society*, n.s. 48, 3 (1958). Good information on the urban population.

———. *Medieval Regions and Their Cities.* Bloomington: Indiana University Press, 1972.

———. "The Metropolitan City Region of the Middle Ages." *Journal of Regional Science* 2 (1960): 55–70.

Sjoberg, Gideon. *The Preindustrial City, Past and Present.* Glencoe, IL: Free Press, 1960.

Trenholme, Norman Maclaren. *The English Monastic Boroughs: A Study in Medieval History.* University of Missouri Studies 2. Columbia: University of Missouri, 1927.

van Werveke, H. "The Rise of the Towns." In *The Cambridge Economic History of Europe.* Vol. 3. Edited by M. M. Postan and H. J. Habakkuk. Cambridge, UK: Cambridge University Press, 1963.

Particular Regions

Conzen, M.R.G. *Alnwick, Northumberland: A Study in Town-Plan Analysis.* Institute of British Geographers 27. London: George Philip, 1960.

Hill, Francis. *Medieval Lincoln.* Cambridge, UK: Cambridge University Press, 1948. The first volume of a magisterial study of an English city.

Leighly, John. *The Towns of Medieval Livonia.* New York: Johnson Reprint Corp., 1968. A valuable study of town foundation in eastern Europe.

Lobel, M. D. *The Borough of Bury St. Edmund's: A Study in the Government and Development of a Monastic Town.* Oxford: Clarendon Press, 1935. An important study of the government of a town that had grown up at the gate of a monastery.

Morris, Rupert H. *Chester in the Plantagenet and Tudor Reigns.* Chester, UK: Printed for the author, 1893. A good case study of urban streets and utilities.

Pirenne, Henri. *Early Democracies in the Low Countries: Urban Society and Political Conflict in the Middle Ages and the Renaissance.* New York: Harper & Row, 1963. A good translation of a standard work on the Flemish cities.

Planitz, Hans. *Die Deutsche Stadt im Mittelalter: von der Römerzeit Bis Zu Den Zunftkämpfen.* Graz: Böhlau-Verlag, 1965.

Raftis, J. A. *A Small Town in Late Medieval England: Godmanchester, 1278–1400.* Studies and Texts 53. Toronto: Pontifical Institute of Mediaeval Studies, 1982.

Reynolds, Susan. *An Introduction to the History of English Medieval Towns.* Oxford: Clarendon Press, 1977. Very good on city government and administration.

Tait, James. *The Medieval English Borough: Studies on Its Origins and Constitutional History.* New York: Barnes and Noble, 1968.

Thrupp, Sylvia L. *The Merchant Class of Medieval London, 1300–1500.* Chicago: University of Chicago Press, 1948.

Urry, William. *Canterbury under the Angevin Kings.* London: Athlone Press, 1967. An intimate study, based upon a voluminous documentation, by the cathedral archivist.

Williams, Gwyn A. *Medieval London: From Commune to Capital.* London: University of London, Athlone Press, 1963.

Urban Social History

Belock, Julius. *Bevölkerungsgeschichte Italiens.* 3 vols. Berlin: De Gruyter, 1937.

Blair, John, and Nigel Ramsay. *English Medieval Industries: Craftsmen, Techniques, Products.* London: Hambledon Press, 1991.

Brooke, C.N.L. "The Missionary at Home: The Church in the Towns, 1000–1250." In *The Mission of the Church and the Propagation of the Faith: Papers Read at the Seventh Summer Meeting and the Eighth Winter Meeting of the Ecclesiastical History Society.* Edited by G. J. Cuming. Studies in Church History 6. Cambridge, UK: Cambridge University Press, 1970, pp. 59–83.

Chevalier, Louis. *Labouring Classes and Dangerous Classes in Paris during the First Half of the Nineteenth Century.* London: Routledge and Kegan Paul, 1973. A translation of a French classic on the medieval underworld.

Clark, Peter, and Paul Slack, eds. *Crisis and Order in English Towns, 1500–1700: Essays in Urban History*. Toronto: University of Toronto Press, 1972.

Colvin, H. M. "Domestic Architecture and Town Planning." In *Medieval England*. Edited by Austin Lane Poole. 2 vols. Oxford: Clarendon Press, 1958, 1:37–87.

Gies, Joseph, and Frances Gies. *Life in a Medieval City*. New York: Crowell, 1973.

Gooder, Arthur. *Criminals, Courts and Conflict*. Edited by Trevor John. Published privately, 2001. A valuable study of criminals and litigation in medieval Coventry.

Knowles, Clifford Cyril, and P. H. Pitt. *The History of Building Regulation in London, 1189–1972: With an Account of the District Surveyors' Association*. London: Architectural Press, 1972.

McCall, Andrew. *The Medieval Underworld*. London: H. Hamilton, 1979.

Mollat, Michel, and Philippe Wolff. *The Popular Revolutions of the Late Middle Ages*. London: Allen & Unwin, 1973.

Mols, Roger. *Introduction à la démographie historique des villes d'Europe du XIVe au XVIIIe siècle*. Gembloux: J. Duculot, 1954–56. The definitive study of urban population during the Middle Ages.

Owen, Dorothy Mary. *Church and Society in Medieval Lincolnshire*. History of Lincolnshire 5. Lincoln: History of Lincolnshire Committee, 1971.

Platt, Colin. *The English Medieval Town*. London: Secker & Warburg, 1976.

Rubin, Miri. *Charity and Community in Medieval Cambridge*. Cambridge, UK: Cambridge University Press, 1987. An in-depth study of the medieval underworld.

Sabine, Ernest L. "Butchering in Mediaeval London." *Speculum* 8, 3 (July 1933): 335–53.

———. "City Cleaning in Mediaeval London." *Speculum* 12, 1 (January 1937): 19–43.

———. "Latrines and Cesspools of Medieval London." *Speculum* 9, 3 (July 1934): 303–21.

Salusbury-Jones, Goronwy Tidy. *Street Life in Medieval England*. Oxford: Pen-in-Hand, 1948.

Sapori, Armando. *The Italian Merchant in the Middle Ages.* Translated by Patricia Ann Kennen. New York: Norton, 1970.

Schofield, John. *The Building of London: From the Conquest to the Great Fire.* London: British Museum Publications, 1983.

Thorndike, Lynn. "Sanitation, Baths, and Street-Cleaning in the Middle Ages and Renaissance." *Speculum* 3, 3 (April 1928): 192–203.

Thrupp, Sylvia L. "Towns." In *Early Medieval Society.* Edited by Sylvia L. Thrupp. New York: Appleton-Century-Crofts, 1967.

Ziegler, Philip. *The Black Death.* New York: John Day Co., 1969.

Urban Archaeology

Barley, M. W. *European Towns: Their Archaeology and Early History.* London and New York: Council for British Archaeology, 1977.

Barlow, Frank, and Martin Biddle. *Winchester in the Early Middle Ages: An Edition and Discussion of the Winton Domesday.* Winchester Studies 1. Oxford: Clarendon Press, 1977.

Carver, Martin O. H. *Medieval Worcester: An Archaeological Framework; Reports, Surveys, Texts, and Essays.* Transactions of the Worcestershire Archaeological Society, 3d ser. 7. Worcester, UK: Worcestershire Archaeological Society, 1980.

Grant, Lindy. *Medieval Art, Architecture, and Archaeology in London.* Conference Transactions for the Year. Oxford: British Archaeological Association, 1990.

Haslam, Jeremy. *Anglo-Saxon Towns in Southern England.* Chichester, UK: Phillimore, 1984.

———. *Early Medieval Towns in Britain, c. 700 to 1140.* Shire Archaeology 45. Cincinnati: Shire Publications, 1985.

INDEX

About the Author

NORMAN POUNDS is an eminent historian of the medieval period and the author of numerous works, including *The Economic History of Medieval Europe, Hearth and Home: A History of Material Culture*, and *The Culture and History of the English People: Iron Age to the Industrial Revolution*.

FIRST DE

Praise for *First Defense*

I first met Dave Hopkins years ago through seeking continued additional personal training, specifically in krav maga. From the many training sessions and time we spent together I learned that Dave was a genuine and sincere person with many diverse life experiences. I was impressed enough with Dave's training techniques that I had him train my son in krav maga as well, and continue to provide his services to people who are interested. I think Dave has written an excellent book covering many areas that can assist people in getting through life.
—Henry Sanchez, US Army professional

First Defense is simply superb—its content transcends the psychological and physiological domains, and it is truly practical in nature. This book has the power to save your life. In the threatening world we wake up to every day, the enemy exists—in movie theaters, schools, churches, parking lots, and restaurants. While we don't have any control over their desires, motives, or actions, we do have the choice to embrace our anxiety and harness the amazing acuity it provides us in fight-or-flight situations. *First Defense* is a technical manual, not in terms of any single fighting technique or martial art, but in the art of transforming our thoughts, feelings, and behaviors into a collective bundle of highly tuned instincts that allows us to fully *experience* anxiety-producing situations by *living in the moment*. This book is a must-read for any soldier or service member going off to combat whose life depends on one's situational awareness and capacity to act on perceived threats instinctively. As the author states, there is no playbook for combative situations. Israeli krav maga is representative of this mantra, and combined with the life practices this book teaches, good people can take back the ground that the enemy infringes upon daily. David Hopkins is a uniquely credible author and patriot who has spent a career and lifetime defending his country. His psychoanalytical insight is rivaled only by his passion to educate and instruct . . . and his undeniable skill to inflict pain on the enemy.
—CPT Zeke Kelly, US Army

First Defense is a brilliant compilation that fuses the mind-body nexus as it concerns the art of hand combat—self-defense. Too often "experts" in the art of self-defense and hand combat dismiss or do not understand the psychophysiological dynamics at play when one is engaged in combat, especially hand combat. Dr. Hopkins does a brilliant job explaining the psychology that affects performance. A keen awareness of these dynamics drastically puts the combatant in charge of the situation, rather than a defender who is always one step behind the opposition. The body cannot be trained until the mind is trained; *First Defense* explains that perfectly!

> —Dale A. Comstock, Special Forces (ret), 3rd Special Forces Group (Green Beret), 1st Special Forces Operational Detachment (Delta Force), 82nd Airborne Division Airborne Infantryman Long Range Reconnaissance Platoon, author of *American Badass*

The area of anxiety and instinct is quite fascinating, and the idea of using your instincts to harness the energy of anxiety that David Hopkins examines in *First Defense* is worthy of study. This book is a welcome addition to the self-defense literature available, as it looks at an area not often, if ever, addressed. This guide on making good decisions in threatening situations with your built-in survival signals fills the void between awareness and physical self-defense skills. The combination of academic research with practical exercises makes this a book to not only read for knowledge, but to use to increase your own sensory awareness, better process information, and make better decisions under threatening situations. I recommend not only studying it, but also incorporating the lessons into your own training.

> —Alain B. Burrese, JD, former US Army, author, safety and self-defense instructor

FIRST
DEFENSE

Anxiety and Instinct for Self-Protection

DAVID HOPKINS, PHD

YMAA Publication Center, Inc.
Wolfeboro, NH USA

YMAA Publication Center, Inc.
PO Box 480
Wolfeboro, NH 03894
800 669-8892 • www.ymaa.com • info@ymaa.com

ISBN: 9781594393426 (print) • ISBN: 9781594393433 (ebook)

Publisher's Cataloging in Publication

Hopkins, David, Jr.

First defense : anxiety and instinct for self-protection / David Hopkins. — Wolfeboro, NH USA : YMAA Publication Center, Inc., [2015]

pages : illustrations ; cm.

ISBN: 978-1-59439-342-6 (print) ; 978-1-59439-343-3 (ebook)
"Make good decisions in threatening situations with your built-in survival signals"—Cover.
Includes bibliography and index.
Summary: We all have a built in weapon system, called anxiety. This book will teach you how to use anxiety as a personal weapon to achieve awareness and avoidance, which are the first two steps learned in self-defense preparedness training, making you more effective and more successful at facing a physical or mental enemy, no matter how large or small that may be.—Publisher.

1. Self-protective behavior. 2. Self-preservation. 3. Self-defense—Psychological aspects. 4. Instinct. 5. Intuition. 6. Anxiety. 7. Crime prevention—Psychological aspects. 8. Fear of crime—Psychological aspects. 9. Violence—Psychological aspects. 10. Victims of crimes—Psychology. 11. Women—Crimes against—Prevention. 12. Children—Crimes against—Prevention. I. Title.

BF397.5.S45 H66 2015   2015947897
155.9/1—dc23   1510

Contents

Foreword

THERE ARE COUNTLESS BOOKS ON THE MARKET today dealing with self-defense. What makes this book unique is the combination of well-grounded psychological concepts relating to combative situations and the practical experience of David in terms of applying these concepts to real-world situations, including threat conditions at the most intense level.

Having served in organizations tasked with applying a combination of both tactical and psychological principles aimed at combatting terrorism and other threats, I can attest to the effectiveness of the methods in David's book. Further, he has designed a no-nonsense training plan that can be used to learn these skills in a short period of time. This book is more than a combination of theories. It is a guide for developing the skill set to literally save lives in combative situations.

David has designed a training program that guides the reader in developing the situational awareness and psychological preparedness for effectively avoiding and, if need be, engaging the enemy. His training plan is well grounded in psychological principles and techniques, tactics and procedures applied in professional security, and other important activities involving assessing and diffusing threats of the most serious kind. In addition to providing instruction, David also provides real-world examples of his own experiences, facing threats both in professional and personal situations. He does so in a humble and specific manner, helping the reader to put the concepts and techniques into practical context. The nature of the experiences and the way he provides them underline the seasoned experience he has as a professional in his unique blend of fields. This combination of detailed instruction coupled with the sharing of these experiences make this book a unique manual for anyone wanting to readily learn these techniques in order to protect themselves and others.

For all of these reasons, this book belongs in the library of any martial artist, law enforcement and military professional, close protection agent, and anyone interested in augmenting their warrior skills.

Tomer Israel
Former captain, Matkal (Israeli Delta Force)
and Shin Bet (Israeli Secret Service and Internal Intelligence),
chief of Israeli Tactical School

Introduction

AS YOU READ THESE WORDS, SLOW YOURSELF down and concentrate fully on your field of vision, not only the words you are reading, but the edges of the pages, beyond the edges to what is in your field of vision just beyond each side of the book, and then out even farther to your peripheral vision in all directions. You are now more aware of what you are actually seeing than you were a few moments ago. Now as you read, pay more attention to what you hear, sounds in your immediate vicinity and other parts of the building, and even what you might hear outside. Now do the same with your sense of smell and touch. Continue reading the words and try to pay even more attention to all of these stimuli coming in each second, making yourself more aware of what is happening around you and in you. Push yourself even further and balance the concentration on the meanings of the words and being truly present in your environment, conscious of what is taking place. It can become difficult to avoid distraction and to know which stimuli are most important and need our attention. Our instincts help us make this decision, and we gain access to them when we learn to gauge our feelings of anxiety.

We all have a built-in weapon system we rarely use. This book will teach you how to develop and use this weapon. Often we are taught that anxiety is something we should avoid, that emotional experiences such as fear, trepidation, and stress are contrary to living a happy life and should be avoided. Further, when it comes to threatening situations, such as self-defense scenarios, we often think we need to control anxiety in order to use techniques. Anxiety increases sensory input. In this book you will learn to effectively use your anxiety with true presence and concentration, feeding your instincts with information vital for survival. This is a key to success in a combative situation. You will also learn to manipulate the anxiety of the enemy in order to weaken his or her abilities.

I made the decision to write this book because I wanted to better understand what I had been doing in situations where I really should have ended up seriously injured or dead. In general, I knew the outcome of these situations was a combination of using my instincts and luck, but after thirty years of combined formal training and experience in martial arts, the military, psychology and psychotherapy, close protection, and investigative and antiterrorism work, there were enough consistencies among the positive outcomes that I intuited that I've been using some kind of "method," and I wanted to delineate for myself what it is.

There were also occasions where I did end up hurt, or I only avoided serious injury or death through luck or being saved by someone else, and these situations also seemed to have a consistency about them that related to less-than-effective methodology. Investigating these ineffective factors also became important for me in order to understand what may or may not work in threatening situations.

Through that personal exploration, gradually a book started to take shape, and I decided then to formulate and organize the ideas into something that might be useful for others. The great psychologist Rollo May once said you can feel the genuine value of a book that has to do with psychological issues when you sense that the author has written the book not simply to push or teach an idea, but instead to discover through the writing process answers to his or her own struggles and searches for truth. It is in this spirit that I share the insights here.

Over the years I have been privileged to work with countless college students as a teacher, with martial arts students as both a practitioner and an instructor, with military hand-to-hand combat trainees, with counseling and psychotherapy clients and peers and supervisors, and with fellow soldiers, all of which have given me the gift of the insights here. A few constants have remained through these disparate areas of operation in terms of the essentials of human interaction.

1. The instincts are the key to making the right decisions for the toughest challenges in our lives.
2. Anxiety is the link between our decision-making process and the instincts.
3. Being fully present in the moment turns us into instruments of the will, which is the mysterious captain of our ship, coordinating the communication between our experiences of anxiety and the effective use of our instincts as we maneuver through the difficulties of life.

Further reinforcing my belief in these truths have also been, of course, those I have encountered who were threats: terrorists and other criminals, stalkers and chance attackers in close protection work, and personal threats I have encountered as a civilian. These experiences have been just as vital in formulating the ideas here as those positive encounters I have had. In fact, writing this is something of a sweet revenge that comes from extracting lessons from those who have violated our basic human right to exist in peace and freedom, even if we are never able to exact direct revenge on an individual enemy. If my aim and the thrust of my will is to grow and deepen no matter what I experience, then there is always hope, even in deep suffering and feelings of loss and victimization. This is not to say criminals or terrorists should get a pass for their actions, but I can benefit from their actions even as I hope they pay for them. No matter what an enemy might take from me, these lessons will always be mine.

So this is not a book about empathizing with the enemy the way I empathize with a psychotherapy client in order to help with healing. Rather, it is about empathizing with the enemy in order to better understand his or her processes, so we can either evade or destroy, depending on the circumstances. I am not saying aggressors, in whatever form they may exist, are incapable of change. I am saying this book is not concerned with that question. It is about strengthening any martial artist's ability to be more successful in facing the enemy.

The book is organized to give the reader a chance to both absorb the concepts and strategies and then to practice the skills necessary to put these concepts and strategies to use in threatening situations. Accordingly, at the end of several chapters there are workbook exercises designed to guide the reader in this process. These skills have to be developed just like any other set of proficiencies in martial arts. You must train, train, train—and train again. The more you practice, the more skilled you will become.

As you will see, the process of using your instincts to harness the energy of anxiety through the will—and skillfully manipulate the enemy in a similar manner—is more than a technique. It is really a way of life, like any martial art when practiced to its full potential. The more we get to know ourselves through developing a relationship with our inner lives, especially that of mobilizing the will to use anxiety in harmony with the instincts, a kind of transcendence occurs—not of being above life and free of its problems, but of being more in life in a palpable way, thereby more in touch with true reality and better able to both enjoy that life and defend ourselves when necessary.

As the great philosopher Arthur Schopenhauer and the mythologist Joseph Campbell both claimed, the more we know ourselves, the more we know others, since the core of human beings is constant. It is my hope that a secondary gain of this work will be that it not only enables others to better defend themselves, but also to deepen their connections to experience and to others.

1

Bringing in Information Accurately
—Mastering Anxiety

EACH SECOND WE BRING IN ELEVEN MILLION BITS of information through
our senses. Under normal circumstances the average person processes
about forty bits of this information in a conscious manner. That is,
at any given moment, if we were to count what we see, hear, smell,
touch, and taste, we could name about forty things.

Where does the rest go? Contemporary methods for measuring sensory and perception response demonstrate that while an individual may
not be aware of the rest of the information coming in, the brain is. For
example, studies using functional MRI technology show that the brain
processes information the individual mechanically brings in through the
senses, even when that individual is not aware of the information. Other
studies indicate people will experience emotions due to being exposed
to a stimulus, although the individual reports not being aware of the
stimulus.

So, even though we are consciously "unaware" of a particular reality, our brains are aware. More importantly, we can gain access to
this information and use it. This is the most important aspect of this

1

phenomenon as it relates to using psychology as a weapon. In a sense we are capable of gaining access to more information about reality than the average person if we are trained to do so. It is almost as if we have our own intelligence-gathering satellite system we can use in potentially dangerous situations to better react to the threat. This has long been a hunch of psychologists and others (think of phrases such as "follow your gut" or "trust your instincts"), and now physical evidence substantiates these beliefs.

The key to accessing this information lies in our capacity for experiencing anxiety. When I use the term *anxiety*, I mean the particular feeling that grips us as if something we have absolutely no control over is about to befall us. We experience anxiety when we are exposed to a stimulus that is outside of our "comfort zone." There are some sources of anxiety we all share, and there are those that are very personal. For example, we all experience the anxiety of our existence: concerns about our careers, intimate relationships, and death—our own death and that of those we love. We may also have personal sources of anxiety, such as public speaking, flying, or particular animals or insects.

In whatever form it comes, we have all felt this very interesting sensation we call anxiety. So with this definition, we can move forward with how this state can help us access more of the information coming into our awareness each second. The process is simple, at least in its concept: if we want access to more of this information, we must be willing to feel anxiety because the information is outside our comfort zone.

This is very important. Those forty bits of information of which we are aware do not come by accident. We help choose which forty bits we pay attention to. Specifically, we all help shape our reality by allowing ourselves access to the information that helps us stay in our comfort zones. For instance, sometimes people will get into relationships with the same type of partner over and over again, unconsciously, although this type of partner is abusive or otherwise unhealthy. Why? Because as they first meet and get to know the person, they unconsciously process the sensory material coming in that matches what they

are used to. They would feel more anxiety if they were to try out a new type of person because that person would be outside their comfort zone and would elicit anxiety. Being willing to experience the anxiety and a new type of person, however, would then lead to the possibility of getting out of this vicious cycle of dysfunctional relationships.

Developing the "Third Ear"

In his book *Listening with the Third Ear*, the psychologist Theodor Reik applies this principle to the process of practicing psychotherapy. He says the proficient psychotherapist must be attuned to the instincts, the third ear, in order to truly understand clients and be sensitive to their needs. In exercising this faculty, we hear what is being said, but another "listening" is taking place as all of the information is coming in through the senses, prompting unconscious responses in the form of associations and spontaneous thoughts and feelings on the part of the therapist.

Think of listening to a song and the memories, thoughts, and feelings that spontaneously arise while hearing it. If you then start to analyze the song, you will lose these sources of information almost immediately. If you simply allow the feelings and thoughts to arise, you will be surprised what you can learn about what you are experiencing in relationship to the themes and feelings in the music.

A similar process happens as we listen to the "music" of another as that person communicates with us verbally and nonverbally. Rather than make assumptions, rather than "analyze" the individual, we open up, experience the unknown, and allow pure information to come in without controlling it. This can only be done when we allow ourselves to feel the anxiety of letting go of control. If we really want to know what the person is communicating, we have no choice but to do this. It is exactly the same in situations of self-defense. If we want to be more proficient in sensing whether a person is a threat, or even to predict what action the person is going to take, we must listen with the third ear.

Instead of avoiding anxiety, then, we must embrace it. If we allow ourselves access to that information through our willingness to feel anxiety, then we have more factual data to make use of in a combative or self-defense situation. This gives us an edge and can mean the difference between life and death.

Psychology at Work: The Dumb Tourist and the Mob Boss

An experience I had while working undercover may help to clarify this process. I was working to gather information about a major organized crime element involved in the trafficking of women for prostitution. I worked the case for a couple of years. There were several times on that job where I am convinced I only survived by relying on my instincts.

On one occasion I was on site for the third time over a two-week period. The location was a restaurant and bar frequented by some of the key personnel of the criminal element. Each time I was there, I sat at the same table outside, on a corner where I could quickly get away if necessary. I was there to collect information, analyze who was doing what, and take pictures.

The target individuals always sat at the same table—several older, more senior guys ordering food and drinks, talking. After a couple of hours, the guy I realized was the actual boss showed up with his bodyguard, checked in and exchanged key info, and then left. He never drank alcohol. His bodyguard was never more than a couple of feet away. This was because another member of this group had been shot and killed by a rival family at the same location a few months before. Later in the evening younger "soldier" types showed up and seemed to set up a casual perimeter for the other senior personnel. As the night came to a close, women working for the group gradually arrived.

On this third occasion everything was going as it always had up to the point of the boss's showing up. I went up to the restroom, and as I came out, I saw the boss had arrived with his bodyguard and with a group of about six of the younger soldiers. They were all sitting at the table directly next to mine. This table was significantly away from the senior group—where the boss normally sat—and it was a table for only four people. They were obviously there for me. Although I had blended in well, I guess I had made them curious.

I didn't react. I walked back to my seat and sat down. The boss was sitting right next to me, my right arm and his left maybe six inches apart, his bodyguard behind him, standing, the soldiers sitting, facing him on the other side of the table.

After a few moments a gypsy woman came by and left a key chain on my table, as she also did with all the other tables. She then went back around and saw who would pay a bit to keep it. I knew this. It was pretty normal in restaurants and bars there. As she left my table, I picked up the key chain and looked at it and then at her, puzzled, but not overdoing it. I nudged the boss next to me and asked in dumb tourist English, "Hey, why did she leave this here?" All I can say that I consciously did was try to speak very authentically, as if I thought he was just some guy, and I was just asking for some help understanding this practice.

All the soldiers looked at me and at him. All conversations stopped. I could feel the massive six-foot-five bodyguard behind us. The boss then responded in very good English and told me I could choose to give her some money for it, that she was poor and needed it for her family. He was actually very sympathetic to her. I responded in kind and took out my wallet, but I had only big bills and asked if any of them had change. A couple of the soldiers pulled out their wallets, showing their large bills, as if we were all saying we didn't carry anything small. The boss had some change and we exchanged money. About ten minutes later they all left.

So what accounts for my actions? Within one or two seconds my senses brought in the fact that the soldiers were there, that the boss was sitting next to my chair, that the table was too small for them all, and that a couple of them were looking at me as I came back out. All

I knew was as I walked those ten seconds from the door to my chair, anxiety hit me, and I totally gave myself over to my instincts. Of course, as I was done and analyzed everything, I realized what I had seen and processed.

The key is I did not think. Had I started trying to control the situation by thinking too much, my hesitation and second-guessing would have led to sure disaster. My anxiety would have been relieved, my awareness not as sharp, and my responses based on faulty information processing. My decision to directly engage the boss was also instinctive, and as I analyzed my actions afterward, I realized it was not haphazard but based on using information I had previously processed.

Why did a guy who was the boss of a huge-money organization appear in normal clothes, check in regularly with his people, never drink on site, never raise his voice, even sometimes, as I remembered later, avoid the other group of men getting drunk? He made an impression as a disciplined, thoughtful, systematic leader. Why does a person like this even become a criminal? Probably partly due to circumstances and partly due to his choice to take a familiar path.

But because he was a person who wore American clothes and who came from a poor country, my hunch was that he would react more positively to an American tourist who also was direct enough to speak to him personally. If I were someone investigating him, if I even knew who he was, I would not nudge him with his bodyguard there and speak directly to him, exposing myself as a foreigner and also breaking the taboo of actually touching him, especially in so casual a manner.

All of this and more played a role in my "deciding" to act as I did, which I am convinced saved my investigation, and possibly my life. In some way my actions with him were so bold it almost seemed impossible that I could be anything other than an American sitting there, not knowing what was going on or who they were.

This last point is another key part of the process of using psychology in threatening situations. We not only use anxiety and instincts as they relate to bringing in information from reality, but also to affect the reality of the other person. What is it we can present to this person at this moment to override his good decision-making ability? How do we mess up, so to speak, his ability to accurately process the information coming in? We take away his anxiety. The enemy who feels safe is a vulnerable enemy.

Imagine you are standing across from an enemy who has a pistol in his belt but who has not yet drawn it. He sees you going for your pistol. He will go for his. What if your pistol were invisible and already in your hand? You can shoot him and he will never know what happened or offer any defense.

This can be done in any number of ways, and what we decide to do goes back to those aforementioned sources of anxiety, those we share commonly or very personal ones. If we can identify what the source of anxiety is for an individual and relieve it, we can take away his ability to accurately read his world and prepare for our attack. The key is that we have to use our anxiety to discern what we need to relieve his anxiety. We bring in all the rich information from our senses and use our instincts to target his weaknesses in a very specific way.

Fear versus Anxiety

In order to use this process effectively, we must understand the difference between fear and anxiety. We often mistake one for the other or think of them as the same emotional process. The experience of anxiety as we are using it here is different from fear. When we feel fear, we react under the control of a stimulus. When we feel anxiety, we are attuned to experiencing in the moment. We are still free, though, to choose our actions. To use anxiety effectively to our advantage, we must learn to think of it as a positive process, a weapon even, rather than a weakness.

Imagine standing on the bank of a river you need to cross. You see the current is fast but not so strong to prevent walking across. You can also see the bottom and that it is about chest high. You can see the other side and that the bank is easily accessible. As you decide to cross, you will experience some fear due to the current and the possibility of slipping and being swept farther down, where you don't know the depth. Now imagine the exact same situation at night with little to no visibility. Same river, same situation—but the experience will be totally different due to anxiety from the unknown factors over which you have no control. What will you feel as you approach the middle, the current becoming stronger, the depth increasing gradually, the other side out of sight? That experience is anxiety.

We want the enemy to be that guy in the middle of the rushing river, in the middle of the night, with absolutely no idea how deep the river will become or how far the other side is. Then we want to drive up next to him in a boat and ask him if he wants a ride across. As he is climbing in, relieved, even grateful, we will handcuff him, bind his eyes and mouth, drive him to the deeper part of the river, and drop him in.

If, however, you drive up to him and say, "Hey, there you are! I have been looking for you and now I got you!" then his immediate fear response will put him on the defensive. Maybe you will be successful anyway, maybe not. If you relieve his anxiety, he will be happy to experience a bit of fear in terms of going with a stranger to escape the situation he is in.

Seeking Deeper Wisdom through a Dialectic

The most complex issues often require us to apply a different kind of thinking than simply taking one side or another. Rather, we look for deeper wisdom by using a dialectic, a method of considering two opposing sides of an issue. When we use the dialectic to come to an understanding of a process or problem, we identify a thesis, or one side of an issue, and then its antithesis, the opposite side. Then we work through that issue until we come to a synthesis, rather than settling for one or the other opposites—which usually serves to appease our anxiety.

The following diagram applies the dialectic to the problem of anxiety. Examining it in this way can help us come to a deeper appreciation for the importance of anxiety in our lives and how we may apply it to the principles here.

Dialectic of Anxiety

When faced with a threatening situation, we can begin simply with reality as it is: a threat exists. Then we move toward the two opposing poles, the thesis and antithesis, in terms of perceiving and engaging the threat psychologically, processing feelings, thoughts, and behavior.

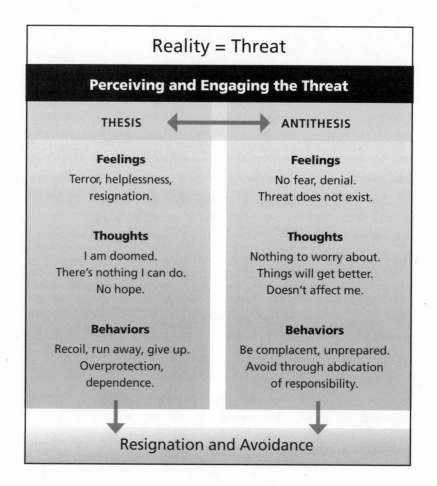

Synthesis

What remains the same here is the general attitude of avoidance. On the thesis side we are resigned to the threat with the attitude that nothing can be done, and on the antithesis side we deny the threat exists at all. Both of these attitudes are, of course, ineffective for dealing with the threat. What is actually being avoided? That a threat exists is an undeniable objective reality. It is not reality that we are avoiding then. Our senses are bringing it in, and there it is. We are *choosing* the manner in which we react to the threat. Avoidance of the threat is impossible. What we are avoiding is the subjective experience, or the feeling of anxiety. However, the fact is that we cannot actually avoid the anxiety. This happens in the first place and leads to the reactions. What we are actually avoiding is consciously feeling the anxiety and the suffering that comes with it.

So, because both reactions are ineffective, we must work on another reaction that is efficient. Since these methods for avoiding anxiety do not work, we must look for a method that does not avoid anxiety because *deciding* to avoid anxiety is like deciding it is not raining while it is pouring down on our heads.

The key to resolving the dilemma of avoidance lies in the central truth manifested in this dialectic, which is the issue of choice. What remains the same in the two opposites is that the individuals are there and choosing how to view objective reality.

We can then return to the process of the dialectic, concentrating this new insight and working through the problem further. In so doing, we take a look at the differences of both sides and exclude them, and instead look for what is the same from both sides.

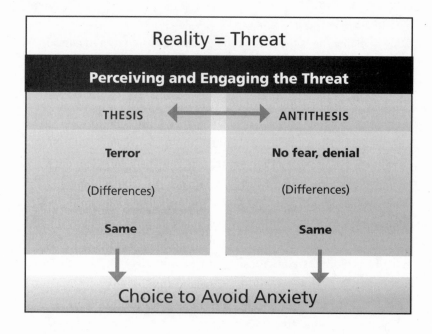

As the next step, we take what remains through the synthesis and work through it further in its two opposites involving choice.

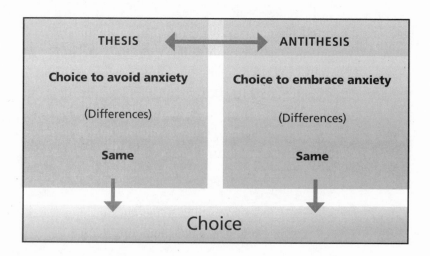

What we are left with, then, is individual choice. The fact is the threat is terrifying and it is not terrifying, depending on how we choose to see it. And if this is true, then we can also *choose* to see the threat in another way: *we recognize its existence, we feel anxiety due to its existence, but we embrace this anxiety rather than avoid it.*

And here is where I part ways with the conventional and even overly simplified medical understanding of anxiety: I see this experience as a fundamental strength rather than a detriment. Anxiety connects us to what is really happening, which enables us to choose the right path based on true reality. The anxiety exists, even right at birth. The only freedom we have is to embrace it.

A Note on the Training Exercises in This Book

In several of the following chapters I offer some suggested activities for practicing and developing the skills discussed in this book. Using psychology as a weapon as I present it is a behavioral activity, just like practicing martial arts, shooting, knife fighting, or any other self-defense or combative method you want to learn. It must be trained, and trained, and trained again, lifelong. The exercises in each chapter should be used in a kind of workbook or journaling format. Please see the appendix at the end of the book, where I have provided example entries to get you started.

Here are some exercises to increase your access to sensory information. As you move through these, you will see you are progressing into more complex tasks, heightening awareness of your senses and feelings. You can begin to combine exercises both daily and weekly over time, but do exercise 1 for several days first until you recognize that your senses increase in intensity. Even after you have moved on to the more complex exercises, continue to return to exercise 1. This is like practicing basic punching or kicking, even after years of practice, and then performing more complex martial arts techniques.

Practical Exercises for Enhancing Sensory Awareness

1. Sit and concentrate on sight, sound, touch, taste, smell—and the sense of everything together and how that changes from moment to moment. Do this each day and keep a journal, recording both sensation and intensity.

EXERCISE 1-1. Enhancing Sensory Awareness

DATE:

RECORD THE EXPERIENCE OF CONCENTRATING ON YOUR SENSES.

2. Do the same as above while conducting activities such as driving, walking, and exercising.

EXERCISE 1-2. Enhancing Sensory Awareness in Motion

DATE:

AFTER PRACTICING THESE SKILLS IN MOTION, RECORD YOUR OBSERVATIONS ON THE EXPERIENCE.

3. Practice these awareness exercises while talking with people and otherwise interacting with them. Later, in your writing, describe the nature of the interaction, including the person with whom you were interacting, the content of the conversation if one occurred, and all other details relating to the interaction.

EXERCISE 1-3. Enhancing Sensory Awareness in Conversation

DATE:

RECORD THE EXPERIENCE OF CONCENTRATING ON YOUR SENSES AS YOU INTERACTED WITH OTHERS.

4. Pay attention to how you feel when doing the first three exercises. Do you start to feel more anxiety or other feelings?

EXERCISE 1-4. Enhancing Sensory Awareness and Evaluating Anxiety

DATE:

DESCRIBE ANY ANXIETY YOU EXPERIENCED WHILE PRACTICING THESE EXERCISES.

5. Now practice the same process in a place where many different types of people potentially enter your reality. Try a public place, such as a café, a park, or a restaurant. Pay attention to your feelings as you watch the actions and hear the voices. What different feelings arise from contact with different people, from their behaviors? Does anyone feel like a potential threat? Why? Do these feelings arise due to your connecting the person with an event in your life, in your past? Or are your feelings based on something the person is doing that could mean he or she poses a potential threat?

EXERCISE 1-5. Enhancing Sensory Awareness in Busy Places

DATE:

DESCRIBE ANY ANXIETY YOU EXPERIENCED WHILE PRACTICING THESE EXERCISES IN PUBLIC.

2

Presence and the Accurate
Processing of Information

THIS RESOURCE OF ANXIETY LIES WITHIN US NATURALLY. We are born with it. The problem is that over time we learn to avoid it rather than to make use of it. Billions of dollars are made each year on pharmaceuticals used to treat "anxiety disorders" of different types. Of course, in extreme circumstances, these disorders do exist; however, the current society within which we live devalues anxiety as a state of being, and any number of products are available, both legal and illegal, to chemically relieve it. Ironically, though, when we think of individuals whom we admire and revere for their contributions to society—Martin Luther King, Jr., Gandhi, the fire and police personnel and other heroes of 9-11, the soldiers who protect our freedoms—these are individuals who have embraced significant anxiety, including that of their own potential deaths.

Being Completely Present in the Moment
The capacity to use anxiety and psychology as weapons, then, lies in each one of us. Our task is to train ourselves in embracing and making

19

use of it, rather than find ways to get rid of it. We must develop the ability to feel anxiety but be comfortable with it so we can gain access to more useful information coming in through our senses. We do this by learning to be completely present in the moment without going into a fear response of panic. All martial arts teach some form of meditation designed to develop complete concentration and focus. Military training also incorporates a similar process of forcing soldiers to focus while undergoing chaotic circumstances. These opposite methods for developing concentration are two poles on the dialectic plane of presence.

In this case, it may appear that practicing peaceful meditation and going through a military drill under simulated battle conditions are two entirely difference experiences. Physically, of course, they are. What we are doing with our bodies, what is happening around us, the nature of sensory experience—these are all different. What remains the same under the two conditions, though, is clear: ourselves. Technically, we, with our minds, our four limbs, our senses, our motor functions, our capacity for emotion, our capacity for thought—all of these are the same in pure mechanical terms. No matter what situation we find ourselves in, we are there. We are an active part of the event. When we realize this fact, we become free to experience anxiety and to better react to situations in our lives, including those that are threatening. We even become capable of influencing the events around us, including the decisions of others.

Of course, we do not choose that someone walks up to us with a knife and threatens our lives. If we do end up getting stabbed, it is not our fault. A victim is never at fault for a violent act. The freedom we do have, however, is the degree to which we experience that event accurately, based on proficiently processing the information our senses are bringing in and then using our instincts to react accordingly.

Whether we are aware of it or not, we are all at every second undergoing a triangular process through which we process our thoughts, feelings, and behaviors. For example, we may have thoughts, which then lead to feelings, which then lead to a particular behavior. We may have a feeling, then a thought resulting from it, which leads to another feeling, and then a resulting behavior. We can also choose to behave, although we may have a particular thought that causes a feeling of fear (as in a dangerous situation), and then the feelings and thoughts change as we act. This process happens naturally, much of it outside our awareness.

We can choose, however, to bring our personal process of thoughts, feelings, and behaviors more into our awareness and more under our control, including how this process functions as we are in threatening situations. We can spend time, for example, keeping a log of the particular thoughts we have as we experience a particular feeling, or what behavior usually results when we have certain thoughts and feelings.

Just like any other training, we have to work intensely enough on this process so it becomes automatic, just like a fighter no longer has to think about how he or she fights—the job just gets done. Soldiers, police, rescue personnel—we expect all these professionals to be so well trained that when the time comes to use their skills, they are able to do so automatically, with focus and precision. Lives depend on it.

In exactly the same way, our own lives depend on our ability to pick up on threats in our environment and protect ourselves. We must become so well trained at reading ourselves that as we allow ourselves to experience anxiety, we automatically process what is coming in through our senses and hear what our instincts tell us is happening.

When I was training to be a therapist, one of the most important skills I had to learn was paying attention to what is called *process* rather than *content*. This means instead of listening to what a person says or what could be called the "what" of communication, we listen to the "how" of communication. This includes tone of voice, mannerisms, and changes in behavior or facial expression, together with particular content elements of the conversation.

We do not pick apart superficial nonverbal behavior. We do not say, for example, that a person folds her arms because she is closed off or guarded, or that because someone looks down he might be hiding something. Doing this is just as useless as only listening to what is being said and taking it as truth. Rather, we act with what the great psychologist Rollo May called "disciplined naiveté." We work with the disciplined and honed skills of being therapists while also abandoning these skills in a mechanical way as we receive messages from our senses. We then trust our instincts to guide our behavior.

I was amazed at how my supervisor would sometimes identify in our sessions what was going on with my psychotherapy patients simply through processing my presence, even though he had never met the patient himself. It was as if I had carried something of the patient with me into his office and into our conversations, or as if the patient were sitting there himself. This happened not when I gave the facts of the case—the "what" of the patient, such as symptoms and history—but instead when he asked me questions like, "How is it to be with this person?" With this type of question I had to search my feelings and suddenly the "how" of the patient entered the room and he or she was sitting there with us. My supervisor could then help me with how to proceed with the patient in a more authentic and meaningful way.

When we are completely present in the moment, we encounter the truth—that is, we experience what is rather than try to analyze what is happening. The many distractions to reality, so to speak, that can distort reality are filtered out, and we fully experience the truth of existence in that moment, instead of simply seeing, hearing, touching, smelling, or tasting.

Instead, we allow all of these sources of information to coalesce into one so we experience reality in its totality, rather than in its parts. The naming of these senses, the splitting of them into separate processes, does not actually exist. We humans have done this in order to make them manageable, controllable, and comprehensible in our intellects. But reality itself does not exist in this way. So, if we want to experience reality, we must embrace the moment fully as it is, rather than the way we would like it to be in order to relieve our anxiety. In psychotherapy this is necessary in order to get to the essential problems the patient may be keeping under the surface due to unawareness or shame. In a combative situation, this is necessary in order to recognize a potential threat, even if a person does not appear to be one, and then to react with focus and precision with every moment as the conflict continues.

In his book, *Listening with the Third Ear*, Theodor Reik discusses the interplay between voluntary and involuntary attention, which directly relates to the discussion here. As soon as we try to *analyze* or *figure out* a person, we decrease the effectiveness of using our instincts. It is as if we look at a group of fifty people and pick one guy who seems dangerous. We focus on this guy because he is the one we believe poses the greatest threat. This objective reality does not actually exist though. Our anxiety level has been raised, and so we automatically concentrate on what we believe is causing it. We gain a sense of control, then, and feel a bit more secure in our anxiety. The fact is, though, forty-nine other people are still there and potential threats, and now we are actually in more danger than before because we are distracted, so to speak, by concentrating on the decided object of our anxiety. If it turns out one of the other individuals is in fact dangerous, then our defensive strategy has failed.

So rather than apply this kind of tunnel vision process, we stay open to experience without trying to control it, even as we acknowledge the potential threat of the individual. The same is true when we are assessing whether an individual is a threat. If we perform TV-inspired pop psychology, analyzing eye contact, mannerisms, tone of voice, pupil dilation, and sweating, then we have already limited our ability to bring reality in as it is. In fact, our behavior of analyzing may change the reality, as it has an effect on the individual.

Voluntary Attention versus Involuntary Attention

Theodor Reik talks about the difference between voluntary attention and involuntary attention in terms of getting at the truth. Voluntary

23

attention relates to thought, to preconceived theories, ideas, and constructs. Involuntary attention is just the opposite. It is allowing reality to work on us while we unconsciously process a wider range of perceptions so we may capture, so to speak, more of the truth. Of course, there are occasions when each is needed, and we also use both in many cases. But it is particularly important when *experiencing* an individual, with all of the complexities of the human being, to tap into involuntary attention. This is the case in both doing therapy and when dealing with potentially threatening individuals. As he states:

> *The quality of attention in psychoanalysis may be well illustrated by the comparison with a searchlight. Voluntary attention, which is restricted to a narrow sector of our field of experience, may be compared in its effect to the turning of the searchlight upon a particular piece of ground. If we know beforehand that the enemy is coming from that direction or that something is going to happen upon that field, then we have anticipated an event, as it were. It is advantageous to illuminate that particular sector brightly. Let us assume a different case, that something, for instance a noise, has turned our attention to a particular zone. Only then do we turn the searchlight upon it. Our attention did not rush on in advance of the perception, but followed it. This is the case of involuntary attention. If we drive at night along a road near New York, we may notice that a searchlight in the middle of the road is scouring the surrounding country uninterruptedly. It illuminates the road, is then directed to the fields, turns toward the town, and swings in a wide curve back to the road, and so repeats its circuit. This kind of activity, which is not confined to one point but is constantly scouring a wide radius, provides the best comparison with the function of free-floating attention. (p. 163)*

He goes on to discuss the advantages and disadvantages of each type of attention. Essentially, what we have is another dialectic. If we stick with one or the other in an extreme manner, we will be lacking in our preparedness. If we only use voluntary attention, we will leave out the realities happening in the shadows, where that searchlight does not shine. If we only use involuntary attention and never focus once our instincts have given us a message of danger, then we will be too open to surprise attack.

In order to solve this dilemma, we might imagine using the unconscious and voluntary and involuntary attention as doing a mission and having a spotter—someone who is positioned with a view of the entire situation, perhaps on top of a building, who can warn us of dangers we cannot see, even as we focus particular attention on our individual task. As Reik states, "'Poised' attention maintains the mean between the two extremes. I cannot escape the danger of surprise, but only attenuate it" (p. 164).

Psychology at Work: Good Cop, Bad Cop

Two occurrences I have had in close protection work and a personal attack against me may help to illustrate the principles in this chapter. In one I was more seasoned and better trained, and I would say I reacted proficiently using my instincts. In the other I learned a valuable lesson.

Once while I was providing close protection services, a woman under my care came under danger by a group of men. We were moving on the street and the group was walking in the other direction, all obviously intoxicated. One became bold enough to approach the woman, and so I stepped between them and identified myself as her security, but this had no effect. He identified himself and the others as police officers. The others laughed, and then he continued to approach. I had no backup nearby, and we would not make it to the vehicle safely if things escalated. I hoped to de-escalate the situation, but he pushed me out of the way and went to her. The others laughed more. At that point I had to act, so I did something I have very rarely done in a civilian setting. I took control of his head, poised to break his neck. I performed the technique but without full force, maybe 50 percent, turning him around and then pushing him toward his group.

Immediately, one of the others in the group took a different approach. He stepped between the others and me and started to deescalate the situation. The target person was in a kind of daze, surprised at what had just happened and no longer wanting confrontation. The second man and I stood discussing the issue for a moment with my principle behind me. I wondered whether I would have to draw my weapon at some point. In the end, though, they left without further incident, and the individual with whom I had the physical confrontation said, "I don't like what you did to my neck." But he said this in a way as if he were still trying to understand what had happened. He was wondering how things had escalated to the point where he very well could have been severely injured or killed.

This is certainly not an example of orthodox self-defense protocol. That they were police officers—if indeed they were—may also make my actions seem reckless. Had I done anything but listen to my instincts at the time, I would not have taken this course of action. The facts are, though, that I was alone protecting a woman, in a foreign country known for not protecting women to the standard most of us expect, and once these guys decided it was OK to continue, I was outnumbered. They were possibly people with a modicum of power as police officers. So who knows what could have happened and whether they were carrying weapons? I had to send a clear message that if they were going to try to rape her, then one or more of them were going to die. That may sound dramatic, but that is what I decided.

I cannot say what changed their minds. Maybe they were afraid that if things escalated, they would be in trouble with their jobs. Who knows? But I am sure the message came through clearly that I was willing to kill to protect her, and that I had decided not to in order to give them a chance to reconsider. I had raised the anxiety level in them, bringing them out of their comfort zones, and then given a chance for it to be appeased by agreeing to no further conflict.

Also, because I acted quickly and with instinct, I gave no warning and no chance to preempt my strategy. They were feeling absolutely no anxiety at the time of my attack, and I attacked right at that moment of vulnerability, rather than stand between her and the assailant, push him, shout—all those prefight steps that may have given them a chance to increase their awareness and aggression. I did almost as lethal an attack as there is while they were feeling perfectly safe. It is like the situation where a group of enemies does not know I am standing outside of a room, and they are sitting around with their weapons leaning against the wall. I do not walk in slowly with my weapon ready and say hello. I attack before they have a chance to react.

I do not believe we can write a playbook for threatening situations on the street or in combat. That works in a game where there are rules, but not when anything goes. This is why I believe if there is one thing we can predict in a combative situation, it is that we can trust our instincts to ground us no matter what situation arises. Of course, we need to have technical training, but even with technical training we are not truly armed as warriors unless we season our ability to experience anxiety and follow it as it guides our actions through accurately reading our world.

What gets in the way of this are the playbooks in our heads. Anyone who has faced a life-or-death situation knows there is this special moment where you ask yourself, "What am I doing here?" For a split second you want to recoil, almost like an infant, and disappear from the threat. This situation is surreal, as if it is not happening. It does not fit our playbook, our everyday lives.

If we want to survive, we have to cross this line. We must keep acting even as we do not want to. If fear seizes us, we will freeze, unable to act with authority. If we tell ourselves the situation is not happening, then we will not be able to act according to reality either. The only path forward is to face the danger with decision and focus, accepting reality and the anxiety we feel, following our instincts.

An Encounter with Drunken Soldiers

Another time I was attacked in a civilian context. I did the exact opposite of what I've described above and did not handle the situation as well as I could have.

I was teaching an evening psychology course on a US Army base at the time. The class had ended around 2100, and after all students had left and I'd gotten my stuff together, I exited the building around 2120. It was dark, with little visibility coming from the few streetlights. As I went out to the main sidewalk leading to the parking lot, a small group of young soldiers approached. I faintly heard one of them say something like "him," but with something preceding it.

Before I had any time to analyze or even see what was going on, this same guy came at me and threw a punch. It missed as I moved, and then we immediately went into a grappling situation as my books and papers fell to the ground. I still don't remember how we ended up that way, but eventually I had him on the ground in a headlock with his jacket over his head. I do remember pulling his jacket over his head while we were standing, but the position we ended up in resulted more by chaotic grappling for position and balance than from any technique, although I wrestled for seven years and have three black belts, including one in judo. I had panicked and all training was out the window.

Anyway, at that point I shouted out to the group that we could stop it all before the military police showed up, and they could leave before anything happened or anyone got hurt. One of them, who I thought at the time was probably an NCO (noncommissioned officer), took charge, agreeing and holding the others in check. I then let the first guy up and backed away a bit as he moved to the group, breathing heavily.

At this point I was completely flustered. I was caught off guard, was winded, and just wanted out of this situation. As I associate to it now—that is, as I connect other thoughts and feelings to this event—I remember several times as a kid in school when I would get my ass kicked because I was so small. At that moment on the Army base, I was a scared kid again, hoping the situation would just go away.

The guy I thought was the NCO then came up to talk and stood between my opponent and me. He said he was sorry, that they were out partying and he would take care of it. The opponent kept saying I used his jacket unfairly and I didn't fight like a man. He wanted another chance. Gradually, as I talked with the leader of the group, the others made their way closer without my realizing. I had tunnel vision, was short of oxygen, and was concentrating mostly on the leader, who was succeeding in easing my anxiety. Then, before I knew what was happening, I saw black and then my own blood flowing all over the sidewalk as I was bent over. I could hear my opponent yelling, "Now I broke your nose, motherfucker!" as they all ran away, laughing.

He was right. My nose was broken—as was my confidence in the many years of martial arts training I had up to that point. What happened in this situation is clear. In that moment I was in panic, not focus. I did not concentrate on being completely present in the moment, without interpreting or trying to control it. I did not allow myself to simply live the how of the experience, allowing the anxiety to flow and fuel my instincts to take over and use my training to defend myself. In fact, I would go so far as to say I was not there in that moment. Instead, the little boy from the playground fights was there, and the situation was too much for him.

Practical Exercises for Processing Information and Being Completely Present

1. One method for developing complete presence and full access to the information coming in through our senses is to practice some type of concentration exercise. I like *zazen*. I connected to it after reading the philosophy of Alan Watts and the great Zen master and teacher Daisetz Suzuki, and it suited me.

   Any type of focus exercise will work. No matter the form, the process should not be one of disappearing, so to speak, through deep relaxation, but instead awakening through complete focus on the moment. You will be amazed at how this takes on a life of its own and works to bring you more awareness of your experience. What often gets in the way is the mind. When we stop moving and just sit and focus, our minds keep racing but we find the freedom to let go.

EXERCISE 2-1. Awakening through Complete Focus

DATE:

RECORD YOUR OBSERVATIONS ON DEVELOPING COMPLETE PRESENCE.

2. In military training one learns to act with complete focus, each step of a particular task or mission painstakingly rehearsed again and again. Complete focus on each action of each second enables precision of task completion. It is only after this precision is reached that speed and power are added. We can learn to develop this type of focus by practicing it when performing everyday tasks. The possibilities are endless.

For example, when you put down this book, concentrate on closing it, setting it down, letting go of it, standing up, walking across the room, whatever it is you do. Try this with different actions each day as time and situation permit. Here, as above, you are training your brain, building neural pathways, to focus on each action of a task. Then pick one task that is not very complex to use for one week. Perform each step slowly, methodically, paying complete attention to each movement, each step.

Start to perform the same actions a little faster, and then still faster, without compromising the precision of each individual action. Then perform smooth, fluid action completion and pay attention to how much more precision your actions have. Move forward in this process as you become comfortable with each step. Record your observations on this process. Then pick one more complex activity you can do each day and for one week practice doing it methodically, step by step, with complete focus, tuning out everything else.

As before, use the same activity so you can see what changes occur in your focus and precision with this activity. Try to choose a task-oriented activity—that is, something that must be done in a correct way. Record your actions. Each week move on to more complex tasks, but continue those that are important to you from the previous weeks. You will find your ability to focus on a task no matter what it is will increase. For example, even if you only work on something as simple as doing one particular martial arts technique, or putting on your uniform, or doing the dishes, this practice in concentration will filter over into other tasks. The act of focusing will cause anxiety about wanting to tend to other tasks, much like the mind wanders in meditation, trying to flee the anxiety of presence and the here and now, so with this practice you will learn to bind the anxiety and complete the task while experiencing it.

EXERCISE 2-2. Training in Slow Motion

DATE:

RECORD YOUR OBSERVATIONS ON THE PRACTICE OF SLOW, DELIBERATE TRAINING.

3. Sit across from another person willing to practice with you and just take each other in, simply looking at each other face to face without talking. This provides practice in being with people, feeling anxiety, focusing, and being present. You learn to read yourself and the other person at the same time, to sense small clues without analyzing and instead listen with the third ear. Combine your practice in being present as described before and apply it now to being with another person completely.

EXERCISE 2-3. Reading Yourself, Reading Another

DATE:

RECORD YOUR EXPERIENCE OF OBSERVING YOUR PARTNER IN THIS EXERCISE. INCLUDE YOUR FEELINGS, THOUGHTS, AND BEHAVIOR. SHARE YOUR OBSERVATIONS WITH YOUR PARTNER IF YOU ARE COMFORTABLE DOING SO.

4. When you are with people under normal conditions, concentrate on how you feel. Is this feeling coming from something in your life or is the feeling coming from this person? If the person makes you feel uneasy, nervous, or anxious, why? Begin to keep a journal of your thoughts, feelings, and actions or potential actions, detailing different situations with others.

EXERCISE 2-4. Examining Associations with Others

DATE:

DESCRIBE YOUR FEELINGS, YOUR ASSOCIATIONS AND ACCOMPANYING THOUGHTS, AND YOUR BEHAVIORAL RESPONSES.

5. Go into one public place each day. While there, practice being completely present and letting your senses pick up on your environment. Scan the area not only with your eyes but with your sense of sound, smell, and touch. Do this without being conspicuous. Do this without consciously analyzing. Let the information feed your instincts.

As you do pick up on peculiarities, register them without immediately making a decision as to why they are peculiar. As you focus on a particular stimulus, whether a person or something else, keep allowing yourself to take in the entire environment at the same time.

Once you leave the environment, record your experiences. Do this as soon as possible, without editing or controlling what you write. Allow your thoughts and feelings to flow. After this, record out of that information your specific thoughts, feelings, and behavior, as well as everything you can recall about the environment and the individuals who came to your attention. Of particular importance are the invisible aspects of your experience, so to speak— that is, the feelings you had about particular individuals or stimuli. Begin to address the what and the why of the situation.

You have already started this process through what you have done, but now fill in any missing elements. What were people doing and why do you suppose they were behaving that way? This includes seemingly minor details such as facial expressions and other body language. What was the situation itself, such as the environment, time of day, weather, temperature, crowd level, and noise level? Address how these factors may have influenced the actions, vibes you picked up from others, and how these factors may have played into how you were thinking, feeling, and behaving.

Maybe a song was playing that caused you agitation or sadness, and then you projected this feeling onto an individual who looked a bit flat, and you assumed he or she was aggressive or angry. Maybe someone reminded you of an actual individual who did you harm or who you simply don't like. Or maybe you will discover you tend to assign positive characteristics to someone who is attractive, seemingly wealthy, or possessing some other desirable quality.

These are just examples of the intimate interplay at work as we engage the world and especially human beings. Maybe my interpretation of them comes from something in me, and they are not actual threats. Don't get bogged down in a never-ending analytical process. Simply write all of this and use it as training material. Then repeat the process again and again in order to hone your ability to be completely present, use your instincts, experience anxiety as it manifests, allow your senses to give you all possible information coming in, and then, in a more sophisticated way, assess the responses of others and yourself. In time you will see through the murkiness of it all to actual threats originating from others and how you react to those threats. You are learning to use your own inner alarm system through physically, cognitively, and emotionally reading yourself as you experience potential threats.

EXERCISE 2-5. Observing Places

DATE:

AFTER COMPLETING THE WRITING DESCRIBED ABOVE, REVIEW YOUR NOTES. WHAT TENDENCIES DO YOU SEE? HOW IS YOUR ATTENTION TO DETAIL EVOLVING?

6. Process associations. Sometimes you can be sitting, having a conversation with someone, and suddenly you have a picture in your head or a song or a specific memory of a person or event. This association may have nothing to do with the content of the conversation taking place. It is a mistake to think the information is simply haphazard and of no value. Often at such moments our unconscious is picking up something the conscious mind is not, and the association is a clue to that information.

Associations are not exactly like regular thoughts. Sometimes they can be in the form of words, such as a quote, song lyrics, or a memory of something someone said. They can also be pictures, sounds, movielike memories—basically anything relating to our sensory experience.

The following diagram comes close to indicating this process, but it is also important to remember the unconscious works somewhat mysteriously, and so it is not to be taken literally. Our thoughts, feelings, and behavior can affect our experience as well, so the process is reciprocal.

Pay attention to your associations for one week and record them together with your thoughts, feelings, behavior, and sensory experience as you have been doing in the other exercises.

EXERCISE 2-6. Processing Associations

DATE:

AFTER PRACTICING THIS EXERCISE FOR ONE WEEK, REVIEW YOUR WRITING. DO YOU NOTICE ANY RECURRING IDEAS OR IMAGES?

7. Go into anxiety-provoking situations that are not dangerous and focus on second-to-second actions while experiencing the anxiety. Perhaps you get anxious in groups of people, or you get anxious when someone else is driving, or perhaps you are going on a first date or a job interview. The key is to be in a real situation that causes anxiety, but not one that could lead to physical harm because you are practicing and developing this skill at this point.

Another way to practice this is simply to think about anxiety-provoking issues and then to pay attention to your thoughts and behaviors. There are certain things that cause all of us anxiety whether we realize it or not. For instance, if you think about your own eventual death, whether you will live your life the way you need to before it comes, this will induce healthy anxiety. Aloneness is another powerful source. If we imagine never having fulfilled our full potential for human relationships, considering that no matter what we achieve in life, in the end we remain completely disconnected, then this usually provokes a healthy anxiety to motivate us toward fixing the problem.

If we have achieved healthy intimacy—marriage, an intimate partner, friendships, children—then these relationships are certainly sources of anxiety as we think about the potential of losing the relationship, and as we think about, particularly in the case of children, whether they will "make it" in terms of life's challenges.

Whatever you use to induce the feeling of anxiety, the task here is to concentrate and push yourself not to seek escape from it. Rather, be completely in the moment and get to know this side of yourself as you are experiencing anxiety: how your body physically reacts, what thoughts you have, what you tend to do to avoid the anxiety. Get to know your anxiety as a companion, your battle buddy that will always be there for you in life's struggles.

EXERCISE 2-7. Understanding Anxiety as a Companion

DATE:

RECORD YOUR OBSERVATIONS ON EXPERIENCING ANXIETY AS DESCRIBED IN THIS EXERCISE.

8. When you spontaneously feel anxiety because of a life situation, focus on every second-to-second action. This happens to all of us, like when we go to work and things get stressful and we start to feel overwhelmed. When you notice this, practice focusing on each individual action, one after the other. I even talk to myself and say, "Now I am driving. Now I am taking out my keys." With practice, you will see how you can regain focus and control over your responses even if circumstances provoke anxiety.

EXERCISE 2-8. Regaining Focus

DATE:

RECORD YOUR OBSERVATIONS ON THE PRACTICE OF SLOWING DOWN AND FOCUSING ON INDIVIDUAL ACTIONS.

3

Nonphysical Reaction to Information

As I HAVE SAID, we all have the ability to use our instincts. The problem is that we often bury that inherent skill under a lot of what we need to learn to get along in contemporary society. So sometimes we may get a warning message about a potential threat, but then we choose to ignore it, perhaps out of doubt in ourselves and our feelings, or perhaps because we just don't want to believe we may be in danger. The first task, then, is to hone our instincts through improving our ability to experience anxiety and to proficiently process the information coming in from our environment.

Knowing what is happening is not enough. We must also be trained in how to react even when not reacting physically. We can do this in two possible situations: before the direct action of the threat takes place or after the direct action has begun.

Nonphysical Defending before Threatening Action

Sometimes we are faced with threats before they become active—that is, before the action is actually taken that can do us harm. If we are able to pick up on a potential threat before it happens, then we are obviously at an advantage. Most of us have experienced this. We sense someone in our immediate vicinity is dangerous, we have a gut feeling someone is untrustworthy or potentially intending harm, or we just get the uneasy feeling something is wrong.

I have an associate who is particularly gifted at reading people and using her instincts to help make decisions about them. Her story is an excellent example of how we can use anxiety and instincts to avoid a potentially dangerous situation. On one occasion she came to me to talk about a man she had been seeing. He was nice, successful, the perfect catch. She enjoyed how he treated her, and they were coming to the point of whether their relationship would move to the next level.

The problem was, despite all the aforementioned positive qualities, she often got sick to her stomach when they were going to meet, especially if they were alone. She first assigned this to other physical problems or to nervousness relating to other issues in her life. Eventually, though, because the problem repeated itself, she began to pay attention to the process. She considered the how instead of the what.

She realized she always got sick to her stomach directly relating to his presence, feeling anxiety so strong it gave her pain and made her nauseated. She made a genius decision based on this message her instincts were sending her. She decided to tell the guy she was not ready to move into the next step to see his reaction.

His other face then began to surface. He became more aggressive, trying to coerce her into what he wanted. The nice guy was gone. She also started paying attention to how he treated other people. When he dealt with people in public, she realized he actually treated them insensitively and sometimes with anger if he didn't get what he wanted. He was Don Juan with her and Darth Vader with others. The message of the process was clear: he was only being nice to her to get what he wanted.

She stopped seeing him, avoided ever being in a potentially threatening situation with him, and later found out he was habitually using women for sex. He sometimes even became violent verbally and over the internet when he did not continue getting what he wanted from women after he had conquered them. Simply put, by allowing herself to experience anxiety and even the physical consequences of it, she also had access to all the information coming in from her senses, and then by paying attention to the process—the how of what was going on— she avoided a dangerous man who would have become a stalker to her as he did to other women.

She had her intelligence satellite, so to speak, helping her gather information on the guy so she could make a better decision. If she had opted to say to herself, "Oh, just enjoy it and trust and stop worrying so much," this would have been like shutting the satellite down.

The price she had to pay is clear. She had to be willing to suffer. When we experience anxiety, it often feels as if some impending doom is threatening us. In the case of my colleague, she actually became physically sick. This is the first step in avoiding a potential threat—being willing to endure the discomfort, allowing anxiety to work on you through its truth.

What she did next is also of paramount importance. She decided to react to the messages and not just recoil. She had a suspicion about this particular person and tested it. When her instincts were confirmed, she walked away. This also required feeling anxiety. She had to experience the aggression he started to show. Sometimes people will remain in threatening situations, not wanting to believe what is happening or afraid it will get worse if they do anything.

There are also many examples in history where groups of people, even nations, have done this, leading to catastrophe. The horrors of Nazi Germany, the growth of the worldwide terrorist threat, and the atrocities of Bosnia and Rwanda are a few instances of this curious phenomenon in human beings. Sometimes we choose to live in denial—to believe the growing problem or potential threat is not as bad as we think it is, rather than face the anxiety and work with it to defeat a threat or prevent one from developing in the first place. The existential philosopher Søren Kierkegaard said anxiety is the road to the truth. We can easily imagine how world events may have been different if groups and world leaders in these examples would have listened to and acted on their anxiety rather than remain comfortable and believe things were not as bad as they seemed.

When our anxiety tells us through our instincts that we are facing a potential threat, we must listen. We must take action to avoid ever being victims of the threat. We ride the anxiety, allowing it to drive us in our resolve. We read our experience through our senses and take action.

Virtual Threats

In contemporary society a completely new danger exists: the virtual threat. These types of threats create unique challenges, both in accurately identifying them and in reacting to them. In our interactions online, we cannot rely on our senses in the classical sense because virtual reality does not give us true sensory information.

In my job I have used fake profiles and e-mail accounts and been tasked with analyzing whether accounts and e-mails were fakes. I have used these types of tools to dupe criminals and terrorists, and I have identified criminals and terrorists hiding behind fake virtual identities. What I have learned through my experiences is that the same principles I have discussed so far also apply in these situations, although we are not provided with the same sensory information as when facing a classical encounter with a person, especially one who is a potential enemy.

Whatever the situation, we must be willing to experience anxiety and follow our instincts. The problem is without being aware of it, we often feel very comfortable sitting behind a computer or a cell phone. We are not facing a person and the usual anxiety that comes with meeting a stranger, and so we relax and drop our guard. So the first step is that we have to consider every person behind a profile, an e-mail, and a text message just as real as if he or she were standing right in front of us.

This is a must, and we have to remind ourselves of it with every single encounter. We cannot trust our senses because, as to physical reality, our senses are only bringing in a computer or cell phone screen. It is impossible for the senses to biologically give us the information we need to perceive reality. We must actively involve ourselves in the thoughts-feelings-behavior process and say, "Do not trust this."

I have friends who are soldiers working in sensitive jobs, and when they have written me from new e-mail addresses, I have asked them what we did or talked about at our last meeting, or some other very personal question before trusting it was really them. Even guys like this, who are all too aware of the threats that exist, laugh in a friendly way at my cautiousness, but I am convinced it is exactly this active control we have to apply to this new type of vulnerability the internet and other forms of communication bring with them.

So being "overly cautious" is the first step. If someone walks up to you with a mask on and wants to get to know you, what do you do? This is the same reaction you should have with online contacts. That said, the internet is here to stay, and platforms like dating websites and social media aren't going anywhere. So I train people in how to identify and avoid the threats inherent in these virtual realities.

We must apply the same commitment to protecting ourselves in a virtual environment as in a real environment. Every profile, every e-mail, every text message comes from a human being. Even a virus or a program is created from the human intellect. If an encounter with a virtual reality is potentially threatening, the essential information you need to know is there because a person is "there."

Imagine you could see through the computer or cell phone and the person is sitting right there in front of you. Obviously, this would be ideal for gaining access to who the person really is. Go further, and you check the identity, criminal background, marital status—everything you need to know. There are, in fact, technologies that can provide this information from an online profile, e-mail address, or cell phone number. These are primarily in the hands of official agencies, however, and so the normal individual cannot benefit from these tools.

In my years of work, I have become convinced that the best "intelligence" tool is not a program, a satellite, or some other technology for gaining information. Rather, the truth about individuals comes from individuals. Even in the professional world of intelligence, failures abound that rely too heavily on signal or other intelligence sources without verification from actual human intellect.

So the simple solution is that you have to actually get to know your virtual acquaintances. There is no better way to find out who they really are. This allows you to use your instincts and judge whether they are threats. I obviously do not mean we should meet a stranger in person to find out who he or she is. Instead, we demand to know all of the same information we would want to know about a person we would be meeting for real: full name, birth date, job, relationship status, criminal background, financial status—these all are essential, and if the individual is not willing to provide this information, then additional contact is a no-go.

Even with all of this biographical information, however, we are still at a disadvantage in terms of knowing the person's quality of character and whether he or she is a threat. When we apply for a job, we have to do more than just provide the factual proof of our qualifications; we also must provide references. The reason for this is obvious. References can help determine whether someone is not only qualified, but a good worker, conscientious, trustworthy, and loyal. The exact same can be used for getting to know someone in an online environment. Think of the process as if the individual is applying for a job. All of the same information should be provided, and more, because developing and maintaining a personal relationship is the most important job any of us has.

Of course, despite these safeguards, we can still be duped. As we saw in the story of my colleague, a person may have good qualifications and references but still be a jerk. She was able to sense this by reading the how of his behavior as they would meet. We can do something very similar in an online environment. For example, we can test the person, so to speak. I see nothing unethical in creating another profile under another name and then corresponding with the individual to see the reaction and whether he or she gives the same information.

If a woman is interested in a man online, she should get all the facts and references we have talked about, and then go through the extra step of checking his character by writing to him as another woman. This will help determine whether he is sincere or feigning interest for the wrong motives.

The possibilities here are endless. The key is to use your instincts, allow yourself to feel anxiety, and attempt to relieve the anxiety of the individual so his or her guard is down. See what behavior then manifests and whether it is consistent with good character.

Of course, there are other possibilities for discovering who a person in a virtual environment really is. Private detectives and other professionals trained in similar activities can find out the information. It is fairly simple to do. The tricky part is accurately evaluating someone's character. We must discipline ourselves to demand a thorough assessment of the individual.

The tendency today to meet and get to know a person we have encountered through the internet is alarming and all too common. We hear one horror story after another of women in particular being duped into affairs with married men, of violent offenders raping, beating, and even murdering victims they have seduced online. "Meeting" people online is a scam. We cannot really know anyone online, and then taking the step to get together with a complete stranger is simply too fraught with danger to make the risk worth the one-in-ten-thousand chance it will become love.

Psychology at Work: The Insecure Gangster

An example of how I have used online identities in my work may help to illustrate how psychological self-defense principles can be used in an online environment—that is, to reduce the anxiety of the individual and get closer to the truth of who the person is.

I once created a profile to get information as to whether a potential criminal was indeed the person we were looking for. First I followed his Facebook account for a while, seeing what he would post, what he would say he was doing, and how he would react to posts from others, all to get a psychological profile of him and then decide the best way to lower his anxiety level and get some information from him.

I created a profile of a female who seemed to fit the type he liked. I don't mean just how she looked, but also her way of talking and her interests. He was a classic psychopath, with some traits of a sexual predator, so I created her as being a bit younger, seductive but submissive, very adoring of how cool he was without overdoing it, and also very sexual.

Before writing him I added several friends to the profile, developing a credible portrait of the character I was playing. Some of these "friends" were also on his list, but they were not actual friends of his. They included a couple of DJs and other public profiles. I created a list of interests, which also aligned with his, without making it too obvious. Tattoos were a primary fascination of "mine," and so when I wrote him to comment on his tattoo, our relationship began.

In short, we wrote for about a week, in which time we became "close." We were set to meet and couldn't wait to have sex, to solidify our relationship. The key to reducing his anxiety was to appeal to his sense of power, to his belief that he was a gangster, that it was cool, that I found it attractive. As long as he was convinced of this, of my adoration of him, and that I would give him all he wanted, he was willing to talk about almost anything. He told me where he was going and what he was doing, giving me an indication of how much money he had. He told me about buying a new car and a handgun, although I knew he was unemployed. After I subtlety indicated how sexy I found it that he was strong, a type of gangster, and that my late father also was one, he was completely relaxed.

Soon I had collected enough information from him to provide probable cause that he was indeed responsible for a recent robbery of a very large sum of money, and when the police raided his house, they found it. I continued to write to him a bit after this to give him the feeling that his arrest had nothing to do with me, and then eventually I simply stopped writing because I was so upset that he was going to jail. After that, I logged into the profile intermittently, just to keep it looking real, and eventually abandoned it.

I have done this many times for different types of jobs. Creating a fake profile is nothing special. People do it all the time. The key is making it look real. The other person must be relieved of anxiety and suspicion.

In this case, the deeper issue was this guy's anxiety about being a nothing, directly related to the lack of love he received from his parents. The sex and conquering of women were simply mechanisms for power—the drive in him to prove he was someone. He was willing to share potentially damaging information relating to his criminal behavior if I was willing to give him what he needed most: proof that his parents were wrong, that he was somebody. This came in the form of my admiration of him. So it was not the promise of sex, and it was not simply the need for acceptance. These are not strong enough to elicit information from a hardened criminal. I had to go to the source of why he was a criminal in the first place, and as a woman relieve this anxiety.

There is no formula for using such a tool to get information about a stranger online. I have always found the method must be tailored to every individual. Of course, love, sex, money, acceptance—these are all, generally speaking, key motivators for most people. However, when we really want to bring out the big guns and get deep, we have to get to the core of someone's very personal pain and anxiety. Relieve that pain and anxiety, and you can gain access to his or her secrets.

Nonphysical Defending after Threatening Action

Sometimes we are not able to do anything to avoid a threat before it manifests. The difference between this circumstance and what we discussed above is that the individual or individuals now have the intention to harm us. It is important to understand the difference between these situations. In the story above, the potential danger existed, but the enemy had not yet thought, "OK, now I am going to hurt you." In these cases we are able to use psychology to avoid a threat. When the intention is there, however, we have a different set of thoughts, feelings, and behavior to contend with.

Imagine the difference between when a bad guy has his gun holstered and when he has it drawn and aimed directly at you. In the first circumstance you "trick" him into not drawing his weapon until you can disappear and avoid him completely. In the second circumstance he has his weapon drawn and you have to use other tactics.

In terms of nonphysical reaction, you do this by manipulating his thoughts, feelings, and behavior so he essentially holsters his weapon and no longer wants to do you harm, or he is distracted and flustered to the degree that he cannot focus and attack as you disengage and disappear.

Essentially, the process is the same as what we have been talking about. Allow yourself to experience anxiety so you are able to accurately react to the reality of the situation. Then manipulate his anxiety to take away his focus and grip on reality.

Let's return to the criminal organization I mentioned in chapter 1, the one involved in trafficking women for prostitution. On another occasion I was again doing surveillance and I found myself in a situation that is a good example of how to react nonphysically to a threatening situation—and of what mistakes can put us in that situation in the first place.

Psychology at Work: Riding the Anxiety

I was at the same restaurant and bar I described before, about six months after the confrontation with the boss and his men. This time all the players were there, with the exception of the young boss. There were also a couple of new individuals. It was winter this time, and the outdoor seating was enclosed in a glass winter garden, so people could still sit outside but stay warm.

It was an uneventful day until one of the group exited the enclosure and stood outside it, directly behind me. I was sitting on the bottom left corner, directly against the glass so I could get away quickly if need be, and so all in the bar were to my front. I did not turn around to look at the guy, but I could feel him behind me. This increased my anxiety, but I did not show any alarm. I had been taking pictures and video with my cell phone, so I put it down, careful not to overreact.

After a few minutes several others of the group also exited and stood behind me, and my anxiety level increased even more, but my instincts told me not to move, not to leave, just to remain calm as if nothing was happening. Then they began talking casually and I could smell smoke. I thought they were just going outside for cigarettes, so I began to calm down. I congratulated myself for not reacting because obviously they were not interested in me and I was not in danger.

I was wrong.

As they all came back in together and returned to their table, I paid only a bit of attention to the fact that the first guy went over to another table away from them. They even asked him what he was doing, and he said he just needed a minute and sat and started to make a phone call. Actually, I only recalled and analyzed this all after the critical events took place. At the time I wasn't paying much attention because I was so relieved that they weren't standing behind me to capture or kill me. Because I allowed myself to stop feeling anxiety, I put down my guard and got myself in a threatening situation.

I continued as before, very cautiously and casually taking pictures and videos as I pretended to write text messages and at times make fake phone calls. I don't know how much time went by, but then, out of habit, I scanned the whole area and realized the guy who had gone to another table to make a call was staring directly at me. His stare was like a rottweiler's. His look said, "Who are you? What are you doing here?"

53

He was a spotter. He had positioned himself to watch me watch them. I don't know if they all planned this, or if he just took the initiative, but it was brilliant. He even played like he was on the phone as he watched me.

In that moment I was under direct threat. I had a choice. Should I run? Attack? I let my instincts guide me, allowing myself to experience the intense anxiety. I only looked at him for a split second, as if his stare were not interesting to me. Then I waived to the passing waiter that I would like a drink, some wine. The waiter brought it and I drank like everything was fine. I didn't look at the guy anymore, other than as one does accidently when in a public place.

I drank one, then two, and started a third glass of wine. I had ordered a bottle, thinking that might at least play a small part in easing the guy's anxiety and bringing down his guard. I hoped it would allow me to get out of the threatening situation without taking physical action. I had little chance of surviving a physical confrontation in that situation, and I also did not want to screw up all the work I had been doing. I wanted him to believe I was no one.

Gradually, it worked and he went back to the other table and seemed to forget me, drinking and enjoying himself with the others as the evening went on.

My instinctive decision to ignore him rather than react physically ended up being the right move. Not only did it probably save my life, but then something happened that proved more beneficial to the mission than I had ever planned. After an hour or so, as it was getting late, the chief of the entire organization arrived. This was a man who did not even live in that country, a man who rarely went out in public. But he walked in and sat down two tables in front of me.

He was accompanied by a younger man known worldwide for his role in an ongoing war between two major criminal organizations. I immediately felt an increase in anxiety, as well as elation at the possibility before me. It was known that the leader would be giving over power of the organization, but to whom was not known. The younger man had never been seen with the boss before and was completely unknown to the investigation until that point.

I had to get a picture. Given the situation that had happened an hour before—and the fact that I had alcohol in my system—it would be a difficult task, but I couldn't pass it up. I actually had wanted to pay and leave, but this was too important.

As they sat down, the boss looked over at me immediately, directly, boldly, checking me out in an intense way, but he did this with other people there as well, so my instincts told me not to react. I just looked away casually. My instincts also told me that there was no way I could just pick up my cell phone, pretend to write a text and click off a couple of photos. The way he looked at me, his alertness, his status, the situation from before—all of this told me I would have to do something different.

I decided to go into the bathroom, but I waited for a bit so he wouldn't think I did it because he had looked at me, and I also waited until they were ordering, so they were distracted. In the bathroom I went into a stall and turned on the video to my camera on my cell phone. I left it running, put it back in my pocket, and then just walked back and sat down at my table.

By this time they were talking and drinking and did not seem to pay attention to my presence at all. After a few minutes, when I could sense that their anxiety levels were down, I slowly pulled out my phone and brought it up in front of me as if writing a text. I took a very short video of them, just long enough to have a clear view, as if taking a picture. At that moment, the boss looked right at me, right at the lens my cell phone camera, as if thinking, "Is that guy taking a picture of us?" His instincts and attention to his environment were amazing.

I pretended not to notice. I just put the phone to my ear and pretended to have a phone call, while sipping more wine at the same time. Gradually, he stopped paying attention to me, and after what felt like an appropriate time to not raise any suspicion, I paid and left.

In both situations with the spotter and the boss, I was under direct threat. They were both thinking something like, "If you are here spying on us, you are dead." When we are in this kind of situation where the psychological intent is there in another to do us harm, we have to attack that psychology. If we can defeat them through easing their anxiety, we can defend ourselves nonphysically as they holster their weapons instead of pulling the trigger. I talk them out of attacking, so to speak, through riding the anxiety, letting it feed me each second with accurate information. Then I take actions to lower their anxiety level and reduce the threat.

Every situation is different. My examples are in no way guidelines for what to do in all circumstances. No matter what anyone says, there is no playbook. You cannot rely on typical self-defense training and say, "Hey, man, I don't want any conflict." Sometimes this type of approach will even trigger an attack. Be present. Be completely in the moment. Allow yourself to feel anxiety so you read the situation accurately— each sound, movement, gesture, smell, everything. Then trust your instincts, which have developed over thousands of years, to guide your actions.

Practical Exercises for Developing Nonphysical Reaction Skills

1. When in public—for example, at a restaurant, in a theater, or on the street—pay attention to your instincts and see if you pick up on behavior of others who may be potentially threatening. Practice doing this without giving off signals that the person actually causes you alarm. Observe the individual discretely.

   As you undergo the situation, ask yourself what you are feeling and thinking, and what you feel like doing. What is it about the person that is setting off alarms and provoking anxiety? Stay calm. Trust your senses and your instincts. Then ask yourself what actions you could take to avoid any possible aggressive action by the individual. Perhaps nothing else is necessary than simply avoiding entering into that person's reality. Perhaps leaving the situation is the right solution. The key is to find a strategy for avoiding the threat before it manifests.

EXERCISE 3-1. Sensing the Behavior of Others

DATE:

RECORD YOUR OBSERVATIONS ON EXPERIENCING ANXIETY IN PUBLIC PLACES.

2. Training to react nonphysically in a threatening situation is complex but essential to any self-defense system. We can design scenarios in which a potential attacker confronts us. The key is that the process needs to be realistic. This is obviously the case in any good training, but the complication here is that there is very little testing of real reaction of the individual unless the training is intensified and there is a real intention on the part of the acting enemy to do harm.

One of the things I do in group training of this skill is to secretly give one student instructions to get angry with another student at some point. I tell the first student to find a reason to get agitated and get to the level just before a fight breaks out. The other individual is then tasked with trying to deescalate and avoid conflict through nonphysical reaction by relieving the anxiety of the other.

As the trainer I control the situation so it does not escalate to an inappropriate level, and in the beginning, I often have to intervene and then tell the other half that it was indeed a test. Then we role-play ways that may have been used to gain an advantage over the threatening person in a nonphysical manner.

Of course, real situations are the best source of experience for developing this skill, but don't go looking for them. That is too dangerous. However, if you happen to spontaneously face such a threatening situation, writing and reflection should help you process the experience later. Describe the situation. Describe your feelings, particularly any anxiety you may have felt. What did you do to avoid the threat?

EXERCISE 3-2. Training Nonphysical Reactions

DATE:

RECORD YOUR OBSERVATIONS ON THE THREATENING SITUATION AND HOW YOU PROCESSED IT LATER.

4

Physical Reaction to Information

SOMETIMES WE ARE NOT ABLE TO USE nonphysical reaction to avoid a threatening situation. We must then be trained to react physically. In employing our physical self-defense techniques, we can use psychology in three possible situations: before the attack, simultaneously as the attack occurs, and after the attack. We may need to use physical methods even when threats are virtual, such as those that come from the internet.

Defending before the Attack

Our right to physically defend ourselves is widely accepted in the contemporary world. Most countries have laws protecting the individual from prosecution when he or she is under direct threat and must defend against bodily harm or even death. What is less clear is the degree to which we are allowed to protect ourselves in that narrow window when an aggressor has decided to attack but has not yet attacked. Using the metaphor from the last chapter, we might say the enemy still has his gun holstered, but his hand is on it, prepared to draw.

The best tool we could have at our disposal at this point would be the ability to read his mind. If we knew 100 percent that he was going to attack, we would, of course, do something to defend ourselves. What we are submitting here as an established fact in psychology is that we have something approaching that ability as a potential weapon. If we are completely present, and we pay attention to our instincts, we can pick up on the enemy's intent to attack before he does so.

Before any part of the enemy's body moves, thereby enabling him to take threatening action toward us, a miniscule amount of movement will take place. This may be in the shoulders, hips, neck, eyes. But something will send a signal. Once we have received the signal, we take disarming actions. We can do this verbally or physically.

Verbal Disarming

Here we perceive the enemy's intent to attack before he does so, and we attempt to take away his edge by relieving his anxiety. We can talk to him, making him feel like we have no intention to attack. We can say things like, "I'm really sorry, man. I don't know what I did, but I don't want any trouble." Or, "Please don't hurt me. I can give you whatever you want." What I actually say is a matter of instinct and it depends on the situation.

This is not, however, a tactic to avoid physical confrontation as described previously. At this point I am convinced he will attack and I will have to defend myself. What I am essentially doing is creating a psychological distraction, tricking him into thinking I do not want to fight. In my mind, however, I have every intention of fighting because I realize we have crossed that line. He has decided to hurt me.

Once again the key is being trained in using my senses to accurately perceive what he is doing and intending to do, second to second. As I speak I am continually reading him. The moment I see an opening, I attack, and attack fiercely. For instance, as I speak, he will listen, whether he wants to or not. As the sound waves enter his ear, his brain will begin processing the information. This is a small diversion, but perhaps enough to give me an edge. Even if I am in midsentence, I will attack, if I do indeed see that he is preoccupied with what I am saying.

This tactic is not new. It has been taught in self-defense for a long time. However, what is not often taught is to be precise, when possible, in what we say. If I simply blabber some words, I will not have the same deterring effect on the enemy as when I say something more meaningful to him. What will relieve his anxiety and disarm him, even for a split second? The right words are like a drug that will relax him, dull his senses, and send the message, "Man, you have nothing to fear from me. In fact, you are going to get whatever you want." And at the moment the drug takes effect, I attack like a lion.

Of course, it can be very difficult to know exactly what will relieve his anxiety in order to give me the edge, especially in an encounter with a stranger. If I know his culture or background, I can use that. But if something more powerful than culture or background is driving him, this won't work. I do not want to give specific formulas for what to use because I believe that would be a setup for failure. Each situation is different because each involves different individuals, and people are simply too complex. This is why I must rely on my instincts in the here and now.

Disarming through Action

We can also use physical action to give us an advantage before an attack. As with verbal disarming, the possibilities are endless, but the method also involves more potential dangers. The wrong movement may actually prompt an attack or give warning of my intentions. An effective disarming action relieves anxiety. An ineffective one raises it. I want the attacker to feel he has nothing to fear from me. I want his sensory experience to be faulty in terms of picking up on my intentions, and I do this by disabling his inner alarm, so to speak, so he is taken by surprise as I attack.

For example, I can feign injury or sickness. I can even start to cry if I can manage it in a natural and realistic manner. It may sound extreme, but I can start to vomit or urinate, both of which are consistent with a fear response. Given the situation, I might even have any of these reactions involuntarily, and so—although my intent is to attack—I can work with these responses to create a diversion to give me the upper hand as the enemy is distracted.

The essential feature of this strategy, no matter what behavior I use, is that I reduce his alarm response and anxiety. I want to point this out because it is sometimes taught in self-defense courses that we can distract an attacker by other types of physical action. For example, we may spit in the attacker's face, look past him to make him think someone is approaching, or use any other technique that diverts his attention and gives us a split-second advantage. Of course, these methods may work. If the attacker becomes distracted and I am able to neutralize him, I am out of danger. But what I am relying on with these methods is very tenuous. What creates a distraction might actually raise an attacker's alarm level. He will certainly be alarmed by something coming at his face, or if he thinks someone is approaching from behind. The distraction will happen, period. But, because I am *raising* his alarm level, I may prompt an instinctive attack reaction. If the attacker is armed with a gun or a knife, this is particularly dangerous. He may decide to shoot or stab me before dealing with the individual approaching from behind, for example.

I am suggesting it is more effective to reduce the alarm response by lowering the enemy's anxiety level. I can create just as useful a sensory distraction through my movements and at the same time affect his biology by reducing the desire to attack that arises naturally in response to feeling alarmed. In other words, if the enemy feels no alarm and is distracted at the same time, I have a maximum advantage when I initiate my attack. If I sell that I am completely nonthreatening through crying and perhaps wetting myself, and at the right moment attack like a lion, I will have a better chance of prevailing.

Simultaneous Attack

Some attacks I can see coming, and then I can use the disarming methods I have described. In other situations I have already been attacked, so I must respond. In still other instances I am confronted with something falling between these two possibilities. I sense the enemy's intention to attack, but only as it actually begins, so I do not have time to do any disarming to relieve his anxiety. Emotionally speaking, his initial assault is completely free of any interference on my part.

Think of defending before the attack as being face to face with a crouching lion about to pounce. I throw a steak to the side of him and he goes after it—then I shoot him. In a simultaneous attack situation, though, I don't see him crouching. I pick up on the attack just as his legs are extending, tightening, launching him onto me. He has initiated the attack, but it has not yet physically reached me.

My reaction at the moment of attack is likely to be more successful if I have intensively developed my ability to be completely present and trust my instincts without panicking. I have a better chance of surviving and prevailing if I remain in a kind of calm fierceness. My mind must be calm, open to messages coming from my senses as I allow myself to experience anxiety, and my actions must be fierce because I have no idea what is coming.

Maybe the attack starts with a punch but will follow with a knife or gun, or more than one attacker. If I have no chance to assess the circumstances, anything could happen. I must react instantaneously, reading the situation from second to second and reacting appropriately, and I must do so without thinking. This requires acting from instinct.

There is no substitute for good training in this situation. That is obviously the case in any self-defense situation, but sometimes we train only under circumstances where we know we will be attacked. In fact, when we go to training, we know we will be attacked, even if "surprise attack" scenarios are part of the training. This is a major flaw in a self-defense training regime. In fact, most attacks on civilians take place under "surprise" conditions. So it makes no sense to conduct planned training only. All military units, whether conventional or elite, undergo surprise-attack training scenarios. The police, the fire department, emergency medical crews—all of these professionals also incorporate surprise scenarios into their training programs. Even kids in schools undergo fire drills and natural disaster training. So why would self-defense training not include the same? I talk later in the chapter about specific ways you can implement surprise-attack scenarios into your training plan.

The point I want to make here is there is a very thin line between psychology and biology. The two work together. I can be a top professional fighter and fall to pieces under the pressure of a surprise attack. My psychology does not match my biology. My brain is programmed to fight, but only under certain psychological conditions. Think of driving a car and all of the body mechanics that go with it. Now think of driving on a narrow road in the mountains of India or Peru. The skills required to drive are the same. The biology is the same. The psychological situation, however, is very different, and this sends the biological programming into chaos.

The key in good training for surprise situations is similar to what we have talked about before relating to content and process. Content is what people say; process is how they say it, or their behavior. The same is true with knowledge acquisition. In therapy we talk about intellectual insight versus emotional insight. Clients may gain intellectual insight into their problems—for example, understand the "why" of their criminal behavior, drug or alcohol use, and dysfunctional relationships—but nevertheless fail to get better.

The "why" alone does not help. They need to feel and gain emotional insight. If I feel the suffering of a dysfunctional series of relationships or of other mistakes I have made, then I am more likely to be motivated to change. This brings us back to our old friend—anxiety. If people do not feel anxiety, they will not change, no matter how much intellectual insight they gain.

So, in the same manner, I can go for twenty years to self-defense training and learn all manner of techniques (the "what" or intellectual insight of training), and be completely ineffective in a realistic situation. I must also be trained in the "way" of combat, the "how" or emotional insight of facing harm and death, and still be able to perform the techniques. I must be able to fight when I am feeling extreme anxiety, both because this is what the psychological situation demands of my biology, and because the anxiety itself is actually my best source of valuable information coming in from my senses—if I have trained myself to use it.

Defending after the Attack

Defending after the attack means the enemy has the advantage from the outset and, unlike in the simultaneous attack, I have already been forced to defend. That is, I am again faced with a surprise attack, but in this case I had no chance to react to the actions preceding the attack. His first assault has been launched and has reached me. If we return to the analogy of the lion, defending after the attack means I did not see the lion crouching, and I did not see him leap into the air. Instead, I only catch his actions as he is almost on me or after he has actually attacked me. There are two possible results in this situation: 1) I am able to react quickly enough to repel the attack, or 2) I am injured in the initial phase of the attack.

If the enemy has already attacked and I am able to offer an initial defense, the key challenge is to immediately follow my defensive action with an appropriate response. A key feature of Israeli krav maga—particularly of the original Israeli Krav Maga Association, Gidon System, to which I belong—is always to attack as I defend. Fighters in this system are trained to go on the offensive in order to minimize the potential for harm. Most of us, until we are trained in such methods, do the opposite. That is, we tend to freeze or recoil when we face a physical assault. This stems from people's tendency to dislike anxiety and avoid it.

The human psyche is fascinating in this respect. We can be faced with any number of anxiety-provoking situations, and we will go to great lengths to ignore them or pretend they do not exist. The psychological term "denial" has become an everyday word for precisely this reason.

We will simply run from a problem to avoid the emotional pain it brings, particularly the anxiety. The same is true here. Who among us wakes up in the morning and says, "Hey, I hope I will be attacked today"? When an attack does occur, we don't want to believe it.

So the first step in developing psychological proficiency in self-defense is to train ourselves out of this mind-set with hard work and discipline, just like we may have to force ourselves to avoid smoking, excessive drinking, too much fast food, or any number of addictions that today keep tens of thousands of psychotherapists securely employed. The human being does not like to feel bad, period. It is no coincidence that psychological treatment in different forms is booming as a business and that the companies that offer any number of addictions to relieve our pain and anxiety are also booming. So I simply accept the fact that I experience anxiety. I just learn to work with it and even embrace it.

If I am attacked, then, I look the situation square in the eye, just as millions of my ancestors have done for tens of thousands of years under many different anxiety-provoking circumstances. I empower myself with all of that history, with all of that human capacity for courage, and I launch an assault that brings to bear the collective energy and experience of those ancestors in me who are my human legacy. The enemy will wish he were someone else at that moment.

Of course, this mind-set and the actions that have to accompany it come through training. I go into detail about the training at the end of this chapter.

Self-Defense and Martial Arts Training

If we do need to defend ourselves physically, we obviously have a better chance at being effective if we have some sort of fight training. Regardless of the particular type of training, the key is that it must be realistic and teach both content and process.

Content means the specific techniques, the particular fighting art; however, techniques alone do not work, no matter how impressive they may seem. The *process* of fighting means the psychological state that exists in dangerous situations. Specifically, we must be conditioned to experience anxiety as we fight. We need training to accurately bring in information each second and react instinctively. This skill develops best under intense training conditions. We must become exhausted, feel pain, fear, and anxiety, and stay in the fight anyway. "Train hard, fight easy" is a phrase many use in this regard, and it needs to be applied seriously.

Another key is the teacher. My mentor in psychology once said we learn more about being a good therapist by being around good therapists than we do from books. I was fortunate to have him and others in this regard, and this statement is profound and wise.

When we observe an expert's proficiency, we absorb it, as well as aspects of his or her character. We internalize these lessons and make them our own. This happens with psychology mentors as well as trainers and coaches in martial arts and self-defense. Their knowledge is really secondary to their "way"—their character and how they carry themselves. Find a good trainer with extensive knowledge, years and years of experience, a lineage, and good character, and then spend as much time around that person as possible.

Further, we absorb from the different styles and characters of different individuals. For instance, my great teacher Haim Gidon of the Israeli Krav Maga Association exudes a calmness that is very difficult to describe. You would never think he would be able to hurt anyone—until you see him fight. He is generous and patient and he listens to his students, and at the same time he is unforgiving in his training regimen. One of his senior instructors, Yigal Arbiv, chief of school security in Netanya, Israel, and a former member of the Israeli Special Forces, also leaves absolutely no doubt about the physical harm he is capable of unleashing. Brand-new students and professional top-tier mixed martial arts fighters alike say they have never met a wrecking machine like him.

Having the privilege of being his friend and working with him in a security firm over the years, I have always been impressed with his gentleness and loyalty. He is a man who will do whatever is necessary to protect the innocent, and his presence makes one humble. I have watched him training children and how this affects their development into true warriors. This ferocity of a killer combined with the gentleness of a caretaker I have come to call the "Yigal factor" in training my students. My goal is to train killing machines with good hearts.

Yet another instructor of mine was a retired Vietnam-era Green Beret. He taught judo and jiu-jitsu in a traditional sense: not as sports, but adapted for military use. His combat experiences and his approach to these disciplines illustrated how real the threats in the world are, and why being a martial artist is a privilege. This path is not a sport or medium for gratifying one's ego. Martial arts exist in their true form to protect the innocent.

I share these examples from my own development to demonstrate what my experiences have been, but everyone must find his or her own teachers, mentors, and guides. In my opinion, however, the task is much more than simply finding a "trainer," and instead is like what Joseph Campbell termed the "hero's journey." Heroes must always have a mentor, or they will never develop their full potential. Mentors must have more than simply the training of the hero as their goal; instead, they must be concerned with, in the words of Robert Bly, the initiated individual's character and soul.

Virtual Attacks

As I pointed out in the previous chapter, we face a new type of self-defense issue today in the form of virtual attacks. The reasons for this are obvious. We are less sure about both the nature of the assailant and in what form the attack may come. On top of that, the degree to which we are legally allowed to defend ourselves is very vague.

I have worked many jobs in close protection and investigations that began as online threats. We talked about virtual threats in chapter 3, but the difference here is that the situation requires physical reaction.

My guidance here will be admittedly controversial. I have simply seen too much psychological and physical damage done, especially to women, by online assailants to limit myself to presenting a politically correct set of guidelines about handling such threats. We have all heard the stories about threats that originated virtually then turned real. The victim ends up terrorized and sometimes physically injured or killed because no one went on the offensive against the assailant. So my resolute opinion is that we must handle virtual threats by taking physical action just as if the enemy were standing directly in front of us.

The first step is, of course, reporting any direct threats to the police. Even given my background and expertise, if someone were threatening me and a police officer were right there, I would let the police officer do his job if he could really protect me. So the first thing we do when someone threatens us online or through some other virtual media is report it to the police.

Of course, in some cases, the police will do nothing unless it continues. OK, but it has now been reported. If the situation escalates and I do what I have to do to defend myself, the police can decide for themselves if they did enough in the first place. At least I reported it. I am not saying we should make a report and then go find the guy and shoot him in the back of the head. I am simply saying that in many, many cases, due to existing laws, the authorities do not do enough to render the enemy incapable of causing harm. And then we have to take preemptive action as if we were face to face with someone who intends to harm us.

There are, of course, laws against threatening to kill a person, over the internet or otherwise. But they are certainly not as stringent as if I were standing there and the guy threatens me directly with a gun or knife. In that situation I am allowed to defend myself physically, and I can be sure he will go to prison. If the threat is online, however, I am not allowed to go find him and attack him, and he will certainly not receive the same punishment as he would when physically threatening me with a deadly weapon. So with these kinds of threats, we have to be particularly creative about protecting ourselves while at the same time not breaking the law.

Psychology at Work: Cornering a Cyberstalker

As before, I do not want to provide a specific formula because every situation is different. We must again trust our instincts. Perhaps one example of a job I worked can provide some guidance on how to handle these particular threats.

I was once consulted because several young teenage girls were being harassed and threatened by an older teenager. They were all around thirteen or fourteen, and he was eighteen. He knew the girls because they all came from the same area but went to different schools. They were not friends nor had he ever had any other kind of relationship with any of them. Nevertheless, he would begin by writing via Facebook and eventually get some of their cell numbers through other acquaintances.

He started off chatting with them amiably, but then as the girls rejected his romantic advances, he became threatening and harassing. He was clever; he did not say he would kill them or anything explicit, but he spoke in generalities about something happening to them. He also created Facebook profiles and groups, using the pictures from the girls and posting very offensive lies about them, or pretending to be them in profiles. This then became known to a wider range of people in the peer group, and the girls were humiliated. He also had several different cell numbers he operated from, and so when one number was blocked, he began with another. All of this was having an impact on the girls and their families; they were afraid to go to public places where he might be, and for some, it affected their grades and even their appetite. The parents had reported everything to the police, but due to the lack of any substantial stalker laws in Germany, nothing was done to help the girls.

I discovered a number that had been used to contact one of the girls, but the parents were not sure if it was his because it was a new number. The suspicion was there though, so I wrote to him from my cell, pretending I was a girl. I was pretty certain he wasn't just doing this with the girls for whom I was working but probably had more potential conquests than he could remember. I sent a simple text like, "Hey, how are you?"

I was confident he would simply believe he had forgotten "me"— the girl I was pretending to be—and say who he was. That way I would know if the number was actually the perpetrator's. When he asked in a text who I was, I said, "Seriously? You don't even know? I guess you have more girls than you can remember. I thought I was special." He took the bait and said he was sorry. Of course he remembered, he said. But I replied that now I was unsure if he was who I thought, and I was afraid to keep talking to him unless he confirmed who he was. Then I just put the known perpetrator's name with a question mark. He confirmed I was right.

I then waited a bit and sent a long text saying I was the chief of an international bodyguard team that specializes in protecting women and children from predators, that we are all highly trained ex-military and police, and that we were hired to protect a group of girls he had been harassing and threatening. I gave him explicit instructions to stop all contact and to erase all Facebook postings and any other online sites or discussions regarding these girls. I told him I already had the parents call the police to report his activity, and if he did not follow my instructions and stop his behavior, we would take further action.

His answer to me was a long "hahahahahahahahaha," and within a few minutes I received about five different texts from different numbers, all threatening me and "laughing." So I said nothing else. I got in my car and drove to his town.

It was a small village in Germany, and first I simply drove around a bit and let my instincts guide me about what to do next. Even going there was instinctive. Something in me said I had to take action, that our phone conversation wasn't going to be enough. He needed to face real consequences.

Once I had taken in the layout of the village, I picked a spot where I could park unseen, not far from a central meeting place where he would also have a difficult time getting away quickly. I then took off my license plates and waited at my observation point. Once I was confident in my plan, I wrote him a text saying I was now in his village with my team, and he could either come down to the meeting place I had picked to talk, or I could drive directly to his house and talk with him and his parents. He said he would come.

While I waited for him to arrive, I scouted the area to make sure he didn't have backup hiding anywhere. The place I picked had a clear shot at all areas of approach to the meeting place, and there was nowhere to hide. I could see anyone he might have as backup.

Once he arrived he sent another laughing text saying he knew it was a bluff. I texted back what he was wearing and that he was riding a scooter. He immediately looked all around in a kind of panic, but there was no way he could see me. I slowly drove out of my observation point and, wearing dark tactical glasses, looked over at him as I drove by. But I could have been anyone. I was about fifty meters from him on another street with a midsized stream between us with no way over. He watched me drive by, staring at him, and then kept looking around, unsure if I was the guy texting him.

I then disappeared. He got spooked and started to slowly pull out. At precisely that moment, I emerged in front of him from another street and texted him that one of my men was now in front of him. This time he didn't answer but drove straight back home and from there said he was going to tell his parents and call the police.

I wrote back that we were now on the job to protect those girls, that we weren't going anywhere, and that we would be observing him and following him for a while. Either follow my instructions, I said, or this is how things are going to be. We would also follow all of his cell phone and online activities, and he would never know with whom he would be writing and texting. We would be a constant presence in his life whether he realized it or not. Or he could simply do what I said and leave the girls alone.

He again threatened to contact the police, but I sensed this was more to save face and not just say "OK," so I didn't respond to it. For a couple of months there was nothing from him to either the girls or me, and then one morning he sent a joke of some sort to one of the girls as a text. I had set up a protocol that any contact from him immediately be sent to me regardless of the time of day, and so within five minutes of his texting her, I texted him and said I had warned him but he had not listened, so now he would have to deal with the consequences.

I then received a call from his mother, and I simply explained the situation to her in the same way I had to him. She was more concerned about his rights and being harassed than for the girls, and so I assured her that he and her family would be under observation constantly to ensure the girls remain safe and that we were a 100 percent protection system between him and them, both virtually and physically.

One factor I had taken into account in my mission planning was the background of the family. Given their tenuous status in Germany, it seemed they might have been in the country for criminal purposes. This meant a chance the girls were in real danger, but it also gave us a way to exploit the family's weakness: they all could have been deported due to his behavior and anything else we might discover as we observed them.

I had further actions in mind if his behavior continued or escalated, but this sufficed. The last text to the girl that day seemed to be a combination of checking to see if I was bluffing and an angry power move as if to say, "I can do what I want."

I made sure for months following that he knew we were around, both virtually and physically, by periodically popping up, so to speak, like a phantom, just walking by, taking a picture as he stood somewhere, and later sending it to him by cell. A couple of times I drove by slowly in the same car as he waited for a bus, or I sent friend requests from

Facebook pages with no photo, but hints at the identity because in my photo album were screenshots of his activity on the internet.

Although this predator was clever, using technology to remain "legal" while carrying out his attacks, he was doing as much damage as if he were physically hurting these girls. The battle, so to speak, had to be brought to a head. He had to be stopped, and no amount of threatening him with legal action was going to accomplish this. It was almost as if he were being told, "OK, you want to fight? Let's fight."

I do not mean this to sound like bravado, and I am not talking about a barroom brawl. This guy was already attacking the girls. He was punching them in the face every day, psychologically speaking. As far as I was concerned, the attack was already taking place. The only question was the right counterattack, and an attack it had to be. He needed to know that whatever he could do to his victims psychologically, my team and I could do ten times better.

At the same time, however, my instincts told me the best way to do this was to also give him an option, a way out of that hell. His anxiety had to be raised to almost a state of paranoia that he was being watched all the time. He needed to feel as if he were no longer free, as if he were in prison (where he actually belonged). And then, if he did what we told him, he would be let out of prison. His anxiety level was raised, and then we had the power to relieve it—as long as he left those girls alone.

Of course, other predators may have immediately lashed out and done physical harm to one of the girls. With that personality type, I would have taken different actions if my instincts dictated it. Each situation has to be assessed individually for all of the factors involved. What this case demonstrates, though, is that virtual attacks can be just as destructive to victims as physical ones, and the response has to be every bit as serious as a physical attack—particularly when current laws actually protect the predator using the internet as a tool for power and destruction. Simply stated, if the law protects the predator, it protects the warrior too, as he or she uses the same tactics against the predator—but with more discipline and skill. The warrior uses anxiety and instinct as tools to accurately manipulate the anxiety responses of the enemy.

Practical Exercises for Developing Physical Reaction Skills

1. In this chapter I discussed the importance of training in self-defense and martial arts. To get the most of this we need to examine the circumstances of our training. What is the content? What are the instructor's qualifications? Are his or her methods appropriate?

EXERCISE 4-1. Evaluating Martial Training

DATE:

HOW CAN YOUR TRAINING BE USED WITH THE CONCEPTS DISCUSSED IN THIS BOOK?

2. It is also important to train in reducing the enemy's anxiety. These scenarios can be role-played and should combine the process of disarming the enemy through relieving his anxiety together with physical attacks. Later, analyze these exercises to evaluate what you have learned and identify areas for improvement. This analysis may include the following questions:

- What did you do to relieve the anxiety of the enemy to gain a tactical advantage?
- What physical techniques did you use?
- How did the psychological tactics and physical techniques function together?
- How effective was your effort?

EXERCISE 4-2. Reducing the Enemy's Anxiety

DATE:

RECORD YOUR OVERALL EVALUATION OF THIS TRAINING, INCLUDING POSSIBLE IMPROVEMENTS. ALSO INCLUDE YOUR THOUGHTS, FEELINGS, BEHAVIOR, AND SENSORY EXPERIENCE.

3. In order to develop complete presence and concentration when fighting, you can use any number of methods designed to practice both being in the moment fully and engaging a threat. Here is an approach I use in training. I assign numbers to individuals and have them line up side by side, all facing me. If a class is very large, I will break it into groups. About ten in a group is a good limit. Then I call out a combination of numbers, such as "six to three." This means number six must move to the left side of number three.

Number six now becomes number four, and those on the left side of four change their numbers accordingly. This goes on and on in different combinations, with the participants having to concentrate on their number, where they need to place themselves, and then how their number changes after doing so.

I start slowly and speed up gradually. Toward the end I am giving new commands almost as fast as the students can react. Once they are warmed up through this exercise, I will do the same thing and then without warning attack one person in the formation. I combine normal types of unarmed attacks (punches, kicks, and chokes) with knife attacks, stick attacks, and pistol and rifle threats, making the attacks more complex as we progress. Any manner of defense tactics can be tested and honed with this method. It aids in the practicing of presence, intellectual concentration, and keeping the instincts open and ready for an attack.

Following the exercise we process the training through discussing presence, sensory experience, concentration, thoughts, anxiety and other feelings, and behavior. The following questions can be helpful in recording and processing this training:

- What was the training scenario?
- What type(s) of attack did you defend against?
- How well were you able to combine the concentration exercise and defending against the attacks?
- What was your experience of anxiety during the training?
- How did anxiety affect your ability to focus?
- What other feelings did you have during the training?
- What effect did they have on you?
- What were your thoughts during the training?
- What was their impact on you—especially on your ability to focus?
- What were your behaviors during the training, both those necessary for completion of the tasks and others?

79

- Did any unnecessary actions impede your ability to accomplish your tasks?
- If so, in what way?

EXERCISE 4-3. *Developing Complete Presence While Fighting*

DATE:

RECORD YOUR OVERALL EVALUATION OF THE TRAINING, INCLUDING POSSIBLE IMPROVEMENTS.

4. Another method I use for generating presence and concentration in the face of attacks is to have one person stand with his or her back to a group of possible attackers. First I tell the person what kind of attack is coming, such as a particular punch, kick, or combination, or an attack with knife, stick, or pistol. I begin with just one person attacking. Then I silently indicate to the group who is to attack. As I say go, the person whose back is to the group turns around and the other person is attacking already.

I will intensify things gradually by having more than one person attack: first two, then three, and more as we progress. As students gain proficiency, attacks will come in different forms, such as a punch or kick or a combination—or with a knife or a stick. The possibilities are endless. The idea is to increase students' abilities to instantaneously use their instincts and senses to assess the threat and react proficiently.

Later I will combine this process with the anxiety-reducing methods, distracting the enemy and reducing his desire to attack.

Of course, I process the experience afterward with the participants. We consider the following questions:

- How well were you able to combine the concentration exercise and defending against the attacks?
- What was your experience of anxiety during the training?
- How did it affect your ability to focus?
- What other feelings did you have during the training and what effect did they have on you?
- What were your thoughts during the training and their impact on you, especially on your ability to focus?
- What were your behaviors during the training, both those necessary for completion of the tasks and others?
- Did any of them impede your ability to accomplish your tasks? If so, in what way?

EXERCISE 4-4. Using Instincts to Assess and React

DATE:

RECORD YOUR OVERALL EVALUATION OF THE TRAINING, INCLUDING POSSIBLE IMPROVEMENTS.

5. Putting all of this together, you can develop a routine to practice defending under different circumstances: before the attack, with the attack, and after the attack. Ideally, your partner would be someone with whom you train regularly, to maximize the quality and safety of the training. That is, the person is able to attack in a proficient manner because he or she is trained, and as you defend, you partner is able to defend against the attack as well, lessening the risk of injury.

If it is not possible to practice with a regular training partner, be sure your temporary partner understands the principles you are developing. Walk through different scenarios and then defend appropriately.

After this initial stage, you can deepen your training relationship to practice your skills outside the normal training environment. That is, you can have an agreement to "test" the other spontaneously under normal life circumstances.

Of course, you need to apply common sense here. Don't initiate an attack scenario in a church, at a staff meeting, or while crossing a busy street. But you can practice while hanging out at home or at the training room, or somewhere else where you won't alarm the general public. You can also set up groups of people to do the same thing with one another so they can repeatedly test each other. The key is to strike a balance between realism and safety.

I run workshops where people are first trained in the techniques for the different scenarios, and then in groups they role-play a scene for a typical situation, such as in the street, at a train station, and in a bar. Specific individuals are secretly assigned the attack role and told what type of attack to initiate. After the role-play, we critique it, slow it down, and replay it until we get it right.

As with exercise 3 above, we should debrief by asking ourselves the following questions:

- What was the training scenario?
- What type(s) of attack did you defend against?

- How well were you able to combine the concentration exercise and defending against the attacks?
- What was your experience of anxiety during the training?
- How did anxiety affect your ability to focus?
- What other feelings did you have during the training?
- What effect did they have on you?
- What were your thoughts during the training?
- What was their impact on you—especially on your ability to focus?
- What were your behaviors during the training, both those necessary for completion of the tasks and others?
- Did any unnecessary actions impede your ability to accomplish your tasks?
- If so, in what way?

EXERCISE 4-5. Practicing Outside the Training Environment

DATE:

RECORD YOUR OVERALL EVALUATION OF THE TRAINING, INCLUDING POSSIBLE IMPROVEMENTS.

5

Being Prepared for Battle

WHILE THIS IS NOT A MARTIAL ARTS or self-defense book in the classical sense—that is, providing self-defense techniques—I do want to cover some physical aspects of self-defense that can give us the edge psychologically. These include aspects related to targets on the attacker, protecting my own targets, and using weapons to my advantage. Soldiers go into battle trained on how and where to attack, with the appropriate protection gear, and armed with weaponry essential to the mission. Without losing the joy for life and turning our everyday experience into battle, we can do the same in order to give ourselves the edge in case we face a threat.

Psychological Targets of Attack

Learning how to use the body as a weapon is only half of what we need to know to fight effectively. We also must know what parts of the enemy's body to target, which is, of course, a basic part of any martial art or self-defense training. What I want to cover here are especially those targets that give us a psychological advantage over the enemy in addition to neutralizing him physically.

Of course, the surest way to neutralize an enemy both psychologically and biologically is to kill him. Then he can't fight, and he is no longer a threat. In most cases, however, killing the enemy is not necessary in civilian situations. Depending on the country in question, you could also end up in legal trouble for doing so. What you can do is work backward from lethal attacks by degree. In other words, for very serious threats, you can attack a target that provides both biological and psychological effects that are close to death, and then move down in severity and degree as the threat itself is less serious in nature.

One mistake often made in fight training is relying too much on pain reactions—in other words, when we target based on how much pain we expect the enemy to feel. In my job and in my training, I have seen people who can continue to act even while experiencing incredible levels of pain. If you were to rely on stopping these individuals only by attacking their groins or nerve points, you would still end up hurt or dead. Their training is such that they learn to absorb pain and keep doing the job. Other individuals on psychoactive substances, especially those correlated with violence, such crystal meth and cocaine, can also endure considerable pain and keep acting violently, in some cases even suffering gunshot wounds and continuing to attack.

I am not saying targets of pain are ineffective. However, we are more likely to affect the enemy psychologically as well as biologically if we bring out the big guns, so to speak. We may not kill the enemy, but we play with his fear of death.

Imagine there are two enemies. You know that both want to kill you. You pull out a shotgun and blast one of them. He is dead. You then make clear to the other one that as long as he stops being a threat, you will spare him. He will stop being a threat.

So, to effectively use targets psychologically on the enemy, we imagine he is really two people. He is the one attacking you, and he is someone else who wants to live. You do something to him that lets him clearly know you could kill him if you wanted, but you will let him live if he stops being a threat. You raise his anxiety level, and then relieve it, as we have discussed.

In chapter 2 I used an example of this as I turned the head of the attacker who claimed to be a police officer. I turned his head enough to demonstrate his vulnerability and to completely control his body motion, but not enough to break his neck or cause serious injury. The amount of pressure I would have had to apply to do this was only just above what he actually felt. His instincts told him this.

So, we are particularly interested in targets that allow us to affect the psychology of the enemy. The enemy thinks you could kill him if you wanted to. The key is to strike a balance. Just because he thinks you could kill him in that moment does not mean you want to or even that the action you take actually would do so. The anxiety of death is often completely different from the reality of possible death. Sometimes people have phobias that they will die from things that are of no significant danger—cleanliness, going outside, and paranoia about other people. What you are playing on with the enemy is his fear of death in order to weaken him.

One of the best ways to do this is with chokes and other attacks affecting airflow. When people cannot breathe, they go into panic. They will do almost anything to regain access to oxygen. But the effective use of chokes must be trained. There is no substitute for working with a top professional trainer in this regard.

There are choking techniques in the IKMA, Gidon System, where one chokes while at the same time applying pressure to break the neck. These techniques can be used without causing any harm whatsoever to the enemy—if he decides to discontinue his attack. In other words, he thinks he will suffocate and get his neck broken, but in reality you control the situation completely, like having your finger on the trigger of a gun. If you do not pull the trigger, nothing happens. If you do, you can either wound him or kill him. In the same way, these techniques can simply stop the enemy by capitalizing on his fear of harm and death, without hurting him at all, or you can choke him until he is unconscious, like placing a bullet strategically to stop an attacker without killing him. You can also suffocate him and break his neck at the same time, like a double tap with a pistol to the chest and head.

Essentially, any method that will play on the enemy's fear of death through inhibiting his breathing can be effective. In addition to chokes, for example, if you are on top in a ground fighting situation, you can smother him by simply hugging his whole head and face into your chest and applying your weight over his mouth and nose. You can also use objects such as a jacket, a belt, dirt from the ground pushed into his mouth and nose, or a plastic bag. All of these can be used to take away the airflow temporarily in order to give a psychological advantage in the fight. Of course, you have to train these methods to make them both effective and to ensure you can control them so you do not apply them lethally when it is not necessary.

Attacking the Senses

Another target is the eyes. When the enemy cannot see, he is not only disadvantaged physically, but there is an automatic response of fear and anxiety relating to potential serious harm or death. We all know this— fear of the dark. Even if there is no danger, we feel anxiety and fear when sight is taken away. This can be used to our advantage in a self-defense situation.

There are many ways to attack the eyes. You can put any number of objects into the eyes, attack the eyes physically with a strike, simply cover the eyes, and also use light from a flashlight to affect the enemy's sight.

Again, this is not a book about self-defense techniques, but I will provide some examples of how we can use physical attacks on the eyes to affect psychology, thereby increasing the effectiveness of the physical attack. As for using objects, there are many options. You are not simply trying to prevent the attacker from seeing, however. Instead, you want to put him in a state of panic. Obviously, pepper spray and similar substances can be effective. Agitating substances like salt, hot beverages, spare change, grass, dirt—basically anything that will both cause pain and affect the enemy's ability to see can give you an edge. You can also directly strike or gouge the eyes if the attack is serious enough to warrant causing more damage and possible permanent blindness, such as when the enemy uses deadly force. If you end up in a grappling situation, you can use a jacket or other piece of clothing, his or yours, to affect his ability to see, which then offers obvious advantages. You can also use a good flashlight to blind the enemy. I always have a tactical light on me—always.

None of these techniques is new. What I am suggesting is adding the psychological aspect. When the enemy is affected by the physical part of the attack on the eyes along with the feeling of being blinded, attack right away, or escape if that is more prudent. Use the physical with the psychological at precisely the right moment.

Sometimes it may be enough to pull out pepper spray—or, better yet, a pepper-spray pistol. If you shine a light in the enemy's eyes, reduce his anxiety by giving him a way out of the situation. Other times you may need to strike right away, just as the dirt thrown into his eyes takes its effect. In a different scenario, it might be best to threaten the use of pepper spray against a potential attacker. When he begins to de-escalate, act as though you will not spray him. When he is no longer on guard, you might decide to hit him with a full blast. We combine these well-known techniques with the principles we have been exploring regarding the use of psychological processes, both ours and the enemy's.

In terms of attacking the sense of touch, fire is one of the best tools for both doing physical damage and for creating a psychological state of panic in the enemy. The feel of fire on the skin has an immediate effect that can give you an advantage. This is why I always have a lighter on me. In fact, I have one in each pocket. Even if an attacker were to apply an effective professional choke as I described above, he will let go immediately when I light his arm on fire. I have worked under-cover in some places where it would have been problematic to carry a traditional weapon, so I carried lighters and lighter fluid inside a nasal spray bottle to disguise what it was.

Another method for attacking the skin is ripping and tearing it. Flesh grabs create significant pain. Dig into the enemy's skin in a circular motion like a cat attacks his prey. You can do this anywhere on the body, but the face and groin are very effective targets. Your teeth are similarly very effective weapons. Biting the face and neck can create significant pain and instill fear and panic in the enemy. You can also use objects that will rip and tear the skin. Knives are an obvious option, but may be unnecessary if the situation is not life threatening. Other objects make potent weapons as well: a cell phone cable, a fork, car keys, or anything that will puncture, rip, and tear the skin. The goal is to create panic and gain the psychological and physical edge when you launch a full attack.

You can also attack the enemy's hearing through sound or striking his ear. Think of war cries. Something in us experiences anxiety when we hear a shrill attack scream. In nature the primal scream is the signal for imminent death, such as from an attacking lion or bear. If the situation has become physical, you can give a war cry combined with your attack.

Striking an enemy's ear will affect his equilibrium. There is a deafening tone that immediately follows a well-placed palm strike to the ear, which then disorients the enemy. Once when trying to arrest a suspect, I was taken up in his huge arms in a bear hug because I was careless in the first part of the altercation. He was immense, and there was a real danger he might break my back or hurt me otherwise. Out of instinct, I screamed as loud as I could into his ear, and he let go just enough so I could apply other methods to defend myself and apprehend him. Of course, I also could have bitten him in the face or neck, but he was drunk and something told me he didn't deserve that kind of reaction. In fact, he was very docile afterward.

Attacks that target several or all of the senses can be especially effective in giving both physical and psychological advantages over the enemy. For example, I carry a 9mm pistol that shoots pepper-spray bullets up to seven meters. It looks, feels, and sounds like a regular Glock, so an attacker is confronted with the threat of a pistol being pointed at him and, if necessary, actually fired at him but without the use of deadly force. However, he hears the blast, which makes him think he has been shot with a real bullet, and then he is confronted with a shot of pepper spray painful enough that his sight and breathing are severely affected. This type of weapon targets all the senses at once, making it especially effective.

Weapons

Being armed can make you more confident about your ability to defend yourself on the one hand and keep you mindful of possible danger on the other. You remain prepared, maintaining a healthy level of anxiety, and at the same time you can actually relax a bit more because you are better equipped should an attack take place.

What weapons we carry to defend ourselves obviously depends on the situation and local laws. I am an American, but I have lived in Germany for many years. The laws in both countries are completely different regarding carrying weapons for self-defense. It is nearly impossible in Germany for a civilian to carry a firearm of any sort, whether pistol or rifle. Similarly, knives are very controlled. It is forbidden to carry any pocketknife you can deploy with one hand, and any knife in general is limited to a very small blade. So to "arm" oneself for self-defense purposes requires some creativity.

I have developed a lot of experience in this regard not only for myself, but for people for whom I have provided close protection services and self-defense training. In some cases, these individuals were under threat from specific stalkers who had already physically attacked them. Even in these cases, they were not allowed to carry a handgun or knife. It is also difficult for close protection agents to get permission here to carry a gun unless the person is a prominent individual, such as a famous celebrity or politician. For this reason, unfortunately, stalking is rampant in Germany, and many victims suffer injury each year due to laws that make it very difficult for them to protect themselves. However, there are ways we can adapt by modifying everyday objects for use in self-defense. In some cases these makeshift weapons offer even better protection than traditional weapons.

One essential tool, as I've mentioned, is a tactical light. I recommend a small high-quality flashlight, tough enough that it won't break when dropped, so it can be used as a striking weapon. The light should be intense, so when you direct it into the eyes of the enemy, he cannot see at all. It should be carried where it is readily deployable. For example, I carry mine in my left pocket or sometimes, especially at night, in my left hand. I do this so my right hand is free to strike or to use a weapon. I can shine the light into the enemy's eyes and then strike him with my right hand while he is blinded.

I also always wear a tactical belt. This adds security by effectively securing weapons, and the belt itself can be used as a weapon for striking, strangling, and binding.

If we reflect on the targets of our attacks, we can adapt everyday items as weapons. For instance, if you want to cut off airflow, you can use some of the items I listed above—a jacket, a belt, a plastic bag. You become proficient at creatively adapting objects to weapons by simply imagining how different items can be used like traditional weapons, and also how you can immediately adapt objects in your environment—utensils, glasses, bottles in a restaurant, magazines and vases in a waiting room. When I fly, I always have my cell cable, a tactical belt, a hardcover book, a strong plastic bag, and my tactical light. Even a menthol lozenge can be a weapon: chew it and spit in an enemy's eye. It burns.

You also need to place your weapons appropriately for smooth deployment, and unless the circumstances require adapting, such as the need to conceal the weapon, you should always have them in the same place so when the time comes to use them, you know where they are. I keep my tactical light in my left pocket, my cell cable in my right pocket, and a lighter in each pocket. I often will also carry some kind of long striking weapon, such as a walking stick or umbrella.

When the security situation is more serious, I carry a small but very robust hammer, razor blades, and the aforementioned nasal spray bottle filled with lighter fluid. I also have an extra belt in my back left pocket or in a cargo pocket to use as a weapon and for tying up the enemy. Sometimes I will have a very small can of hair spray that fits into a pocket. This combined with the lighter has a well-known effect. This must be practiced and trained though, because the can may explode.

Invisibility as a Weapon

The most effective weapon I have is my own invisibility. I am best prepared when I do not exist to the enemy.

Once when I was in Netanya, Israel, for training, I was walking down the street at night. Despite its incredibly beautiful beaches, Netanya is known as a kind of Wild West in Israel due to organized crime and terrorist elements operating in and around it. One has to be vigilant there. I am always assessing people who approach my space, determining whether they are potential threats. When I saw a man coming toward me on the same side of the street, I immediately assessed him. He walked without any indication of looking for trouble, with his hands in his pockets, just a normal-looking guy.

As we got closer to each other, he talked to me. If I hadn't known him, I would have considered him absolutely benign. If I were an offender, for example, looking for a fight or a robbery victim, he would have been the perfect target. I was completely free of anxiety in that moment and unprepared. However, in reality that man was Haim Gidon, chief of the Israeli Krav Maga Association, one of the most lethal killers in the world.

In *The Art of War*, Sun Tzu says the ideal spy is the absolute opposite of what the enemy would expect but at the same time capable of exactly what will defeat the enemy. That is the way we want to prepare physically and psychologically as warriors.

Protective Gear

Just as with weapons, protective gear can serve psychologically to raise our confidence for dealing with a potential attack and to remind us that attacks can occur. Soldiers who go into battle wear armor to protect vital targets. Without overdoing it, we can do the same to give ourselves an advantage. We should wear shoes that provide good traction for running and fighting and that can also cause harm if we choose to deliver a kick. Our other clothing should be strong but loose enough to allow movement for fighting and running.

I won't go into details here about the technical qualities of fireproof and bulletproof clothing. We have to decide what is reasonable and necessary under different circumstances, and technical questions are not actually the point of this book. But we should give some thought as to how we can protect the same set of targets we go after on the enemy. In potentially dangerous situations, you should have eye protection, clothing thick enough to provide protection against blades, your neck covered with, for instance, a jacket or scarf, groin protection if possible, and quality gloves. One can very easily research and acquire the right protective equipment for a given situation.

Summary

This is not about being paranoid and always thinking there is danger around every corner. It is simply about being prepared for the real dangers that do exist. When you face that reality, you experience anxiety and take steps to protect yourself and those for whom you are responsible. When you allow yourself to feel the anxiety of danger and even mortality, you become assertive in your life and will yourself to take responsibility. In his book *Love and Will*, Rollo May talks about the care for oneself that manifests from honestly conceptualizing the difficulties we face and embracing the anxiety and suffering inherent in life.

When we begin to care for ourselves, we take responsibility for ourselves without malice toward others. We embrace anxiety rather than let it close us off. While May's words relate to the psychology of relationships, we can see the wisdom in them for our identities and actions as warriors. We can be prepared in caring for our own existence without being aggressive or shutting ourselves off from relationships or experience. At one extreme, passiveness and believing all is well with the world is naive and is not caring for oneself. At the other extreme, aggressiveness will actually invite danger and limit experiences in life to one violent encounter after another. This is not caring for oneself either. The synthesis of the two is assertiveness—caring for yourself and those for whom you are responsible through active preparedness.

I had a student once who said before she went to the first training at my school she had been training a considerable amount of time in another discipline but she felt apprehensive about actually fighting. She did not feel she could be aggressive and would freeze up when actually faced with the enemy.

I invited her to a five-hour seminar at which the others were seasoned fighters from my club. To make a long story short, her skills were well developed for the style she had trained, and as we started to spar, she unleashed hell not only on my students—all young, fit, and proficient male fighters—but on me as well when I demonstrated some techniques on her. What was remarkable about her was not that she understated her abilities, but that her humility actually kept her cognizant of her shadow—that is, her tendency to underestimate and doubt her abilities. So instead of falling prey to this "weakness," she acted in the opposite direction and was an absolute lioness whose ferociousness was intimidating to anyone in her sights.

Her resolute act of will to become what she wanted to be reminded me of a quote my mentor repeated regularly: "We are not what we feel. We are what we do." She felt vulnerable, unsure, and intimidated by conflict. Did she manifest the behavior connected with these feelings through withdrawing, becoming passive, freezing? No. She willed herself to be a warrior, period. She became what she wanted to be despite her doubts. I would go so far as to say this: if she had not accepted and recognized her "weakness," this would not have been possible.

What makes us "weak" is what makes us warriors. A warrior is not a cold-blooded killer. A warrior is a defender of those who cannot defend themselves. And to be willing to defend in the true spirit of defending—in contrast to being a quasi-video-game action-film figure who feels cool about himself by popping off rounds and pouncing in full battle gear—it is necessary to empathize with the weakness of those whom we are defending. If we are just killers, then we are only pseudo-warriors, mimicking an ideal formulated by others.

To be true warriors and defenders, we must be intimately linked, deep in our marrow, to those whom we defend: the man next to us in battle, our families, our countrymen, or, in the highest order of defending, any human being who suffers under tyranny and abuse. The true test of a warrior is not his or her hardness or ability, but the degree to which that warrior feels compassion for the suffering of others under oppression and acts despite all instincts for self-preservation to protect what transcends the individual ego—our brothers, our sisters, regardless of origin, united through suffering.

So, the psychologically prepared warrior is invisible. He or she is equipped with all the necessary gear for a threatening situation, physically trained, alert and using the instincts through sensory input, but completely benign in appearance. The combined effect of being prepared while at the same time not posturing or *looking for a fight* creates readiness and integrity, both of which bring confidence and self-respect, leading to centeredness and presence, strengthening the ability to accurately read and act on reality as it is happening in the moment.

6

After-Action Assessment

WE CAN SHARPEN ANY SET of skills when we take time after employing them to assess what went well, what did not go well, and what we can do to improve. Soldiers, professional athletes, psychotherapists, and professionals in all areas do this. In a self-defense situation, we need to do the same. It is not enough to simply review our physical tactics. We need to assess what we felt before, during, and after the event, particularly regarding our anxiety. We also need to consider the feelings of the enemy before, during, and after, including his or her anxiety and accompanying actions. After this, we need to role-play the event, going step by step through it again, seeking to improve our actions, including considering how well we allowed ourselves to experience anxiety and bring in and process information from our senses, reacting to the information and situation without panic. We then role-play the event further, under intense conditions, to develop deeper, instinctive proficiency and "thicker skin" for facing similar situations in the future.

Processing the Event in Stages
Considering an attack situation in terms of how we felt before, during, and after is much the same as what a psychotherapist does with a

client who is processing a traumatic event. No event can be understood as a complete experience when broken into these parts. The event has its own integrity, its own reality, regardless of how we pick it apart. This is especially true with events that evoke intense feeling. If we want to learn from a situation, we must have respect for this fact. In order to make sense of it, we break it down, but at the same time, we allow ourselves to be open to reality as it speaks to us. We don't need to reduce that reality, neatly packaged for our intellect. We work through the dialectic, analyzing the event as separate stages, while at the same time understanding that, in reality, there are no stages.

Our need to intellectualize and understand events is due to our anxiety. We believe if we can understand a traumatic event, we will have control over it. And we do in some ways. That is the purpose for working through it. All that we do, in terms of understanding any phenomenon, is limited by the ability of our senses to bring reality in and the ability of our intellect to process that reality. The reality itself remains. So, if we are too sure of ourselves as we are breaking down an event, we can be certain we will not be prepared for the next challenge we face.

The mistakes made in military campaigns throughout history testify to this. One would think that after much analysis of mistakes made in failed campaigns, we would be fully prepared when we face similar situations again on the battlefield. As we all know, however, this is not the case. In my opinion, one reason for this is that we rely too much on our intellect and our analyzing of events, and we then reduce our anxiety through thinking we have control. If only one element changes, though, the entire reality changes. Therefore, we must analyze and understand an attack while at the same time feeling anxiety. We must be open to elements of the situation we may not want to recognize because they cause anxiety.

Reflect again on Kierkegaard's words: anxiety is the road to the truth. If I process a traumatic event and do not feel anxiety, I am avoiding the truth. I am leaving out something of vital importance, something that causes me anxiety. No traumatic event is without anxiety, so if I try to do an after-action review without this feeling accompanying me, it is like listening to a song with the volume turned down too low to hear the words or the small nuances in the melody and harmony.

It is useful, however, to start by breaking down the situation into stages. First we can write the basic details. Next we go through the entire assessment. I have set this framework in "Practical Exercises for After-Action Review," which appears at the end of this chapter.

Stage 1: Before the Event

The first stage involves processing what was going on just before the event took place. We need to assess everything we can remember about the enemy, ourselves, and the overall situation, including location, time, weather, and all other factors associated with the experience.

In considering the enemy, we need to ask ourselves questions regarding his behavior preceding the event. Were there signs of possible aggression we might have ignored? Did we talk ourselves out of seeing some impending danger to avoid anxiety? How was he dressed? How did he move? How did he speak? All aspects of his behavior need to be brainstormed and written down. Did he seem intoxicated or influenced by some physiological process that may have led to aggression? What thoughts and feelings do we think he was experiencing? This is obviously very tricky, but it should be considered and also written down to help assess the big picture.

Who else was involved just before the event, and what role did they play?

We also need to assess what we were thinking, feeling, and what behaviors we exhibited prior to the event. In what ways did these thoughts, feelings, and behaviors relate to the behavior of the enemy and to the other factors mentioned above? What role did anxiety play before the event took place? Did we perhaps send signals that may have had a part in triggering the behavior of the enemy? If so, what were they?

Stage 2: During the Event

Next we need to ask the same kinds of questions regarding the incident itself. How did the enemy attack? Or if there was no physical action, what did he do specifically? What thoughts and feelings may have been behind the actions? What other factors played a role? Did anyone else become involved?

What was our response? What methods did we use? What were we thinking and feeling as we acted? Did we use any weapons? What role did the external factors play—for example, location, weather, and time? Were our actions limited by any of these factors or did they help?

Stage 3: After the Event

Now we do the same for the phase following the event. What did the enemy do, feel, and think immediately after? How did the event actually come to an end? Were others involved in stopping it if there was an actual altercation? Were the police or other first responders involved? How did we feel immediately following, and what were our thoughts? What behaviors did we manifest, and what physiological responses did we have?

Processing the Event in the Now

After documenting and analyzing the event in stages, we then process it in the moment. What I mean by this is that we actually try to relive the event. One of the best ways for doing this is to role-play it. If we have others to help us with this, all the better. One person can play the enemy and others can play the parts of additional individuals who were in the situation.

Now that we have reflected in stages on what we can remember about the situation, we go through replaying it step by step. In as realistic a way as possible, we reenact each stage. We should do our best to manifest the same feelings and thoughts, although this is, of course, impossible to do with perfect accuracy.

What is very important, though, is to actually feel as we now role-play the event. It is especially crucial to get back in touch with the anxiety we experienced. We relive the moment in a true sense, emotionally speaking. This is key. Any purely objective assessment of a situation without also going through the feelings again will result in an ineffective evaluation of what happened and of how we might improve our actions. So as we manifest the feelings again through role-playing, we let ourselves go, so to speak, and brave the experience once more, even if it was traumatic.

Once we have done this for each stage, we immediately record our thoughts, feelings, and behavior as especially the anxiety is still working through us. Then we assess more deeply the thoughts, feelings, and behavior of the enemy through gaining feedback from the person role-playing the enemy. We do the same for any others who may have been involved in the situation. Following this, we go through the event again, without breaking it into stages, but rather from start to finish, and then analyze and process it as before.

Assessment of Possible Improvements

Improving proficiency in self-defense and combative situations has to do with two issues: technical performance and emotional processing. Although it is important to identify improvements in both areas, they are actually interconnected; improvement in one area automatically increases proficiency in the other.

For instance, if we experience a situation in which we "fail" to correctly use a fighting technique to defend ourselves, we train hard and under realistic conditions and then use the particular technique correctly. This increases our confidence (emotional processing) for dealing successfully with future conflicts. The key to accomplishing this is far more psychological than physical due to the debilitating nature of shame, guilt, and other feelings associated with failure. So we must change our view of "failure" if we want to evolve into better warriors.

Perhaps the most difficult self-defense situations to review are those in which we have been victimized and "lost" the fight. We want to control the situation in retrospect. We wonder what we did wrong, how we got into the situation, why we were attacked, and why we didn't prevail. What we are doing in asking all these questions is trying to appease our anxiety about something similar happening again and also about our feeling "weak." It is a natural reaction as an emotion.

What is not natural are the thoughts that often accompany the process. Many times we berate ourselves and reinforce feelings of weakness and failure. We would rather believe we had some control over the situation than simply accept that chaos is indifferent to our efforts to control it. The fact that we are so vulnerable that nothing we do can keep us from being hurt can provoke incredible anxiety, and so we convince ourselves we are at fault. We believe that if we are at fault, we can do something to prevent it from happening again.

I have been hurt several times in close protection and military situations, and I remember having thoughts like, "What the hell? I am trained as a professional killer, and I got my ass kicked." Sometimes I even questioned why I should continue training if it wasn't going to work anyway. Of course, I have the benefit of being a psychologist, so I know the power negative cognitive processes can have, and I know they occur automatically out of self-preservation and often should not be given any weight. However, this knowledge did not stop them from occurring in me. In fact, I had to do exactly what I am describing here: identify the thoughts, process the truth and untruth of them, and reconstruct and role-play the event to help me grow as a warrior and as a human being. That is the power and freedom we have no matter what happens to us. We can choose how the experience affects us, however terrible it was.

The key to getting past our minds—that is, the cognitive processes that berate us with messages of weakness and failure—is to operate from a dialectic compass. Nearly every issue has two sides, a thesis and antithesis. Often, in order to avoid feelings of anxiety, we humans hold vigorously to one of these poles. Good or evil, "good guys" and "bad guys," strong or weak, winner or loser, love and hate—these are just some obvious examples of how we categorize and separate very complex issues in order to give us some sense of control over them, to relieve or minimize our anxiety.

The same is true when it comes to combative and self-defense situations. We either win or lose a fight. We either win or lose in Afghanistan or Iraq. We will win or lose the War on Terror or the War on Drugs. This type of either/or thinking, when carried out with too much surety or what the Greeks called hubris, often leads to further difficulty and preventable tragedy because reality itself does not care what we humans think in order to minimize our anxiety.

There is a saying in judo that if two masters stand across from each other, there will be no fight. This is because judo is based on using the movements and momentum of the attacker against him. Because judo is literally the "gentle way," however, no attack will ever take place because a gentle warrior does not attack unnecessarily. Judo is a fighting method. Judo is not a fighting method. These two statements are thesis and antithesis. This makes no sense to us. As we consider the synthesis, though—the higher wisdom, so to speak—we can say that judo is a fighting system, the goal of which is to prevent a fight from ever happening again between two human beings. If two masters stand across from each other, there will be no fight.

This same type of tried and tested wisdom must be applied to reviewing what has happened in a self-defense or combative situation. There is no winner or loser in a fight. When we win, we lose. When we lose, we win.

Those who "win" a fight and fully celebrate this through pride put up a wall to their own improvement. What I mean is that if we are fully satisfied with ourselves, we will not even begin the process of assessing what improvements we can make as warriors. We will continue on to the next possible combative situation without having learned anything from the situation we "won." Further, in order to celebrate a victory such as this, the enemy must be fully dehumanized to the extent that we do not feel any compassion for the defeated fellow human being.

This last use of language is controversial. I have come into contact with people in my work who traffic women and children, are involved in terrorism, or are rapists and murderers. I have often found it difficult to think of them as human beings. But this does not matter. The fact is they are human beings. If I allow my abhorrence and sometimes even feelings of rage and hate to block my accurate assessment of reality, then I will not improve my ability to combat these perpetrators. It is as simple as that. This is not a moral issue; it simply concerns reality and my ability to improve myself based on reality and not my passions.

If I force myself to see even the most abhorrent enemy as a human being, I will be better able to assess his possible weaknesses and strengths, and especially how to use his anxiety against him. To do that, I must have compassion for him, as difficult as this may be. This is one side of the dialectic compass for improving myself as warrior: I must have compassion for my enemy as a human being. In some situations I am compassionate not because I care for him but to improve my ability to defeat him.

On the other side is the compassion I must have for myself as a human being. As discussed above, we often berate ourselves and feel shame, guilt, vulnerability, and weakness after we have been the victim of an attack and have "lost" a fight. When we develop compassion for ourselves, however, and begin the assessment process of our performance as a warrior from this standpoint, we are better able to process and change the negative thought processes that can debilitate us as warriors. In doing so, we can assess more objectively and clearly the possible improvements we can make. So even if we lost a fight, we have won because we have a powerful new source of thoughts, behaviors, and feelings that can teach us how to improve. Compassion for ourselves moves us to take care of ourselves and gives us motivation to become better as warriors in order to better protect ourselves.

So we must have compassion for the enemy and for ourselves. The synthesis of the dialectic of the enemy versus me, of losing versus winning, is acting with compassion even as I act as a warrior, including the act of killing. I operate from compassion for humanity, and so my actions will be guided by both my ferocity in battle and the motivation to only use that ferocity for good. This requires me to feel anxiety because the reality of battle does not fit the simple standpoint of dealing with the combative reality as it is, not as I wish it to be. I must be willing to face the truth and operate from compassion, which then evokes anxiety because someone is going to get hurt. Thinking again of the two proverbial judo masters, I hope my potential enemy is also operating from compassion so no fight will occur.

So as we consider ways of improving our tactics in a self-defense or combative situation, what is paramount is the motivation from which we do so. In role-playing we can practice better combative and psychological tactics, such as those described in previous chapters, but with the motivation of having compassion for the enemy and for ourselves. This will ensure we are developing as warriors based on reality and with the full potential to heal even as we improve.

All combative situations involve some level of trauma, even when we "win." Assessment through the motivation of compassion provides the best chance for healing from the trauma as we develop. In a somewhat magical way compassion leads to thoughts and behavioral responses that have to do with the "good" in human beings, and in this way we do not lose hope in the "good" of the world. Such a loss is often at the core of severe psychological trauma resulting from violence. We lose hope in humanity and in ourselves.

Visualizing Improvement and Possibilities: A Warrior Must Have Hope and Foster Initiative

Dale Comstock is a former Delta Force operator, author, and physical training and alternative healing coach. He discusses the power of visualizing a reality that has not yet manifested to then make it happen. He explains how this has been an important principle in shaping his reality on and off the battlefield. This process is far more subtle and powerful than the classical concept of setting a goal and working toward it.

You actually decide that something is real, and then your unconscious will work toward making it real. The pioneering psychologist Carl Jung proposed basically the same concept when he said we must "trick" the brain to manifest what we need despite the many obstacles life inevitably puts in our way.

Paradoxically, the brain holds the power to destroy us or to elevate us to levels we never realized were possible. On the one hand, it wants to be satisfied, comfortable—no hunger, no thirst, no pain, no worries. This has something to do with our survival instincts. The brain wants us to relieve the anxiety manifested when an alarm goes off, signaling that all is not OK. Of course, this is necessary and useful. But if we only live from this kind of motivation, we never push ourselves beyond a very crude biological survival. Many issues related to obesity, substance abuse, lethargy, and apathy can be attributed to a life orientation based on this perspective.

So sometimes we must actually will ourselves to go beyond what our biology wants. We forsake comfort in order to reach our full potential and, in threatening situations, to defend ourselves. Learning to fight is far more than learning technique, as we all know. In the course of our development as warriors, whether as beginners or experts, we must continually will ourselves to believe there is an even stronger fighter in us, and this is particularly important when conducting an after-action review. We must will ourselves to visualize a future successful outcome.

Rollo May said we must conceive in order to perceive. This is crucial, for example, in psychotherapy. When clients come to me, I must first convince them there is hope; if they can conceive of a new life, that life will become possible. I do the same in training new fighters. I have seen the most timid, wounded people come in, and through courage over time, become absolutely lethal if they are threatened. I'll quote my mentor again: "We are not what we feel. We are what we do."

Faith in this creed is vital, particularly in the beginning of training or a program of personal development. The goal is to make the will, not biology, the deciding factor in development and destiny. To get there, one must push beyond pain, doubt, fatigue, fear, apprehension, and the big one—anxiety.

Post-Traumatic Stress Disorder and the Warrior

Some people believe they do not need therapy after traumatic experiences in combat. Others seek healing in perfecting technique. The "need" to choose one of these perspectives is often counterproductive. As far as I am concerned, there is no difference between taking part in physical training and going to therapy. To become effective warriors, we need both. In fact, I would go so far as to say unless we do the work of processing our suffering, especially anxiety, we are not yet the warriors we are capable of becoming.

If healing from trauma meant gaining empowerment by creatively working through emotions with the overall goal of becoming stronger—just like working out physically—therapy would be a lot more successful. It would especially open the door for men, who may feel therapy is for the weak. Nobody says, "Hey, I am heading to the dojo because I am weak," or "I am going to the firing range because I am weak." But men often think, "I am going to therapy, so that means I am weak."

Working Through versus Curing

The medical model identifying post-traumatic stress disorder (PTSD) as a disease that needs to be cured, whether through medication or otherwise, is too limited in its approach. There are definitely those who have suffered to such an extent that significant biological changes have taken place in the brain and medication is necessary. But it is all too often the primary help given. I worked in a psychiatric clinic in the military as a counselor, and one of the primary directives we were given was that long-term psychotherapy was to be avoided.

Instead, those diagnosed with PTSD were given medication. More often, no diagnosis was made—despite obvious symptoms—in order to avoid prescribing a psychotropic medication for a soldier who may be carrying a weapon. This was the primary approach in military and Veteran's Administration mental health care for our veterans suffering from PTSD. It was, in my opinion, very unethical. The best model for diagnosis and treatment is that of the American Psychiatric Association and the diagnostic criteria of the *Diagnostic Statistical Manual*.

One significant change to the diagnosis of PTSD over the years was adding the requirement that one must have specifically faced an event that could potentially lead to serious injury or death. This may seem logical, but determining whether a person really experienced the emotional shock that can lead to PTSD is basically up to the person doing the assessment. For example, suppose a soldier is deployed for an extended period and is never personally engaged in combat; perhaps he or she is far enough in the rear to be out of any real danger. This soldier may, though, be witness to wounded and killed fellow service members or may even know some of them. This prolonged exposure to death and suffering is obviously enough to cause trauma.

Many mental health workers operating solely or primarily from the above model will not make the diagnosis, and then soldiers do not get the treatment they need. I myself have witnessed this. Often, these soldiers are instead diagnosed with an adjustment disorder. This is blatantly unethical and it shows a lack of respect for the service they have provided and their suffering.

There are two ways to deal with any psychological struggle. One is to look to the medical model of assessment and diagnosis and then follow the treatment plan. The other is to understand the individual and help him or her work through the suffering. When I use the term "understand," I mean suspending judgment, analysis, and diagnosis and instead listening to and being open to the person who is suffering.

Even if he or she can be identified as having a problem fitting a particular diagnosis, the mystery of that individual changes everything, both in terms of the way symptoms manifest and what methods will work to facilitate healing. The psychoanalyst Otto Rank astutely applied Einstein's insights into physics to psychology when he said the psyche is no different from matter—personality and diagnosis are relative to how an individual lives those phenomena and also relative to how the therapist approaches that individual's struggles and diagnoses.

What we call PTSD was not handed down by God with the Ten Commandments. It is a theoretical construct formulated by individuals, with all the preconceptions individuals have, including those behind the scientific method. If you were to speak with a psychiatrist, a clinical psychologist, a licensed counselor, and a social worker, you would get differing opinions about the causes and appropriate treatment of any psychological problem because each of these professionals has different preconceptions and theories. Additionally, there are vastly different theories within the professions themselves. A psychoanalyst, a behaviorist, a systems therapist, and a humanist all have differing opinions about what causes psychological problems and what should be done about them.

The problem is that most people who go for help don't know this. They think whatever they are told is a scientific standard, like when they go in for a sore throat. When I worked at a military psychiatric clinic, people would call or be referred for help and the secretary would then schedule that person with the next available mental health worker. Depending on the luck of the draw, the individual would end up seeing a psychiatrist, social worker, psychologist, licensed professional counselor, or a paraprofessional premaster's level counselor. All of these individuals have different training and different assumptions, as well as different methods of diagnosis and treatment, as I said above. But the client is unlikely to know this. So he or she may end up being prescribed medication, undergoing psychoanalysis, doing family systems work, engaging in Rogerian client-centered counseling, and the list goes on, all depending on the practitioner available.

What often fails, in my opinion, in treating PTSD is that professionals get hung up on their own particular theories and academic backgrounds. These become the focus, and the client becomes secondary, a collection of symptoms needing treatment based on a particular paradigm.

What people who are suffering really need is to be understood, and through the genuine empathy of the therapist, to be honored for their suffering. Through this process, the client undergoes a corrective emotional experience that can gradually lead toward healing. What is often shared, irrespective of the events and other causes underlying the suffering, is a sense of guilt and shame on the part of the client, particularly survivor's guilt in the case of veterans. In addition, there is often a sense of distrust of others and the world in general, a feeling that the world is an unsafe place. Hope and meaning in life begin to diminish. To rectify this, the relationship between the therapist and the patient is paramount—not the therapist's theoretical background.

If we apply this discussion to combative situations—that is, when we develop PTSD due to a traumatic event involving an attacker—we need to remember what made us sick, so to speak, was a human interaction. The solution, then, must also be human, not merely medical or the application of some kind of method. Medication may help, but not alone. Neither will behavioral approaches, cognitive reprogramming to replace negative thoughts with positive ones, or any other purely mechanical way of changing an individual or relieving symptoms. Negative human experiences challenge our feelings of hope for all humankind. The only solution is proof that humans are indeed good, and this proof comes when the therapist takes the time to listen to and understand the suffering client.

So when we decide as part of our training that we may need treatment for a traumatic event, we must take the process very seriously. Warriors must be warriors in caring for themselves. The same drive we put into training and fighting should be applied to demanding quality mental health care, as well as to our own efforts in the healing process.

The following is a checklist about what you should ask a mental health professional about his or her competencies before entering a therapy relationship. As I said before, the process of working through trauma and developing proficiency in psychological tactics is just like getting fight training. Would you go to a substandard trainer to improve fighting skills? You would want to know that trainer's background and experience, but you would also want to know he or she is a good person. The same should be demanded of a mental health worker when seeking treatment.

What to Ask Mental Health Professionals

1. What is their education level and what licenses do they have?
2. What is the specific theory or theories from which they work?
3. How many years of experience do they have, and approximately how many people have they worked with?
4. What experience do they have with trauma and PTSD?
5. What do they expect from you and what are they able to offer you?

Competent and confident professionals will have no problem answering these questions. For example, not only will they be willing to discuss education level and licensure, but they should be willing to explain the differences among psychologists, counselors, social workers, and psychiatrists. If they are not willing to have this discussion, then they are either morally or professionally unprepared to treat PTSD. Look elsewhere.

There is no reason why quality professionals cannot say that if you work hard, you will get better under their care. Even with a well-qualified and dedicated therapist, we must be willing to do the work. We as warriors are not weakened by stopping to assess, to integrate our wounds, losses, and failures. Instead, we develop a wiser toughness, a courage that lets go of ego, making energy available for greater strength. Resisting our feelings takes energy and dams a massive power that builds up from suffering. Open that dam and an immeasurable rush of energy is released. The direction it takes is critical. This is why the relationship between the therapist and the warrior is important. Rollo May said that the therapist is like Virgil leading Dante through hell in the *Inferno*. Virgil knew the way, but if Dante had not been willing to make the journey, he would not have made it out and to paradise.

Practical Exercises for After-Action Review

1. When military and law enforcement professionals have been involved in a critical incident, it is common for them to conduct an after-action review. During this process they examine the details of what took place, which aspects were successful, which were not, and what they could do better next time. This is a good practice for soldiers, officers, and civilians alike.

   Below is a list of points to consider in your own after-action review. This process is helpful with anything from a lethal confrontation to a potentially dangerous encounter on the street.

Before the Threatening Event

- Describe the scene of the threatening event. Include environment, time, weather, others present—essentially everything taking place.
- Describe everything you perceived about the attacker before the incident.
- Were you able to anticipate an attack or was it unexpected?
- What was your experience of anxiety before the threatening event? Be as specific as possible in terms of when and to what degree you felt it.
- How did it affect your ability to focus?
- What other feelings did you have before the event?
- How did they affect you, especially your ability to focus?

- What were your thoughts before the event?
- How did they affect you, especially your ability to focus?
- What were your behaviors before the event?
- Did any of them impede your ability to focus and use your instincts? If so, in what way?
- Describe your sensory experience and how it related to your thoughts, feelings, behaviors, and ability to remain present and focused.
- How could you have improved your response before the threatening event?

During the Threatening Event

- Were you able to defend yourself using the psychological methods described in this book?
- Were you able to defend yourself using martial arts or self-defense techniques?
- What was your experience of anxiety during the threatening event? Be as specific as possible in terms of when and to what degree you felt it.
- How did it affect your ability to focus?
- What other feelings did you have during the event?
- How did they affect you, especially your ability to focus?
- What were your thoughts during the event?
- How did they affect you, especially your ability to focus?
- What were your behaviors during the event?
- Did any of them impede your ability to focus and use your instincts? If so, in what way?
- Describe your sensory experience and how it related to your thoughts, feelings, behaviors, and ability to remain present and focused.
- How could you have improved your response during the threatening event?

After the Threatening Event

- What was your experience of anxiety after the threatening event? Be as specific as possible in terms of when and to what degree you felt it.
- How did it affect your ability to focus?
- What other feelings did you have after the event?
- How did they affect you, especially your ability to focus?
- What were your thoughts after the event?
- How did they affect you, especially your ability to focus?
- What were your behaviors after the event?
- Did any of them impede your ability to focus and use your instincts? If so, in what way?
- How can you improve your response after the threatening event?

EXERCISE 6-1. Reviewing a Critical Incident

DATE:

AFTER WORKING THROUGH THE PROMPTS ABOVE, RECORD YOUR OVERALL EVALUATION OF THE THREATENING EVENT.

2. After processing the before, during, and after of the event, role-play what happened. Do this with a partner or simply by yourself.

Before the Role-Play

- What was your experience of anxiety before the role-play? Be as specific as possible in terms of when and to what degree you felt it.
- How did it affect your ability to focus?
- What other feelings did you have before the role-play?
- How did they affect you, especially your ability to focus?
- What were your thoughts before the role-play?
- How did they affect you, especially your ability to focus?
- What were your behaviors before the role-play?
- Did any of them impede your ability to focus and use your instincts? If so, in what way?

During the Role-Play

- What was your experience of anxiety during the role-play? Be as specific as possible in terms of when and to what degree you felt it.
- How did it affect your ability to focus?
- What other feelings did you have during the role-play?
- How did they affect you, especially your ability to focus?
- What were your thoughts during the role-play?
- How did they affect you, especially your ability to focus?
- What were your behaviors during the role-play?
- Did any of them impede your ability to focus and use your instincts? If so, in what way?

After the Role-Play

- What was your experience of anxiety after the role-play? Be as specific as possible in terms of when and to what degree you felt it.
- How did it affect your ability to focus?
- What other feelings did you have after the role-play?
- How did they affect you, especially your ability to focus?
- What were your thoughts after the role-play?
- How did they affect you, especially your ability to focus?

- What were your behaviors after the role-play?
- Did any of them impede your ability to focus and use your instincts? If so, in what way?

EXERCISE 6-2. Role-Playing a Critical Incident

DATE:

AFTER WORKING THROUGH THE PROMPTS ABOVE, RECORD YOUR OVERALL EVALUATION OF THE ROLE-PLAY. HAS IT IMPROVED YOUR UNDERSTANDING OF THE THREATENING EVENT?

7

Specific Issues Relating to Women and Children

ACCORDING TO THE WORLD HEALTH ORGANIZATION, one in three women worldwide will be the victim of violence, including sexual violence. Over twenty-two million women in the United States have been sexually assaulted. The FBI estimates only 46 percent of these assaults are reported. These statistics tell us it is vital for every woman and girl to take courses in combatives, both armed and unarmed. This may seem drastic, but facts are facts, and the danger is real.

It is also important to use the data to gain insight into the potential enemy. While not all violent crimes committed against women fit easily into categories, we can say with confidence that the vast majority have to do with power issues relating to violent men and their female victims.

Society's Messages to Women
The first step is to challenge the cultural programming of women, who often accept a subordinate position toward men or even believe at some level that they exist only for a man's entertainment. And yet, precisely

for that reason, this may yield a certain advantage for women—that is, the anxiety level of the man is already down due to his sense of power, and we already know the advantages given when the enemy's anxiety level is down. He is less likely to be aware of what we might do to evade or attack.

I want to be clear that I am not saying we should consider women warriors on a sliding scale simply because they are women. This makes no more sense than saying that men are all the same or that there exist basic principles about men that make them better or worse warriors, depending on personal traits or fighting styles. Rather, I am saying we need to consider the possible belief systems a woman may have internalized regarding her relationship to men in society, particularly regarding power relationships, abuse, and violence. Further, in thinking about strategy and tactics we need to consider the enemy, and here we are especially concerned with psychological issues relating to male attackers and women as potential victims.

While it is acknowledging a stereotype to say women are more passive than men, I will say it is absolutely the case that women are, and have been for a long time, bombarded with the messages in many societies that their position is secondary to men's, that they are to follow rather than lead and listen rather than be heard. If a woman is a victim of a sexual assault, moreover, there remains the primitive attitude that perhaps she was inviting the behavior through flirting and the way she dressed. As a psychologist and martial arts instructor, I have been witness to and myself have worked with different types of "assertiveness" training, both for relationships and life in general. I also, of course, have much experience in training for the more aggressive type of assertiveness needed for physically defending oneself. Often, such programs are targeted especially at women.

I believe this is a mistake. The supposition is often that women are passive and therefore need training to be assertive. Starting from that assumption as a trainer indicates a prejudice and perhaps even a type of sexism from the outset. I am not saying there is a conscious disregard for the inherent strength in women, but often that is the attitude.

Rather than training women in assertiveness, I concentrate on helping them rediscover their natural assertiveness. Obviously, we all have different temperaments, men and women alike, and even as children we show differences in shyness and other traits that may have to do with assertiveness, but to say that girls are more passive than boys at birth is based on absolutely no hard scientific evidence. Rather, depending on the particular environment a female grows up in and the experiences she may have had, her capacity for asserting herself might be stifled. This can also have a detrimental effect on her ability to defend herself in a threatening situation.

Before we talk about how this may be corrected, it is important to clarify what assertiveness is. Let's return to the model of the dialectic (thesis, antithesis, synthesis). In this case we will consider the mind-set of a woman who has internalized a subordinate position and who struggles to assert herself.

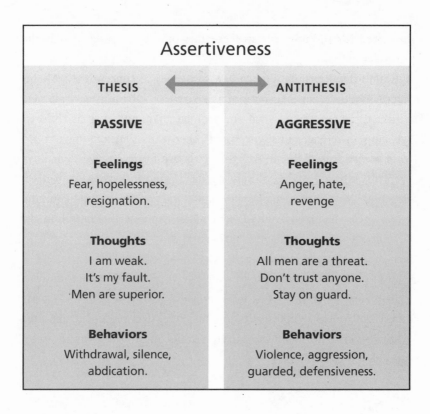

When we compare these two opposing sides, we see the core issue that remains the same is the reality that thoughts, feelings, and behavior are all related to men. In other words, a woman operating from either of these extremes is basing her entire psychology and being on her belief about the orientation of men toward women.

Of course, it would be impossible for men to have no impact on women's psychology. Men are inextricably part of a woman's reality. But a woman can change her psychological orientation toward men. She can recognize that men exist, but not base her orientation to men on her belief about the orientation of men toward women. She is free to choose what her orientation is. Otherwise, these opposites—passivity versus aggression—could not exist.

Again, returning to the general process of the dialectic, we take the next step toward the truth by keeping what remains the same in the two opposing sides, which is once again the individual's power to choose.

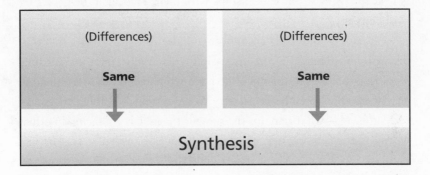

A Woman's Existence Is Based on Men

Now we turn this into a thesis and work it against its antithesis. Without listing the obvious thoughts, feelings, and behaviors that are different in each, we can see clearly what is the same in both:

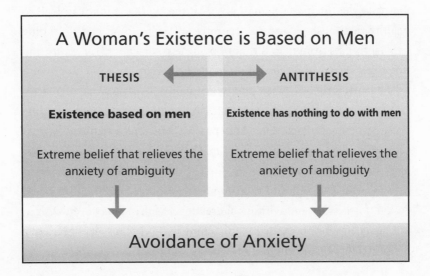

So what is the same in both belief systems is that a woman is choosing to avoid anxiety by holding to an extreme belief that helps her avoid the complexity of having to consider men as individuals rather than prejudging them as all the same. When a woman holds either of these extreme beliefs, she is not considering her identity for its own sake but is instead basing it on relationships with men. This again helps her to avoid anxiety.

We do not need to construct another dialectic process to see that this discussion is identical to the discussion we had in chapter 1 regarding anxiety as it relates to threats. Whether a woman chooses to avoid anxiety or chooses to embrace anxiety to an extreme—leading to excessive suffering—what remains the same is that she is *choosing*. In other words, she is defining her reality, and in fact, she is being *assertive* in doing so. Specifically, she is *asserting* her *will* to take the position she wants regardless of what reality actually is, and the reality is that some men are bad and some men are good, which makes assessing an individual man more anxiety provoking.

As I said above, then, women do not need to be trained to be assertive. They already are. Some may simply be assertive in the wrong direction—that is, in avoiding the complexity of ambiguity relating to men and the threats they may pose. So the synthesis that can lead to healthy relationships and to accurately picking up on and defending against threats from men is that of being *assertive based on reality* and not *assertive based on the desire to avoid anxiety*.

The truth is that, for men and women alike, being passive or aggressive does not lead to positive results in human interactions, including those involving threats. When I am passive, I become a victim of aggression, and when I am aggressive, I make someone else a victim of that aggression. When I am assertive, I act with resolution and determination to defend myself and those under my charge, with aggression of action if necessary, but without aggression of spirit. I may even wish to kill my enemy, not because I would enjoy it, but because it is necessary for protecting those who might become victims.

That which makes passiveness and aggressiveness essentially the same is the avoidance of anxiety. When I become passive in a conflict, I am in some way freezing or avoiding the confrontation so as not to have to carry through with the battle and ride the anxiety as it relates to the reality at hand. Acting with blind aggression is the same. Rather than experiencing the anxiety of the conflict as we deal with the threat in a measurable and appropriate way, we can simply give over to pure hate and rage, both of which drown out the more constructive emotion of anxiety.

Taking either of these paths is akin to taking a drug: passiveness and withdrawing can function like an opiate or depressant; acting with blind aggression can function like a stimulant. In both cases, the body responds with chemicals that give a subjective experience similar to the psychoactive functions of these drugs.

Assertiveness, however, requires that we face reality by engaging the anxiety, binding it without denying it or pushing it away, and using it with resolution to face the issue at hand, including a threat. There is no relief for this suffering, only the honest experiencing of it and doing what needs to be done, no matter how we feel.

If society or my immediate environment has sent me the message that my role is to be passive, I can end up in a kind of self-fulfilling prophecy. That is, I feel anxiety as I face a threat, I sense the need to assert myself, but then I berate myself with thoughts like, "This is my fault." "How did I get into this?" "If I would have only . . ." "Why did I provoke him?" These messages serve to appease my anxiety, although that may at first be difficult to see. Specifically, by taking the blame for a situation that is actually out of my control, I give myself a false sense of control. This relieves the anxiety of being in a situation where I am simply a victim and have no power over the behavior of the other.

Child Victims of Abuse

This process is especially common in victims of abuse, particularly children. For example, they may unconsciously think, "This must be my fault because if it is my fault, then I can do something to fix it, and then it won't happen to me again." This gives them a sense of control and thereby relieves some of the anxiety of helplessness.

In abused children the process is almost automatic because depending on age, they have not yet developed the abstract cognitive skills or emotional maturity to see anything happening as out of their own control. To think they are helpless and may have to suffer abuse again and again is simply too much for them to process, so they assign the blame to themselves, believing they then have some control over it. Whether this kind of process takes place in childhood or adulthood, it can then lead to problems with assertion, including in a threatening situation.

Women and Negative Self-Talk

For women in our society, depending again on individual experience, it is important to investigate and make explicit any thought processes that may reinforce a self-destructive attitude toward experiencing threats or actual acts of abuse. Thoughts that relate to passiveness are particularly likely if the types of messages we discussed before have been reinforced.

My mentor sometimes had adult clients wear a puppet on their hands and use it to talk to themselves in front of other group members, verbalizing their actual thoughts about the feelings they were experiencing. The puppet was an alligator that ate away at their self-concepts and feelings of self-respect. It is amazing what kinds of cruel things we will say to ourselves silently, particularly when we feel weak, inadequate, or like losers. In these instances, he had the clients take their other hand and cover the mouth of the puppet, shutting it up physically, and then say aloud the healthy thoughts that accompanied their feelings from then on.

In some cases he also had them write the negative and persecuting thoughts on a piece of paper, take it outside the room, and throw it away. I have used this method as well, even having clients burn the paper in an ashtray. These symbolic actions are important. Persecuting thoughts are more powerful than we may think. They plague us throughout each day, and we must become aware of them.

In cases like the ones we have been discussing here, women should become aware of those thoughts that reinforce feelings of being secondary to men, of not having a right to voice their opinions, of feeling responsible for any kind of abuse. These feelings come from having a pervasively passive orientation to life. Sit down, write them out as they emerge, and then burn them in an ashtray. Replace them with assertive and positive thoughts consistent with your natural and given right to exist and assert yourself.

Intimate-Partner Threats

Intimate-partner threats for women are unfortunately all too common and pose their own special types of problems. Sometimes you can simply end up having bad luck: you trust the wrong person and become the victim of a threat or an attack. For example, you meet a guy and things seem fine over a long enough period that you trust being in a potentially vulnerable position with him, and then the threat or abuse happens. At some point we all trust the wrong person. We can only learn from the experience and move on, either processing the event individually or seeking professional help if abuse did occur and we feel traumatized.

However, when this becomes a pattern, other work needs to be done. I mentioned earlier in the book that all of us can end up staying in unhealthy relationships because doing so is simply remaining within our comfort zones. I have seen this with clients more times than I can count. Oftentimes, this is a sad cycle the sufferers themselves don't understand and wish they could change.

The first step in becoming assertive in this situation and then changing it is simply being willing to experience the anxiety. We must move outside our comfort zones concerning the type of partner we seem to attract and choose. People tend to draw to themselves, and also actively seek, partners who give them a sense of familiarity. So sometimes both women and men will stay in abusive relationships—even though they know they are abusive—simply to avoid the unknown. The thought of developing a new relationship with a person who makes us feel something different can cause anxiety. Avoiding this anxiety can keep us stuck in our old relationship habits.

Many times we choose to live in familiar misery rather than risk an even worse misery by coming out of our comfort zones.

While I was studying to be a psychologist and therapist, I underwent therapy myself. Based on the insights I gained, I deliberately decided to avoid relationships that made me comfortable, that seemed familiar, and instead sought out relationships that brought me anxiety. Before this conscious choice, I unconsciously sought out relationship partners who were an unhealthy match for me. At the same time, I felt sure at my very core that I was meant to be with them. The result was that I had been in one unhealthy relationship after another.

We are discussing the value of anxiety in relationships, but, of course, we must not confuse anxiety with fear. If someone makes you afraid, that is anxiety telling you there is danger. But we can feel anxiety about something good. Think of the job you always wanted, the degree you hope to get, surviving a dangerous situation . . . these are sources of anxiety that lead to something enriching and deepening. So there is at the end of the path of anxiety a reward, so to speak, when we talk about the essentials in life.

Who does not feel anxiety over a sick child, or the future of the child when considering his or her safety, success, and happiness? To lack this anxiety would lead to shallow parenting. In fact, it is through parenting that we perhaps learn more about the difference between fear and anxiety than through any other activity. If we parent out of fear, it is because we simply want control and to avoid suffering. We overprotect our kids, controlling their decisions to avoid something befalling them that will cause us to suffer.

The anxiety involved in parenting is different. This anxiety seizes us, keeps us up at night, and raises our blood pressure, but also motivates us to read parenting books, to seek therapy and parenting classes, to learn how to be a parent just as we would learn any other skill, so that we can do the job without having to control and stifle. Fear leads us to set rigid rules, control freedom, dictate, berate, and manipulate—all in order to avoid the anxiety of suffering. This is the difference between fear and anxiety in terms of how each drives our behavior.

If you are a woman in an abusive relationship, the answer is simple, but the road is difficult. Who are you? Why were you born? To be the outlet for someone else's anxiety over low self-esteem? Who were you as a little girl? What were your dreams before they were stripped from you? Look in the mirror and answer these questions out loud, and any others you can think of that relate to your fundamental existence. Any answer you come up with that does not cause you anxiety is wrong— the right answers will lead you toward loving yourself and pursuing a full life. This will cause you anxiety because you will finally start to value your life and then feel the constructive anxiety to live it well before it is too late.

The power this will manifest in your will to defend yourself, using psychology, cannot be explained in words. It is very similar to what leads to fighting for your buddy in battle. No one thinks about politics or orders in those situations. You fight for the person on your side. And in this regard, the person on your side is you. Lock and load and start to fight for her.

Special Issues for Kids

Psychology as it relates to children and self-defense or the martial arts has to do with development. That is, children think and feel differently at different stages in their development, and, of course, they are much weaker as young children. So when training them and when considering their special vulnerabilities in attacks, we need to take some important factors into account.

131

Training Issues for Kids

Kids can be trained to be lethal fighters, despite their size. Just take a look at some videos from children training who are Shaolin monks. Of course, this is an extreme example, but the point is clear. In fact, due to the nature of neurological development in childhood, kids are capable of learning complex subjects—languages for example—far more easily than adults. The same is true in martial arts.

When it comes to training, the difference, in my opinion, is the pressure applied. Of course kids need discipline, but just as task-oriented development is still at an early stage in kids, so is the development of self-esteem and self-concept. I myself have been guilty of making more than one child cry in training because I forgot that important fact. Generally speaking, children think in concrete terms, more so than do adults. That is, they see things in simple terms. If you are too hard in criticizing a particular technique, for them you are criticizing their whole being.

The key is to get them excited and committed to the training. If we force them to become killers, it will affect their self-image later and lead to difficulties. We may end up providing them with some tools for protection in childhood but decrease their ability to trust their instincts in adulthood because they don't trust themselves due to the excessive criticism we subjected them to in childhood. I am not writing this to point the finger at others. I am writing it to myself. I have done this several times, and so I know what I am talking about. It does not work.

We can argue back and forth about discipline and guidance, but the fact is we must engage with children where they are. Why is this training relevant to their lives? We can tell them it is for their safety, but this argument does not mean much to kids. They think concretely, not abstractly, even into late adolescence, so if we want to make them good fighters, we must do so with a kind of trick. We must make them fighters but by making the training fun and relating to the value system they can understand at their developmental level. By all means, make training effective, but make it also build their self-concepts, their hunger for adventure and knowledge, and their natural inclination to excitement and fun. Make it practical. Not every child can be a Shaolin monk.

Several of the children I have trained to fight cried at some point. I always felt miserable. I always knew I failed. I trained them the way I did because I was operating from the fear that they would not be able to defend themselves. I pushed too hard, afraid I was not up to the task. Instead, I should have understood they were children, with sensitive and developing egos. That is a challenge that elicits some anxiety in me.

We require schoolteachers to have more knowledge than simply the content of their subjects. You can have a degree in math, English, or science, but you cannot be a teacher unless you get a license, awarded for your knowledge of child development and pedagogy. How many martial arts schools operate without the trainer having this same kind of knowledge? This is a problem.

Training kids in the principles in this book is also highly effective. Kids are very open to learning about feelings. However, as we just discussed, we need to match the training to their psychology. Kids need to be taught in a very concrete way what they are feeling. For example, pictures of faces with the names of feelings under them can be helpful and easy to understand. You can also use magazines and books with pictures of people showing emotions and talk with kids about what the people are feeling. There are countless tools available to help kids identify feeling states.

Kids also respond well to stories that illustrate concrete examples. Fairy tales, heroic tales, and other stories that involve threats and anxiety-provoking situations and are simple enough for kids to understand can help them learn to modulate their feelings. Plus, they will stay interested in the "training" because of the stories. *Grimm's Fairy Tales*, for instance, are very helpful because they often include danger and threats. But then, in many cases, there is a happy ending. This over time and with repetition can unconsciously reinforce a sense of hope and a feeling that, even in times of anxiety and fear, things will work out.

Other stories I have used include *Black Beauty, The Hobbit, The Lord of the Rings, The Chronicles of Narnia*, stories from the Bible, and, in some cases, books that are designed for kids who have undergone specific forms of trauma or loss. The possibilities are numerous, and with a little research you can find the right stories for the right child. Movies can be very helpful as well. The *Star Wars* series, *The Lord of the Rings* and *The Hobbit*, cartoons like *The Land before Time* . . . these are just a few examples. Kids can easily identify with a protagonist's need to endure anxiety when facing adversity. At the end of this chapter is an exercise giving guidance on the use of different kinds of stories for kids.

The Special Vulnerability of Kids

Depending on age and size, kids are simply more vulnerable to attack by adults. For that reason they are also sometimes targets for older or bigger kids. When we consider their particular vulnerability to the enemy, then, I believe kids, once old enough, should always be armed— with age-appropriate weapons, of course.

For example, I once volunteered to train girls living in a neighborhood where a convicted child rapist had returned after his prison sentence. I taught them the use of a tactical light combined with pepper spray, a pocketknife, and a pistol adapted to shoot pepper-spray bullets up to seven meters.

Obviously, the right "weapon" for the particular child is relative and needs to be given particular attention. I am not talking about giving kids pistols or knives to take to school—or pistols under any circumstances in the case of young children. But how do you tell a thirteen-year-old girl in Rojava, Syria, that she should not carry a weapon after many of her friends and family have been raped and slaughtered by terrorists? This is obviously an extreme example, but it is happening. I am not advocating that kids in the United States should carry weapons. But the point is clear. We must as adults use our instincts to accurately gauge the threats to our kids, and, rather than live in denial, get them the training they need to defend themselves in what is unfortunately a dangerous world.

Every kid in every school in the United States should be carrying a tactical light and know how to use it to blind an attacker—as well as other methods of self-defense. Through the kind of training in anxiety processing I have discussed, children should be conditioned to deal with all kinds of threats. At the end of this chapter, there are exercises you can conduct with kids for training these skills.

Online Threats and Kids

We discussed online threats in chapters 3 and 4, but I want to elaborate on the topic here, particularly with a focus on young people.

Social media has made it easier for both predators and peers to endanger children and teenagers. It is important to have a strategy and set of tactics for both kids and those responsible for them to employ when any of these types of threats manifest.

The first step is to take these threats seriously. Sometimes we may be inclined to believe an online threat is not as dangerous as when a child is approached by a stranger or bullied face to face. When we return to the principle of knowing the enemy, however, it becomes clear that this kind of threat is in some ways even more dangerous. First, in some cases, basic legal protections are not there to support potential victims. Depending on the particular country, or state or city, laws are still lacking to stop online predators and bullies. One result of this is that even if the perpetrator never makes a physical threat, the victim is left psychologically traumatized. Tragically, in some instances this can even lead to suicide or other destructive behaviors, such as alcohol or drug abuse.

Second, those who engage in this kind of threatening behavior online are demonstrating an impulse-control problem and a reality-denial problem, both of which are indicative of a particularly dangerous character disorder. While in some ways it is easier for any of us to voice an opinion online than directly to another person, threatening other people in this way is something altogether different. In terms of impulse control, it demonstrates that these individuals are not concerned about their words being recorded and perhaps used against them if their identities are discovered. In some cases, particularly bullying by peers, no effort is made to mask their identities. There is almost a kind of pride, as they bask in the glory of threatening or bullying.

This is a different behavioral profile than when, for example, a spontaneous argument or fight happens face to face. I am not excusing or minimizing the latter, but my experience has been that habitual online perpetrators, whether strangers acting as predators or peers being bullies, tend to have the personality profiles of true criminals, and this makes for a special kind of enemy.

When I refer to someone with a reality-denial problem, I mean the type of person who is so narcissistic that he sees the world only through his own eyes. There is no sense of what others might think about the behavior. There is no concern regarding who might be privy to the behavior or the fact that, because it takes place online, it is all documented. This means a reduced capacity for any kind of empathy or feelings of guilt, raising the potential for even more serious acts of violence.

This is a kind of insanity, a quasipsychosis, not of the type relating to psychotic disorders such as schizophrenia, but of the type where the person is fully capable of planning a violent act while at the same time being incapable of empathizing with the victims.

In his book *The Mask of Sanity*, the pioneering criminal-personality psychologist Hervey Cleckley gives a thorough, no-nonsense description of the personality structure of these kinds of individuals. These are the most dangerous types of criminals because they will go to church each Sunday, take care of their aging grandma, volunteer at a homeless shelter, serve as president of the PTA, coach the local baseball team, be a model father and husband, but in those shadow moments of their souls, rape, abuse, and even murder. If physical action seems too risky, the internet is the perfect option for acting out their lust for power, rage, and control.

If we want to protect our kids from these and other types of threats, we must consider the themes we have discussed here, particularly as they relate to anxiety. We must as parents be capable of picking up signals through our senses as we allow ourselves to experience the anxiety of knowing something may not be right with our children. This means we must be willing to experience anxiety at any given moment, even if we do not consciously know a problem exists.

This is no different from being in a public place and suddenly feeling anxiety because a threat is somewhere around me, even though I may not have consciously recognized it yet. My senses have picked up the threat and my instincts are setting off an alarm. The same process can alert us to problems with our kids. They may not want to tell us about being bullied on the internet, or that they are being inappropriately propositioned by a stranger. They may feel ashamed or afraid they will get in trouble. If, however, we have nurtured a relationship wherein they feel they can come to us and tell us anything, then we will be in a better position to protect them from online threats.

Once, during a therapy session with a concerned and caring father who was himself a psychotherapist, the great existential psychotherapist James Bugental continued to direct the client back to his own feelings and processes whenever he tried to get into the content of the fights with his son. When the father wanted to talk about whether he was right or wrong on the issues, Dr. Bugental got the father to focus on what he was feeling in the here and now, to work on his ability to be present in the moment, just as we have been discussing. The content was not the core issue. It was the father's difficulties with staying present in his relationships. He was not able to pick up on messages from his son and authentically communicate what he was feeling, to the detriment of their relationship.

Our relationship with our kids is the greatest weapon we have in protecting them. If that relationship is strong, we are more likely to pick up on problems and then send the message to them that we are available to hear them, understand them, and leave our judgment at the door. We will be modeling for them the process of being present and trusting the instincts since we will be actually doing this with them. This will teach them to do the same as they live their lives and have to face their own struggles and the inevitable threats with which they will have to contend.

Practical Exercises for Training Children

Training kids in the principles discussed in this book can raise complex issues, so I have provided the following training protocols.

1. As I have said, we need to be especially critical of self-defense or martial arts training for kids. We must consider the particular style and its content, and we must also evaluate the knowledge and the character of the instructor. What preparation and training does he or she have in child development and safety issues relating to training children?

EXERCISE 7-1. Evaluating Training for Children

DATE:

RECORD YOUR ANALYSIS OF THE TRAINING AND THE INSTRUCTOR.

2. For a child's training in the methods in this book, it is important to assess the way we model and teach how to process feelings, especially anxiety, and how to use the instincts. As I have said, it is very important not to force kids into a training program. They will likely become overwhelmed and frustrated. Instead, look for possibilities to engage them and teach them the skills as they have a real need for them in their lives.

We should be aware of everyday situations that allow this, and we should seek opportunities for children to practice and deepen their abilities. It is also helpful to research other appropriate resources—stories and movies, for example—to help them process feelings, discuss, and learn the methods.

It is important to reflect on the stories we choose and how model the concepts in this book. We should ask ourselves about the thoughts, feelings, and behaviors the story elicits in us. Did experiencing the story or movie together increase the level of presence and connection between you and the child? If so, how? If not, why?

Finally, what else resulted from the experience, such as discussions or other behaviors related to the experience? What was the benefit for the child and what could you improve for next time?

EXERCISE 7-2. Modeling the Process for Children

DATE:

CREATE A LIST OF EVERYDAY ACTIVITIES THAT ALLOW YOU THE OPPORTUNITY TO EXPERIENCE ANXIETY AND PROCESS IT IN WAYS YOU CAN MODEL FOR YOUR CHILD.

3. Games can be helpful for practicing the techniques described in this chapter. There is one called the Nurturing Game that incorporates excellent, well-grounded questions on thought, feeling, and behavior. The game is simple, even for small kids. It can be played by the whole family or just a couple of people. You throw the dice and move on a board, and the parents and kids move on two different paths that cross at times. You land on a square that corresponds to different cards designed for parents, kids, or for both.

The questions are not just touchy-feely. One is, "What could I do better as a parent to understand my kids?" which you then have to answer in front of your children. There are also "praise squares." When you land on one, you must pick someone in the family and say something you like about him or her. Then there are squares that direct you to pick one person to hug. Both create a way to give a person, child or adult, individual special affirmation and affection, which is essential in our family relationships.

The game helps us do the hard work of processing thoughts, feelings, and behavior as they relate to the very difficult and delicate subject of intimate relationships. It also ensures an overall climate of support and understanding, and kids in particular need this. In my opinion, the Nurturing Game is one of the best out there for modeling the methods I discuss in this book.

But any games your kids enjoy will work as long as they facilitate connection, presence, and the processing of feelings. Physical games work as well, and martial arts training is absolutely perfect if done correctly. Other rituals might include going for a walk, having a meal, camping, or visiting an important site such as a grave or memorial. These are just a few ideas of how to set up time and space to work in an authentic way on the issues we have been discussing.

You know your kids better than anyone else. Pick what you believe will lead to immediate presence and connection, and to learning the principles in this book. If something doesn't seem to work for them, move on to something else.

EXERCISE 7-3. *Making a Game of It*

DATE:

RECORD YOUR THOUGHTS AND OBSERVATIONS ON HOW GAMES AND RITUALS CAN HELP US WORK THROUGH ANXIETY AND MODEL THAT BEHAVIOR FOR CHILDREN.

4. When children face threats, we must help them learn to process them. This way they learn to address situations in their own lives in ways that help them to work through feelings, especially those prompting anxiety and feelings of being victimized or threatened. Of course, obvious examples include being bullied at school or being made fun of. But we can also use less obvious situations to condition them to process difficult feelings relating to anxiety and other forms of suffering.

Once we start paying attention to and identifying these opportunities, we realize how much anxiety our kids actually go through on a daily basis. It is a bit humbling and will usually motivate us to work even harder as parents. Some fairly common examples include anxiety about school performance or other important performance-based events in their lives, such as sports or other extracurricular activities. Other common concerns include feeling belittled by their peers, teachers, or authority figures, or family situations such as moving or welcoming a new child.

Whatever the circumstance, there are essentially two types of anxiety-provoking situations: those they can "solve" on their own but with our assistance and those where we need to intervene because the level of threat or suffering is beyond their ability to cope effectively.

When reflecting on these situations, it is important to write about your thoughts and feelings, as well as what you observed from the child. Describe your experience of anxiety. How did you process it? How did you model that processing? What other feelings did you experience, and how did they influence the situation?

Once you have answered these questions for yourself, use them to assess the child's reactions.

Finally, review what you did to help the child process the problem and resolve it. Did you need to intervene directly? If so, how, and did this provide a model for the child for dealing with these kinds of problems or threats in the future? What was the benefit for the child, and what could you improve next time?

EXERCISE 7-4. Helping Children Learn to Process Anxiety

DATE:

WHAT DO YOU BELIEVE WAS THE BENEFIT FOR THE CHILD, AND WHAT COULD YOU IMPROVE FOR NEXT TIME?

8

Motivation of the Warrior

THE MOTIVATION OF THE INDIVIDUAL or group plays an integral role in determining the final outcome when facing a combative or self-defense situation. Intention that is positively grounded increases focus, strength, speed, and endurance. Think of a mother lion defending her cubs. She experiences anxiety but is fearless in protecting them. People are the same. Through my years of experience, I am convinced that when we are motivated by what is good, we will eventually prevail over those who are not. We all choose to live by either service, which we might even call love, or power.

Power and the Warrior

It is for this reason that I do not consider using psychology as a weapon to be unethical. In fact, manipulation of other people for the sake of power is antithetical to these methods and always leads to failure. No matter how apparently successful they are in the beginning, those who employ power and control in order to manipulate others for selfish reasons will eventually succumb to a blindside—a blindside caused by their lack of anxiety. We need only think of the many dictators in history who seemed invincible for a time—Hitler, Mussolini, Saddam

Hussein—but then suffered defeat through underestimating their enemies and overestimating their own abilities. As I have mentioned, the Greeks, wise in war, called this hubris. Similarly, Sun Tzu in *The Art of War* stated that we must know ourselves and we must know our enemy. If either of these elements is missing, we will eventually fail.

The problem is that there may be times where I intend to act or believe I am acting from the motivation of service but instead am acting for the sake of power. As a psychologist and psychotherapist, I believe we all do this from time to time, particularly in intimate relationships. Much of the work in psychotherapy is about helping individuals to understand and work through how they are preventing themselves from developing true intimacy and love. The majority of that process entails increasing the capacity for experiencing anxiety.

I act with power in order to control, to keep the other from hurting me, to prevent having to experience suffering. If I do this, though, I can hardly get close to the other individual in a true sense. I will never really get to know another person if that individual is never able to share with me intimate thoughts and feelings because he or she is always under my control.

This is a master-slave relationship, not one of love. People did not follow Hitler because they loved him. They followed him out of fear or because he helped relieve them of their anxiety. He sold them a fantasy that allowed them to avoid doubts about their existence. He said they were the master race. He was a good salesman, like any other cult leader.

On the other hand, people followed Martin Luther King, Jr., because they loved him. They endured despite the intense anxiety they had to face as they supported his cause, including the anxiety of death. The more successful of these two individuals is clear, in terms of a lasting, heroic legacy.

We all have the potential to be a Hitler or a Martin Luther King, Jr. Being humble about this helps us to avoid the pitfalls of hubris and to act with the wisdom of Sun Tzu—knowing both ourselves and our enemy. For this reason I believe intensely that the abilities of true warriors are increased when they undergo some form of self-exploration as a part of their overall training.

As I have said, when I was training to be a therapist, I went through my own therapy. I am convinced this has increased my ability to operate as a warrior. It heightened my capacity to feel (particularly anxiety), give my feelings names, and observe myself even as I act. It made me more capable of reading and empathizing with the feelings of others, and then in some situations, manipulating an individual's anxiety in order to defend others or myself. It also forced me to accept and pay attention to the potential in myself to do harm.

In *Listening with the Third Ear*, Theodor Reik states, "The unconscious does not know the word or concept 'no.' The frontiers of the personality reach farther in both directions: into what is commonly called good and into what is commonly called evil" (p. 174). This is why we must tap into the unconscious to be effective in threatening situations: our conscious side is more likely to freeze or fail to recognize the threat. This is also why it is vital to be in touch with our demons, our own aggressive impulses. By conditioning ourselves to the "bad guy" in ourselves, we are better able to recognize and react to this force in the enemy and make ourselves more capable of forgetting ourselves in serving as warriors.

The philosopher Arthur Schopenhauer once asked why a person would jump in front of an oncoming train, sacrificing him- or herself to save a complete stranger. The reason, he said, is in that moment you forget that you and the other individual are separate and instead are bonded to the core of humanity—or soul, or whatever we may call it. You realize then that you and the other are one. Lecturing on this issue, the mythologist Joseph Campbell related Schopenhauer's example to helicopter pilots in Vietnam and how they put their lives on the line to rescue wounded fellow soldiers.

If we apply the right motivation of service and the dialectic compass of compassion to using psychological principles in self-defense and combative situations, we will be acting as true warriors. No matter the outcome, we can then live with a sense of honor. To go even further, it is only a warrior who acts with honor, and so those motivated by power will not be able to apply these principles at all. They simply will not work because they are not based on cheap interpretations of psychological principles for use in "psychological operations," but instead on the difficult process of experiencing anxiety and braving reality as it is when facing the enemy.

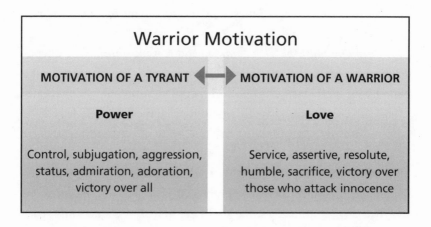

Which of these profiles leads to friendships, connections based on mutual respect, fulfillment, and meaning? Which has to do with the people involved and not their status or position? The answer is obvious. In a combative situation, victory per se is not defined by results. It never was. Valor, honor—these words have never had to do with only the actual defeating of the enemy in battle.

The Mark of the True Warrior

If we want to identify one trait that distinguishes warriors from people who can simply fight, I believe we can narrow it down to this: warriors, in the act of protecting, completely forget themselves. They forget they are individuals or that they even exist. Warriors become instruments of a long history of those known or unknown who have served to protect the innocent. No titles, no trophies, no fame, no medals . . . just pure service.

I don't believe any of us lives up to this ideal all of the time. It is best to remain humble—it is healthiest—but to some extent we would all like attention, acknowledgement, and praise. Show me a person who says he is all service and no kudos, and I will show you a person heading for a fall.

What we can do, then, to maximize our effectiveness as warriors is to be humble about and keep an eye on our innate drive to be the top gun, no matter what. That last phrase is important. I believe wholeheartedly in the effectiveness of integrating competition into training, especially training that entails life-and-death situations, such as military training. It pushes us to achieve greater levels of mastery than we know lies within us. But when being the top gun becomes the guiding value in training and our lives, problems will ensue. Teamwork and loyalty become less important than selling oneself and one's experiences for the sake of personal fame and acclaim. In some cases this even leads to breaches in sensitive information regarding military operations, techniques, tactics, and procedures.

I know a guy who has become a mentor for me who served twenty-five years as an enlisted soldier in the Rangers and other elite units in the US military. No one knows him. He continues to serve in a civilian capacity on the forefront of the War on Terror and just does his job—that's it. I even asked if he wanted to write a book together about hand-to-hand combat in these special types of units, and he politely declined. I have known him for several years, trained with him, and worked with him, and even as a writer, I find no words to describe the depth of his humility despite what he has accomplished and endured. There are no words for such service. You just bow and feel thankful.

I am not saying admiration for warriors, be they professional fighters, famous martial artist actors, or former military, is always a negative. I am saying you can tell pretty quickly who is about pushing his own fame versus providing genuine service by sharing knowledge and mentoring.

How? Effectiveness. The individual concerned with his own ego is burning energy that could be used for continuing to develop competence. The warrior is only concerned with continuing to develop warrior competence in all of its components. Films and books abound in the martial arts and military communities, and it is fairly easy to sense which ones are there to sell a personality, and which are there out of a continuing developmental process on the part of the warrior to deepen his or her proficiency and effectiveness to serve.

Conclusion

As I was considering how to end this book, a colleague of mine consulted with me about a situation involving his daughter. I have known this colleague so long that I have seen his daughter grow up. They are like family to me.

She had been approached in a gym by a guy around forty or older who was overly aggressive in hitting on her. It went beyond the normal flirting she had experienced in that environment, and so she was shaken up. I told him I would talk with her and see what we could do. She told me the whole story, including how she told the guy that because she was eighteen, he was too old for her. He replied that his last girlfriend was seventeen, and without going into detail, let's just say his continued approach to her was lecherous and intrusive. He talked with her and treated her like a stripper, as if she were in the gym for his entertainment, and at her refusal to go out drinking with him, his arrogance and subtle aggression became more pronounced.

It would be easy to simply dismiss this as a jerk with no respect hitting on a younger girl and unable to accept a polite rejection. Because

153

I directly talked with her, however, I had access to her feelings. What I mean is as I had her describe in detail the conversation and everything else that happened, it was as if I were transported into the event itself, and I could feel the process beyond the content. She was visibly and palpably frightened, and although I didn't push her then to fully communicate these feelings, I could feel her vulnerability about having to relive the incident.

The first thing I told her was anytime she left the gym she should use the front door. There were always a lot of people in front of the building, so I told her to park there too. There was a main crossing to a train station as well, which had a constant flow of people going back and forth and regular patrols of police officers. In the area around the back entrance she had been using, there was less security.

I also reassured her that she had asserted herself well and handled the situation perfectly, and that I could imagine how she had felt. I wasn't just trying to boost her confidence. I meant it. She had asserted herself in a very controlled way, leaving no doubt that she had no interest in the guy and did not want to talk with him anymore. But she was afraid of what might happen next. I told her she could call anytime if she was there and felt scared, whether she knew the guy was around or not, and I would come. Then I told her about carrying a pistol that shoots pepper-spray bullets and offered to train her in the use of it, as well as in krav maga.

I decided that all this—plus checking out who the guy was from the bits of information she was able to gather—was enough. That night, however I dreamed she actually had been raped by the man. When I got up and analyzed the dream by allowing myself to feel anxiety and going with my instincts about it, I became more aggressive about finding the guy and working up a plan. Somehow, in concentrating on being very present with her as she spoke, my senses fed my instincts with information about the depth of her terror, which I only realized as my unconscious revealed it to me in my dream.

I researched the gym and the types of people who went there, including the guy in question. I recommended she change gyms immediately, even if she had to pay more.

I also developed a series of plans to put myself between her and the guy. This included making use of his self-doubt that stemmed from his age and made him target young females. I played on that anxiety and what seemed to be a hidden hunger anxiety that came from being a former soldier who now worked at a movie theater but spent a lot of time in the gym, working on a soldier's figure without actually having that status anymore—or any money.

As one part of the overall plan, I decided to join the gym for a month and gradually and naturally introduce myself to him as a fellow former soldier with my own firm, looking for big strong guys like him to help me do close protection for prominent celebrities. The celebrities we would protect would, of course, include attractive young females. In this way, I would gain control over him along with further information about his background and personality.

I end the book with this story because it brings out some key points about the concepts and techniques discussed throughout. This girl was as close as it gets to being my own daughter. I think any father can imagine how he would feel in this situation. As she told me the story, I thought immediately about just finding the guy and talking to him face to face. Without consciously wanting to, I thought of the different ways I could kill him if he did anything to her.

Two to three minutes into my conversation with her, I went into the zone I go into when, for instance, I am directly in contact with terrorists or other serious criminals. The content of the conversation did not warrant this in and of itself, but what I felt coming from her certainly did. What actually happened was different from what words on paper can communicate. He had used his power to intimidate, belittle, and in my opinion even abuse her. And that is how she was left feeling.

So one key point I am trying to make is that as we use anxiety and our instincts in threatening situations, process is paramount. What we experience is more important than facts alone. If I went to the police or even the managers of the gym, nothing would happen because it was on the edge of what could be considered harassment. But how do you assess the look in a huge forty-year-old man's eyes, the tone of his voice, and his posture as he aggressively closes the distance on a young girl? This is exactly what we do as more skilled warriors when we assess our enemy.

Another key point I want to make is how I felt in the situation. As I said, I wanted to directly attack this guy and had many spontaneous visions of how I could do it. I can say with confidence I had absolutely no fear about a confrontation with him. But I did feel anxiety within two or three minutes of her beginning to speak, as I said. The anxiety I had was, however, not about getting hurt. It was of her getting hurt. This became especially pronounced in my dream.

At the same time, I know if I had been walking down the street, for example, and this individual picked a fight with me, I would have experienced fear just before fighting him. I have almost always felt fear when I have faced an enemy who was a threat to me. On the other hand, whenever I have been in a situation where my duty was to protect someone else, I did not have that same fear. I have felt anxiety, but I go into some mode where I do not exist anymore, and I am instead an instrument of the task before me. The fear will come and go, with the thoughts of myself getting hurt or killed, but when I am not thinking about myself, I do not feel that fear. This is much more complicated than it sounds, and I do not think it is the same in every individual. But when we protecting others, when we serve something greater than ourselves, we human beings are capable of remarkable feats.

As for the aggressive jerk at the gym, I cannot say yet how the situation will resolve. Perhaps the measures I've described will suffice, but my job is to plan for the worst, no matter how overexaggerated the threat may seem to most people. Preparing for the worst is more than simple protocol when you are responsible for accomplishing a mission. Even the planning provides a psychological sense of security for the person under threat. What I want in situations like this is for it to be as though I have a gun pointed at the threat's head without his knowing it, and then if he escalates, I pull the trigger before he can do any harm to the potential victim.

Perhaps I also chose to use this situation in the conclusion because it is a very personal one, and I suspect most people reading this book and wanting to apply its principles will be protecting themselves and those closest to them. The irony is that when threats do occur close to home, we are faced with two opposing forces: motivation to defend in its most intense form versus being so close to the problem that we can end up giving in to the passions of pure rage and intense fear. Some will act out hastily in such a case, and others will freeze facing the danger of loss and suffering. The middle way is to harness the rage and fear through balanced and guiding anxiety. We then mobilize our will, using our instincts to fight with purpose—but also with selflessness. Somehow we become lost in this kind of force and become instruments of good, devoid of ego, operating as true warriors to protect those in our care.

However strong our instinct for defending may be, we must also develop it through training and discipline, just like developing any true fighting skill. Learning a few self-defense tricks or going to the shooting range with a pistol for a day does not prepare one to fight. The same is true for this method. This is a perishable skill. If I develop it to a proficient level but then get complacent, it will fade over time.

Going even further, I believe this skill, just like any martial art, must actually become a way of life in order for us to discover its full potential. The skills we learn will assist us in areas other than self-defense. The use of presence and empathy can help us in deepening and improving our relationships, getting a job, and performing that job better. Nearly everything we do in life requires human contact and interaction, so improving our ability to better understand how we are feeling and reading our own processes as well as those of others can only enrich us. Becoming more present and having access to more of the information coming in through our senses also creates a subjective experience of being more alive. This you have already noticed if you have completed the exercises in this book.

Learning to be present, to feel anxiety, and to think and act in difficult circumstances, these are the initial challenges. But making them part of daily life is something else altogether. Any martial artist who trains over a significant period with sustained practice and with great intensity knows there is a threshold where you don't really think about doing technique anymore. You become an instrument of something else—as in any art, such as writing, painting, and playing music. Art cannot be forced and cannot be produced out of ego. The instrument, the individual, must give himself or herself over to something much more powerful and mysterious.

The process I have presented in this book is intended to be practiced and developed in the same way. Discipline, together with precise and diligent practice, is necessary for developing presence, effectively using anxiety to lead us to the truth and to follow our instincts. At some point you will stop thinking about *doing* and simply *become* this process. You will switch on hypersensitivity at the appropriate moments in order to accurately read what is going on around you, in you, and with others who may be potential threats.

It is important to continually work on this skill. You will see for yourself the deepening that presence can bring, allowing you to be more in the reality you are living in the here and now. Daisetz Suzuki talks about the *satori* being the experience at the core of Zen practice, the awakening to reality, including to yourself—pure experience without analyzing what it is or what it means. The samurai knew the value of this in their combative training, and what we are talking about here is much the same, though built on contemporary psychological models.

This process is not about psychological tricks. It concerns a transformation in ourselves to both deepen our human experience and, as warriors, to better defend through selfless service.

Acknowledgments

I WOULD LIKE TO THANK all those mentors and colleagues who have over the years supported and been part of my personal and professional development: Dr. David F. F., SFC D. Parritt (US Army Special Forces, retired), 1SG H. "Chez" Sanchez (US Army Special Operations, retired), HH, MNR, DH, JM, MH, Grandmaster Haim Gidon, JH, Yigal Arbiv, 1LT JS (US Army Airborne), CPT M. "Zeke" K. (US Army Airborne), and Marco Behnke.

Appendix: Practical Exercises—Examples

THROUGHOUT THIS BOOK I HAVE PROVIDED EXERCISES to help you sharpen your awareness, improve your sense of presence, and ask critical questions about your training and execution. In this appendix I offer a few sample responses to exercise 1-1, "Enhancing Sensory Awareness."

Session 1 is an example of the writer's first experience with this exercise. In session 2, as the writer becomes more familiar with the process, we see his or her skills of observation improving.

In all of these exercises our writing should be free and informal, allowing our senses and instincts to lead the way.

Session 1
Sight
The more I concentrated, the more things I began to see in detail and in my peripheral vision. I was able to see more specific colors

on objects and shapes. As people came into view, I noticed more details in terms of type and color of clothes, hair color.

Sound

I began to hear other noises outside my immediate area, including people talking, cars passing, animals. I could also hear my own breathing and the sounds as I would shift body position and the sounds of other mannerisms from people around me.

Touch

I sensed in more specific ways how my body was feeling, touching the chair, the floor. I also noticed the feel of my hat, my clothes, and faint sensations such as feelings and some pains from chronic injuries. I could also feel the wind on my face in a more specific way.

Taste

As I focused, I could faintly taste some smells, such as the coffee I had not started drinking yet, and then more specifically the taste of the sugar and milk in the coffee.

Smell

I could smell the coffee much stronger, and even the sugar as I opened it to pour it in the coffee. I could also smell the cologne of a guy walking by and some food people ordered a couple of tables down. I also picked up more strongly on the exhaust smell of cars driving by.

Altogether

In general, I felt more alive, alert, and stimulated by all the different sensations coming in. I found myself jumping from one to the other in terms of reaction—that is, my attention would focus on a particular smell or sound or something catching my eye, all of it at once stimulating but a bit overwhelming.

Session 2

Sight

In the second session, after a few minutes, I experienced more specifics than in the one before, such as specific types of clothes, facial expressions, body language, jewelry people were wearing.

Sound

I could better gauge the tones and volumes of voices. I could also hear movements outside my immediate environment, conversations between people, footsteps, car doors closing, cars starting.

Touch

I could sense someone walk behind me and brush lightly against me. I also became more aware of my feeling states, physically sensing how my stomach and chest would feel when picking up on anxiety, like a slight fullness in my chest accompanied by heat.

Taste

I found I could taste smells, things I knew were based on scent, but with an increased experience of them, such as someone nearby smoking and the food people were eating.

Smell

My sense of smell was very intense, picking up on the food people were eating, people smoking even at a distance, as well as coffee and other scents from the location.

Altogether

Again I was a bit overwhelmed by all the sensations at once, but I was better able to ground myself and just take it all in and try to pick up and concentrate on those more prominent while not dismissing the others. I felt a little more comfortable with the process and enjoyed it more.

Bibliography

Bugental, James. *The Art of the Psychotherapist*. New York: W. W. Norton & Company, 1992.

Cleckley, Hervey. *The Mask of Sanity: An Attempt to Clarify Some Issues about the So-Called Psychopathic Personality*. Eastford, Connecticut: Martino Fine Books, 2015.

Comstock, Dale. *American Badass*. Zulu 7 Publishing, 2013.

Kano, Jigoro. *Kodokan Judo*. New York: Kodansha USA, 2013.

———. *Mind over Muscle: Writings from the Founder of Judo*. New York: Kodansha USA, 2013.

Kierkegaard, Søren. *The Concept of Anxiety: A Simple Psychologically Orienting Deliberation on the Dogmatic Issue of Hereditary Sin*. Princeton: Princeton University Press, 1981.

———. *The Essential Kierkegaard*. Princeton: Princeton University Press, 2000.

May, Rollo. *Love & Will*. New York: W. W. Norton & Company, 2007.

———. *The Meaning of Anxiety*. New York: W. W. Norton & Company, 1996.

Nietzsche, Friedrich. *Basic Writings of Nietzsche*. Translated by Walter Kaufmann. New York: Modern Library Classics, 2000.

Reik, Theodor. *Listening with the Third Ear*. New York: Farrar Straus & Giroux, 1983.

Sun Tzu. *The Art of War*. Translated by Samuel B. Griffith. New York: Oxford University Press, 1971.

Yalom, Irvin. *The Theory and Practice of Group Psychotherapy*. 5th ed. New York: Basic Books, 2005.

Recommended Reading

Kano, Jigoro and Naoki Murata. *Mind Over Muscle: Writings from the Founder of Judo*. New York: Kodansha USA, 2013.

As the founder of judo, Jigoro Kano's books are more than simply "how to" instruction on technique or training. You actually feel through his writing what he meant by the "gentle way." At the same time his ferocity as a warrior is clear. This book is relevant to any warrior, regardless of the art he or she practices.

Reik, Theodor. *Compulsions to Confess: On the Psycho Analysis of Crime & Punishment*. North Stratford, New Hampshire: Ayer Company Publishers, 1977.

Similar to *The Unknown Murderer*, Reik demonstrates in this book how unconscious impulses such as blushing and stumbling over words can act as compulsions of the individual to confess repressed impulses while at the same time punishing the individual for having them. The application for assessing whether someone is telling the truth is obvious. (Note: This book was also published with the title *The Compulsion to Confess*.)

———. *Listening with the Third Ear*. New York: Farrar Straus & Giroux, 1983.

This is one of the core books for the ideas in *First Defense*. I would even go so far as to say without *Listening with the Third Ear*—and working with my mentor, who was an expert in Reik's method—I would have never written this book.

———. *The Unknown Murderer*. London: Hogarth Press, 1936.

This is another book applying Reik's method to analyzing crime scenes for clues to the personality profile of the criminal. He postulates that the criminal unconsciously leaves clues behind in a compulsion to be caught, and by using the processes described in *Listening with the Third Ear* we can gain clues as to the perpetrator of a crime.

Suzuki, D. T. *An Introduction to Zen Buddhism*. New York: Grove Press, 1994.

———. *Zen and Japanese Buddhism*. Clarendon, Vermont: Charles Tuttle, 1958.

———. *Zen and the Samurai*. New York: Macmillan Audio, 1995.

All three of these titles communicate better than anything I have ever read about the process of the essence of satori, or awakening to the moment through Zen practice. This experience is central to the ideas of presence in *First Defense*.

Watts, Alan. *Beyond Theology: The Art of Godmanship*. New York: Vintage, 1973.

———. *Psychotherapy East and West*. New York: Vintage, 1975.

———. *The Way of Zen*. New York: Vintage, 1999.

Alan Watts is a Westerner who intensely studied Zen. In his writing he makes the essentials of Zen philosophy and practice easy to understand and brings them to the Western reader. His comparisons of psychological principles underlying Eastern and Western visions of the human psyche and behavior are excellent.

Resources

Bodyguards Without Borders
https://m.facebook.com/profile.php?id=153859771358361
Bodyguards Without Borders (TM) (SM) is dedicated to the mission of providing professional protection to those who most need it but who often cannot afford it. Of particular importance to their efforts is the protection of children and women, including those suffering under human trafficking and slavery.

Child Exploitation Investigations Unit, Department of Homeland Security
http://www.ice.gov/predator

Human Exploitation Rescue Operative (HERO) Corps
http://www.ice.gov/hero
This program offers training to special operations veterans who are wounded, injured, or ill. It allows them to start a new career in investigating and combating online child exploitation.

Office of Women's Health, Department of Health and Human Services
http://womenshealth.gov/violence-against-women/get-help-for
-violence/resources-by-state-violence-against-women.html
This is a list of resources by state for female victims of violence.

Stalking Resource Center, the National Center for Victims of Crime
https://www.victimsofcrime.org/our-programs/stalking-resource
-center

Index

About the Author

DR. DAVID HOPKINS is a psychologist with twenty-one years of experience, combining psychological principles relating to violence and psychotherapy with martial arts, self-defense, close protection, and in investigative work against terrorists and criminal elements, including organized crime. He has taught psychology relating to violence at universities in both the US and overseas, and is chief of the Israeli Krav Maga Association, Gidon System, in Germany. He holds black belts in judo and jiu-jitsu and is the head of an international high-risk close protection and intelligence-gathering team operating against terrorist and organized crime elements. He also serves as a consultant to an international paramilitary and close protection team and is co-owner of Israeli School Security, a school security consulting and training firm.

BOOKS FROM YMAA

continued on next page . . .

DVDS FROM YMAA

more products available from . . .

YMAA Publication Center, Inc. 楊氏東方文化出版中心

1-800-669-8892 • info@ymaa.com • www.ymaa.com

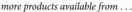